Contents

ADVANCED COMPOSITION:

A BOOK OF MODELS FOR WRITING

JOHN E. WARRINER
Head of the English Department
Garden City High School
Garden City, New York

RICHARD M. LUDWIG
Associate Professor of English
Princeton University
Princeton, New Jersey

FRANCIS X. CONNOLLY
Professor of English
Fordham University
New York, New York

HARCOURT, BRACE & WORLD, INC.

New York · Chicago · San Francisco
Atlanta · Dallas

THE AUTHORS, *Advanced Composition: A Book of Models for Writing*—**JOHN E. WARRINER** has taught English for 30 years, in junior and senior high schools and in college. He is the author of *Handbook of English: I and II*, co-author of *English Workshop*, and a reader for the College Entrance Examination Board. **RICHARD M. LUDWIG**, who received his Ph.D. at Harvard University, is Associate Professor of English at Princeton University. His publications include *Essays Today*, *Nine Short Novels* (with Marvin Perry), and *Major American Writers* (with Howard Mumford Jones and Ernest E. Leisy). **FRANCIS X. CONNOLLY** is Professor of English at Fordham University, where he received his Ph.D. Among his publications are *Poetry: Its Power and Wisdom*, *A Rhetoric Case Book*, *The Types of Literature*, *Sentences in Context* (with Donald Sears), *Harbrace College Handbook* (with John Hodges).

The photograph on the cover of this book shows part of a type case containing the printing type Perpetua, a face designed in 1932 by the English artist Eric Gill. The chapter headings throughout the book are set in this type. Cover photograph by Lew Merrim from Monkmeyer.

ADVANCED
COMPOSITION

INTRODUCTION

How this book will help you to write better.

The purpose of this book is to teach writing. We learn to write in three ways: (1) by studying grammar, sentence structure, mechanics, and organization; (2) by studying the writing of professional writers; and (3) by practicing in our own writing the skills we have learned. This book provides you with many different types of good prose to examine and to use as models and suggests many topics for you to write about.

The essays and stories that follow are divided for your convenience into four parts: Description, Exposition, Narration, and Models Without Analysis. As you come to each of the first three parts, you will find first a general discussion of what is meant by "description" or "exposition" or "narration," and then, in the chapters that follow, a variety of models to illustrate the characteristics of the type of writing. As you read each model, examine it to see what the writer's purpose is, how he has handled his material, how he commands his reader's attention. The critical "Analysis" and the "Questions on Content" and "Questions on Technique" which follow each selection will guide you in your study.

You will find that most of the rhetorical terms used in the analyses are defined in context where they first occur. When a rhetorical term recurs, it is marked with a circle, thus: °, which directs you to the Glossary on page 523 for explanation. Here all rhetorical terms used in the text are listed in alphabetical order. They are defined in more detail than in the text itself and illustrated with additional examples. Difficult words, proper names, and allusions occurring in the models are also marked with a circle, referring you to a footnote which explains how the author is using the term or what the reference means. Words marked with an asterisk, thus: *, are suggested additions to your vocabulary. They, together with frequently used words marked with °, are repeated in a brief section called "Add to your vocabulary" after the model.

After you have carefully studied a model, you are ready to write. Suggestions for writing follow the questions on content and technique. Many of the models deal with topics about which you yourself have ideas, or they may remind you of experiences of your own. As you try your hand at an expository or a descriptive or a narrative piece, apply the technique you observed in the model. This does not mean that you should imitate slavishly the author whose piece you have studied. But every good writer, regardless of style, employs certain techniques which the models in this book exemplify, and which you too must master if you would learn to write well. These techniques are highlighted by the "Questions on Technique."

Writing means planning.

In undertaking any writing assignment, you will want to progress by several stages. You will not want to plunge into your subject at once, uncertain of where you are going. If you do this, your essay will be built on shifting ground, a house of words with a weak foundation. Suppose, for example, that your assignment is to describe a memorable personal experience. As a subject you have chosen your first journey alone away from home. As a working title you have chosen "Stranger on a Train." How shall you begin?

First, you will want to recall and make notes on *specific* details: how old were you, where were you going, why, how long was the journey, what happened? How did things in the train look, feel, smell, sound? Your title at first glance suggests *you* were the stranger, since it was your first journey by yourself; but you have, perhaps, someone else in mind: the man in the derby who asked to share your seat on the train. You will need to recall *more* specific details: who was he, what did he look like, what was he carrying, why were you suspicious of his behavior? Stage one, then, is the assembling of your material: who, when, what, where. These rough notes are a beginning.

Second, you will want to decide in what order you will use this material. You may organize it chronologically, progressing from your leaving home to your arrival at your destination. Or you may begin in the middle of the incident with the stranger walking toward you down the aisle. Or you may organize the composition not as a story, but as an essay, beginning with why this event was memorable and going on to describe the event and its effect on you. No matter which approach, which ordering of events you choose, a complete outline or plan is of great importance. You must have your conclusion clearly in mind before you begin writing.

Third, you need to decide where your main emphasis will lie. Although you are writing in the first person, is this a story about you, about the stranger, or about a journey? Let us suppose the man in the derby is the center of interest. You will want, therefore, to focus attention on him fairly soon. You cannot afford to waste words on unimportant details if your reader is to *see* this stranger, to *feel* your reaction to what happens after he sits down beside you and begins to talk. Following your outline will keep all details in the right order. You must also decide in advance which detail is to be the center of the composition.

Writing means thinking.

All these steps involve clear thinking. In fact, good writing begins with clear thinking. It is impossible to separate the two processes. That is not to say that every author elaborately outlines his work before he puts words on paper. Professional writers are able to organize their source material rapidly and concisely, sometimes out of sheer force of habit. But these professionals have had practice in establishing the primary ideas in their writing, in arranging their sentences for strongest emphasis, in cutting away all unnecessary words and phrases. Much of their outlining is done mentally. Clear thinking and deep concentration are habitual with them.

A final word about Part Four of this book: Models Without Analysis. The four pieces in this section were selected to give you the opportunity to test your reading and interpretation without aid from anyone. Having learned in your study of Parts One through Three how to criticize writing, you launch into analysis on your own.

PART ONE

DESCRIPTION

Perhaps the first kind of writing we attempt, as we are growing up, is descriptive, the kind of writing that tells us how things appear. If not purely descriptive, it is at least a mixture of sights and sounds we know with a simple narrative of what happened and when. From an early age we make our conversation and our letters *describe* as well as *tell*. The neighbors have a new dog. What does he look like? Relatives visit in a new car. What color is it, what size, what model?

Careful observation.

Good descriptive writing begins with careful observation of details. Putting these details into your writing does not mean a mere heaping up of adjectives. One precise adjective will serve far better than four carelessly chosen. In fact, nouns and verbs are more important to descriptive writing than adjectives and adverbs, and they, too, need to be selected carefully if we are to give the reader an accurate impression of what we see and hear. Our conversation is generally repetitive; our writing should not be. When our friends listen to a description of a mountain lake, they have the advantage of our gestures, inflections, and facial expressions to augment our words. They can *see* the log cabin, the rocky path down to the dock, the gold shimmer on the water at sunset because we have used more than words to describe them. When we come to write that description, in a letter

5

or a diary, words alone must re-create the impression. They must *show* us as well as *tell* us.

Appeals to all senses.

How do professional writers develop atmosphere and impressions through descriptive writing? Do they want us only to *see* or do they depend on the other senses as well? Let us look at the opening paragraphs of two novels. The English novelist Joseph Conrad begins *Lord Jim* with a primarily visual description of the hero.

> He was an inch, perhaps two, under six feet, powerfully built, and he advanced straight at you with a slight stoop of the shoulders, head forward and a fixed from-under stare, which made you think of a charging bull. His voice was deep, loud, and his manner displayed a kind of dogged self-assertion which had nothing aggressive in it. It seemed a necessity, and it was directed apparently as much at himself as at anybody else. He was spotlessly neat, appareled in immaculate white from shoes to hat, and in the various Eastern ports where he got his living as ship-chandler's water-clerk he was very popular.

Conrad uses common words to create an effective first impression. A "fixed from-under stare" is a simple but memorable way of indicating bullishness in a man. To have Jim's loud voice "directed apparently as much at himself as at anybody else" is the first subtle indication of character in an otherwise physical portrait. Conrad will have much more to say about Jim's psychological qualities as the story unravels. For the moment he wants simply to *show* us the man. Dressed "in immaculate white from shoes to hat" he is a great contrast to the hurly-burly of the docks on which he works.

But *seeing* is not the whole problem. Good descriptive writing uses all the senses, and it extends naturally to places, emotions, and experiences as well as to persons. In *A Walker in the City*, Alfred Kazin recalls his childhood in Brownsville, in east Brooklyn. As he describes his mother's kitchen, "the warm odor of a coffeecake baking in the oven" pervades his memory. It is the expected detail. But as he continues, another odor, more unusual, identifies another member of his family.

My great moment came at six, when my father returned from work, his overalls smelling faintly of turpentine and shellac, white drops of silver paint still gleaming on his chin. Hanging his overcoat in the long dark hall that led into our kitchen, he would leave in one pocket a loosely folded copy of the New York *World;* and then everything that beckoned to me from that other hemisphere of my brain beyond the East River would start up from the smell of fresh newsprint and the sight of the globe on the front page. It was a paper that carried special associations for me with Brooklyn Bridge. They published the *World* under the green dome on Park Row overlooking the bridge; the fresh salt air of New York harbor lingered for me in the smell of paint and damp newsprint in the hall. I felt that my father brought the outside straight into our house with each day's copy of the *World.*

The English novelist C. S. Forester writes that he was "brought up in the wrong part of London, the dull part where nothing ever happened," yet in his essay, "Hornblower's London," he makes Peckham Road, in south London, sound like a feast for a small boy's senses.

Peckham Road in those days was a wonderful place (and I suppose still is to little boys not yet in their teens) . It was incredibly noisy; the steel-tired wheels of the cart rumbled like thunder over the granite setts ° and macadam, and the trampling of the horses added to the din. The horses added considerably to the dirt as well; on a rainy day the vast hoofs of the dray horses, coming down ponderously into the puddles, would splash a loathsome mixture all about, sometimes as high as the upper windows. . . . But the horse trams disappeared quite early in the cen-

setts: squared paving stones, usually granite.

tury—1905 would be my guess. . . . Thereafter electric trams sailed up and down the Peckham Road,
singing what to a little boy were magnificent melo-
dies as they boomed along; at night they were like
great ships of light cleaving a way through the darkness.

From rumbling carts to singing trolley cars—Forester
slips out of one era and into another through a simple
auditory description.

Other examples of descriptive writing come to mind:
the now famous opening paragraph of *Moby-Dick* in
which Melville describes Ishmael's state of mind and why
it leads him to sea again; the nineteenth chapter of the
Adventures of Huckleberry Finn in which Mark Twain
makes us see and hear the Mississippi River at dawn
just as Huck saw it; the wooden jail with "rust on the
ponderous ironwork of its oaken door" in the opening
chapter of Hawthorne's *The Scarlet Letter*. But the list
is unending. Every good writer uses description.

Dominant impression.

In the essays which follow, under the general heading
of description, the dominant impression the writers wish
to leave is what it looked like or how it felt or what
it meant, what it was worth. They approach their material differently, and so it is convenient to divide them
into four groups. The essays in Chapter 1 concern entirely personal subjective experience. The writers use
the first person pronoun, as we would expect. It would
be awkward to write about our childhood or adolescence
in any other way. The essays in Chapter 2 concern more
nearly objective or impersonal experience, although
complete objectivity is difficult to find outside of the
laboratory. Writers choose the pronouns, the vocabulary,
and the style which best fit their intentions. Here again
the division is not absolute. As sensory impressions °
merge in descriptive writing, so does subjective writing

sensory impressions: See Glossary.

merge with objective writing. For convenience only, we have divided the primarily objective description into the single subject and the complex subject. What is important for you to remember is not what category your writing falls into but what dominant impression you wish to create. Once you have chosen your subject and your approach, you are ready to arrange in some kind of order the significant details. All of the descriptive essays that follow are full of vivid, memorable sensory impressions.

CHAPTER I

Primarily subjective experience

OBSERVATIONS: CHILDHOOD

LAURIE LEE · *A Winter Treat*

Laurie Lee is an English poet and musician who was born in the Cotswolds, in Gloucestershire. In 1959, he published his recollections of his boyhood in the west of England (called The Edge of Day *when it appeared in this country) in which he fondly describes his little village, the country school, the Squire's Big House, and especially his own family—an intrepid mother and seven children; the father had disappeared.*

One of his chapters is devoted to outings and festivals, memorable times for all young boys. "The year," he writes, "revolved around the village, the festivals round the year, the church round the festivals, the Squire round the church, and the village round the Squire." He gets them all into this recollection of a post-Christmas party which begins with rehearsals and anticipation. Eileen Brown is a neighbor; Marjorie is Lee's eldest sister; the Squire is the town's chief citizen. Note how every detail is seen through a small boy's eyes.

"A Winter Treat" from *The Edge of Day*, William Morrow and Co., Inc. © 1959 by Laurie Lee. Reprinted by permission of William Morrow and Co.. Inc.

1   The Parochial Church Tea and Annual Entertainment was the village's winter treat. It took place in the schoolroom, round about Twelfth Night, and cost us a shilling to go. The Tea was an orgy of communal gluttony,* in which everyone took pains to eat more than his money's worth and the helpers ate more than the customers. The Entertainment which followed, home-produced and by lamplight, provided us with sufficient catch phrases for a year.

2   Regularly, for a few weeks before the night, one witnessed the same scenes in our kitchen, the sisters sitting in various corners of the room, muttering secretly to themselves, smiling, nodding, and making lah-di-dah gestures with a kind of intent and solitary madness. They were rehearsing their sketches for the Entertainment, which I found impossible not to learn, too, so that I would be haunted for days by three nightmare monologues full of one-sided unanswered questions.

3   On the morning of the feast we got the school ready. We built a stage out of trestles and planks. Mr. Robinson was in the cloakroom slicing boiled ham, where he'd been for the last three days, and three giggling helpers were now forking the meat and slapping it into sandwiches. Outside in the yard John Barraclough had arrived and set up his old field kitchen, had broken six hurdles across his knee and filled up the boiler with water. Laid out on the wall were thirty-five teapots, freshly washed and drying in the wind. The feast was preparing; and by carrying chairs, helping with the stage, and fetching water from the spring, Jack and I made ourselves sufficiently noticeable to earn a free ticket each.

4   Punctually at six, with big eating to be done, we returned to the lighted school. Villagers with lanterns streamed in from all quarters. We heard the bubbling of water in Barraclough's boiler, smelt the sweet wood smoke from his fire, saw his red face lit like a turnip lamp ° as he crouched to stoke up the flames.

5   We lined up in the cold, not noticing the cold, wait-

turnip lamp: the hollow rind of a turnip employed as a lantern.

ing for the doors to open. When they did, it was chins and boots and elbows, no queues; we just fought our way in. Lamplight and decorations had transformed the schoolroom from a prison into a banqueting hall. The long trestle-tables were patterned with food: fly-cake, brown buns, ham sandwiches. The two stoves were roaring, reeking of coke. The helpers had their teapots charged. We sat down stiffly and gazed at the food; fidgeted, coughed and waited. . . .

6   The stage curtains parted to reveal the Squire, wearing a cloak and a deer-stalking hat. He cast his dim, wet eyes round the crowded room, then sighed and turned to go. Somebody whispered from behind the curtain. "Bless me!" said the Squire, and came back.

7   "The Parochial Church Tea!" he began, then paused. "Is with us again . . . I suggest. And Entertainment. Another year! Another year comes round! . . . When I see you all gathered together here—once more—when I see—when I think . . . And here you all are! When I see you here—as I'm sure you all are—once again . . . It comes to me, friends!—how time—how you—how all of us here—as it were . . ." His moustache was quivering, tears ran down his face, he groped for the curtains and left.

8   His place was taken by the snow-haired Vicar, who beamed weakly upon us all.

9   "What is the smallest room in the world?" he asked.

10   "A mushroom!" we bawled, without hesitation.

11   "And the largest, may I ask?"

12   "ROOM FOR IMPROVEMENT!"

13   "You know it," he muttered crossly. Recovering himself, he folded his hands: "And now, O bountiful Father . . ."

14   We barked through grace and got our hands on the food and began to eat it in any old order. Cakes, buns, ham, it didn't matter at all, we just worked from one plate to the next. Folk by the fires fanned themselves with sandwiches, a joker fried ham on the stove, steaming brown teapots passed up and down, and we were so

busy there was small conversation. Through the lighted windows we could see snow falling, huge feathers against the dark. "It's old Mother Hawkins a-plucking her geese!" cried someone; an excellent omen. Twelfth Night, and old Mother Hawkins at work, up in the sky with her birds; we loosened our belts and began to nod at each other; it was going to be a year of fat.

¹⁵ We had littered the tables with our messy leavings of cake crumbs and broken meat; some hands still went through the motions of eating, but clearly we'd had enough. The Vicar rose to his feet again, and again we thanked the Lord. "And now, my friends, comes the—er—feast for the soul. If you would care to—ah—take the air a moment, willing hands are waiting to clear the hall and prepare for the—um—Entertainment. . . ."

¹⁶ We crowded outside and huddled in the snow while the tables were taken away. Inside, behind curtains, the actors were making up—and my moment, too, was approaching. The snow whirled about me and I began to sweat; I wanted to run off home. Then the doors re-opened and I crouched by the stove, shivering and chattering with nerves. The curtains parted and the Entertainment began, with a comic I neither saw nor heard. . . .

¹⁷ "For the next item, ladies and gentlemen, we have an instrumental duet, by Miss Brown and—er—young Laurie Lee."

¹⁸ Smirking with misery I walked to the stage. Eileen's face was as white as a minim.° She sat at the piano, placed the music crooked, I straightened it, it fell to the ground. I groped to retrieve it; we looked at one another with hatred; the audience was still as death. Eileen tried to give me an A, but struck B instead, and I tuned up like an ape threading needles. At last we were ready, I raised my fiddle; and Eileen was off like a bolting horse. I caught her up in the middle of the piece—which I believe was a lullaby—and after playing the repeats, only

minim: a provincial expression for minnow, a tiny, silvery white fish.

twice as fast, we just stopped, frozen motionless, spent.
¹⁹   Some hearty stamping and whistling followed, and a
shout of "Give us another!" Eileen and I didn't exchange
a glance, but we loved each other now. We found the
music of "Danny Boy" and began to give it all our emotion, dawdling dreamily among the fruitier chords and
scampering over the high bits; till the audience joined
in, using their hymn-singing voices, which showed us the
utmost respect. When it was over I returned to my seat
by the stove, my body feeling smooth and beautiful.
Eileen's mother was weeping into her hat, and so was
mine, I think. . . .
²⁰   Now I was free to become one of the audience, and
the Entertainment burgeoned * before me. What had
seemed to me earlier as the capering of demons now
became a spectacle of human genius. Turn followed turn
in variety and splendor. Mr. Crosby, the organist, told
jokes and stories as though his very life depended on
them, trembling, sweating, never pausing for a laugh,
and rolling his eyes at the wings for rescue. We loved
him, however, and wouldn't let him go, while he grew
more and more hysterical, racing through monologues,
gabbling songs about shrimps, skipping, mopping, and
jumping up and down, as though humoring a tribe of
savages.
²¹   Major Doveton came next, with his Indian banjo,
which was even harder to tune than my fiddle. He
straddled a chair and began wrestling with the keys,
cursing us in English and Urdu.° Then all the strings
broke, and he snarled off the stage and started kicking
the banjo round the cloakroom. He was followed by a
play in which Marjorie, as Cinderella, sat in a goose-
feathered dress in a castle. While waiting for the pump-
kin to turn into a coach, she sang "All alone by the
telephone."
²²   Two ballads came next, and Mrs. Pimbury, a widow,
sang them both with astonishing spirit. The first invited us to go with her to Canada; the second was addressed to a mushroom:

Urdu: Hindustani as spoken by Mohammedans in India.

> *Grow! Grow! Grow! Little mushroom, grow!*
> *Somebody wants you soon.*
> *I'll call again tomorrow morning—*
> > *See!*
> *And if you've grown bigger you will just suit* ME!
> *So Grow! Grow! Grow! little mushroom—Grow!*

²³ Though we'd not heard this before, it soon became part of our heritage, as did the song of a later lady. This last—the Baroness von Hodenburg—sealed our entertainment with almost professional distinction. She was a guest star from Sheepscombe and her appearance was striking; it enshrined all the mystery of art. She wore a loose green gown like a hospital patient's, and her hair was red and long. "She writes," whispered Mother. "Poems and booklets and that."

²⁴ "I am going to sink you," announced this lady, "a little ditty I convected myself. Bose vords und music, I may say, is mine—und zey refer to ziss pleasant valleys."

²⁵ With that she sat down, arched her beautiful back, raised her bangled wrists over the keyboard, then ripped off some startling runs and trills, and sang with a ringing laugh:

> *Elfin volk come over the hill!*
> *Come und dance, just vere you vill!*
> *Brink your pipes, und brink your flutes,*
> *Brink your sveetly soundink notes!*
> *Come avay-hay! Life is gay-hay!*
> *Life—Is—Gay!*

²⁶ We thought this song soppy, but we never forgot it. From then on, whenever we saw the Baroness in the lanes we used to bowl the song at her through the hedges. But she would only stop, and cock her head, and smile dreamily to herself. . . .

²⁷ After these songs the night ended with slapstick; rough stuff about babies, chaps dressed as women, broad Gloucester exchanges between yokels and toffs,* with the

yokels coming off best. We ached with joy, and kicked at the chairs; but we knew the end was coming. The Vicar got up, proposed a vote of thanks, and said oranges would be distributed at the gate. The National Anthem was romped through, we all began coughing, then streamed outdoors through the snow.

[28] Back home our sisters discussed their performances till the tears dripped off their noses. But to us boys it was not over, not till tomorrow; there was still one squeeze left in the lemon. Tomorrow, very early, we'd go back to the schoolroom, find the baskets of broken food—half-eaten buns, ham coated with cake crumbs—and together we'd finish the lot.

ANALYSIS

Laurie Lee has a keen ear for dialogue. The Squire's fumbling speech is wondrous syntax (or rather lack of good sentence structure); the Vicar's is typically hesitant; the Baroness von Hodenburg's is unforgettable because we can hear her urge us to "brink your sveetly soundink notes." But good description does not depend upon dialogue. What Lee does here so successfully is to combine children's language with descriptive phrases a literate adult would use in recollecting a childhood party. His sisters made "lah-di-dah gestures"; three giggling helpers were "forking the meat and slapping it into sandwiches"; the Vicar said grace and "[we] got our hands on the food and began to eat in any old order"; Eileen and Laurie "found the music of 'Danny Boy' and began to give it all [their] emotion, dawdling dreamily among the fruitier chords and scampering over the high bits."

This is fine, colloquial (or informal, conversational) language. It brings a youthful zest to the description. And yet Lee can call the tea "an orgy of communal gluttony," the long trestle-tables are "patterned with food," he "tunes up like an ape threading needles," Baroness von Hodenburg "sealed our entertainment with almost professional distinction"—clearly not a child's vocabulary. It is a measure of Lee's skill in writing that the two "vocabularies" do not jar. Quite clearly he is recollecting an occasion here, but the reader feels he is sitting with the young Laurie Lee enjoying it *now*. His details are specific and accurate; their effect is instantaneous.

Even more important than Lee's vocabulary is his good sense of proportion. This essay has a beginning, a middle, and an end. The author is always in control and the reader always knows where he is. The first paragraph identifies the occasion, the second cites the preparation; together they make a simple introduction. The next three paragraphs start the festival. The Squire and the Vicar are, properly, the first to speak. Then comes food. Then the cleaning away of the food. Then entertainment. Note that Lee promised this order in his first sentence, when he gave us the name of the festival. We come quickly to Lee's part in the entertainment. Call it foreshortening of the description, if you wish; that is, he could well have described *all* the acts, but he chose, for emphasis on the first person narrative, to come quickly to his own. We race through the description just as Lee and Eileen raced through the music; the verbs are almost staccato, their impact swift. Then he writes that "now I was free to become one of the audience." The pace slackens, and we meander through the middle section of the essay. Two paragraphs from the end Lee literally announces the end. We hear briefly of the slapstick comedy and are soon streaming "outdoors through the snow." As a coda he gives us the last squeeze of the lemon: the "half-eaten buns," the "ham coated with cake crumbs," will make a second feast tomorrow. Lee has written of his festival so well we feel that we want to share the leftovers with these Cotswold boys in their schoolroom.

Questions on Content

1. Why do you suppose the entertainment takes place in the schoolroom and not in the church?
2. In what way is the time of year important to the atmosphere Lee creates?
3. What adjectives would you use to describe the humor of this essay?

Add to your vocabulary: gluttony, burgeoned, toff. What is a trestle-table?

Questions on Technique

1. This essay is written in the first person, yet Lee incorporates other "performers" and includes considerably detailed description of their contributions. Would he have written a better essay if he had described only himself?

2. Find passages in which Lee makes effective use of sensory impressions ° other than those of sight. Show that they help us to experience the events fully.

3. Inspect the verbs in any of the longer paragraphs. Show that Lee achieves through the use of verbs what many writers try for adjectively. What other words might he have chosen?

4. Could we eliminate without loss the words to Mrs. Pimbury's and Baroness von Hodenburg's songs? Why do you think so?

5. If you were asked to state the dominant impression this essay leaves with you, what would you call it: how one boy reacted to a festival; how an English village entertains itself; local talent on stage; small-town humor?

Suggestions for Writing

1. In 400 words, describe a single event that you remember well from your childhood. Do not just narrate the action; recall the details "around" it. Try to give the impressions you had as a child.

2. When did you first "perform" before an audience? Do you remember the state of your nerves, the faces in the crowd, the response to the performance? Write a 400-word essay about it.

3. Describe a church supper, a Sunday School picnic, an organized hike or camping trip from their culinary aspects, in 400–500 words.

4. Laurie Lee is reveling in familiar sights and sounds, familiar to his village, that is. Describe briefly a visit you made to a *strange* place as a child and what your reactions were.

sensory impressions: See Glossary.

THOMAS SANCTON · *The Silver Horn*

Putting a Cotswold festival on stage, as it were, is somewhat more difficult than merely "turning back the pages" to recall "how it was then." Laurie Lee showed us a remarkably large number of his neighbors in a short space. Thomas Sancton, a newspaperman in his native city of New Orleans, turns this recollection of his youth into equally vivid prose even though his locale is simply a Boy Scout summer camp on a Louisiana bayou, his style is in a low key, his friends remain nameless. Sancton wants us to see and feel what he saw and felt as a young boy, but he does not parade his material as Lee does.

This is another sort of descriptive writing. We might call it descriptive reflection, for Sancton attempts to answer here, as he says, when and where it was that he "first began to believe what [he] now believe[s] about the Southern world, . . . about democracy, about America, about life and death, about men and all their curious fates." The temptation for most writers, on such an occasion, would be to moralize or to argue the reader into sharing a point of view, but Sancton avoids both. He is as relaxed in his writing as he was at the summer camp. When he does offer us a judgment, he does it tentatively. There is always a fine balance between the events and what they meant to him. "Little things that happened during these years," he writes, "seemed of great importance."

As you read this reminiscence, consider the tense of the verb seemed. *Could not Sancton also be suggesting, although indirectly, that even now, in his adult years, these little things* seem *important because he did his "first real thinking in this camp"? This descriptive essay*

is written in the first person. It begins as reminiscence.
It quickly develops into more than that.

¹ The scene is a Boy Scout summer camp, thickly grown
with pines and cypress. There is a row of green clapboard
cabins, with clean floors and neat double-decker bunks;
there is an open field and a flag hanging still in the
heavy air; and at the field's edge the land drops down a
little to the dark water of a bayou.° I spent five summers
here, from the time I was twelve until I entered college.
I did my first real living and my first real thinking in
this camp.

² And I think of it now. Like some reader of a long
novel who turns back through the pages to find a forgotten part of the plot, and who comes with a flash of recognition across old scenes and dialogues, and characters
who have gone out of the narrative but whose personalities and substance once filled pages and pages, I have
gone turning back through the pages of my life. When
was it and where was it—I have been asking—that I first
began to believe what I now believe about the Southern
world I left not many years ago, about Negroes, about
democracy, about America,. about life and death, about
men and all their curious fates? This search has been
long and turning. Often it has led me back to the years
of my early teens and to the summers I spent in the camp.

³ I was born to the sidewalks and asphalt of the largest
city and the widest street in the South. In New Orleans,
broad Canal Street was never empty of speeding automobiles and streetcars, even late at night, and of people
walking by, their footsteps echoing on the sidewalk. But
here on the bayou another world existed. In the morning
it was the strange, thin call of a bugle that broke into
our sleep. Almost before we were awake we could smell
the wet exercise field and the forest. Birds popped from
tree to tree, plump and colorful, bluejays, mockingbirds,
cardinals, flickers—Audubon had painted in these woods.
Rabbits ran into the bushes. Snakes we had no fear of,

bayou: a creek or minor river tributary to another body of water.

long thick blue racers and speckled king snakes, slid through the weeds at our approach.

⁴ Standing in the wet grass, still yawning and sleepy, we took the morning exercises. Night chill was in the air, but behind our backs the sun was rising, and its warmth crept onto our shoulders. After the exercises we raced along a wagon road to the swimming pool, and as we ran up, shouting and excited, two or three startled frogs made tremendous leaps and plumped beneath the glassy surface of the water. After the swim we dried our skinny sunburned bodies and ran to the mess hall.

⁵ Most of us in the camp were poor boys, or boys who were almost poor. It was not a welfare camp, but the fees were low, less than a dollar a day for a camper. As a consequence it was filled with boys from modest New Orleans neighborhoods and also from the tough ones. There was always a smattering of the democratic rich: the son of the traction company president came every summer. So did his cousin from Texas, a wild, hard towhead with plenty of money and the soul of a true picaroon.° He fascinated and dominated the rest of us. He was the first colorful outlaw I ever knew. But most of the well-to-do families sent their boys to camps in the Maine woods or the North Carolina mountains. Our camp was only forty miles from the city. Department store clerks, streetcar motormen, little grocers could afford the fees.

⁶ We had no saddle horses, no golf course, and only a weed-grown tennis court which no one used. For diversion we fell back on nature. In the morning we performed a work detail, cutting a patch of weeds or hauling dirt in wheelbarrows to mend a road. After this we were free to swim, to paddle on the bayou in slender little Louisiana boats called pirogues, to fish for the boisterous black bass and yellow perch and fat blue catfish, and to work for our Boy Scout medals and merit badges, tracking through the grassy cut-over pine lands, cooking dough and bacon on sweet-gum spits, bandaging one another with first-aid splints.

picaroon: a rogue or pirate.

⁷ These little medals and bits of colored ribbon meant a great deal to us. We wrote home enthusiastic letters about our progress, describing in detail how we had passed the tests, forwarding the comments of some eighteen-year-old camp officer as though it really mattered. Our parents, most of whom did not have very big events happening in their own lives, were just as eager and simple-hearted about these things, and one or two of the fathers were foolishly ambitious to have their sons win the highest number of merit badges in the area.

⁸ Little things that happened during these years seemed of great importance. I remember that in my first year at camp I wore an ill-fitting Boy Scout hat. One of the councilors, a boy five years my senior who seemed to me to belong already to the grown-up world of brilliance and authority, began, in a pleasant way, to tease me about the hat. Every morning for a week he led us to the abandoned logging road and clocked us as we walked and trotted a measured mile. My hat was anchored down by a heavy chin strap; it flopped and sailed about my head as I ran to the finish line. The boy began to laugh at me. He waved his arms and called out, "Come on, you rookie!" The other kids took it up and Rookie became my first nickname. I loved it. I tingled when someone called it out. I painted it on my belt, carved it in my packing case, inked it into my hatband, and began to sign it to my letters home. Years later when we were grown I knew this camp officer again. The gap between our ages had vanished and in real life now he seemed to me a rather colorless young lawyer. He did not remember about the hat.

⁹ At mealtime we ate ravenously in the mess hall. There were steaming platters of pork and beans and cabbage and stew. As we walked to the long clapboard building with our hair freshly combed and water glistening on our faces, which we washed at the flowing pipe of a big artesian well, we existed in a transport of driving hunger. In the steamy fragrance of the mess hall we set up a clatter of knives and forks and china, and afterward we went to our cabins and flopped on the bunks in a state of

drowsy satisfaction. Somehow, fat never formed on our skinny frames. We ran too much. We paddled in the boats. We swam. We cut firewood and played softball after supper. When there was nothing else to do we climbed in the rafters of our cabins, trying to invent complicated monkey swings that no one else could do. Every year some campers broke their arms.

II

10   During those summers in camp a love grew up in me for the rhythms of nature, for tropical rains that came sweeping through the pines and oaks, for the fiery midday sun, for long evenings, and the deep black nights. Great campfires were lit beside the bayou and a rushing column of luminous smoke and sparks ascended to the cypress trees. Fire gleamed in the water where bass were sleeping in the stumps. Campers wandered toward the meeting place, their flashlights swinging in the woods. We sat about the fire, singing, beating deep rumbling tom-toms made of hollowed oak logs, performing an ageless repertoire of skits and mimicry. And after these sessions one leader took the Protestant boys and another the Catholics and, standing in the open fields, in our separate groups, we prayed aloud.

11   My heart had strayed already from the formal, repetitious praying. A towering pine tree at the field's edge made a silhouette in the starry sky. I knew the constellations, the Giant, the Dipper, the Bear. I looked for the two inseparable stars, Misar and Alcar, horse and rider, and sensed the fact that Arabs named these stars a thousand years before me, and even in my boy's ignorance I felt aware of man's long and varied time upon the earth. I knew this night-filled wilderness had stretched beneath these stars for endless ages before Frenchmen had come in boats to build New Orleans. I thought of the Indians who had fished and hunted here, whose bones and broken pottery we sometimes found in grassy mounds. I felt worshipful of the earth, the pine tree, the night itself.

12   Sometimes we packed provisions and tents and

mosquito bars and paddled down the bayou to the lake, ten miles away. The lake was a great inland finger of the Gulf of Mexico, twenty miles long, ten wide. Twenty miles below us, in prehistoric times, the mouth of the Mississippi River had built up new land, and these watery prairies had pinched off the small inland gulf and made a lake of it, but it connected still through a series of passes with the Mexican Gulf. The lake teemed with croakers, catfish, shrimp, and big blue-clawed crabs. At the northern end, where we camped, a network of tributary bayous emptied into the lake. For the last mile or so of their crooked lengths, where the brackish * water of the lake crept into the slow-moving bayous, fish and small life were abundant, bass fed in the rushes, and muskrats built their cities of the plains.

13   There was a relatively high, sandy point near the mouth of the bayou, where we camped. The sun went down red into the lake and left a long, clear twilight. A few stars came out. A salty wind blew in from the Mexican Gulf; it came out of the south every night. The breeze swept over the rushes and made small waves break on the sandy, grassy shore. There was a red beacon light on weather-beaten piles out in the lake and its long reflection shimmered in the water. We sprayed our mosquito netting with citronella ° and built up a driftwood fire and lay down on canvas bedrolls spread upon the thin, tough grass and sand. The trade wind blew through our tents throughout the night. We listened to the waves. We could smell the vast salt marshes far below us. A yellow moon came out of the gulf. Far down the lake we could see the lights of a railroad bridge. We felt the beauty of this wilderness like a hunger.

14   After two days of fishing and swimming in the lake, our shoulders and faces darker from the sun, we paddled back up the winding bayou.

citronella: a fragrant grass of southern Asia, used in making perfumes and insect repellent.

III

¹⁵ One summer when I was sixteen a party of us, paddling upstream to buy some candy at a crossroads store, came upon three young girls who were bathing in a sandy cove.* There were four of us in the long pirogue, all of an age. For a long moment we were speechless. At last we said hello, and they answered in warm gay voices. We drifted the boat into the cove and began to speak to them. Two of the girls were sisters. The three of them had come to visit a relative who kept a fine summer lodge in the woods across the bayou from the camp. One of the sisters was fifteen and the others were seventeen. They were aglow with fresh and slender beauty, and their bathing suits were bright flags of color. Their impact upon us was overwhelming. We grew silly, tongue-tied, said foolish things we did not mean to say, shoved one another about in the boat, and finally overturned it. The loreleis ° laughed musical little laughs. They seemed unbearably beautiful. We had no idea what to do about it.

¹⁶ The girls had been at the lodge for a week. They missed their beaux in New Orleans, they missed the dating and the dancing and the music. It was a gay town in the summertime. The older girls looked upon us as children; but still—they must have reflected—we were not such children at that. The younger sister, a slender child with thick brown hair and heavily crimsoned lips, sat on the bank and regarded us with a happy open face.

¹⁷ At last we took courage and asked if we could call on them that night.

¹⁸ "Oh, yes!" they cried eagerly. Life at that moment was dazzling.

¹⁹ Making this rendezvous was an impulsive thing to do, for it was midweek and we should have to steal away after taps and walk down a path without flashlights

loreleis: In German legend, the Lorelei was a siren who lured sailors to destruction by singing from a rock on the Rhine River.

through a snake-infested lowland and—because the boats were counted and chained at nightfall—swim across the bayou, holding our clothes above our heads.

20 We crept from our cabins at ten o'clock that night and met in the pine woods. One of us intoned * a counting-out rhyme; the loser had to walk first down the path through the snake hole. He cut a long gum sapling and rattled it down the path ahead of us. We walked bunched tightly together, tense with fear, giggling at our own unbelievable audacity, trembling in our eagerness. At the bayou's edge we slipped out of our shorts and shirts and sneakers and, holding them above our heads with one hand, we felt our way round the knees and along the sunken roots of a cypress tree, and pushed off into the bayou and began to swim.

21 The moon had not yet risen. We had only the silhouettes of trees to guide us. We swam closely together, cautioning one another to silence, bursting into convulsive squeals as water lilies brushed against our bodies or when a fish broke the surface near us. We swam upstream from the camp, past two bends, and waded from the water in the cove where we had met the girls. Now we were laughing with relief and excitement, and popping one another on the backsides. We scraped the glistening water from our bodies, dressed, and combed our wet hair and hurried off down the wagon path into the woods. Long ago the cove had been a landing stage for small schooners which came to load pine firewood for New Orleans.

22 The girls were waiting for us, dressed in bright print cotton dresses and wearing hair ribbons. The soft light gave age and mystery to their youthful shoulders, to their slender bodies; and, like nameless night-blooming vines in the woods about us, they bore a splendid fragrance all their own, a fragrance of youth and cleanliness and fresh cosmetics. They were playing a phonograph on the wide porch of the lodge. This was the summer of Maurice Chevalier's ° great success in Ameri-

Maurice Chevalier: French-born singer and movie star.

can movies. The little sister sang his song, rolling her eyes, turning out her soft pink lip:

> *If ze night-ting gail*
> *Good zing lak you . . .*

And she sang another:

> *. . . you make me feel so grand*
> *I want to hand the world to you.*
> *You seem to understand*
> *Each foolish little dream I'm dreaming, scheme I'm*
> * scheming . . .*

[23] I was so in love with her I could hardly catch my breath. I was in love with the other sister too, and with their friend. All of the boys were in love with all of the girls; the girls—so they said—had crushes on each of us. Our hearts were afire.

[24] We walked hand in hand down the wagon trail to the cove and built a bonfire. We stretched out on blankets, laughing, singing. We sang the songs that people always sing by rivers and campfires, "There's a Long, Long Trail A-Winding," "The Sweetheart of Sigma Chi," all the rest. We kissed the girls and they held fast to us. Before this night we had been only boys, holding hands with girls in movies, not quite sure why we pursued them and acted silly. Now, lying beneath the open sky, for the first time we understood the poignance * and the beauty of the human heritage.

[25] Every night for two weeks we came to see them. And when they told us good-by the last kiss was as much a discovery as the first, and we knew that love was a thing that could never grow old. After they had gone we would steal from our cabins to sit on the back porch of the camp hospital, on a hill, where we could see the bayou and the cove and the woods where we had found them; and we sat there talking late into the night, like daemon lovers in the ballads of old. I never passed the cove again, even years later when I would paddle down

the bayou fishing, without remembering our meetings with a suddenly racing heart. First love is unforgettable.

IV

²⁶   I had no lessons to do in those summer months of camp life. There was plenty of time to think. I was living a communal life with other boys. Among us were embryonic bullies, scoundrels, cheats, promoters, Babbitts,° and stuffed shirts; and there were also the boys of good heart, the unselfish, the humorous, the courageous, boys who were the salt of the earth, but who, often in their later lives, would be misled and preyed upon and set against one another by the sharp ones. One and all we lived together, ate together, slept together. Our personalities clashed, fermented, or formed amalgams.° Sitting together at night in the lamplit cabins, with darkness and towering woods closing in upon us, we had our first grave talks about religion, about death, about sex. The future stretching before us was wide and fathomless. And all about us, in the grass, in the underbrush, in towering summer skies, we beheld the face of nature and the earth's wide harmonies as they had never been revealed in our city lives. At night we could stretch out upon the field, observe the stars, and grasp for the first time the fact that some were vastly deeper in space than others. In our star-study courses we heard phrases like "light years." It began to seep into the consciousness of many of us that a hundred years or the life of an individual had little meaning in the total universe; and from this point some of us began our first gropings after moral philosophy, gropings for a belief that could give the total universe a meaning in our own lives.

²⁷   There was a bugler in our camp who was the first consummate * expert, in any field, that I had known. He had no other talent but his music. He was a good-natured, chubby, curly-headed Italian boy, rather lazy,

Babbitts: from Sinclair Lewis' novel, *Babbitt,* whose hero was an unimaginative "go-getting" businessman.
amalgams: compounds of different things.

and when he was not back in the woods practicing his cornet he walked round with a dreamy look, as though our own handicrafts could not possibly be of interest to him.

28 Paolo had a silver trumpet and he preferred it to the bugle. He wanted to be a great musician. He would take his horn and music back into a pine clearing a quarter of a mile from the camp and all day long we could hear him practicing the runs. He blew the trumpet with a clear, sweet tone. We had supreme confidence as we stood at attention on the parade grounds and the flag came down the creaking flagpole pulley in the late afternoon sunlight, and Paolo stood alone, with everyone watching, and bugled. We were proud of him when visitors came. He had that ability of experts to create a sense of possessiveness in others.

29 It was at bedtime that Paolo gathered up into his clear, thin music all the ineffable ° hungering of our awakening lives. At ten o'clock he climbed a high ladder to a life-guard platform we had nailed into the branches of a tall cypress tree beside the bayou. Paolo lived for this moment and, with the whole camp silent and listening below him in the darkness, he blew taps with a soft and ghostly beauty all his own. Somehow the music spoke for us, uttered the thing we knew but had no words for, set up a wailing in the pine trees of the brevity and splendor of human life. Lying in our bunks in the darkness of the cabin, some of us fell into sleep; but some lay in silence thinking longer, alive to the night, and I was one of these.

30 One night some ten years later I entered a smoke-filled tavern in another city where Paolo was playing in a band. By this time he had made a small reputation as a boy with a hot trumpet. I watched his now older face as he tore through the hot routines. He was tired. The silver horn made noise but, though I knew little about it, I could see that he was not a great jazz musician.

31 I did not go to see him any more. I wanted to re-

ineffable: indescribable.

member Paolo before he had lost something, before any of us had lost it, a kind of innocence. I wanted to remember him in the land of our first discoveries, when he had climbed into a cypress tree to blow his horn, and there was a kind of Gothic ° night-drench in our lives.

ANALYSIS

Sancton divides his essay into four parts. The first might be subtitled "Cast of Characters." In a pleasantly indirect manner, he introduces us to his camp friends and their daily routine. Part II is more personal and the style is richer with descriptive adjectives. We could call it "Faces of Nature," keeping in mind that the author is telling us as much about himself as he is about camping on the bayou. Call the third part "Escapade," in both meanings of the word. Sancton narrates an incident here, but he also describes young love. It is a good example, as we said earlier, of how descriptive writing merges into narrative on occasion. In the last part, which we are not encouraged to sub-title since it gives the title to the whole essay, Sancton returns to his initial motive in recalling these days. He says, "There was plenty of time to think." Remember that he introduced this aspect of his essay in his topic sentence,° at the end of the first paragraph: "I did my first real living and my first real thinking in this camp." How is he to illustrate (rather than merely to enumerate) what he thought about? By describing the communal life of the camp? By talking of stargazing late at night in the open fields?

These serve, but he chooses Paolo—the only camper he feels it necessary to name—both as "the first consummate expert, in any field, that [he] had known" and as a symbol of lost innocence. Through Paolo, Sancton is able to say many things: the early respect he had for skill, and devotion to that skill, the way music "spoke for" the boys at taps, the isolation of a young boy as he lay in his bunk, thinking, unable to sleep. But most of all, Paolo serves as a rude awakening and forceful con-

Gothic: wild. unrestrained.
topic sentence: See Glossary.

clusion, simultaneously. Sancton wishes to end this reminiscence in time present, as it began. We plunge, therefore, from taps at camp to a "smoke-filled tavern," from a "clear, thin music" to a "hot trumpet." If the contrast is not sharp enough, if you perchance miss his point, he spells it out in the final paragraph: "I did not go to see him anymore. . . . I wanted to remember him in the land of our first discoveries."

We might call this kind of organization discursive or rambling, quite different from Laurie Lee's; yet it suits Sancton's purpose. He does not wish to proceed from a fixed point in time through a single incident, building his description of people and places on a chronological pattern. He uses chronological flash-backs, it is true, but we could more accurately describe the structure of this essay as elaboration of topic paragraph or theme with variations. The incidents span five years, from the time Sancton was twelve until he entered college. The last variation, the concluding elaboration is Paolo; and consciously or not we are led to agree with Sancton that the "clear, sweet tones" in a cypress bayou, and all they stood for, are gone with his youth. The carefully detailed descriptions all point toward this conclusion. The essay is discursive but never uncontrolled.

Questions on Content

1. Why does Sancton not name his camp, nor its location, nor his friends, except for Paolo? Does it make any difference to you, as reader? What details of location and daily routine do you remember?

2. How much of what Sancton writes about do you think is typical of only a Southern camp? Would you call this a regional essay?

3. Why should "Rookie" be such an apt nickname for this author?

4. Sancton concludes his third section with this sentence: "First love is unforgettable." What descriptive details bear out this conclusion? Near the end of this section, he writes: ". . . for the first time we understood the poignance and the beauty of the human heritage." What has this idea to do with first love?

Add to your vocabulary: brackish, cove, intoned, poign-ance, consummate, ineffable.

Questions on Technique

1. The opening paragraph of this essay is a model of declarative statement and simple announcement of purpose. How do the second and third paragraphs develop Sancton's initial ideas?
2. How could the train of events in this essay have been organized in a different way? Would your suggested organization improve the essay?
3. What particular seasonal details does Sancton use to describe a summertime camp? What part do certain sounds play in creating the atmosphere the author wishes to share with us? What do the lyrics of popular songs add to the third section?
4. Sancton twice uses references to the stars, in the second and the fourth part. What more does he make of them than *mere* reference? What else is he trying to say? Does this technique—saying one thing in terms of another—apply to any other elements of the essay?

Suggestions for Writing

1. It is your first day at camp or at a new school. In 400 words, record your impressions as you remember them.
2. In four or five paragraphs, describe a childhood friend who possessed a skill you much admired, such as dancing, horseback riding, diving, singing.
3. What childhood possession can you think of that was, now that you look back, a symbol of some strong feeling, that stood for something more than just an-other toy or gift or handmade object? Explain its meaning to you in three or four paragraphs.
4. What did the Boy Scouts or Girl Scouts (or any group with whom you went camping) mean to you as a child? Describe in 500 words one occasion which illus-trates your feelings about these days.
5. Can you select from your childhood an experience which taught you an important lesson, perhaps about behavior or about life or about human beings? If you

can recall such an experience, describe it in detail so that the reader will understand in what way it was important to you.

RUTH McKENNEY · *A Loud Sneer for Our Feathered Friends*

As a humorist and reporter in the nineteen twenties and thirties, Ruth McKenney was not widely known in America. Her book My Sister Eileen *first appeared in 1938. Years later, Leonard Bernstein and others made a brilliant Broadway musical from it, called* Wonderful Town. *The film was equally successful. Not all of the chapters of the McKenney autobiography were utilized on stage, however. Ruth and Eileen also went to camp. They hated it. No pirogues on the bayou, no silver horns, no speculation on the stars for them. In the reminiscence that follows, we see the other side of "living with nature." The girls hated camp councilors, Indian lore, organized recreation, and particularly birds. Ruth McKenney is not one to conceal her loathing. In fact, this essay is a splendid mixture of satire ° and humor with a description of an old-fashioned girls' camp. The language is colloquial,° the attitudes flippant.*

¹ From childhood, my sister and I have had a well-grounded dislike for our friends the birds. We came to hate them when she was ten and I was eleven. We had been exiled by what we considered an unfeeling family to one of those loathsome girls' camps where Indian lore is rife and the management puts up neatly lettered signs reminding the clients to be Good Sports. From the mo-

satire: See Glossary.
colloquial: See Glossary.

ment Eileen and I arrived at dismal old Camp Hi-Wah, we were Bad Sports, and we liked it.

² We refused to get out of bed when the bugle blew in the morning, we fought against scrubbing our teeth in public to music, we sneered when the flag was ceremoniously lowered at sunset, we avoided doing a good deed a day, we complained loudly about the food, which was terrible, and we bought some chalk once and wrote all over the Recreation Cabin, "We hate Camp Hi-Wah." It made a wonderful scandal, although unfortunately we were immediately accused of the crime. All the other little campers *loved* dear old Camp Hi-Wah, which shows you what kind of people they were.

³ The first two weeks Eileen and I were at Camp Hi-Wah, we sat in our cabin grinding our teeth at our councilor and writing letters to distant relatives. These letters were, if I say so myself, real masterpieces of double dealing and heartless chicanery.° In our childish and, we hoped, appealing scrawl, we explained to Great-Aunt Mary Farrel and Second Cousin Joe Murphy that we were having such fun at dear Camp Hi-Wah making Indian pocketbooks.

⁴ "We would simply L-O-V-E to make you a pocketbook, dear Aunt Mary," we wrote, "only the leather costs $1 for a small pocketbook or $1.67 for a large size pocketbook, which is much nicer because you can carry more things in it, and the rawhide you sew it up with, just exactly the way the Indians did, costs 40 cents more. We burn pictures on the leather but that doesn't cost anything. If we O-N-L-Y had $1 or $1.67 and 40 cents for the rawhide, we could make you the S-W-E-L-L-E-S-T pocketbook."

⁵ As soon as we had enough orders for Indian pocketbooks with pictures burnt on them, we planned to abscond * with the funds sent by our trusting relatives and run away to New York City, where, as we used to explain dramatically to our cabin-mates, we intended to

chicanery: trickery.

live a life of sin. After a few days, our exciting plans for our immediate future were bruited ° all over the camp, and admirers came from as far away as Cabin Minnehaha, which was way down at the end of Hiawatha Alley, just to hear us tell about New York and sin.

⁶ Fame had its price, however. One of the sweet little girls who lived in our cabin turned out to be such a Good Citizen ("Camp Hi-Wah Girls Learn to Be Good Citizens") that she told our dreadful secret to our councilor. Our mail was impounded * for weeks, and worst of all, we actually had to make several Indian pocketbooks with pictures burnt on them. My pictures were all supposed to be snakes, although they were pretty blurred. Eileen specialized in what she believed to be the likeness of a werewolf,° but Cousin Joe, who had generously ordered three pocketbooks, wrote a nice letter thanking Eileen for his pretty pocketbooks with the pretty pictures of Abraham Lincoln on them. We were terribly disgusted by the whole thing.

⁷ It was in this mood that we turned to birds. The handicraft hour at Camp Hi-Wah, heralded by the ten-thirty A.M. bugle, competed for popularity with the bird walks at the same hour. You could, as Eileen had already somewhat precociously * learned how to say, name your own poison. After three weeks of burning pictures on leather, we were ready for anything, even our feathered friends.

⁸ So one hot morning in July, the two McKenney sisters, big and bad and fierce for their age, answered the bird-walk bugle call, leaving the Indian-pocketbook teacher to mourn her two most backward pupils. We were dressed, somewhat reluctantly, to be sure, in the required heavy stockings for poison ivy and brambles, and carried, each of us, in our dirty hands a copy of a guide to bird lore called *Bird Life for Children*.

⁹ *Bird Life for Children* was a volume that all the Good Citizens in Camp Hi-Wah pretended to find en-

bruited: reported, rumored.
werewolf: a person transformed into a wolf.

grossing. Eileen and I thought it was stupefyingly dull.
Our favorite literary character at the time was Dumas'
Marguerite de Valois,° who took her decapitated lover's
head home in a big handkerchief for old times' sake.
Eileen, in those days, was always going to name her first
girl child Marguerite de Valois.

10   *Bird Life for Children* was full of horrid pictures in
full color of robins and pigeons and redbirds. Under
each picture was a loathsomely whimsical paragraph describing how the bird in question spent his spare time,
what he ate, and why children should love him. Eileen
and I hated the book so, we were quite prepared to
despise birds when we started off that morning on our
first bird walk, but we had no idea of what we were going to suffer, that whole awful summer, because of our
feathered friends. In the first place, since we had started
off making leather pocketbooks, we were three weeks
behind the rest of the Hi-Wah bird-lovers. They had
been tramping through blackberry bushes for days and
days and had already got the hang of the more ordinary
bird life around camp, whereas the only bird I could
identify at the time was the vulture. Cousin Joe took
me to a zoo once, and there was a fine vulture there, a
big, fat one. They fed him six live rats every day in lieu
of * human flesh. I kept a sharp eye out for a vulture all
summer, but one never turned up at Camp Hi-Wah.
Nothing interesting ever happened around that place.

11   On that first bird walk, Eileen and I trotted anxiously along behind the little band of serious-minded
bird-lovers, trying desperately to see, or at least hear,
even one bird, even one robin. But alas, while other
bird-walkers saw, or pretended to see—for Eileen and I
never believed them for a moment—all kinds of hum-
mingbirds and hawks and owls and whatnot, we never
saw or heard a single, solitary feathered friend, not one.

12   By the time we staggered into camp for lunch, with

Dumas' Marguerite de Valois: Alexandre Dumas, *père*, wrote *Marguerite de Valois*, a novel, in 1845. The real Marguerite de Valois
was the wife of Henry IV of France.

stubbed toes, scratched faces, and tangled hair, Eileen and I were soured for life on birds. Our bird logs, which we carried strapped to our belts along with the *Guide*, were still chaste and bare, while all the other little bird-lovers had fulsome * entries, such as "Saw and heard red-bird at 10:37 A.M. Molting."

¹³ Still, for the next three days we stayed honest and suffered. For three terrible mornings we endured being dolts * among bird-walkers, the laughing-stock of Camp Hi-Wah. After six incredibly tiresome hours, our bird logs were still blank. Then we cracked under the strain. The fourth morning we got up feeling grim but determined. We sharpened our pencils before we started off on the now-familiar trail through the second-growth forest.

¹⁴ When we got well into the woods and Mary Mahoney, the premier bird-walker of Camp Hi-Wah, had already spotted and logged her first redbird of the morning, Eileen suddenly stopped dead in her tracks. "Hark!" she cried. She had read that somewhere in a book. "Quiet!" I echoed instantly.

¹⁵ The bird-walkers drew to a halt respectfully and stood in silence. They stood and stood. It was not good form even to whisper while fellow bird-walkers were logging a victim, but after quite a long time the Leader, whose feet were flat and often hurt her, whispered impatiently, "Haven't you got him logged yet?"

¹⁶ "You drove him away," Eileen replied sternly. "It was a yellow-billed cuckoo."

¹⁷ "A yellow-billed cuckoo?" cried the Leader incredulously.

¹⁸ "Well," Eileen said modestly, "at least *I* think it was." Then, with many a pretty hesitation and thoughtful pause, she recited the leading features of the yellow-billed cuckoo, as recorded in *Bird Life for Children*.

¹⁹ The Leader was terribly impressed. Later on that morning I logged a kingfisher, a red-headed woodpecker, and a yellow-bellied sapsucker, which was all I could remember at the moment. Each time, I kept the bird-

walkers standing around for an interminable period, gaping into blank space and listening desperately to the rustle of the wind in the trees and the creak of their shoes as they went from one foot to another.

20   In a few days Eileen and I were the apple of our Leader's eye, the modest heroes of the Camp Hi-Wah bird walks. Naturally, there were base children around camp, former leading bird-walkers, who spread foul rumors up and down Hiawatha Alley that Eileen and I were frauds. We soon stopped this ugly talk, however. Eileen was the pitcher, and a very good one, too, of the Red Bird ball team and I was the first base. When Elouise Pritchard, the worst gossip in Cabin Sitting Bull, came up to bat, she got a pitched ball right in the stomach. Of course it was only a soft ball, but Eileen could throw it pretty hard. To vary this routine, I tagged Mary Mahoney, former head bird-walker, out at first base, and Mary had a bruise on her thigh for weeks. The rumors stopped abruptly.

21   We had begun to get pretty bored with logging rare birds when the game took on a new angle. Mary Mahoney and several other bird-walkers began to see the same birds we did on our morning jaunts into the forest. This made us pretty mad, but there wasn't much we could do about it. Next, Mary Mahoney began to see birds we weren't logging. The third week after we joined the Camp Hi-Wah Bird Study Circle, everybody except the poor, dumb Leader and a few backward but honest bird-lovers was logging the rarest birds seen around Camp Hi-Wah in twenty years. Bird walks developed into a race to see who could shout "Hark!" first and keep the rest of the little party in fidgety silence for the next five minutes.

22   The poor bird-walk Leader was in agony. Her reputation as a bird-lover was in shreds. Her talented pupils were seeing rare birds right and left, while the best she could log for herself would be a few crummy old redbirds and a robin or so. At last our Leader's morale collapsed. It was the day when nearly everybody in the study circle swore that she saw and heard a bona-fide nightingale.

²³ "Where?" cried our Leader desperately, after the fourth nightingale had been triumphantly logged in the short space of five minutes. Heartless fingers pointed to a vague bush. The Leader strained her honest eyes. No notion of our duplicity * crossed her innocent, unworldly mind.

²⁴ "I can't see any nightingale," our Leader cried, and burst into tears. Then, full of shame, she sped back to camp, leaving the Camp Hi-Wah bird-lovers to their nightingales and guilty thoughts.

²⁵ Eileen and I ate a hearty lunch that noon because we thought we would need it. Then we strolled down Hia-watha Alley and hunted up Mary Mahoney.

²⁶ "We will put the Iron Cross on you if you tell," Eileen started off, as soon as we found Mary.

²⁷ "What's the Iron Cross?" Mary squeaked, startled out of her usual haughty poise.

²⁸ "Never mind," I growled. "You'll find out if you tell."

²⁹ We walked past Cabin Sitting Bull, past the flag-pole, into the tall grass beyond the ball field.

³⁰ "She'll tell," Eileen said finally.

³¹ "What'll we do?" I replied mournfully. "They'll try us at campfire tonight."

³² They did, too. It was terrible. We denied every-thing, but the Head of Camp, a mean old lady who wore middy blouses and pleated serge bloomers, sen-tenced us to no desserts and eight-o'clock bedtime for two weeks. We thought over what to do to Mary Ma-honey for four whole days. Nothing seemed sufficiently frightful, but in the end we put the wart curse on her. The wart curse was simple but horrible. We dropped around to Cabin Sitting Bull one evening and in the pres-ence of Mary and her allies we drew ourselves up to our full height and said solemnly in unison, "We put the wart curse on you, Mary Mahoney." Then we stalked away.

33   We didn't believe for a moment in the wart curse, but we hoped Mary would. At first she was openly contemptuous, but to our delight, on the fourth evening she developed a horrible sty in her eye. We told everybody a sty was a kind of a wart and that we had Mary in our power. The next day Mary broke down and came around to our cabin and apologized in choked accents. She gave Eileen her best hair ribbon and me a little barrel that had a picture of Niagara Falls inside it, if you looked hard enough. We were satisfied.

ANALYSIS

Anyone who has seen *Wonderful Town* knows that explosiveness is one of its main ingredients. In a milder way, Ruth McKenney etches her reactions to Camp Hi-Wah. The essay bristles not with sensory images or carefully wrought physical description but with blunt opinionated judgments, usually negative. The tone, that is, the attitude of the writer toward her subject, is wholly consistent: "We were Bad Sports, and we liked it." The details of the essay are indirectly aimed at proving the thesis. But be assured that as Thomas Sancton permits his memory to color simple fact, so does Ruth McKenney. She knows how to embellish, to exaggerate, to undercut. Where Sancton recalls happy days, she remembers only gloom, and because the gloom is exaggerated we laugh easily at what she writes.

How she writes is our concern here. Let us, with this essay, inspect the language rather than the structure. Cast your eye over the first seven paragraphs. Note some of the verbs she uses; they rend the air: "we had been exiled by what we considered an unfeeling family"; "we refused . . . we fought . . . we sneered . . . we complained"; "we sat in our cabin grinding our teeth"; "we planned to abscond with the funds"; "our exciting plans . . . were bruited all over the camp"; "our mail was impounded for weeks"; "we turned to birds." These are not only vigorous verbs (*abscond, bruited, impounded* shape the exaggerated tone), they set the stage for the main incident of the reminiscence. Ruth and Eileen obviously turned to birds in desperation. Witness the title.

The adjectives she employs in the bird-watching episode work equally well for her in establishing a negative, disapproving attitude—the basis of good satire.° Nothing would change their opinion of this camp: with "dirty" hands they read *Bird Life for Children,* full of "horrid" pictures; the descriptions of the birds were "loathsomely whimsical"; after their first bird-hike, they staggered into camp with "stubbed" toes, "scratched" faces, and "tangled" hair; on the fourth morning they got up feeling "grim but determined." These adjectives are unusually ordinary, but they are always apt and, compared with the verbs, unobtrusive. The temptation to overstress one's feelings with harsh adjectives is great here, but the author avoids it.

We could finish reading the essay with close attention to the nouns she uses: the birds are always "victims"; the sisters become "modest heroes" of Camp Hi-Wah; in retaliation their enemies spread "ugly talk"; in counter-retaliation the sisters put "the wart curse" on Mary Mahoney. But the good writer does not consciously "noun" it or "verb" it. He describes graphically, he evokes a feeling, he makes us see, he shares his antipathies or enthusiasms. Miss McKenney is doing that here, in a free, natural style, filled with simple colloquialisms. The style is welded to the occasion she recounts. It would not do for an essay on a Cotswold village or a Boy Scout camp on a bayou; it fits the McKenney sisters perfectly because they wish to satirize Camp Hi-Wah, to make us share their loathing for it.

Questions on Content

1. The camp, we are told, is loathsome. In what ways did it offend Ruth and Eileen?
2. Do we ever hear the other side of the story: what Camp Hi-Wah thought of the McKenney sisters? Why do you suppose the author sounds so biased?
3. What picture have you of the councilors of this camp?

Add to your vocabulary: abscond, chicanery, impounded, precociously, in lieu of, fulsome, dolts, duplicity.

satire: See Glossary.

Questions on Technique

1. This essay abounds in colloquialisms: "a few crummy old redbirds"; "a mean old lady"; "dismal old Camp Hi-Wah." Find more of them. Do they sometimes border on worn-out phrases, what we call clichés? ° Would you eliminate them if you were re-writing this essay?

2. Of what use are the digressions Miss McKenney employs: Dumas' Marguerite de Valois; the vulture Cousin Joe showed Ruth at the zoo?

3. As readers, we do not always laugh at the same things. Where do you think Miss McKenney is writing most humorously?

4. "If we o-n-l-y had $1" is an old stylistic device, that is, a way of emphasizing. Do you think it is apt here? Why?

5. Thomas Sancton's essay is for the most part devoid of names; Miss McKenney's is rife with them. Has she chosen effective names (assuming that they are most likely substitutes for the real ones)?

6. What effect has the last paragraph, particularly the last sentence, on you as reader? How would you have ended the essay?

Suggestions for Writing

1. In four or five paragraphs, describe a person or a place you know well, paying close attention to the adjectives you use. Then describe a simple incident involving a person or place (do not tell a story, only set a scene) in which you strive to select forceful verbs.

2. One's first descriptive writing is usually in praise. Now write a 500-word satiric essay on a sport you dislike, a camp you were forced to attend, a boring trip you took with relatives.

3. Write an essay called "That Isn't the Way I Remember It" or "Papa Thought He Knew Best" or "Honesty Is Sometimes the Best Policy"—reversals of what you expect in autobiography.

4. In an essay, contradict from your own experiences what Miss McKenney says about camping and bird study.

clichés: See Glossary.

OBSERVATIONS: ADOLESCENCE

LINCOLN STEFFENS · *I Become a Student*

Born in 1866 and brought up in San Francisco, Lincoln Steffens was educated—perhaps he would object to the verb—at the University of California and in several European universities. His Autobiography, *published in 1931, is a colorful record of his early life, his career as a young journalist in New York, his years as muckraker, editor of* McClure's Magazine, *war reporter, and social critic. The essay which follows is a single chapter from that remarkable book. When Steffens entered the University of California it was a young and fairly small institution. "Berkeley, the beautiful," he writes, "was not the developed villa community it is now; I used to shoot quail in the brush under the oaks along the edges of the college grounds."*

That was in 1885. We wonder what he would say today about the size not only of the University of California but of scores of state universities across our country, and of their student bodies, their athletic plants, especially their educational policies. As he tells us here of how he became interested in learning, we watch a mind awakening, a young man determining what he wants to do with his life. We might call this kind of essay a portrait of a mind as well as school-days reminiscence. The opening sentence sets the tone.° Steffens took nothing on hearsay, in school or in life.

tone: See Glossary.

"I Become a Student," from *The Autobiography of Lincoln Steffens,* copyright, 1931, by Harcourt, Brace & World, Inc.; renewed, 1959, by Peter Steffens. Reprinted by permission of the publishers.

1 It is possible to get an education at a university. It has been done; not often, but the fact that a proportion, however small, of college students do get a start in interested, methodical study, proves my thesis, and the two personal experiences I have to offer illustrate it and show how to circumvent the faculty, the other students, and the whole college system of mind-fixing. My method might lose a boy his degree, but a degree is not worth so much as the capacity and the drive to learn, and the undergraduate desire for an empty baccalaureate is one of the holds the educational system has on students. Wise students some day will refuse to take degrees, as the best men (in England, for instance) give, but do not themselves accept, titles.

2 My method was hit on by accident and some instinct. I specialized. With several courses prescribed, I concentrated on the one or two that interested me most, and letting the others go, I worked intensively on my favorites. In my first two years, for example, I worked at English and political economy and read philosophy. At the beginning of my junior year I had several cinches in history. Now I liked history; I had neglected it partly because I rebelled at the way it was taught, as positive knowledge unrelated to politics, art, life, or anything else. The professors gave us chapters out of a few books to read, con, and be quizzed on. Blessed as I was with a "bad memory," I could not commit to it anything that I did not understand and intellectually need. The bare record of the story of man, with names, dates, and irrelative events, bored me. But I had discovered in my readings of literature, philosophy, and political economy that history had light to throw upon unhistorical questions. So I proposed in my junior and senior years to specialize in history, taking all the courses required and those also that I had flunked in. With this in mind I listened attentively to the first introductory talk of Professor William Cary Jones on American constitutional history. He was a dull lecturer, but I noticed that, after telling us what pages of what books we must be prepared in, he mumbled off some other references "for those that may care to dig deeper."

³ When the rest of the class rushed out into the sunshine, I went up to the professor and, to his surprise, asked for this memorandum. He gave it to me. Up in the library I ran through the required chapters in the two different books, and they differed on several points. Turning to the other authorities, I saw that they disagreed on the same facts and also on others. The librarian, appealed to, helped me search the book-shelves till the library closed, and then I called on Professor Jones for more references. He was astonished, invited me in, and began to approve my industry, which astonished me. I was not trying to be a good boy; I was better than that: I was a curious boy. He lent me a couple of his books, and I went off to my club to read them. They only deepened the mystery, clearing up the historical question, but leaving the answer to be dug for and written.

⁴ The historians did not know! History was not a science, but a field for research, a field for me, for any young man, to explore, to make discoveries in and write a scientific report about. I was fascinated. As I went on from chapter to chapter, day after day, finding frequently essential differences of opinion and of fact, I saw more and more work to do. In this course, American constitutional history, I hunted far enough to suspect that the Fathers of the Republic who wrote our sacred Constitution of the United States not only did not, but did not want to, establish a democratic government, and I dreamed for a while—as I used as a child to play I was Napoleon or a trapper—I promised myself to write a true history of the making of the American Constitution. I did not do it; that chapter has been done or well begun since by two men: Smith of the University of Washington and Beard (then) of Columbia (afterward forced out, perhaps for this very work). I found other events, men, and epochs waiting for students. In all my other courses, in ancient, in European, and in modern

history, the disagreeing authorities carried me back to the need of a fresh search for (or of) the original documents or other clinching testimony. Of course I did well in my classes. The history professors soon knew me as a student and seldom put a question to me except when the class had flunked it. Then Professor Jones would say, "Well, Steffens, tell them about it."

⁵ Fine. But vanity wasn't my ruling passion then. What I had was a quickening sense that I was learning a method of studying history and that every chapter of it, from the beginning of the world to the end, is crying out to be rewritten. There was something for Youth to do; these superior old men had not done anything, finally.

⁶ Years afterward I came out of the graft prosecution office in San Francisco with Rudolph Spreckels, the banker and backer of the investigation. We were to go somewhere, quick, in his car, and we couldn't. The chauffeur was trying to repair something wrong. Mr. Spreckels smiled; he looked closely at the defective part, and to my silent, wondering inquiry he answered: "Always, when I see something badly done or not done at all, I see an opportunity to make a fortune. I never kick at bad work by my class: there's lots of it and we suffer from it. But our failures and neglects are chances for the young fellows coming along and looking for work."

⁷ Nothing is done. Everything in the world remains to be done or done over. "The greatest picture is not yet painted, the greatest play isn't written (not even by Shakespeare), the greatest poem is unsung. There isn't in all the world a perfect railroad, nor a good government, nor a sound law." Physics, mathematics, and especially the most advanced and exact of the sciences, are being fundamentally revised. Chemistry is just becoming a science; psychology, economics, and sociology are awaiting a Darwin,° whose work in turn is awaiting an Ein-

Darwin: Charles Darwin (1809–1882), British naturalist and author of *On the Origin of Species* (1859).

stein.° If the rah-rah boys in our colleges could be told this, they might not all be such specialists in football, petting parties, and unearned degrees. They are not told it, however; they are told to learn what is known. This is nothing, philosophically speaking.

8 Somehow or other in my later years at Berkeley, two professors, Moses and Howison, representing opposite schools of thought, got into a controversy, probably about their classes. They brought together in the house of one of them a few of their picked students, with the evident intention of letting us show in conversation how much or how little we had understood of their respective teachings. I don't remember just what the subject was that they threw into the ring, but we wrestled with it till the professors could stand it no longer. Then they broke in, and while we sat silent and highly entertained, they went at each other hard and fast and long. It was after midnight when, the debate over, we went home. I asked the other fellows what they had got out of it, and their answers showed that they had seen nothing but a fine, fair fight. When I laughed, they asked me what I, the D.S., had seen that was so much more profound.

9 I said that I had seen two highly trained, well-educated Masters of Arts and Doctors of Philosophy disagreeing upon every essential point of thought and knowledge. They had all there was of the sciences; and yet they could not find any knowledge upon which they could base an acceptable conclusion. They had no test of knowledge; they didn't know what is and what is not. And they have no test of right and wrong; they have no basis for even an ethics.

10 Well, and what of it? They asked me that, and that I did not answer. I was stunned by the discovery that it was philosophically true, in a most literal sense, that

Einstein: Albert Einstein (1879–1955), German-born American physicist and mathematician. He is best known for his principle of relativity and contributions to the development of atomic physics.

nothing is known; that it is precisely the foundation that is lacking for science; that all we call knowledge rested upon assumptions which the scientists did not all accept; and that, likewise, there is no scientific reason for saying, for example, that stealing is wrong. In brief: there was no scientific basis for an ethics. No wonder men said one thing and did another; no wonder they could settle nothing either in life or in the academies.

11 I could hardly believe this. Maybe these professors, whom I greatly respected, did not know it all. I read the books over again with a fresh eye, with a real interest, and I could see that, as in history, so in other branches of knowledge, everything was in the air. And I was glad of it. Rebel though I was, I had got the religion of scholarship and science; I was in awe of the authorities in the academic world. It was a release to feel my worship cool and pass. But I could not be sure. I must go elsewhere, see and hear other professors, men these California professors quoted and looked up to as their high priests. I decided to go as a student to Europe when I was through Berkeley, and I would start with the German universities.

12 My father listened to my plan, and he was disappointed. He had hoped I would succeed him in his business; it was for that that he was staying in it. When I said that, whatever I might do, I would never go into business, he said, rather sadly, that he would sell out his interest and retire. And he did soon after our talk. But he wanted me to stay home and, to keep me, offered to buy an interest in a certain San Francisco daily paper. He had evidently had this in mind for some time. I had always done some writing, verse at the poetical age of puberty, then a novel which my mother alone treasured. Journalism was the business for a boy who liked to write, he thought, and he said I had often spoken of a newspaper as my ambition. No doubt I had in the intervals between my campaigns as Napoleon. But no more. I was now going to be a scientist, a philosopher.

He sighed; he thought it over, and with the approval of my mother, who was for every sort of education, he gave his consent.

ANALYSIS

"It is possible to get an education at a university. . . . The two personal experiences I have to offer illustrate it." In the first sentence Steffens tells us what he wants to do in this brief chapter. He hopes to take his reader off guard, of course, with the adjective "possible." Even though he is writing in the early 1930's, about an educational experience in 1885, the doubts he raises are still applicable today. "The whole college system of mind-fixing" is not, Steffens argues, synonymous with education. Seeking a degree is not seeking knowledge, although some knowledge may cling in the process. He calls education "the capacity and the drive to learn" rather than the accumulation of facts. When his professors gave him chapters to "read, con, and be quizzed on" he blamed a bad memory for his failure. In time he discovered he had to "understand and intellectually need" what he was reading in order to assimilate it. 'Assimilation" is the right word. As the body absorbs food, as a community absorbs new residents—this was the method Steffens had to discover; and, he tells us, "my method was hit on by accident and some instinct."

This essay, then, is a good illustration of statement and development of theme.° Let us look briefly at the development. His two experiences were "the first introductory talk of Professor William Cary Jones on American constitutional history" and "two highly trained well-educated Masters of Arts and Doctors of Philosophy disagreeing upon every essential point of thought and knowledge." The incident concerning Rudolph Spreckels is only a digression. Note that Steffens gives us only the barest of details about these two occasions. Note also the title of his chapter. Is there any connection? It is clear that Steffens, at once and always, is the subject of his autobiography; he is not loath to remind us that experience in relation to *him* is the chief con-

theme: See Glossary.

cern. This insistence is not egotism. It is merely one way of focusing the reader's attention. Thus we can see where this essay is taking us: a university *should* educate; the University of California did not hold Steffens' interest; three separate professors did awaken his mind to what "disagreeing authorities" can mean to a young student; after four years he could see that "as in history, so in other branches of knowledge, everything was in the air"; graduation from Berkeley meant "commencement" of learning for Steffens and he was ready to begin with Europe, with his parents' blessing.

Whether we agree with all he says is unimportant. This is forceful descriptive writing, partly because Steffens is *not* trying to force us to accept his point of view. His was not a unique educational experience. Had he entered the University of California in 1945 instead of 1885, he might have had a very different kind of experience; but Steffens, being the strong individualist he was, would doubtless have made his own discoveries in his own way. That individualism comes through strongly in his writing. It is the source of the strength of this essay. We listen attentively to the description of a state of mind.

Questions on Content

1. What did Steffens first study at college? When did he begin his study of history?
2. What is the point he wishes to make in the Rudolph Spreckels digression? Could it be omitted from the essay?
3. What does Steffens mean when he says, "Everything in the world remains to be done or done over"?
4. Why does Steffens think it unwise for students to seek only the facts and certainties and never to "read the books over again with a fresh eye"?
5. Could the last paragraph of this essay be removed without damage to Steffens' point of view? How did Steffens' father hope to tempt him away from Europe? What did Europe mean to Steffens at this age?

Questions on Technique

1. How successful is Steffens' opening paragraph in capturing your attention? (Remember that this essay

is a chapter in an autobiography; it is preceded by "I Go to College" and followed by "Berlin: Philosophy and Music.")

2. Do you feel Steffens should give us more details of his curriculum? Why choose only his history courses to discuss specifically?

3. In what ways does the vocabulary of this essay suit the subject matter? How would you describe Steffens' attitude: authoritative, questioning, self-centered, flippant?

Suggestions for Writing

1. Using Steffens' title, write a brief essay on your own educational "awakening."

2. Under the title "Why I Want to Go to College," discuss what you think the college curriculum should ideally offer you.

3. The high school curriculum aims at diversity; the college curriculum allows considerable specialization. Discuss in 500 words the difference between a broad and a narrow education as preparation for your future.

4. Describe in five or six paragraphs a teacher or a book which had a strong influence on your mental growth. Choose the details to illustrate the awakening or the growth rather than the physical attributes of the subject.

5. Write a 400-word essay called "Choosing a Profession." It is not important whether you are fully certain this choice is the final one. Describing your state of mind and how you reached your decision is the main object.

6. Write an evaluation of your own education thus far. You may write a critical essay of it as a whole or describe one period or one aspect of it. State your purpose in the beginning, as Steffens did, and then develop it in terms of specific experiences.

JAMES THURBER · *University Days*

James Thurber believes "humor is a kind of emotional chaos told about calmly and quietly in retrospect." He has been practicing it with enormous success for over thirty years, mainly in the pages of the New Yorker. *In 1945, he published* The Thurber Carnival, *a retrospective cross-section of his genius—short stories, fables, satirical ° essays, and his distinctive line drawings—beginning with excerpts from his first volume,* My World— and Welcome to It.*

The Thurber world is very special indeed. Though born in Columbus, Ohio, he has spent most of his life in New York and Connecticut writing of "the little perils of routine living." His habitat is the metropolis and the "secret life" man must develop (like Walter Mitty) to face the forces of mechanization. He knows the weakness of our civilization almost more acutely than he has a right to. He says of his drawings that they "sometimes seem to have reached completion by some other route than the common one of intent." Be assured that Thurber always knows where his writing is taking him, discursive though it may seem at first glance. His sense of form and style are unfaltering. Like excellence in most things, his descriptive ease in writing hides much hard work in "laying out" his subject and, one guesses, considerable re-writing to find the one perfect word or simile.° Thurber, like Steffens, attended a state university, but there the similarity ends. We are plunged at once into Thurber's botany class, without any theorizing or explanations.

satirical: See Glossary.
simile: See Glossary.

"University Days" by James Thurber, from *The New Yorker*, September 23, 1933. Permission the author, 1933. © The New Yorker Magazine, Inc.

¹ I passed all the other courses that I took at my university, but I could never pass botany. This was because all botany students had to spend several hours a week in a laboratory looking through a microscope at plant cells, and I could never see through a microscope. I never once saw a cell through a microscope. This used to enrage my instructor. He would wander around the laboratory pleased with the progress all the students were making in drawing the involved and, so I am told, interesting structure of flower cells, until he came to me. I would just be standing there. "I can't see anything," I would say. He would begin patiently enough, explaining how anybody can see through a microscope, but he would always end up in a fury, claiming that I could *too* see through a microscope but just pretended that I couldn't. "It takes away from the beauty of flowers anyway," I used to tell him. "We are not concerned with beauty in this course," he would say. "We are concerned solely with what I may call the *mechanics* of flars." "Well," I'd say, "I can't see anything." "Try it just once again," he'd say, and I would put my eye to the microscope and see nothing at all, except now and again, a nebulous * milky substance—a phenomenon of maladjustment. You were supposed to see a vivid, restless clockwork of sharply defined plant cells. "I see what looks like a lot of milk," I would tell him. This, he claimed, was the result of my not having adjusted the microscope properly; so he would readjust it for me, or rather, for himself. And I would look again and see milk.

² I finally took a deferred pass, as they called it, and waited a year and tried again. (You had to pass one of the biological sciences or you couldn't graduate.) The professor had come back from vacation brown as a berry, bright-eyed, and eager to explain cell structure again to his classes. "Well," he said to me, cheerily, when we met in the first laboratory hour of the semester, "we're going to see cells this time, aren't we?" "Yes, sir," I said. Students to right of me and to left of me and in front of me were seeing cells; what's more, they were quietly drawing

pictures of them in their notebooks. Of course, I didn't see anything.

3   "We'll try it," the professor said to me, grimly, "with every adjustment of the microscope known to man. As God is my witness, I'll arrange this glass so that you see cells through it or I'll give up teaching. In twenty-two years of botany, I—" He cut off abruptly for he was beginning to quiver all over, like Lionel Barrymore,° and he genuinely wished to hold onto his temper; his scenes with me had taken a great deal out of him.

4   So we tried it with every adjustment of the microscope known to man. With only one of them did I see anything but blackness or the familiar lacteal opacity,* and that time I saw, to my pleasure and amazement, a variegated * constellation of flecks, specks, and dots. These I hastily drew. The instructor, noting my activity, came back from an adjoining desk, a smile on his lips and his eyebrows high in hope. He looked at my cell drawing. "What's that?" he demanded, with a hint of a squeal in his voice. "That's what I saw," I said. "You didn't, you didn't, you *did*n't!" he screamed, losing control of his temper instantly, and he bent over and squinted into the microscope. His head snapped up. "That's your eye!" he shouted. " You've fixed the lens so that it reflects! You've drawn your eye!"

5   Another course that I didn't like, but somehow managed to pass, was economics. I went to that class straight from the botany class, which didn't help me any in understanding either subject. I used to get them mixed up. But not as mixed up as another student in my economics class who came there direct from a physics laboratory. He was a tackle on the football team, named Bolenciecwcz. At that time Ohio State University had one of the best football teams in the country, and Bolenciecwcz was one of its outstanding stars. In order to be eligible to play it was necessary for him to keep up in his studies,

Lionel Barrymore: a Hollywood star (1879–1954) noted for playing irritable old men.

a very difficult matter, for while he was not dumber than an ox he was not any smarter. Most of his professors were lenient and helped him along. None gave him more hints, in answering questions, or asked him simpler ones than the economics professor, a thin, timid man named Bassum. One day when we were on the subject of transportation and distribution, it came Bolenciecwcz's turn to answer a question. "Name one means of transportation," the professor said to him. No light came into the big tackle's eyes. "Just any means of transportation," said the professor. Bolenciecwcz sat staring at him. "That is," pursued the professor, "any medium, agency, or method of going from one place to another." Bolenciecwcz had the look of a man who is being led into a trap. "You may choose among steam, horse-drawn, or electrically propelled vehicles," said the instructor. "I might suggest the one which we commonly take in making long journeys across land." There was a profound silence in which everybody stirred uneasily, including Bolenciecwcz and Mr. Bassum. Mr. Bassum abruptly broke this silence in an amazing manner. "Choo-choo-choo," he said, in a low voice, and turned instantly scarlet. He glanced appealingly around the room. All of us, of course, shared Mr. Bassum's desire that Bolenciecwcz should stay abreast of the class in economics, for the Illinois game, one of the hardest and most important of the season, was only a week off. "Toot, toot, too-tooooooot!" some student with a deep voice moaned, and we all looked encouragingly at Bolenciecwcz. Somebody else gave a fine imitation of a locomotive letting off steam. Mr. Bassum himself rounded off the little show. "Ding, dong, ding, dong," he said, hopefully. Bolenciecwcz was staring at the floor now, trying to think, his great brow furrowed, his huge hands rubbing together, his face red.

6   "How did you come to college this year, Mr. Bolenciecwcz?" asked the professor. "*Chuf*fa chuffa, *chuf*fa chuffa."

7   "M'father sent me," said the football player.

8   "What on?" asked Bassum.

⁹ "I git an 'lowance," said the tackle, in a low, husky voice, obviously embarrassed.

¹⁰ "No, no," said Bassum. "Name a means of transportation. What did you *ride* here on?"

¹¹ "Train," said Bolenciecwcz.

¹² "Quite right," said the professor. "Now, Mr. Nugent, will you tell us—"

¹³ If I went through anguish in botany and economics—for different reasons—gymnasium work was even worse. I don't even like to think about it. They wouldn't let you play games or join in the exercises with your glasses on and I couldn't see with mine off. I bumped into professors, horizontal bars, agricultural students, and swinging iron rings. Not being able to see, I could take it but I couldn't dish it out. Also, in order to pass gymnasium (and you had to pass it to graduate) you had to learn to swim if you didn't know how. I didn't like the swimming pool, I didn't like swimming, and I didn't like the swimming instructor, and after all these years I still don't. I never swam but I passed my gym work anyway, by having another student give my gymnasium number (978) and swim across the pool in my place. He was a quiet, amiable blond youth, number 473, and he would have seen through a microscope for me if we could have got away with it, but we couldn't get away with it. Another thing I didn't like about gymnasium work was that they made you strip the day you registered. It is impossible for me to be happy when I am stripped and being asked a lot of questions. Still, I did better than a lanky agricultural student who was cross-examined just before I was. They asked each student what college he was in—that is, whether Arts, Engineering, Commerce, or Agriculture. "What college are you in?" the instructor snapped at the youth in front of me. "Ohio State University," he said promptly.

¹⁴ It wasn't that agricultural student but it was another a whole lot like him who decided to take up journalism, possibly on the ground that when farming went to pot he could fall back on newspaper work. He didn't realize,

of course, that that would be very much like falling back full-length on a kit of carpenter's tools. Haskins didn't seem cut out for journalism, being too embarrassed to talk to anybody and unable to use a typewriter, but the editor of the college paper assigned him to the cow barns, the sheep house, the horse pavilion, and the animal husbandry department generally. This was a genuinely big "beat," for it took up five times as much ground and got ten times as great a legislative appropriation as the College of Liberal Arts. The agricultural student knew animals, but nevertheless his stories were dull and colorlessly written. He took all afternoon on each of them, because he had to hunt for each letter on the typewriter. Once in a while he had to ask somebody to help him hunt. "C" and "L," in particular, were hard letters for him to find. His editor finally got pretty much annoyed at the farmer-journalist because his pieces were so uninteresting. "See here, Haskins," he snapped at him one day, "why is it we never have anything hot from you on the horse pavilion? Here we have two hundred head of horses on this campus—more than any other university in the Western Conference except Purdue—and yet you never get any real lowdown on them. Now shoot over to the horse barns and dig up something lively." Haskins shambled out and came back in about an hour; he said he had something. "Well, start it off snappily," said the editor. "Something people will read." Haskins set to work and in a couple of hours brought a sheet of typewritten paper to the desk; it was a two-hundred-word story about some disease that had broken out among the horses. Its opening sentence was simple but arresting. It read: "Who has noticed the sores on the tops of the horses in the animal husbandry * building?"

15   Ohio State was a land grant university and therefore two years of military drill was compulsory. We drilled with old Springfield rifles ° and studied the tactics of the

Springfield rifles: officially designated *United States rifle, Model of 1903*. They were breech-loading magazine .30 caliber rifles of the bolt type.

Civil War even though the World War was going on at the time. At 11 o'clock each morning thousands of freshmen and sophomores used to deploy over the campus, moodily creeping up on the old chemistry building. It was good training for the kind of warfare that was waged at Shiloh but it had no connection with what was going on in Europe. Some people used to think there was German money behind it, but they didn't dare say so or they would have been thrown in jail as German spies. It was a period of muddy thought and marked, I believe, the decline of higher education in the Middle West.

[16] As a soldier I was never any good at all. Most of the cadets were glumly indifferent soldiers, but I was no good at all. Once General Littlefield, who was commandant of the cadet corps, popped up in front of me during regimental drill and snapped, "You are the main trouble with this university!" I think he meant that my type was the main trouble with the university but he may have meant me individually. I was mediocre at drill, certainly —that is, until my senior year. By that time I had drilled longer than anybody else in the Western Conference, having failed at military at the end of each preceding year so that I had to do it all over again. I was the only senior still in uniform. The uniform which, when new, had made me look like an interurban railway conductor, now that it had become faded and too tight, made me look like Bert Williams ° in his bellboy act. This had a definitely bad effect on my morale. Even so, I had become by sheer practice little short of wonderful at squad maneuvers.

[17] One day General Littlefield picked our company out of the whole regiment and tried to get it mixed up by putting it through one movement after another as fast as we could execute them: squads right, squads left, squads on right into line, squads right about, squads left front into line, etc. In about three minutes one hundred

Bert Willams: a blackface comedian, part of the Williams and Worker team.

and nine men were marching in one direction and I was marching away from them at an angle of forty-five degrees, all alone. "Company, halt!" shouted General Littlefield. "That man is the only man who has it right!" I was made a corporal for my achievement.

18 The next day General Littlefield summoned me to his office. He was swatting flies when I went in. I was silent and he was silent too, for a long time. I don't think he remembered me or why he had sent for me, but he didn't want to admit it. He swatted some more flies, keeping his eyes on them narrowly before he let go with the swatter. "Button up your coat" he snapped. Looking back on it now I can see that he meant me although he was looking at a fly, but I just stood there. Another fly came to rest on a paper in front of the general and began rubbing its hind legs together. The general lifted the swatter cautiously. I moved restlessly and the fly flew away. "You startled him!" barked General Littlefield, looking at me severely. I said I was sorry. "That won't help the situation!" snapped the general, with cold military logic. I didn't see what I could do except offer to chase some more flies toward his desk, but I didn't say anything. He stared out the window at the faraway figures of co-eds crossing the campus toward the library. Finally, he told me I could go. So I went. He either didn't know which cadet I was or else he forgot what he wanted to see me about. It may have been that he wished to apologize for having called me the main trouble with the university; or maybe he had decided to compliment me on my brilliant drilling of the day before and then at the last minute decided not to. I don't know. I don't think about it much any more.

ANALYSIS

Although this essay is built around disparate episodes in Thurber's college career, it easily divides into five sections. The first four paragraphs describe botany class; then he moves on to economics, gymnasium class, journalism, and military drill. It is not a survey of a college course nor is it meant to be. What holds the sections together is the first person pronoun, Thurber's delicious sense of humor, and above all his sense of timing. Note how each section ends with no waiting for a laugh, with an abrupt switch to another subject: "You've fixed the lens so that it reflects! You've drawn your eye!" or "What college are you in?" the instructor snapped at the youth in front of me. "Ohio State University," he said promptly. Thurber depends on our appreciating his own awkwardness or the comical forthrightness of his fellow students. The obvious is often the source of humor. He plays upon it here with a fine hand for building a climax, for describing an incident "just as it happened," for omitting any unnecessary editorial or explanatory comment. Steffens built up his essay from a thesis, through examples, to a conclusion. Thurber has no conclusion, just as he has, in effect, no introduction.

How, then, is this effective writing? First, the essay demonstrates a relaxed organization, well-fitted to writing *about* college days, rather than surveying a four-year course. Thurber wants to give us facets of life at Ohio State seen through *his* eyes. A personal view may be a distorted view (he says elsewhere that his badly-focused, gold-rimmed glasses forever needed straightening so he saw not two of everything but one and a half) yet the author's personality lies in these very distortions.

Second, Thurber's style is based on skillful repetition of words. Notice in the opening sentence how the ear and eye pick up the last word, "botany." Thurber then repeats "botany" in the next sentence, and introduces two naturally allied words, "microscope," both in the middle and the end of the sentence, and "cell." Sentence three uses both words again—"I never once saw a cell through a microscope"—thereby firmly establishing in our minds what this first episode is about. Follow this technical device through the first four paragraphs and you will notice these words emphasized through repetition: "sea," "adjust," "milk," and the pronoun "we" (when the instructor, like the nurse who asks if we are ready to take our medicine, clearly means "you"). In each succeeding section he plays on a word or words: "transportation," "swim" and "swimming," "horses" and "horse barn," "drill," and "swatter." This repetition gives an almost painful obviousness to the point someone in the episode is trying to make, which is exactly the response Thurber desires.

Third, Thurber is not afraid of exaggeration. He does not exactly depart from what we might accept as credible, but he makes effective overstatement: "As God is my witness, I'll arrange this glass so that you see cells through it or I'll give up teaching," or "Once in a while he had to ask somebody to help him hunt. 'C' and 'L,' in particular, were hard letters for him to find," or "Some people used to think there was German money behind it. . . . It was a period of muddy thought and marked, I believe, the decline of higher education in the Middle West." Thurber knows we will not take him wholly seriously, and we know that he knows—an altogether happy relationship between author and reader. Were he to use ordinary hyperbole—such gross exaggeration as a million when he meant fifteen—he would lose all the humor implicit in these half-serious overstatements. Thurber's instincts are sound. He has the good taste to write it "straight" most of the time. Indeed his "straight" writing is the bulk of this essay. We finish with a feeling that Thurber enjoyed Ohio State University, in spite of microscopes and swimming and drill.

Questions on Content

1. Thurber writes of his botany instructor that "his scenes with me had taken a good deal out of him." How does he convince us this is true?
2. Of gymnasium work, he writes "I don't even like to think about it." Why doesn't he?
3. What is wrong with the agricultural student's basic approach to journalism?
4. In speaking of using a microscope, what does he mean by not seeing anything but "blackness or the familiar lacteal opacity"?

Add to your vocabulary: nebulous, opacity, variegated, husbandry.

Questions on Technique

1. For what reasons do you think Thurber sometimes uses dialogue in this descriptive essay? Why does he wish to combine anecdotes with descriptive writing?
2. What kind of humorous effect does he get from "Choo-choo-choo," "Toot, toot, too-tooooooot," and "*Chuf*fa chuffa, *chuf*fa chuffa"? from "the sores on the tops of the horses"? from Springfield rifles and Civil War tactics?
3. Thurber makes excellent use of similes: "like falling back full-length on a kit of carpenter's tools." Find two other similes.

Suggestions for Writing

1. Describe in 400 words a single incident that illustrates your own attitude toward physical education, or some other aspect of your schooling.
2. Describe your most difficult course in high school and explain why you had difficulty.
3. Try your hand at humorous writing, keeping it descriptive but using yourself (as Thurber does) as the butt of the humor. Suggested subjects: learning to speak a new language, learning to play a musical instrument, your first date, your first public speech, an adult dinner party.
4. Organize an essay called "High School Days." What will you include? eliminate? Write the essay in 500 words.
5. Inspect several college humor magazines to determine the kind of article they print. Write a 500-word essay you could submit to one of them.

CHAPTER 2

Primarily objective experience

THE SINGLE SUBJECT

LEE STROUT WHITE · *Farewell, My Lovely!*

*Automobiles today are more than means of transporta-
tion. They are almost necessities. Sixty years ago Henry
Ford's horseless carriage was only beginning to change
the face of our nation. Richard Lee Strout, of the* Christian Science Monitor, *and E. B. White, long a member
of the* New Yorker *staff, have never been able to forget
what a challenge and a joy the Model T Ford was. First
built in 1909, it was described as capable of going anywhere except into society. It was still going in 1927.*

*Under the pseudonym of Lee Strout White, these two
admirers of Ford's miraculous invention join to mourn
the passing of the Model T. "Celebrate" might be a better word because this essay is a love letter to a car. When
the Model T first appeared, Ford declared his impatience*

with "a tendency to keep monkeying with styles and to spoil a good thing by changing it." Ford buyers agreed. In less than two decades, Henry Ford had sold more than fifteen million "Tin Lizzies." Strout and White recall every important detail of their automobile. They will admit it was homely, without pretensions; but it had a will of its own and every owner knew it. This essay is written with affection, "the tribute of the sigh that is not a sob." The authors patently regret that these days are gone forever. To hold them in memory they want, they say, to make a few "random entries."

1 I see by the new Sears Roebuck catalogue that it is still possible to buy an axle for a 1909 Model T Ford, but I am not deceived. The great days have faded, the end is in sight. Only one page in the current catalogue is devoted to parts and accessories for the Model T; yet everyone remembers springtimes when the Ford gadget section was larger than men's clothing, almost as large as household furnishings. The last Model T was built in 1927, and the car is fading from what scholars call the American scene—which is an understatement, because to a few million people who grew up with it, the old Ford practically *was* the American scene.

2 It was the miracle God had wrought. And it was patently the sort of thing that could only happen once. Mechanically uncanny, it was like nothing that had ever come to the world before. Flourishing industries rose and fell with it. As a vehicle, it was hard-working, commonplace, heroic; and it often seemed to transmit those qualities to the persons who rode in it. My own generation identifies it with Youth, with its gaudy, irretrievable excitements; before it fades into the mist, I would like to pay it the tribute of the sigh that is not a sob, and set down random entries in a shape somewhat less cumbersome than a Sears Roebuck catalogue.

3 The Model T was distinguished from all other makes of cars by the fact that its transmission was of a type

known as planetary—which was half metaphysics,° half sheer friction. Engineers accepted the word "planetary" in its epicyclic * sense, but I was always conscious that it also meant "wandering," "erratic." Because of the peculiar nature of this planetary element, there was always, in Model T, a certain dull rapport * between engine and wheels, and even when the car was in a state known as neutral, it trembled with a deep imperative and tended to inch forward. There was never a moment when the bands were not faintly egging the machine on. In this respect it was like a horse, rolling the bit on its tongue, and country people brought to it the same technique they used with draft animals.

4 Its most remarkable quality was its rate of acceleration. In its palmy days the Model T could take off faster than anything on the road. The reason was simple. To get under way, you simply hooked the third finger of the right hand around a lever on the steering column, pulled down hard, and shoved your left foot forcibly against the low-speed pedal. These were simple, positive motions; the car responded by lunging forward with a roar. After a few seconds of this turmoil, you took your toe off the pedal, eased up a mite on the throttle, and the car, possessed of only two forward speeds, catapulted directly into high with a series of ugly jerks and was off on its glorious errand. The abruptness of this departure was never equaled in other cars of the period. The human leg was (and still is) incapable of letting in a clutch with anything like the forthright abandon that used to send Model T on its way. Letting in a clutch is a negative, hesitant motion, depending on delicate nervous control; pushing down the Ford pedal was a simple, country motion—an expansive act, which came as natural as kicking an old door to make it budge.

5 The driver of the old Model T was a man enthroned.

metaphysics: the branch of philosophy which treats of first principles, including the science of being and the structure of the universe.

The car, with top up, stood seven feet high. The driver sat on top of the gas tank, brooding it with his own body. When he wanted gasoline, he alighted, along with everything else in the front seat; the seat was pulled off, the metal cap unscrewed, and a wooden stick thrust down to sound the liquid in the well. There were always a couple of these sounding sticks kicking around in the ratty sub-cushion regions of a flivver. Refuelling was more of a social function then, because the driver had to unbend, whether he wanted to or not. Directly in front of the driver was the windshield—high, uncompromisingly erect. Nobody talked about air resistance, and the four cylinders pushed the car through the atmosphere with a simple disregard of physical law.

[6]   There was this about a Model T: the purchaser never regarded his purchase as a complete, finished product. When you bought a Ford, you figured you had a start—a vibrant, spirited framework to which could be screwed an almost limitless assortment of decorative and functional hardware. Driving away from the agency, hugging the new wheel between your knees, you were already full of creative worry. A Ford was born naked as a baby, and a flourishing industry grew up out of correcting its rare deficiencies and combating its fascinating diseases. Those were the great days of lily-painting. I have been looking at some old Sears Roebuck catalogues, and they bring everything back so clear.

[7]   First you bought a Ruby Safety Reflector for the rear, so that your posterior would glow in another car's brilliance. Then you invested thirty-nine cents in some radiator Moto Wings, a popular ornament which gave the Pegasus touch to the machine and did something godlike to the owner. For nine cents you bought a fan-belt guide to keep the belt from slipping off the pulley.

[8]   You bought a radiator compound to stop leaks. This was as much a part of everybody's equipment as aspirin tablets are of a medicine cabinet. You bought special oil to prevent chattering, a clamp-on dash light, a patching outfit, a tool box which you bolted to the running board,

a sun visor, a steering-column brace to keep the column rigid, and a set of emergency containers for gas, oil, and water—three thin, disc-like cans which reposed in a case on the running board during long, important journeys— red for gas, gray for water, green for oil. It was only a beginning. After the car was about a year old, steps were taken to check the alarming disintegration (Model T was full of tumors, but they were benign). A set of anti-rattlers (98¢) was a popular panacea.* You hooked them on to the gas and spark rods, to the brake pull rod, and to the steering-rod connections. Hood silencers, of black rubber, were applied to the fluttering hood. Shock-absorbers and snubbers gave "complete relaxation." Some people bought rubber pedal pads, to fit over the standard metal pedals. (I didn't like these, I remember.) Persons of a suspicious or pugnacious turn of mind bought a rear-view mirror; but most Model T owners weren't worried by what was coming from behind because they would soon enough see it out in front. They rode in a state of cheerful catalepsy.° Quite a large mutinous clique among Ford owners went over to a foot accelerator (you could buy one and screw it to the floor board), but there was a certain madness in these people, because the Model T, just as she stood, had a choice of three foot pedals to push, and there were plenty of moments when both feet were occupied in the routine performance of duty and when the only way to speed up the engine was with the hand throttle.

[9] Gadget bred gadget. Owners not only bought ready-made gadgets, they invented gadgets to meet special needs. I myself drove my car directly from the agency to the blacksmith's, and had the smith affix two enormous iron brackets to the port running board to support an army trunk.

[10] People who owned closed models built along different lines: they bought ball grip handles for opening doors, window anti-rattlers, and deluxe flower vases of the cut-

---

catalepsy: a morbid physical state characterized by muscular rigidity and suspension of sensation.

glass anti-splash type. People with delicate sensibilities garnished their car with a device called the Donna Lee Automobile Disseminator—a porous vase guaranteed, according to Sears, to fill the car with a "faint clean odor of lavender." The gap between open cars and closed cars was not as great then as it is now: for $11.95, Sears Roebuck converted your touring car into a sedan and you went forth renewed. One agreeable quality of the old Fords was that they had no bumpers, and their fenders softened and wilted with the years and permitted the driver to squeeze in and out of tight places.

[11] Tires were 30 x 3½, cost about twelve dollars, and punctured readily. Everybody carried a Jiffy patching set, with a nutmeg grater to roughen the tube before the goo was spread on. Everybody was capable of putting on a patch, expected to have to, and did have to.

[12] During my association with Model T's, self-starters were not a prevalent accessory. They were expensive and under suspicion. Your car came equipped with a serviceable crank, and the first thing you learned was how to Get Results. It was a special trick, and until you learned it (usually from another Ford owner, but sometimes by a period of appalling experimentation) you might as well have been winding up an awning. The trick was to leave the ignition switch off, proceed to the animal's head, pull the choke (which was a little wire protruding through the radiator), and give the crank two or three nonchalant upward lifts. Then, whistling as though thinking about something else, you would saunter back to the driver's cabin, turn the ignition on, return to the crank, and this time, catching it on the down stroke, give it a quick spin with plenty of That. If this procedure was followed, the engine almost always responded—first with a few scattered explosions, then with a tumultuous gunfire, which you checked by racing around to the driver's seat and retarding the throttle. Often, if the emergency brake hadn't been pulled all the way back, the car advanced on you the instant the first explosion occurred and you would hold it back by leaning your weight against it. I

can still feel my old Ford nuzzling me at the curb, as
though looking for an apple in my pocket.

13 The lore and legend that governed the Ford were
boundless. Owners had their own theories about everything; they discussed mutual problems in that wise, infinitely resourceful way old women discuss rheumatism.
Exact knowledge was pretty scarce, and often proved less
effective than superstition. Dropping a camphor ball into
the gas tank was a popular expedient; it seemed to have
a tonic effect on both man and machine. There wasn't
much to base exact knowledge on. The Ford driver flew
blind. He didn't know the temperature of his engine,
the speed of his car, the amount of his fuel, or the pressure of his oil (the old Ford lubricated itself by what was
amiably described as the "splash system"). A speed-
ometer cost money and was an extra, like a windshield-
wiper. The dashboard of the early models was bare save
for an ignition key; later models, grown effete,° boasted
an ammeter ° which pulsated alarmingly with the throbbing of the car. Under the dash was a box of coils, with
vibrators which you adjusted, or thought you adjusted.
Whatever the driver learned of his motor, he learned
not through instruments but through sudden developments. I remember that the timer was one of the vital
organs about which there was ample doctrine. When
everything else had been checked, you "had a look" at
the timer. It was an extravagantly odd little device,
simple in construction, mysterious in function. It contained a roller, held by a spring, and there were four
contact points on the inside of the case against which,
many people believed, the roller rolled. I have had a
timer apart on a sick Ford many times, but I never really
knew what I was up to—I was just showing off before
God. There were almost as many schools of thought as
there were timers. Some people, when things went wrong,
just clenched their teeth and gave the timer a smart crack
with a wrench. Other people opened it up and blew on

effete: as used here, lacking the vigor or the energy of the Model T.
ammeter: an instrument for measuring electric current.

it. There was a school that held that the timer needed large amounts of oil; they fixed it by frequent baptism. And there was a school that was positive it was meant to run dry as a bone; these people were continually taking it off and wiping it. I remember once spitting into a timer; not in anger, but in a spirit of research. You see, the Model T driver moved in the realm of metaphysics. He believed his car could be hexed.

14   One reason the Ford anatomy was never reduced to an exact science was that, having "fixed" it, the owner couldn't honestly claim that the treatment had brought about the cure. There were too many authenticated cases of Fords fixing themselves—restored naturally to health after a short rest. Farmers soon discovered this, and it fitted nicely with their draft-horse philosophy: "Let 'er cool off and she'll snap into it again."

15   A Ford owner had Number One Bearing constantly in mind. This bearing, being at the front end of the motor, was the one that always burned out, because the oil didn't reach it when the car was climbing hills. (That's what I was always told, anyway.) The oil used to recede and leave Number One dry as a clam flat; you had to watch that bearing like a hawk. It was like a weak heart—you could hear it start knocking, and that was when you stopped and let her cool off. Try as you would to keep the oil supply right, in the end Number One always went out. "Number One Bearing burned out on me and I had to have her replaced," you would say, wisely; and your companions always had a lot to tell about how to pamper Number One to keep her alive.

16   Sprinkled not too liberally among the millions of amateur witch doctors who drove Fords and applied their own abominable cures were the heaven-sent mechanics who could really make the car talk. These professionals turned up in undreamed-of spots. One time, on the banks of the Columbia River in Washington, I heard the rear end go out of my Model T when I was trying to whip it up a steep incline onto the deck of a ferry. Something snapped; the car slid backward into the mud. It

seemed to me like the end of the trail. But the captain of the ferry, observing the withered remnant, spoke up.

17 "What's got her?" he asked.

18 "I guess it's the rear end," I replied, listlessly. The captain leaned over the rail and stared. Then I saw that there was a hunger in his eyes that set him off from other men.

19 "Tell you what," he said, carelessly, trying to cover up his eagerness, "let's pull the so-and-so up onto the boat, and I'll help you fix her while we're going back and forth on the river."

20 We did just this. All that day I plied between the towns of Pasco and Kennewick, while the skipper (who had once worked in a Ford garage) directed the amazing work of resetting the bones of my car.

21 Springtime in the heyday of the Model T was a delirious season. Owning a car was still a major excitement, roads were still wonderful and bad. The Fords were obviously conceived in madness: any car which was capable of going from forward into reverse without any perceptible mechanical hiatus ° was bound to be a mighty challenging thing to the human imagination. Boys used to veer them off the highway into a level pasture and run wild with them, as though they were cutting up with a girl. Most everybody used the reverse pedal quite as much as the regular foot brake—it distributed the wear over the bands and wore them all down evenly. That was the big trick, to wear all the bands down evenly, so that the final chattering would be total and the whole unit scream for renewal.

22 The days were golden, the nights were dim and strange. I still recall with trembling those loud, nocturnal crises when you drew up to a signpost and raced the engine so the lights would be bright enough to read destinations by. I have never been really planetary since. I suppose it's time to say good-by. Farewell, my lovely!

hiatus: break or interruption.

ANALYSIS

It is unlikely that anyone who has driven it could describe a Model T objectively. When Strout and White say they are setting down random entries, they do not mean they are eliminating the first person. This essay is both a personal reminiscence and an elaborately detailed description, with emphasis on the latter. It is not the owners but the car that we will remember. The picture of what it was like to cope with a Model T comes through clearly because of the authors' enthusiasm. The picture of the car as a vehicle, a twentieth-century phenomenon, is the main achievement of the essay.

Strout and White move easily from a two-paragraph introduction to a description of the transmission, of the method of acceleration, of refueling, and of decorating the car. The last third of the essay (paragraphs 13–22) might be called "lore and legend." They are not exactly random entries, then, but we can see what Strout and White mean. They are not trying to sell us this model. They are not arguing a thesis about motor vehicles and their development. They are merely enjoying a romp through their memories. This is what she was like; this is what happened when. . . .

One of the delights of this essay is the zest Strout and White bring to the words they use. We like to be presented with specific images (word pictures): the Ruby Safety Reflector, the Donna Lee Automobile Disseminator, radiator Moto Wings, anti-rattlers, hood silencers, clamp-on dash lights. They are equally specific in describing motion: "The car responded with a lunging roar" or "It trembled with a deep imperative and tended to inch forward." Personifying ° the car is, of course, inevitable: "A Ford was born naked as a baby," "Model T was full of tumors," "The trick was to leave the ignition switch on, proceed to the animal's head," "I can still feel my old Ford nuzzling me at the curb." Strout and White also possess a lovely sense of whimsy, a fanciful turn of phrase. They can speak of a transmission as "planetary—which was half metaphysics, half sheer friction." Letting in the clutch was "a simple, country mo-

personifying: See Glossary.

tion—an expansive act, which came as natural as kicking an old door to make it budge." Ford owners rode in "a state of cheerful catalepsy." The car's fenders "softened and wilted with the years and permitted the driver to squeeze in and out of tight places."

Other simple descriptive phrases are equally exact and vivid. The driver was a man "enthroned." The chassis was "a vibrant, spirited framework." You roughened the tube with a "nutmeg grater" before you spread on the "goo." To "Get Results" with the crank you had to give it plenty of "That." You kept your gasoline measuring stick down in "the ratty sub-cushion regions of a flivver." In short, Strout and White more than remember these days and this car. They re-create the Model T before our eyes. And that is one chief object of good descriptive writing.

Questions on Content

1. What part does the Sears Roebuck catalogue play in the essay?
2. What do Strout and White call "the most remarkable quality" of the Model T?
3. Why was the driver like a man "enthroned"?
4. With what kind of gauges or instruments was the car *not* equipped? What steps were taken to check "the alarming disintegration" after the car was about a year old?

Add to your vocabulary: epicyclic, rapport, panacea, effete.

Questions on Technique

1. In what ways do Strout and White illustrate this sentence in their second paragraph: "As a vehicle, it was hard-working, commonplace, heroic"?
2. What do the authors make of the word "planetary" in the third paragraph? That is, how do they treat the subject of the transmission humorously and seriously at the same time? Are there two meanings of this word?
3. What adjectives in particular do you find vividly descriptive?

4. What are your reactions to the "lore and legend" section of this essay (paragraphs 13–22) ? What parts do you think are exaggeration?

Suggestions for Writing

1. Compare your family's car with the Model T as Strout and White describe it. What great changes have taken place in terms of the shape, performance, and equipment of modern cars? (Perhaps someone in the class can bring in pictures of the Model T.)
2. Describe in 500 words your own first car, bicycle, motor scooter, or outboard motor and what it meant to you as a possession.
3. Project a description of the cars of the future, or what you would like to drive in the future.
4. Describe another "institution" in American social life: radio, television, movies, comic strips. Try, if you can, to make a comparison of what the medium was like when you first encountered it with what it has now grown into.

JOHN STEINBECK · *The Turtle*

The Grapes of Wrath *was one of the most popular novels to be published in America in the 1930's. It appeared late in the decade, in 1939. Steinbeck had gone to live among the migrant farmers in their transient California tent camps in order to know their plight at first hand. The novel was an explosive indictment, and it was damned and banned as often as it was praised. The story of the Joad family sold widely in many countries. It reached millions more when John Ford made his remarkable film of Steinbeck's novel.*

Steinbeck broke his novel into two kinds of chapters, alternately—first a chapter describing the countryside or the people or nature in general, then a chapter telling

*the story of the Joads. His general descriptions are full
of commentary, frequently oblique, on the migrant labor
problem or human nature under stress or the animal
world. This brief essay, "The Turtle," is the third chapter of the novel. The highway could be Route 66, but
the place does not matter. Steinbeck is writing for all
time, all places.*

¹ The concrete highway was edged with a mat of tangled, broken, dry grass, and the grass heads were heavy
with oat beards to catch on a dog's coat, and fox-tails to
tangle in a horse's fetlocks, and clover burrs to fasten in
sheep's wool; sleeping life waiting to be spread and dis-
persed, every seed armed with an appliance of dispersal,
twisting darts and parachutes for the wind, little spears
and balls of tiny thorns, and all waiting for animals and
for the wind, for a man's trouser cuff or the hem of a
woman's skirt, all passive but armed with appliances of
activity, still, but each possessed of the anlage ° of movement.

² The sun lay on the grass and warmed it, and in the
shade under the grass the insects moved, ants and ant
lions to set traps for them, grasshoppers to jump into the
air and flick their yellow wings for a second, sow bugs
like little armadillos,° plodding restlessly on many tender
feet. And over the grass at the roadside a land turtle
crawled, turning aside for nothing, dragging his high-
domed shell over the grass. His hard legs and yellow-
nailed feet threshed slowly through the grass, not really
walking, but boosting and dragging his shell along. The
barley beards slid off his shell, and the clover burrs fell
on him and rolled to the ground. His horny beak was
partly open, and his fierce, humorous eyes, under brows
like fingernails, stared straight ahead. He came over the
grass leaving a beaten trail behind him, and the hill,
which was the highway embankment, reared up ahead of

anlage: foundation or rudiment.
armadillos: a variety of burrowing animals with bony plates covering their body.

him. For a moment he stopped, his head held high. He blinked and looked up and down. At last he started to climb the enbankment. Front clawed feet reached forward but did not touch. The hind feet kicked his shell along, and it scraped on the grass, and on the gravel. As the embankment grew steeper and steeper, the more frantic were the efforts of the land turtle. Pushing hind legs strained and slipped, boosting the shell along, and the horny head protruded as far as the neck could stretch. Little by little the shell slid up the embankment until at last a parapet ° cut straight across its line of march, the shoulder of the road, a concrete wall four inches high. As though they worked independently, the hind legs pushed the shell against the wall. The head upraised and peered over the wall to the broad smooth plain of cement. Now the hands, braced on top of the wall, strained and lifted, and the shell came slowly up and rested its front end on the wall. For a moment the turtle rested. A red ant ran into the shell, into the soft skin inside the shell, and suddenly head and legs snapped in, and the armored tail clamped in sideways. The red ant was crushed between body and legs. And one head of wild oats was clamped into the shell by a front leg. For a long moment the turtle lay still, and then the neck crept out and the old humorous frowning eyes looked about and the legs and tail came out. The back legs went to work, straining like elephant legs, and the shell tipped to an angle so that the front legs could not reach the level cement plain. But higher and higher the hind legs boosted it, until at last the center of balance was reached, the front tipped down, the front legs scratched at the pavement, and it was up. But the head of wild oats was held by its stem around the front legs.

⁵ Now the going was easy, and all the legs worked, and the shell boosted along, waggling from side to side. A sedan driven by a forty-year old woman approached. She saw the turtle and swung to the right, off the highway,

parapet: a protective wall or barrier.

the wheels screamed and a cloud of dust boiled up. Two wheels lifted for a moment and then settled. The car skidded back onto the road, and went on, but more slowly. The turtle had jerked into its shell, but now it hurried on, for the highway was burning hot.

⁴ And now a light truck approached, and as it came near, the driver saw the turtle and swerved to hit it. His front wheel struck the edge of the shell, flipped the turtle like a tiddly-wink, spun it like a coin, and rolled it off the highway. The truck went back to its course along the right side. Lying on its back, the turtle was tight in its shell for a long time. But at last its legs waved in the air, reaching for something to pull it over. Its front foot caught a piece of quartz and little by little the shell pulled over and flopped upright. The wild oat head fell out and three of the spearhead seeds stuck in the ground. And as the turtle crawled on down the embankment, its shell dragged dirt over the seeds. The turtle entered a dust road and jerked itself along, drawing a wavy shallow trench in the dust with its shell. The old humorous eyes looked ahead, and the horny beak opened a little. His yellow toe nails slipped a fraction in the dust.

ANALYSIS

This essay is as simple and direct as objective ° description can be. Steinbeck lets graphic visual images build the whole picture. He does not need to intrude as author. The first person pronoun has no place here.

He could easily begin this essay with a description of the turtle. Why introduce first seeds and their dissemination, then the smaller insects, before reaching the main subject? Perhaps he wishes to give a sense of continuity in the natural world: nothing exists in isolation. Perhaps he wants to tie his first paragraph to his last: the turtle unknowingly deposits the seeds on the other side of the road. The life process continues. Why introduce in so brief a description, we might also ask, not one but two motorists? Perhaps Steinbeck intends to comment

objective: See Glossary.

obliquely, or indirectly, on human nature—the thoughtful and the thoughtless—and to make the turtle impervious to both, as it were. There is a splendid inevitability about the turtle's progress. It is painfully slow, but only in comparison with man's clocks, not with nature's. The "old humorous eyes looked ahead" and the turtle moved on. Steinbeck comes to no conclusions. He only describes a simple daily event. If he has his own opinions about what this turtle might stand for—the common people?—he is not giving them.

Questions on Content

1. What particular attributes do the seeds described in the first paragraph possess?
2. How do the turtle's legs work: independently or in unison?
3. What does the red ant add to this description?

Questions on Technique

1. What differences do you note between the vocabulary of the first paragraph and the rest of the essay?
2. What effect does Steinbeck achieve with this idea: ". . . at last a parapet cut straight across its line of march, the shoulder of the road, a concrete wall four inches high." Why is "wall" the perfect word here?
3. Why bother to tell us the sedan is driven by a forty-year-old woman? Could not this paragraph be omitted?
4. Why repeat the description of the turtle's "humorous" eyes?

Suggestions for Writing

1. Select an animal you know well from observation and describe it as graphically as you can, but limit the description to activity. For instance, describe a cat stalking (and perhaps capturing) a bird. Describe each movement that brings the cat close to the bird, the capture of the bird, or its escape, and so forth.
2. Write an essay wherein you compare the method in which a number of animals move. For example, the chipmunk, the bear, the cat, the snake, and the cow. How closely related to the means of locomotion is the size of each animal?

3. Project Steinbeck's descriptive method to the sight of three small children trying to cross a busy city street.
4. Describe the driver of the light truck in terms of the rest of his trip down the highway.

EDWIN WAY TEALE · *Winged Bullets*

John Steinbeck is primarily a novelist, but we need only look at his Sea of Cortez *(written with Edward F. Ricketts, published in 1941) to know that marine biology is one of his hobbies. Edwin Way Teale is primarily a roving naturalist, but he is also a dedicated writer and photographer. He has been awarded the John Burroughs Medal for distinguished nature writing and is a member of numerous scientific organizations, including the Explorers Club and the New York Entomological Society.*

In "Winged Bullets," which first appeared in Grassroot Jungles, *Teale describes one of the insect pioneers of our world, the dragonfly. He tells us in the opening sentence that years ago he spent a winter near Santa Monica, near "the tar pits of Rancho La Brea, the so-called Death Trap of the Ages." In the preface to his recent* Adventures in Nature, *he has to admit that "La Brea Tar Pits, in California, which I knew in the 1920's as an isolated, rather lonely stretch of wasteland on the outskirts of Los Angeles, are now on a main artery, in a business center of the city, set amid towering buildings and surrounded by a barrier of high wire-mesh."*

Time changes all things, including the dragonfly. What this amazing insect was like in the Carboniferous Age and what it is like now, many millions of years later, is the subject Teale wishes to explore. His talent for

"Winged Bullets" from *Adventures in Nature: Selections from the Outdoor Writings of Edwin Way Teale.* Copyright 1937, 1944 by Dodd, Mead & Company, Inc. Reprinted by permission of the publishers.

making us see, feel, and understand is enormous. He describes with the eye of a photographer; he teaches us from a wide range of natural history.

1   One winter, years ago, I lived in a house on the road to Santa Monica. Less than a mile away, in an open California field, lay the tar pits of Rancho La Brea, the so-called Death Trap of the Ages. The great beasts of the earth—the saber-toothed tiger, the dire wolf, the imperial elephant—had been caught there like insects on flypaper.

2   Even now, tar, heavy and glistening, oozes from the ground and creeps away down the slope into great pools where bubbles rise, expand, and burst in rainbow hues. Here, one day when the air was filled with the stillness which precedes a downpour, I encountered a fleeting moment of drama. Time slipped backward a hundred million years and I watched an event occurring before the initial word of written history.

3   A dragonfly, slanting over the pool on glittering wings, had swooped too low. Writhing and twisting, it lay gripped by the black glue of the tar pit, its long segmented body straining first to one side, then to the other. Finally its struggles ceased. Quiescent *, it sank deeper and deeper into the tar just as, long ago, so many of its ancestors had done at this identical spot on the changing, eroding face of the earth.

4   For the dragonflies, with the silverfish and the cockroaches, were insect pioneers, one of the earliest forms to appear. In the prehistoric jungles of the Carboniferous Age ° dragonflies as big as hawks soared through the steaming air. Their fossil remains have been discovered in the Permian rocks of Kansas, in the Jurassic forma-

Carboniferous Age: Geologic time is divided into five great eras: Archeozoic, Proterozoic, Paleozoic, Mesozoic, and Cenozoic. Each era is divided into several periods. The Carboniferous Period (in the Paleozoic Era, the age of invertebrates and marine forms) began approximately 230 million years ago. The Permian Period marks the end of the Paleozoic Era. The Jurassic Period is one of three divisions of the Mesozoic Era. The Miocene Period is a division of the Cenozoic, or most recent, Era.

tions of Siberia, in the Miocene beds of Colorado, and in the coal deposits of Belgium. Possessed of wings that measured nearly thirty inches from tip to tip they were the largest insects that ever lived.

⁵ The towering trees of that day have been dwarfed to the club moss and the ground pines of the present. And the dragonfly has shrunk with them. The largest of the 2,000 and more species known has a wingspread of approximately seven and a half inches.

⁶ In their long existence on earth many have been the changes seen by these familiar "snake feeders," "devil's darning needles," "mosquito hawks," "gauze flies," "virgins of the water"—to give but a few of the many names by which the dragonfly is known. It has lived on while the dinosaurs passed from the earth; while cavemen, mound builders, and cliff dwellers evolved into modern man. Yet, in many of its habits and characteristics, the dragonfly is still a creature from the distant past.

⁷ Often it rushes through the air, scooping up its victims in a basket formed of spine-fringed legs, sucking their bodies dry and letting the carcasses fall to the ground, all without slackening its headlong pace. Its great compound organs of sight may contain as many lenses as the eyes of 15,000 men. Its head, resembling half of a hollowed-out marble, is attached to the slender body by a sort of ball-and-socket joint that enables the dragonfly to turn its head almost completely around and see below as well as above. Its veined and transparent wings, moving on the average twenty-eight times a second, can carry it through the air at speeds approaching sixty miles an hour.

⁸ Probably no other insect is so much a creature of the air. It has legs but it never walks. Its jointed and spine-bordered limbs, bunched far forward, enable it to cling and climb. When it leaves the earth, its awkwardness falls away; it becomes the acme of grace, swooping, turning, zooming at will. It can dive like a pursuit plane or hover like an autogiro. As soon as the sun lifts above

the horizon, the dragonflies are a-wing. Only one Oriental species hunts at night. Most other members of the family are children of the sun.

9 So true is this that certain species alight if the sun even goes under a cloud. I remember one sultry morning when I was working my way slowly through a dense stand of flags bordering a swamp pond. With beads of moisture clinging to the vegetation at the base of the tangle, the flags rose like a thick head of hair on a perspiring scalp. I had paused motionless to watch a small gray insect which had fallen into the pond. Its feeble struggle sent tiny ripples running across the surface. Then all was still.

10 Over the spot swept the shadow of a dragonfly, a zigzagging back and forth above the stagnant water. A cloud passed before the sun. Instantly the dragonfly, a shining little fellow with delicate, red-spotted wings, swept toward me, seemed to halt in amazement with wings aquiver, and then dropped lightly to the tip of a flag almost within reach of my hand. Without difficulty I caught it and, after a momentary struggle, it clung to my finger and even rode along as I moved slowly through the flags. The cloud passed by, the brilliance of the sunshine struck us once more and, as though actuated by a spring, my little passenger leaped into the air and darted away.

11 So completely is the dragonfly a creature of the air that the female often remains upon the wing when laying her eggs. Unlike the gangling crane fly, which soars aloft scattering its eggs through the air, she usually bumps along the surface of a pond, dipping the tip of her abdomen in the water at intervals, leaving behind clumps of tiny eggs. During the hottest days of summer I have seen dragonflies in the heart of New York City making their characteristic bumping flights amid the fumes and noise of traffic on Fifth Avenue, as though laying eggs on a smooth black river of asphalt. Sometimes the female dives completely under the surface to

attach her eggs to the leaves or stems of plants. She is incased in a film of air which enables her to remain submerged long enough to complete the work.

[12] A small relative of the dragonfly, the frail and gauzy damselfly, follows an even stranger procedure in depositing her eggs beneath the surface of a pond. Because the female, alone, would have difficulty breaking through the surface film on returning to the air, the male accompanies her, flying ahead and gripping her with the "pincers" at the tip of his abdomen, pulling like a locomotive attached to a train. Flying tandem in this way, they dive into the water and when the eggs have been deposited break through the surface, the male gaining his freedom first and using his wings to drag the female after him.

[13] The shape of the dragonfly's egg varies. Some are stubby, like roundish grains of wheat; others are elongated, like kernels of rice. The latter are almost always deposited in slits in the stems or leaves of underwater plants. Nobody knows how many eggs a dragonfly is capable of laying. Dr. Leland O. Howard tells of finding 110,000 separate eggs in a single clump.

[14] What would happen if all these eggs hatched out and reached maturity is indicated by the "dragonfly year" of 1839. Over a large part of the continent of Europe, and especially in Germany, France, and the Netherlands, immense swarms of the insects followed the rivers and darkened the sky. The superstitious believed them harbingers * of famine and war. But scientists pointed out that preceding springs had been unusually rainy. Rivers and lakes had overflowed, providing wide areas of shallow water where the dragonfly nymphs were relatively safe from the fish that usually attacked them. As a consequence, increased numbers had become winged adults and hunger drove millions to seek new feeding grounds.

[15] Occasionally dragonflies migrate in great numbers, especially when droughts dry up ponds and swamps. One of the biggest of these migrations occurred in 1881. Over southern Illinois the air was reported "literally alive with

dragonflies," all streaming southwest, some flying only a foot from the ground, others soaring almost out of sight. Drought was thought to have caused the mass movement of the insects. Off the coast of Europe, vessels have sometimes sighted small swarms far out at sea.

16 Under normal conditions the many enemies of the dragonfly keep down the number of these insects. Even before the eggs are hatched, one curious foe, a certain hymenopterous ° parasite, begins its work, laying its eggs in those of the dragonfly. To reach the ones hidden away in slits in underwater plants, the almost microscopic fly descends far beneath the surface. It uses its wings as oars and carries with it tiny bubbles of air that keep it alive until it reaches the surface again.

17 If the eggs survive the dangers that beset them, they hatch into insect ogres, the underwater nymphs of the dragonfly. With dirty gray-green bodies making them inconspicuous, they lie in the mud or lurk among the pond weeds. The thin walls of the lower intestines are formed into gills which absorb oxygen from the water. Curiously, the nymph breathes and swims in the same manner. When it expels water forcibly from the lower end of the food canal, after absorbing the oxygen, the recoil drives it ahead. Thus, like a tiny submarine rocket, the nymph progresses across the mud bottom of the pond.

18 Almost as strange as its method of locomotion is its manner of catching prey. Unlike the adult dragonfly, the nymph is sluggish and captures its living food by stealth. It lies in wait until some mayfly or mosquito larva, some caddis worm or water bug swims too close. Then an underlip, so long it folds down under the body and between the nymph's front legs when not in use, shoots out. At its end are sharp pincers which grip the victim and pull it into the wide mouth of the insect goblin. Then the underlip folds down again and the mouth disappears behind a

hymenopterous: belonging to a large, highly specialized group of insects, including wasps, beetles, and ants.

chitinous ° mask which gives the creature the appearance of wearing a frozen, perpetual smile.

¹⁹ The nymphs are insatiable * cannibals, devouring each other and even catching and destroying newly emerged adults before their wings have a chance to harden. As they grow older, the nymphs are able to overpower tadpoles and small fish. Larger fish, in turn, hunt them down and they form an important item in the diet of trout and other game fish.

²⁰ Most smaller dragonflies pass a year in the water as nymphs. Larger species are often two or even three years old before they are "born" as aerial insects. During this long wait they may molt from ten to fifteen times. The transformation from the underwater nymph to the aerial dragonfly is almost as amazing as though a trout should suddenly shed its skin and become a robin.

²¹ Usually this miracle occurs during the heat of the day, although a few dragonflies emerge at night. In either case they climb from the water and cling to the bank, a stick or weed, while the suit of chitin armor splits down the back and the wings, damp and crumpled, unfold. Then, when the glistening coat has hardened, the insect darts into the sunshine. It leaves behind the ghost of its other self, a brown, translucent shell which continues to cling to the spot of transformation, a chitinous monument to Nature's miracle.

²² The shining wings, on which the dragonfly rides, are supported by a vast network of veins. In a single wing there may be as many as 3,000 separate cells between the veins. The insect skims through the air with one goal in sight, appeasing an insatiable appetite for living food. This appetite is approached by only two other insects I know: the praying mantis and the robber fly.

²³ The most surprising experience I ever had with a dragonfly occurred one day when I was holding one of the insects by its tough, parchment-like wings. I was

chitinous: of or like a horny substance secreted by the upper layers of skin and forming the hard outer covering of insects.

watching the metallic segments of the abdomen moving in and out in rhythm with the insect's breathing. Sud denly the body curled upward, the tip reached the dragonfly's mouth, and the insect calmly began eating off its own tail! I was almost as astonished as if I had seen a man crunching off his fingers or making a meal of his arm. Since then I have read that hungry dragonflies will consume parts of their own bodies to appease the craving for food.

24 Many other instances attest to the abnormal appetite of these insects. Dr. Howard tells of one specimen which had been chloroformed and mounted. Evidently the anesthetic was insufficiently strong, for the insect revived after it had been secured to a board by a large pin thrust through the thorax. In spite of this terrible injury it ate ravenously when flies were placed within reach of its jaws. The pleasure of swallowing food seemed to make it forget the pin thrust completely through its body. As long as the feeding continued, it made no effort to escape.

25 In a space of two hours one dragonfly was seen to devour more than its weight in horseflies. Sometimes these predatory creatures will swoop down and pick small moths from twigs and leaves. With their needle-sharp teeth, they attack bees and wasps without hesitation. Frequently larger dragonflies will catch and consume smaller species and, on at least one occasion, a dragonfly was seen with a large swallowtail butterfly in its grasp. However, mosquitoes and gnats form the bulk of its diet, thus making it an invaluable ally of man. At dusk some species of these winged hunters cruise back and forth in squadrons, looking for swarms of gnats and mosquitoes.

26 When aquatic insects become scarce, the larger dragonflies will sometimes travel miles inland from the nearest water in their search for food. The larger the dragonfly, the higher it hunts in the air. The smaller species skim so low above the water that trout and other game fish sometimes leap into the air and catch them on the wing. Bullfrogs also snap them up when they come

too close, and the webs of spiders snare the smaller drag-onflies. The larger ones, however, break through and es-cape. In the words of an Old Japanese poem: "Through even the spider's fence, it has force to burst its way."

[27] Like all other insects, dragonflies have their in-dividual traits. Some are wild and shy; others are sociable and inquisitive. I remember one in particular, a big fel-low with blue metallic body, which hovered near a raft on which I was fishing in a lonely little lake far back in the woods of Maine. The bottom of the lake was strewn with rotting logs and among these skeletons of trees swam great black leeches, undulating like ribbons. Gaunt pine stubs, killed by some fire of long ago, lined the shore. Clinging to them were scores of nymph skins, some new, some old, some light tan, some weathered to a chocolate brown. All around us, on these dead pines, creatures of the mud had been transformed into creatures of the air.

[28] This particular dragonfly of which I speak would perch on the raft beside me, circle around and around my rod, make passes at the line as I reeled it in. Several times it dashed at flies buzzing about my head, picking them out of the air and then stopping still in front of me like a matador who had killed a bull and was taking his applause. Fishing became dull in comparison to watching this neighborly insect, and, much to the disgust of my guide, I reeled in my line and turned to tossing bits of wood into the air for the dragonfly to swoop upon.

[29] How a similar ruse is used to capture elusive dragon-flies is told in Lafcadio Hearn's *A Japanese Miscellany.* Children attach tiny pebbles to the ends of long hairs and throw these miniature bolas into the air where dragonflies are circling. When one of the insects pounces upon the passing object, the hair twists about its body and the weight of the pebbles brings it to earth.

[30] After more than a hundred million years on earth the dragonfly asks no more of life today than it did in the age of the dinosaurs. Sunshine and living insects are the twin needs of its existence. In a world of infinite change, its wants have remained the same.

31 During the evenings of one whole week, years ago when I was a boy on an Indiana farm, I pored over the pages of a mail-order catalogue, making a list of everything in the world I wanted. The total cost, as I remember it, was only $392.80. Today how strangely small is the satisfaction of knowing that, if I wished, I could buy the list complete. Successive years have brought new wants. "Man," says Henry George, "is the only animal whose desires increase as they are fed; the only animal that is never satisfied."

32 But the dragonfly, so perfectly fitted for its small and transitory existence, desires no other food or home than its ancestors have had through the ages. For it, life is simple and direct.

33 In northern states the first cold of fall kills off these children of the sun. Only the nymphs remain in their underwater home to carry on the chain of life. Lingering old age is virtually unknown in the world of insects. There is no wasting decrepitude *; no long deterioration of powers. For the dragonfly there is only the swoop of an enemy or the numbing anesthetic of autumn cold. Death, for it, is also simple and direct.

ANALYSIS

If we begin with the title of this essay, we have a clue to the author's intention. He is, frankly, charmed and amazed by this insect, the dragonfly, and especially by its speed of flight. He wants us to know it, to see it as he has. In order not to burden his reader with too many technical details too quickly, he builds his essay in several stages.

The first five paragraphs are a kind of historical introduction. Paragraph 6 begins a general description: first its common names, then its anatomical details, its habits in the air, and an incident the writer experienced. Paragraph 11 begins a section on dragonfly eggs, their hatching, and their enemies. Paragraphs 17–22 are devoted to what Teale calls "insect ogres, the underwater nymphs of the dragonfly." He uses the word "nymph" here in its zoological, not its mythological, meaning: an insect in its pre-adult stage, with incomplete metamorphosis. Paragraphs 23–29 are not digressions; Teale is illuminating the more fantastic talents of the dragonfly by means of a few experiences. We shall not easily forget this insect's appetite because of Teale's descriptive powers. Finally he gives four brief paragraphs (30–33) to an easy, graceful conclusion. Note that here he is not above bringing himself as a small boy into the text of basically objective ° writing. He wishes to make the point he announced in his introduction: the dragonfly has changed in size, not in habits or habitat. Man is the dissatisfied animal. Insects do not know old age, deterioration, decrepitude. Death is simple and direct. These last two adjectives might also describe Teale's literary talents.

Questions on Content

1. Exactly how much has the dragonfly diminished in size since the Carboniferous Age?
2. What anatomical details impress you most in Teale's description?
3. What are damselflies? How do they lay their eggs?
4. Describe the nymph's method of locomotion, its manner of catching prey, its "birth" as an aerial insect.
5. What do dragonflies eat?
6. What individual traits was Teale able to observe in these insects?

Add to your vocabulary: quiescent, harbinger, insatiable, decrepitude.

Questions on Technique

1. Why does Teale bother to tell us about the tar pits of Rancho La Brea? Why is this an apt introduction to an entomological essay?
2. What do the common names in paragraph 6—"mosquito hawks," "gauze flies," and the others—add to the anatomical description of paragraph 7? Which paragraph makes you *see* this insect?
3. Paragraph 11 describes a "creature of the air." What details does Teale choose to give us?

objective: See Glossary.

4. How does Teale impress upon us this insect's phe-
   nomenal appetite?
5. Is the conclusion to this essay an anti-climax for you?
   Would you have written it differently? Why?

Suggestions for Writing

1. Those of us who are not naturalists would have great
   trouble describing an insect in as much detail as
   Teale does. But we do have eyes to observe the natural world. Select a subject with which you are familiar—a flower, a reptile, an insect, an animal—and
   make your reader see some of its characteristics. You
   may want to weave into your observations some facts
   obtained from reference books.
2. What unusual traits in animals or birds have you observed? Describe them in 500 words.
3. In nontechnical language, rewrite Teale's essay in
   600 words.

THE COMPLEX SUBJECT

JAMES RAMSEY ULLMAN · *Kilimanjaro!*

*The answer to the common question, why climb
mountains, is the now-familiar, because they are there.
Jungfrau, Matterhorn, Annapurna, Everest—they have
challenged men in the past; they will continue to entice
men to climb them. James Ramsey Ullman is a celebrated writer on men and mountains. His novel* The
White Tower *(1945) deserved its great popularity because Ullman could not only tell a superb adventure*

"Kilimanjaro!" by James Ramsey Ullman from *Holiday*, November, 1957.
Copyright 1957 by the Curtis Publishing Company. Reprinted by permission
of Harold Matson Company.

story, of six, oddly assorted people and a Swiss mountain, but could also write out of personal experience. He fills the pages of High Conquest: The Story of Mountaineering and The Other Side of the Mountain: An Escape to the Amazon *with his own exploits. It was only a matter of time before he would be tempted by Kilimanjaro,. "the apex of Africa."*

To divorce a description of this great mountain from the narration of his climbing is, for Ullman, impossible. "Kilimanjaro!" is a combination of portrait and story. Every reader will agree, however, that what remains after he has experienced this climb vicariously is the feeling not of the energy Ullman expended or the dangers involved but of Kilimanjaro's size and imperturbable dominance. "Raise our eyes, wherever we were," he writes, "and there it was. . . . Changeless above change unending, the white ghost in the sky." This is the mountain Ernest Hemingway immortalized in 1936 in his short story "The Snows of Kilimanjaro." In the intriguing epigraph to that story, Hemingway records that "its western summit is called the Masai 'Ngàje Ngài,' the House of God. Close to the western summit there is the dried and frozen carcass of a leopard. No one has explained what the leopard was seeking at that altitude."

Ullman and Thomas, his Wachagga guide, conquered Kilimanjaro in three and a half days. It is likely that our memories of this description will last far longer. We feel we are there, in the village of Marangu, at Pieter's Hut, at Mawenzi and Kibo. We can see the whole of Africa "lying clear and bright in crystal space."

[1] It has been called the House of God. It has been called the High One. The Cold One. The White One. On close acquaintance, by climbers, it has been called a variety of names rather less printable. But to the world at large it is Kilimanjaro, the apex of Africa and one of the great mountains of the earth.

² For two weeks we had been on safari in southern Kenya and northern Tanganyika, and it was a realm of glorious variety. We moved from the red lands of Tsavo to the white lands of Amboseli; from prairie to parkland to forest to swamp to desert. We rode out from the towns of the settlers, through the villages of the Masai, into the domain of the lion, the rhino, and the elephant, and everywhere was something new and fresh and different from what we had seen before. Only one thing remained constant. Raise our eyes, wherever we were, and there *it* was. Above the giraffes' ears, above the baobab trees,° above the bright white cloud puffs in the African sunlight. Changeless above change unending, the white ghost in the sky.

³ Slowly we circled it, and the circle grew tighter. "They say it's one of the easiest big mountains in the world," I said to son Jim; and Jim nodded, but awkwardly, because his neck was craned back so far. "And it's only a mile higher than the Matterhorn," I added cheerfully.

⁴ Our white hunter, to whom mountaineers were a stranger breed than albino zebras, kept pointing off in sundry directions across what he affectionately called MMBA. Translation: Miles and Miles of Bloody ° Africa. But by now we were incapable of focusing on anything except the center of our magic circle, the Miles and Miles of Bloody Kilimanjaro.

⁵ It is a thing of contradictions; a long-dead volcano built up from the plains in vast gentle slopes and known to expert cragsmen as a "nothing" mountain, an antagonist that calls for neither rope nor ax nor crampon * nor any special climbing skills. It is, at the same time, an awful lot of nothing. The surrounding plains are at a mere 3000-foot elevation, its summit at 19,340—and Ev-

baobab trees: broad-trunked African timber trees of the silk-cotton family; they bear a gourd-like fruit.

Bloody: British slang, difficult to approximate, but close to our use of damned or detestable.

erest itself boasts no such three-mile leap from base to tip. A German scientist, Dr. Hans Meyer, first conquered Kilimanjaro in 1889, and since then it has been challenged by more climbers than any peak of its size on earth. Few have ever fallen from it, but well over half its challengers, through the years, have run out of gas on its upper flanks and had to turn back defeated.

6 Until a little more than a century ago the very existence of Kilimanjaro was unsuspected by the outside world. It was during the great European land grabs in Africa, when Kenya fell to the British and Tanganyika to the Germans, that it was discovered that the highest point of the continent stood flush on their borders. In a moment of generosity, Queen Victoria (who had plenty of mountains in her realm) presented a gift to her nephew the Kaiser (who had none) by authorizing a bulge in the boundary whereby the peak became all German. But the British got it back, with compound interest, in the first World War, and it has been theirs ever since.

7 Road's end was the village of Marangu, sprawled on the mountain's southern flank at about the 5000-foot level. There Jim and I bade temporary farewell to jeep and white hunter (no neck-craner he), picked up our provisions and equipment, and joined forces with our porters. These added up to nine: a headman-guide, a cook, and seven rank-and-file load bearers. All were men of the Wachagga tribe (called Chaggas for short), and they ranged in age from a sixteen-year-old boy, who was having his first go at the mountain, to Thomas, the headman, who, at fifty-four, would be making his uncounted-hundredth ascent. Of the lot of them only Thomas had the job of going all the way to the top—*if* his employers were able to follow him. We also joined forces with a third *bwana:* ° Fred Hughes, an official in

bwana: master or boss, in Swahili, a language common to Central Africa.

the Tanganyika Forestry Service and secretary of the local mountaineering club.

8   If we followed the usual schedule we would be gone five days: three and a half up, one and a half down. "Got your dark glasses for the snowfields?" Fred asked. And it was a startling thought in that tropical world of black Africa. We were in shorts and T shirts. We sweated. We plodded. We hiked ten miles to climb the three thousand feet of our first day's ascent.

9   During the first two hours we were in inhabited country—primitive but not squalid or poverty-stricken. On the contrary, it had a bright multihued Land of Oz quality, a mixture of sunshine and greenery and gay clothing and chatter and laughter.

10   Then we entered the forest. This was pure jungle-land: a maze of black boles,° dense shrubbery, ferns, fronds ° and lianas.° Orchids and begonias winked on and off like lights in the surrounding shadow. Birds cawed. Monkeys jabbered. Jabbering right back at them, our long file wound its way between the great green-bearded trees.

11   By now we were strung out loosely, each going at his own pace, meaning that Fred and Jim were up ahead, well out of my ken, and I dead last in the procession. Well, next to dead last. Headman Thomas considered it his duty to stay with the feeblest of his *bwanas* and crept loyally behind me.

12   Unfortunately there was not much communication between us. Thomas' English was pretty well limited to his own name, presumably acquired in a mission house. And my mastery of the African tongues was somewhat less than that. Our major attempt at conversation came during a brief stop, when Thomas pointed at me and inquired, "Nairobi?"

13   "No, America," I told him.

boles: trunks or stems of trees.
fronds: leaves, especially of palm trees.
lianas: climbing plants that root in the ground.

[14] "Ah," he said, "missionary."

[15] And we let it go at that.

[16] The lowest of Kilimanjaro's three huts, at about 9000 feet, is called the Bismarck. The head of our column took four hours to reach it. I needed about five.

[17] The second day's trek, to Pieter's Hut, was another ten-odd miles, another 3000-plus feet higher. At first we were still in dense forest, but then the vegetation began to thin, we came out onto great moorlike slopes, and the surrounding world swung slowly into view. To the east, and the Indian Ocean, a cloud bank spread away beneath us into blue miles, gleaming white and frozen as a polar snowfield. To south and west, there was not white but brown, no cloud but only distance—an incredible sweep of MMBA stretching to horizons so distant that the eye faltered trying to reach them.

[18] Then the eye turned. It looked north. It looked up. And there, again, was Kilimanjaro. It is not a single tapering peak but a huge and sprawling massif, almost a range in itself. To our right—the east—was the lesser of its two ultimate summits, called Mawenzi, an ancient volcanic core of red crumbling rock, raising its jagged towers to a height of some 17,000 feet. Then to the west, and directly above us, its walls leveled out into a long skyline saddle which swept on for some seven miles before beginning to rise again—this time into the slopes of Kibo. Kibo is *the* top of the mountain, and utterly unlike Mawenzi: a symmetrical truncated cone, perpetually snow-capped, and so vast it dwarfs its rival. This is the Kilimanjaro of the stories, the legends, the photographs: the fabulous white-topped pudding athwart the equatorial sky.

[19] I have, in my day, described the great silences on certain mountains, but there were no silences that day on Kilimanjaro. The porters jabbered; they laughed; they told each other stories at a distance of a quarter of a mile. And though almost all were barefoot, they moved like chamois over rocks and gravel that were trying hard

to tear my stout boots to ribbons. On their heads, nonchalantly, swayed their forty-pound loads of foodstuffs, utensils, and blankets. Two men, I noted, carried fine new capacious * knapsacks—presumably the gifts of previous employers—but even these went balanced atop their craniums.

20   And so up we went, now through long slanting meadows, with Alpine flowers bright around us, and by the time my private rear guard reached Pieter's Hut it was midafternoon. Here at 12,300 feet, it was cold even in the sunshine, and when night came we sat huddled in blankets long before turning into our bunks. Far below us, on the plains, we could see the pinprick lights of towns and villages, and in the emptiness beyond them the orange glow of bush fires. From the Chaggas' lean-to, bursting with smoke and stench, came a low, slow singsong that was half mission-house hymn and half ancient tribal chant.

21   In the morning the fires below were invisible. But there was fire above: the ice-white summit of Kibo ablaze in the rising sun. In the stainless clarity of air, it seemed close enough to reach out and touch, but there was still another full day's climb ahead of us before we would be even at the base of the final cone. Toward noon we reached our first major goal: the great 14,000-foot saddle between Kibo and Mawenzi. Seven miles long and almost as broad, it is utterly barren and flat as a ball field, and I had been told by previous climbers how terribly the wind could blow across its unprotected wastes. Our luck held, however. We had no wind. Only sun.

22   The trail came out close to the base of Mawenzi, and its tattered spires rose sheer above us. Then we turned our backs and slogged across the saddle. At this altitude, I knew all too well, a whole encyclopedia of ailments can afflict the climber, among them headache, nausea, sore throat, thumping heart. But so far I was all right; and even after we crossed the seven flat miles and

began the ascent of Kibo's skirts, my anatomy continued to hold together. Right foot, left foot. Right, left. Perhaps a hundred steps—ten seconds' rest—a hundred more. Ahead, a slowly emerging speck on the scree ° slopes, was Kibo Hut—about 16,500 feet up, higher than the highest peak of the Alps.

23 Kibo Hut was tiny. It was dirty. It was freezing. Here there was neither water nor firewood, and all we had brought up was the minimal amount needed for drinking and cooking. Such problems, however, did not prevent our cook, Samuel, from dispensing a de luxe tea and supper, complete with serving cloth and napkins. And for the eighth time in eight meals he hopefully set out the prize item in his larder—a jar of ferocious-looking mustard pickles that, to his great distress, no one had yet deigned to touch.

24 "Jim, don't you think we owe it to Samuel—"

25 That was as far as I got. Suddenly I was conscious of something even yellower than the horrid pickles, and that something was Jim's face.

26 "Ex-cuse me," he mumbled weakly, and lurched from the hut.

27 It was the demon Altitude, striking without warning; and from then on Jim had no respite from nausea and racking headaches. We gave him aspirin. No effect. Sundry other pills. No effect. "A night's sleep will fix you up," we told him. But there was no sleep for poor Jim. When I awoke at 3:30—the grim hour of up-and-at-it—it was to find him miserably climbing back into his bunk after still another bout of sickness outside.

28 It was obvious that he could go no higher.

29 "Don't feel too bad about it," Fred comforted him. "Even George Mallory—the *Everest* Mallory—got sick up here at Kibo and had to go back."

30 This information didn't seem to cheer Jim greatly, but he was realist enough to know the score, and it was

scree: a pebble; a stone; also a heap of stones or debris.

decided that at daylight he would go down to Pieter's. Fred, too, would be going no higher, but this was according to plan. He had already been up the mountain three times. So now it was I alone who bestirred myself, sloshing down the tea that Samuel brought me and pulling on my heavy clothing in the cold candlelit hut.

31 Then the door opened and Thomas stomped in, dressed now in heavy boots, woolen helmet, and a too-small British-army overcoat that must have dated from the Zulu Wars. And a moment later there were just we two—and Kilimanjaro.

32 It was still full night, but the stars and a late-waning moon gave light enough to see by, and above us Kibo's snow dome loomed like a great beacon lighted from within. There remained some 3500 vertical feet to go to the top—no more, to be sure, than we had climbed on each of the previous days, but now the angle of ascent steeped sharply. There was no solid rock, but only loose scree and crumbled lava in which one floundered and backslid maddeningly. And with each foot gained the lungs struggled harder and more futilely for breathable air.

33 Step—slip. Step—slip. Multiplied a hundred times, and then a thousand.

34 We followed a long shallow gully up to our left; then another to the right. My rests were no longer at hundred-step intervals but at fifty, and then thirty and then twenty. Yet, basically, there was no sign of *real* trouble. Heart, lungs, and legs, to be sure, were working overtime—but still working. My stomach behaved, and aspirin dissolved a gathering headache. Best of all, the mountain was keeping its sharpest claws sheathed, for there was neither wind nor bitter cold.

35 As we climbed on, the night thinned and the stars faded. For perhaps half an hour we crept on in gray twilight, and then the grayness was shattered by the wildest, most savage sunrise I have ever seen. The whole eastern horizon was banded with crimson. Mawenzi, its

summit already beneath us, flamed red as fire. And Kibo's snowcap, above us, was suddenly no longer a mountaintop but a vast spectrum, itself a sun in the gleaming sky. I put on dark goggles, and so did Thomas. But even through their green film the light seemed too brilliant for mere human eyes.

36 We were at 17,000 feet—seventeen-five—eighteen. Kibo's walls now rose up smoothly. No gullies, no humps or ridges; only an endless hateful grind of scree and lava.

37 At the end of the endlessness, clamped into the sky above, were the rocks of Gillman's Point, lowest notch in the crater's rim, and through the minutes, and then the hours, it seemed to remain exactly the same distance above us.

38 Step—slip. Step—slip. I was half convinced we were not moving at all. But apparently we were, for around us there were changes. Red Mawenzi was remote below. To the left and right were snow slopes and glaciers. And to the right, too, and only a little below the rim, we could see the bulge in the mountainside known as Leopard Point. Kibo's famous leopard is no legend. He was not invented by Ernest Hemingway for "The Snows of Kilimanjaro," but was right there for years, a carcass frozen amid the ice and rock—with no one knowing how, or why, he had climbed to it. And the reason he is there no longer is that he was gradually hacked to bits by climbers and carried away as souvenirs.

39 Leopard Point is at 18,500 feet, and now it was below us. Gillman's is at 18,635, and at last it seemed closer. It was very close. We had almost reached it. We *had* reached it. We were standing, not on scree but on solid rock, and before us the mountain no longer climbed skyward but fell sharply away into its summit crater.

40 "Is O.K., *bwana,*" said Thomas. (The altitude brought out his English.)

41 "Yes, O.K."

42   O.K.? It was marvelous. It was heaven. To be there, to stand there. To *sit down.*

43   Kilimanjaro's crater, like the rest of the mountain, is on the grand scale. More than a mile across and some three and a half in circumference, it is a double crater whose deepest point is about 900 feet lower than the highest summit. Gillman's Point, where we now were, is on the crater scarp.* Six hundred feet down steep walls is the crater floor, a piebald * sweep of black and white, lava and snow, almost perfectly level, except for a number of huge and fantastic ice masses that have been given such names as the Dome, the Battleship, and the Cathedral. At the center of this circle, like a bull's-eye in a target, is the inner crater, another 300 feet deep, complete with a second scarp, steep walls and, at the very bottom, the volcano's cold core, called the Ash Pit.

44   I would have liked to go down and see the Ash Pit, but there was something I wanted more—and that something was not down but up. In the rulebook of Kilimanjaro, Gillman's Point "counts"; if you reach it you have climbed the mountain. But it is not the top. *The* top is some 700 feet higher and a mile and a quarter distant to the south and west, along the ups and downs of the crater rim. It is still known by its old German name, the Kaiser Wilhelm Spitze, and it is only there that all of Africa is beneath you.

45   Par for the climb from Kibo Hut to Gillman's is five hours. It had taken me seven, and I was thoroughly conscious that I had not spent the morning in bed. In all honesty, I had not expected to get this far. I was surprised and delighted that I had, and decided the only sane course was to leave well enough alone. "Gillman's counts," I told myself. "It's enough, and we'll go down." Then Thomas looked at me inquiringly, and my hand, quite on its own, pointed up.

46   The hateful scree was below us. We were on blessed solid rock. For all of ten steps, that is. Then we came off

the rock onto snow, the snow was soft and crustless in the midday sunshine, and we sank in to the knee, the thigh, the waist. I lurched. I floundered. In no time my mouth was open like a boated fish's, gasping for air, and my heart was pounding fit to crack my ribs.

⁴⁷ Even Thomas was not quite superhuman. He sank in too. But sinking or not, he was able to keep going steadily, whereas my ratio of movement to rest was about one to three. On the downslopes of the ragged rim my gait was a stumbling crawl. On the upgrades, which of course predominated, the crawl seemed in comparison to have been a light-footed sprint.

⁴⁸ We searched for snowless rock. But now there was snow everywhere. Ahead, on the endless hummocks ° of the rim; to the right, choking the crater; to the left, falling away endlessly in billowing waves of glacier. The snow gleamed. The snow glared. The billows were no longer static but undulating, and from their crests darted long white lances of light that struck blindingly into my eyes. I fumbled in a pocket for my goggles but didn't find them. I had them on. The whiteness beat against their green lenses as if it would crack them with its force.

⁴⁹ In that frozen world it was not cold. It was warm, even hot. Sweat was trickling on my back and down my forehead, under the goggles, into my eyes. My eyes were bothering me even more now than legs, lungs, or heart. Sweat and snow seemed to mingle, forming patterns and images that wove before me. Soon the whole mountain-top was weaving. Crater and rim revolved slowly in space, like an enormous wheel.

⁵⁰ I was terribly tired, and the snow was soft. It was a great pillow, a featherbed, all around me, and in the deep drifts, leaning against it, I closed my eyes. I had read, sometimes even written, of climbers overwhelmed by sleep at high altitudes, and now for the first time it

hummocks: ridges of ice, as in an ice field.

was actually happening to me. With eyes closed, the awful glare was gone. Resting motionless in my featherbed, I felt breathing and heartbeat ease, and I sank gently, deliciously, into a shadowed doze. Luckily the shadows never closed in entirely. My head jerked back. My eyes opened. I crept on again, willing myself to move, my eyes to stay open.

51 I had estimated an hour from Gillman's Point to the summit, but now, after twice that, we seemed to be nowhere at all. All recognizable features of rim and crater were gone. There were the endless humps, the snow, the sky; and now something was happening to the sky, too, for it was no longer blue but white. Like the mountain, it was covered with snow—or was it cloud? Yes, it was cloud, I decided. And then suddenly, through a rent in the cloud, I saw a sight that I thought was hallucination: a soaring plane. It was not silver, as a plane should be, but gleaming amber, and it moved high and still, like a specter, and then vanished in the gulfs of space.

52 It had not been illusion, I learned later; Thomas had seen the plane too. But then I didn't know. I couldn't even find Thomas. Like the spectral thing in the sky, he had disappeared, too, into the whiteness. And then a second hallucination: a black disk. The disk was not in the sky but on the rim before me. It grew larger as I approached. It was Thomas's face, and he had turned and was waiting.

53 Down—up. Up—down. Then up and more up. The cloud seemed to be gone, and there was only the rim and the crater spinning around me. Then they, too, dissolved, as I tripped and fell headlong into the snow. When I arose it was to see still another hallucination. In the whiteness ahead, there was something that was not white. On a hump of snow there was what seemed to be a pile of stones—a pile fashioned not by nature but by man—and rising from the stones two bamboo poles. I climbed another few steps and the pile didn't vanish.

I reached out to touch it, and it was there. *We* were there. On the Kaiser Wilhelm Spitze, 19,340 feet high. I shook hands with Thomas and sat down. Or maybe I sat down first.

⁵⁴ After a few minutes my head was clear, my breathing normal. I smoked a cigarette, and it was good. From beneath the stones I pulled a black metal box, took out the summit register and signed it; and that was good, too, except that I wished Jim were there to sign with me.

⁵⁵ Then I looked slowly around. MMBK lay all below us. MMBA lay all around us. If I say I could see the Indian Ocean, Johannesburg, the Nile, the Congo, I am obviously lying. But I would not have thought so then, for it seemed to me I could see *everything*—the whole of Africa—lying clear and bright in crystal space. There are few men in the world as happy as the mountaineer atop his mountain, and for half an hour, on that magical summit, I savored my reward to the full.

⁵⁶ Then—*"Bwana—"*

⁵⁷ "Yes, Thomas."

⁵⁸ He pointed at my wristwatch. There was still a full installment of the price to be paid: those Miles and Miles of Bloody Kilimanjaro in reverse.

⁵⁹ I shall make it brief, which it wasn't. First there was the crater rim again: the humps, the whiteness, the ups, the downs; but now, at least, the downs predominated. There was our self-made trail to follow; and in half the time of our upward crawl we were back on the rocks of Gillman's Point. Here I was greeted by another hallucination. A figure was moving. A voice was speaking. Presently they turned into Fred Hughes, and Fred said, "Have some chocolate." Then he added, "I thought I'd amble up and see how you were doing."

⁶⁰ "So the worst is over," I thought—and failed to hear the sound of off-stage laughter. But I heard it clearly enough during the hours that followed, as I crept and lurched and stumbled down the endless slopes of scree

and lava. The proper way to descend a mountain like Kilimanjaro is on the double-quick—sliding, almost running, as gravity pulls you along. But for me gravity was no ally, for I had not the strength to brace against it. Every time I tried to advance at more than a crawl, my knees buckled, and I swayed and fell.

61 So a crawl it was. Down the miles. Through the hours. Sometimes Fred and Thomas were with me; sometimes they were no more than specks far below. But always there were knees, calves, feet, toes. There were stones, stones, stones. There was an ache spreading upward that would have been almost unendurable if I had not been at least half asleep from fatigue.

62 Day was ending; Kibo Hut appeared. But this was not journey's end. Not only Jim but all the porters had gone on down to Pieter's, taking our food and blankets along.

63 "Can you keep going?" Fred asked me.

64 "I most certainly cannot," I assured him. But after an hour's rest, somehow, I did; and on through the night I went, hobbling into Pieter's Hut a little before midnight.

65 This time it was Jim who was the nurse and I the patient.

66 Then came the last day—the walk down to Marangu. "There's nothing to it," Fred and Jim reminded me cheerfully. But by now there was nothing much to me either. My face was round and swollen as a red balloon; my knees jerked and twitched like a puppet's; and my toes wore monstrous blisters.

67 Hobble, hobble, hobble. Sway, stumble, trip. I tried walking pigeon-toed; I tried walking duck-footed. No good. Nothing was any good. At every step the rocks in the path seemed to rise gleefully and kick me, and I kicked them savagely back, and groaned.

68 "Snows!" I thought. Mr. Hemingway could have his snows. What I would remember would be the *toes* of Kilimanjaro.

⁶⁹ Still, all things have an end—even MMBK. And at five that afternoon our 1957 Kilimanjaro Expedition had passed into history. We were on the terrace of the hotel at Marangu. I was barefoot. I was pouring the third beer into my swollen face. I was swearing silently that in the rest of my life I would climb nothing higher than New York's Murray Hill.

⁷⁰ Then our white hunter joined us.

⁷¹ "Well, how was it?" he asked.

⁷² "It was wonderful," I heard myself saying, and the darndest thing is that I was telling the truth.

ANALYSIS

Ullman faces two problems in writing this essay. Since his subject is the mountain, not the climb, his reader deserves geographical and historical orientation. How can he best dispense it? And second, how can he keep his narrative (what happened) from dominating his description (what it looked like, how it felt)?

He solves the first problem handily. The mountain presides over the first six paragraphs. We learn its size, its history, its many names, its location (though it is in northern Tanganyika it can be seen in Kenya). Ullman slowly intrudes himself and his friends into this general introduction. The transition to the climb itself is thus easily made.

The second problem (keeping the narrative from dominating the description) is more difficult. Ullman's solution is to describe, whenever possible, who was climbing, what equipment they carried, what conditions they met, what reactions they experienced. Never does the reader ask, are they going to make it. Ullman underplays the climbers' role constantly. He stresses the fatigue not the difficulty. He describes the terrain, the altitude, the view and not the skill it takes to reach 19,000 feet. The accumulative effect is MMBK. Expert cragsmen may call it a "nothing" mountain, but from the terrace of the hotel at Marangu (where we end this essay) it looks huge and exhausting, tormenting and exhilarating. Ullman sums up his own reaction in an easy pun on Hemingway's title: "What I would remember would be the *toes* of Kilimanjaro."

Stylistically this account of an expedition has much to commend it, more than we can point out here. In the first paragraph Ullman introduces one of his most effective devices: staccato sentences or phrases. Note how successfully he uses them in paragraphs 10, 18, 23, 27, and especially 42, where he gains the reader's smile and respect through his honest anticlimax: "It was marvelous. It was heaven. To be there, to stand there. To *sit down*." When he comes to paragraph 59, he is ready to let the short sentence take over in order to make his descent brief. But like all good writers, Ullman knows the value of variety. Paragraph 60 breaks the staccato rhythm long enough to "slide" for a few sentences.

There are other devices he employs. For humor he uses MMBA, MMBK, and his conversations with Thomas; for verisimilitude, young Jim's sudden nausea on the ascent and Ullman's own twitching knees and swollen face on the descent; for contrast, paragraphs 46–53, the snow fields above the scree and crumbled lava; for a memorable conclusion, the expected reverse-twist—"'It was wonderful,' I heard myself saying, and the darndest thing is that I was telling the truth." The professional writer has many such devices to bring variety and zest to his prose. What he learns early to avoid is overusing them.

Questions on Content

1. What vital statistics about Kilimanjaro do we learn from Ullman's essay?
2. What details do you recall of this group of twelve men as they set off for the ascent?
3. How does the summit Mawenzi differ from Kibo, *the* top of the mountain?
4. How does Ullman describe Kilimanjaro's crater and Gillman's Point?
5. What kind of man was Thomas, the guide?
6. What satisfaction and pleasures Ullman experienced served to counteract the hardships?

Add to your vocabulary: crampon, capacious, scarp piebald.

Questions on Technique

1. Ullman divides the essay into four parts. What is the function of each division?
2. What makes his description of Kibo Hut and what happened there (paragraphs 22–31) effective?
3. What senses are important in this description of mountain climbing? List several examples.
4. Why does he devote only one paragraph (55) to a description of the whole reason for the effort: the summit?

Suggestions for Writing

1. Describe in 500 words a climbing expedition you participated in. How many were in the party, how high was the mountain, what equipment did you use, what were your feelings on the way up and at the top?
2. Not only mountain climbing needs perseverance. What experience have you had that challenged your endurance or courage? Describe your physical reactions; do not simply narrate the event.
3. Describe in 500 words any especially colorful scene you have witnessed: a sunset, a parade, a storm, a stadium during a big game.

HANSON W. BALDWIN · *R.M.S.* Titanic

The sinking of the Titanic *off the Grand Banks of Newfoundland in April, 1912, is an event that has been told many times and in many media. Hanson W. Baldwin, since 1929 a member of the news staff of the New York* Times, *published this version in 1934. As a graduate of the U.S. Naval Academy, he possesses a knowledge of ships that is something more than amateur. As a reporter, he knows how to muster facts, how to build a story, where to place emphasis to hold his reader's atten-*

"R.M.S. *Titanic*" by Hanson W. Baldwin from *Harper's Magazine*, January, 1934. Copyright 1934 by Hanson W. Baldwin. Reprinted by permission of Willis Kingsley Wing.

tion. What is so remarkable about Baldwin's essay is the obvious fact of its not being an eye-witness report. Baldwin was only nine years old when the Titanic *sank, yet he makes his research come alive, through a variety of techniques.*

The Titanic *left Southampton, England, on April 10, 1912. It sank at 2:20* A.M. *on April 15, less than three hours after striking an iceberg. Of the 2,201 persons on board, almost 1,500 lost their lives. These are the facts Baldwin had to begin with. How he holds our attention to this descriptive account—suspense is obviously not one method—is worth close study. This essay is full of graphic details. Distinguish, as you read, their variety.*

¹ The White Star liner *Titanic,* largest ship the world had ever known, sailed from Southampton on her maiden voyage to New York on April 10, 1912. The paint on her strakes ° was fair and bright; she was fresh from Harland and Wolff's Belfast yards, strong in the strength of her forty-six thousand tons of steel, bent, hammered, shaped, and riveted through the three years of her slow birth.

² There was little fuss and fanfare at her sailing; her sister-ship, the *Olympic*—slightly smaller than the *Titanic*—had been in service for some months and to her had gone the thunder of the cheers.

³ But the *Titanic* needed no whistling steamers or shouting crowds to call attention to her superlative qualities. Her bulk dwarfed the ships near her as longshoremen singled up her mooring lines and cast off the turns of heavy rope from the dock bollards.° She was not only the largest ship afloat, but was believed to be the safest. Carlisle, her builder, had given her double bottoms and had divided her hull into sixteen water-tight compartments, which made her, men thought, unsinkable. She had been built to be and had been described

strakes: the planking or plates on the sides or bottom of a vessel.
bollards: vertical posts on which mooring rope is tied.

as a gigantic lifeboat. Her designers' dreams of a triple-screw giant, a luxurious, floating hotel, which could speed to New York at twenty-three knots, had been carefully translated from blue prints and mold loft lines at the Belfast yards into a living reality.

4   The *Titanic's* sailing from Southampton, though quiet, was not wholly uneventful. As the liner moved slowly toward the end of her dock that April day, the surge of her passing sucked away from the quay the steamer *New York,* moored just to seaward of the *Titanic's* berth. There were sharp cracks as the manila mooring lines of the *New York* parted under the strain. The frayed ropes writhed and whistled through the air and snapped down among the waving crowd on the pier; the *New York* swung toward the *Titanic's* bow, was checked and dragged back to the dock barely in time to avert a collision. Seamen muttered, thought it an ominous start.

5   Past Spithead and the Isle of Wight the *Titanic* steamed. She called at Cherbourg at dusk and then laid her course for Queenstown. At 1:30 P.M., on Thursday, April 11, she stood out of Queenstown harbor, screaming gulls soaring in her wake, with 2,201 persons—men, women and children—aboard.

6   Occupying the Empire bedroom and Georgian suites of the first-class accommodations were many well-known men and women—Colonel John Jacob Astor and his young bride; Major Archibald Butt, military aide to President Taft, and his friend, Frank D. Millet, the painter; John B. Thayer, vice-president of the Pennsylvania Railroad, and Charles M. Hays, president of the Grand Trunk Railway of Canada; W. T. Stead, the English journalist; Jacques Futrelle, French novelist; H. B. Harris, theatrical manager, and Mrs. Harris; Mr. and Mrs. Isidor Straus; and J. Bruce Ismay, chairman and managing director of the White Star line.

7   Down in the plain wooden cabins of the steerage class were 706 immigrants to the land of promise, and trimly stowed in the great holds was a cargo valued at

$420,000: oak beams, sponges, wine, calabashes,° and an odd miscellany of the common and the rare.

8   The *Titanic* took her departure on Fastnet Light and, heading into the night, laid her course for New York. She was due at Quarantine the following Wednesday morning.

9   Sunday dawned fair and clear. The *Titanic* steamed smoothly toward the west, faint streamers of brownish smoke trailing from her funnels. The purser held services in the saloon ° in the morning; on the steerage deck aft the immigrants were playing games and a Scotsman was puffing "The Campbells Are Coming" on his bagpipes in the midst of the uproar.

10   At 9 A.M. a message from the steamer *Caronia* sputtered into the wireless shack:

Captain, *Titanic*—Westbound steamers report bergs growlers and field ice in 42 degrees N. from 49 degrees to 51 degrees W. 12th April.

Compliments—
Barr

11   It was cold in the afternoon; the sun was brilliant, but the *Titanic,* her screws turning over at 75 revolutions per minute, was approaching the Banks.

12   In the Marconi cabin Second Operator Harold Bride, ear-phones clamped on his head, was figuring accounts; he did not stop to answer when he heard *MWL,* Continental Morse for the nearby Leyland liner, *Californian,* calling the *Titanic.* The *Californian* had some message about the icebergs; he didn't bother then to take it down. About 1:42 P.M. the rasping spark of those days spoke again across the water. It was the *Baltic,* calling the *Titanic,* warning her of ice on the steamer track. Bride took the message down and sent it up to the bridge. The officer-of-the-deck glanced at it; sent it to the bearded master of the *Titanic,* Captain E. C. Smith,

calabashes: gourds, or bottles made from gourds.
saloon: a large room for the common use of passengers on a passenger vessel.

a veteran of the White Star service. It was lunch time then; the Captain, walking along the promenade deck, saw Mr. Ismay, stopped, and handed him the message without comment. Ismay read it, stuffed it in his pocket, told two ladies about the icebergs, and resumed his walk. Later, about 7:15 P.M., the Captain requested the return of the message in order to post it in the chart room for the information of officers.

[13] Dinner that night in the Jacobean dining room was gay. It was bitter on deck, but the night was calm and fine; the sky was moonless but studded with stars twinkling coldly in the clear air.

[14] After dinner some of the second-class passengers gathered in the saloon, where the Reverend Mr. Carter conducted a "hymn sing-song." It was almost ten o'clock and the stewards were waiting with biscuits and coffee as the group sang:

> *O, hear us when we cry to Thee*
> *For those in peril on the sea.*

[15] On the bridge Second Officer Lightoller—short, stocky, efficient—was relieved at ten o'clock by First Officer Murdoch. Lightoller had talked with other officers about the proximity of ice; at least five wireless ice warnings had reached the ship; lookouts had been cautioned to be alert; captains and officers expected to reach the field at any time after 9:30 P.M. At 22 knots, its speed unslackened, the *Titanic* plowed on through the night.

[16] Lightoller left the darkened bridge to his relief and turned in. Captain Smith went to his cabin. The steerage was long since quiet; in the first and second cabins lights were going out; voices were growing still, people were asleep. Murdoch paced back and forth on the bridge, peering out over the dark water, glancing now and then at the compass in front of Quartermaster Hichens at the wheel.

[17] In the crow's nest, Lookout Frederick Fleet and his partner, Leigh, gazed down at the water, still and unruffled in the dim. starlit darkness. Behind and below

them the ship, a white shadow with here and there a last winking light; ahead of them a dark and silent and cold ocean.

18   There was a sudden clang. "Dong-dong. Dong-dong. Dong-dong. Dong!" The metal clapper of the great ship's bell struck out 11:30. Mindful of the warnings, Fleet strained his eyes, searching the darkness for the dreaded ice. But there were only the stars and the sea.

19   In the wireless room, where Phillips, first operator, had relieved Bride, the buzz of the *Californian's* set again crackled into the ear-phones:

> *Californian:* "Say, old man, we are stuck here, sur-rounded by ice."
> *Titanic:* "Shut up, shut up; keep out. I am talking to Cape Race; you are jamming my signals."

20   Then, a few minutes later—about 11:40 . . .

II

21   Out of the dark she came, a vast, dim, white, mon-strous shape, directly in the *Titanic's* path. For a mo-ment Fleet doubted his eyes. But she was a deadly real-ity, this ghastly *thing*. Frantically, Fleet struck three bells—*something dead ahead.* He snatched the telephone and called the bridge:

22   "Iceberg! Right ahead!"

23   The First Officer heard but did not stop to acknowl-edge the message.

24   "Hard-a-starboard!"

25   Hichens strained at the wheel; the bow swung slowly to port. The monster was almost upon them now.

26   Murdoch leaped to the engine-room telegraph. Bells clanged. Far below in the engine-room those bells struck the first warning. Danger! The indicators on the dial faces swung round to "Stop!" Then "Full speed astern!" Frantically the engineers turned great valve wheels; an-swered the bridge bells . . .

27   There was a slight shock, a brief scraping, a small

list to port. Shell ice—slabs and chunks of it—fell on the foredeck. Slowly the *Titanic* stopped.

28   Captain Smith hurried out of his cabin.

29   "What has the ship struck?"

30   Murdoch answered, "An iceberg, sir. I hard-a-starboarded and reversed the engines, and I was going to hard-a-port around it, but she was too close. I could not do any more. I have closed the water-tight doors."

31   Fourth Officer Boxhall, other officers, the carpenter, came to the bridge. The Captain sent Boxhall and the carpenter below to ascertain the damage.

32   A few lights switched on in the first and second cabins; sleepy passengers peered through porthole glass; some casually asked the stewards:

33   "Why have we stopped?"

34   "I don't know, sir, but I don't suppose it is anything much."

35   In the smoking room a quorum of gamblers and their prey were still sitting around a poker table; the usual crowd of kibitzers looked on. They had felt the slight jar of the collision and had seen an eighty-foot ice mountain glide by the smoking room windows, but the night was calm and clear, the *Titanic* was "unsinkable"; they hadn't bothered to go on deck.

36   But far below, in the warren of passages on the starboard side forward, in the forward holds and boiler rooms, men could see that the *Titanic's* hurt was mortal. In No. 6 boiler room, where the red glow from the furnaces lighted up the naked, sweaty chests of coal-blackened firemen, water was pouring through a great gash about two feet above the floor plates. This was no slow leak; the ship was open to the sea; in ten minutes there were eight feet of water in No. 6. Long before then the stokers had raked the flaming fires out of the furnaces and had scrambled through the water-tight doors into No. 5 or had climbed up the long steel ladders to safety. When Boxhall looked at the mailroom in No. 3 hold, twenty-four feet above the keel, the mailbags were already floating about in the slushing water. In No. 5

boiler room a stream of water spurted into an empty bunker. All six compartments forward of No. 4 were open to the sea; in ten seconds the iceberg's jagged claw had ripped a three-hundred-foot slash in the bottom of the great *Titanic*.

37   Reports came to the bridge; Ismay in dressing gown ran out on deck in the cold, still, starlit night, climbed up the bridge ladder.

38   "What has happened?"

39   Captain Smith: "We have struck ice."

40   "Do you think she is seriously damaged?"

41   Captain Smith: "I'm afraid she is."

42   Ismay went below and passed Chief Engineer William Bell fresh from an inspection of the damaged compartments. Bell corroborated the Captain's statement; hurried back down the glistening steel ladders to his duty. Man after man followed him—Thomas Andrews, one of the ship's designers, Archie Frost, the builder's chief engineer, and his twenty assistants—men who had no posts of duty in the engine room but whose traditions called them there.

43   On deck, in corridor and stateroom, life flowed again. Men, women, and children awoke and questioned; orders were given to uncover the lifeboats; water rose into the firemen's quarters; half-dressed stokers streamed up on deck. But the passengers—most of them—did not know that the *Titanic* was sinking. The shock of the collision had been so slight that some were not awakened by it; the *Titanic* was so huge that she must be unsinkable; the night was too calm, too beautiful, to think of death at sea.

44   Captain Smith half ran to the door of the radio shack. Bride, partly dressed, eyes dulled with sleep, was standing behind Phillips, waiting.

45   "Send the call for assistance."

46   The blue spark danced: "CQD—CQD—CQD—CQ—"

47   Miles away Marconi men heard. Cape Race heard it, and the steamships *La Provence* and *Mt. Temple*.

48   The sea was surging into the *Titanic's* hold. At

12:20 the water burst into the seamen's quarters through a collapsed fore and aft wooden bulkhead. Pumps strained in the engine rooms—men and machinery making a futile fight against the sea. Steadily the water rose.

[49] The boats were swung out—slowly; for the deckhands were late in reaching their stations, there had been no boat drill, and many of the crew did not know to what boats they were assigned. Orders were shouted; the safety valves had lifted, and steam was blowing off in a great rushing roar. In the chart house Fourth Officer Boxhall bent above a chart, working rapidly with pencil and dividers.

[50] 12:25 A.M. Boxhall's position is sent out to a fleet of vessels: "Come at once; we have struck a berg."

[51] To the Cunarder *Carpathia* (Arthur Henry Rostron, Master, New York to Liverpool, fifty-eight miles away): "It's a CQD, old man. Position 41–46 N.; 50–14 W."

[52] The blue spark dancing: "Sinking; cannot hear for noise of steam."

[53] 12:30 A.M. The word is passed: "Women and children in the boats." Stewards finish waking their passengers below; life-preservers are tied on; some men smile at the precaution. "The *Titanic* is unsinkable." The *Mt. Temple* starts for the *Titanic;* the *Carpathia,* with a double-watch in her stokeholds, radios, "Coming hard." The CQD changes the course of many ships—but not of one; the operator of the *Californian,* nearby, has just put down his ear-phones and turned in.

[54] The CQD flashes over land and sea from Cape Race to New York; newspaper city rooms leap to life and presses whir.

[55] On the *Titanic,* water creeps over the bulkhead between Nos. 5 and 6 firerooms. She is going down by the head; the engineers—fighting a losing battle—are forced back foot by foot by the rising water. Down the promenade deck, Happy Jock Hume, the bandsman, runs with his instrument.

[56] 12:45 A.M. Murdoch, in charge on the starboard side,

eyes tragic, but calm and cool, orders boat No. 7 lowered. The women hang back; they want no boat-ride on an ice-strewn sea; the *Titanic* is unsinkable. The men encourage them, explain that this is just a precautionary measure: "We'll see you again at breakfast." There is little confusion; passengers stream slowly to the boat deck. In the steerage the immigrants chatter excitedly.

57   A sudden sharp hiss—a streaked flare against the night; Boxhall sends a rocket toward the sky. It explodes, and a parachute of white stars lights up the icy sea. "God! Rockets!" The band plays ragtime.

58   No. 8 is lowered, and No. 5. Ismay, still in dressing gown, calls for women and children, handles lines, stumbles in the way of an officer, is told to "get out of here." Third Officer Pitman takes charge of No. 5; as he swings into the boat Murdoch grasps his hand. "Good-by and good luck, old man."

59   No. 6 goes over the side. There are only twenty-eight people in a lifeboat with a capacity of sixty-five.

60   A light stabs from the bridge; Boxhall is calling in Morse flashes, again and again, to a strange ship stopped in the ice jam five to ten miles away. Another rocket drops its shower of sparks above the ice-strewn sea and the dying ship.

61   1:00 A.M. Slowly the water creeps higher; the fore ports of the *Titanic* are dipping into the sea. Rope squeaks through blocks; lifeboats drop jerkily seaward. Through the shouting on the deck comes the sound of the band playing ragtime.

62   The "Millionaires' Special" leaves the ship—boat No. 1, with a capacity of forty people, carries only Sir Cosmo and Lady Duff Gordon and ten others. Aft, the frightened immigrants mill and jostle and rush for a boat. An officer's fist flies out; three shots are fired in the air, and the panic is quelled. . . . Four Chinese sneak unseen into a boat and hide in its bottom.

63   1:20 A.M. Water is coming into No. 4 boiler room. Stokers slice and shovel as water laps about their ankles —steam for the dynamos, steam for the dancing spark!

As the water rises, great ash hoes rake the flaming coals from the furnaces. Safety valves pop; the stokers retreat aft, and the water-tight doors clang shut behind them.

⁶⁴ The rockets fling their splendor toward the stars. The boats are more heavily loaded now, for the passengers know the *Titanic* is sinking. Women cling and sob. The great screws aft are rising clear of the sea. Half-filled boats are ordered to come alongside the cargo ports and take on more passengers, but the ports are never opened—and the boats are never filled. Others pull for the steamer's light miles away but never reach it; the lights disappear, the unknown ship steams off.

⁶⁵ The water rises and the band plays ragtime.

⁶⁶ 1:30 A.M. Lightoller is getting the port boats off; Murdoch the starboard. As one boat is lowered into the sea a boat officer fires his gun along the ship's side to stop a rush from the lower decks. A woman tries to take her Great Dane into a boat with her; she is refused and steps out of the boat to die with her dog. Millet's "little smile which played on his lips all through the voyage" plays no more; his lips are grim, but he waves good-by and brings wraps for the women.

⁶⁷ Benjamin Guggenheim, in evening clothes, smiles and says, "We've dressed up in our best and are prepared to go down like gentlemen."

⁶⁸ 1:40 A.M. Boat 14 is clear, and then 13, 16, 15 and C. The lights still shine, but the *Baltic* hears the blue spark say, "Engine-room getting flooded."

⁶⁹ The *Olympic* signals, "Am lighting up all possible boilers as fast as can."

⁷⁰ Major Butt helps women into the last boats and waves good-by to them. Mrs. Straus puts her foot on the gunwale of a lifeboat, then she draws back and goes to her husband: "We have been together many years; where you go I will go." Colonel John Jacob Astor puts his young wife in a lifeboat, steps back, taps cigarette on fingernail: "Good-by, dearie; I'll join you later."

⁷¹ 1:45 A.M. The foredeck is under water, the fo'c'sle head almost awash; the great stern is lifted high toward

the bright stars; and still the band plays. Mr. and Mrs. Harris approach a lifeboat arm in arm.

72   Officer: "Ladies first, please."

73   Harris bows, smiles, steps back: "Of course, certainly; ladies first."

74   Boxhall fires the last rocket, then leaves in charge of boat No. 2.

75   2:00 A.M. She is dying now; her bow goes deeper, her stern higher. But there must be steam. Below in the stokeholds the sweaty firemen keep steam up for the flaring lights and the dancing spark. The glowing coals slide and tumble over the slanted grate bars; the sea pounds behind that yielding bulkhead. But the spark dances on.

76   The *Asian* hears Phillips try the new signal—SOS.

77   Boat No. 4 has left now; boat D leaves ten minutes later. Jacques Futrelle clasps his wife: "For God's sake, go! It's your last chance; go!" Madame Futrelle is half-forced into the boat. It clears the side.

78   There are about 660 people in the boats, and 1,500 still on the sinking *Titanic*.

79   On top of the officers' quarters men work frantically to get the two collapsibles stowed there over the side. Water is over the forward part of A deck now; it surges up the companionways toward the boat deck. In the radio shack, Bride has slipped a coat and lifejacket about Phillips as the first operator sits hunched over his key, sending—still sending—"41–46 N.; 50–14 W. CQD—CQD—SOS—SOS—"

80   The captain's tired white face appears at the radio-room door: "Men, you have done your full duty. You can do no more. Now, it's every man for himself." The captain disappears—back to his sinking bridge, where Painter, his personal steward, stands quietly waiting for orders. The spark dances on. Bride turns his back and goes into the inner cabin. As he does so, a stoker, grimed with coal, mad with fear, steals into the shack and reaches for the lifejacket on Phillips' back. Bride wheels about and brains him with a wrench.

[81] 2:10 A.M. Below decks the steam is still holding, though the pressure is falling—rapidly. In the gymnasium on the boat deck the athletic instructor watches quietly as two gentlemen ride the bicycles and another swings casually at the punching bag. Mail clerks stagger up the boat-deck stairways, dragging soaked mail sacks. The spark still dances. The band still plays—but not ragtime:

> *Nearer my God to Thee,*
> *Nearer to Thee . . .*

[82] A few men take up the refrain; others kneel on the slanting decks to pray. Many run and scramble aft, where hundreds are clinging above the silent screws on the great uptilted stern. The spark still dances and the lights still flare; the engineers are on the job. The hymn comes to its close. Bandmaster Hartley, Yorkshireman violinist, taps his bow against a bulkhead, calls for "Autumn" as the water curls about his feet, and the eight musicians brace themselves against the ship's slant. People are leaping from the decks into the nearby water—the icy water. A woman cries, "Oh, save me, save me!" A man answers, "Good lady, save yourself. Only God can save you now." The band plays "Autumn":

> *God of Mercy and Compassion!*
> *Look with pity on my pain. . .*

[83] The water creeps over the bridge where the *Titanic's* master stands; heavily he steps out to meet it.

[84] 2:17 A.M. "CQ—" The *Virginian* hears a ragged, blurred CQ, then an abrupt stop. The blue spark dances no more. The lights flicker out; the engineers have lost their battle.

[85] 2:18 A.M. Men run about blackened decks; leap into the night; are swept into the sea by the curling wave which licks up the *Titanic's* length. Lightoller does not leave the ship; the ship leaves him; there are hundreds like him, but only a few who live to tell of it. The funnels still swim above the water, but the ship is climbing

to the perpendicular; the bridge is under and most of the foremast; the great stern rises like a squat leviathan.° Men swim away from the sinking ship; others drop from the stern.

86 The band plays in the darkness, the water lapping upwards:

> *Hold me up in mighty waters,*
> *Keep my eyes on things above,*
> *Righteousness, divine atonement,*
> *Peace and everlas . . .*

87 The forward funnel snaps and crashes into the sea; its steel tons hammer out of existence swimmers struggling in the freezing water. Streams of sparks, of smoke and steam, burst from the after funnels. The ship upends to 50–to 60 degrees.

88 Down in the black abyss of the stokeholds, of the engine-rooms, where the dynamos have whirred at long last to a stop, the stokers and the engineers are reeling against hot metal, the rising water clutching at their knees. The boilers, the engine cylinders, rip from their bed plates; crash through bulkheads; rumble—steel against steel.

89 The *Titanic* stands on end, poised briefly for the plunge. Slowly she slides to her grave—slowly at first, and then more quickly—quickly—quickly.

90 2:20 A.M. The greatest ship in the world has sunk. From the calm, dark waters, where the floating lifeboats move, there goes up, in the white wake of her passing, "one long continuous moan."

III

91 The boats that the *Titanic* had launched pulled safely away from the slight suction of the sinking ship, pulled away from the screams that came from the lips of the freezing men and women in the water. The boats were poorly manned and badly equipped, and they had

leviathan: any huge marine animal, also anything of huge size, as a ship.

been unevenly loaded. Some carried so few seamen that women bent to the oars. Mrs. Astor tugged at an oar handle; the Countess of Rothes took a tiller. Shivering stokers in sweaty, coal-blackened singlets and light trousers steered in some boats; stewards in white coats rowed in others. Ismay was in the last boat that left the ship from the starboard side; with Mr. Carter of Philadelphia and two seamen he tugged at the oars. In one of the lifeboats an Italian with a broken wrist—disguised in a woman's shawl and hat—huddled on the floor boards, ashamed now that fear had left him. In another rode the only baggage saved from the *Titanic*—the carry-all of Samuel L. Goldenberg, one of the rescued passengers.

92 There were only a few boats that were heavily loaded; most of those that were half empty made but perfunctory * efforts to pick up the moaning swimmers, their officers and crew fearing they would endanger the living if they pulled back into the midst of the dying. Some boats beat off the freezing victims; fear-crazed men and women struck with oars at the heads of swimmers. One woman drove her fist into the face of a half-dead man as he tried feebly to climb over the gunwale. Two other women helped him in and stanched the flow of blood from the ring-cuts on his face.

93 One of the collapsible boats, which had floated off the top of the officers' quarters when the *Titanic* sank, was an icy haven for thirty or forty men. The boat had capsized as the ship sank; men swam to it, clung to it, climbed upon its slippery bottom, stood knee-deep in water in the freezing air. Chunks of ice swirled about their legs; their soaked clothing clutched their bodies in icy folds. Colonel Archibald Gracie was cast up there, Gracie who had leaped from the stern as the *Titanic* sank; young Thayer who had seen his father die; Lightoller who had twice been sucked down with the ship and twice blown to the surface by a belch of air; Bride, the second operator, and Phillips, the first. There were many stokers, half-naked; it was a shivering company. They stood there in the icy sea, under the far stars, and sang and prayed—the Lord's Prayer. After a while a lifeboat came and picked them off, but Phillips was dead then or died soon afterward in the boat.

94 Only a few of the boats had lights; only one—No. 2—had a light that was of any use to the *Carpathia,* twisting through the ice-field to the rescue. Other ships were "coming hard" too; one, the *Californian,* was still dead to opportunity.

95 The blue sparks still danced, but not the *Titanic's.* *La Provence* to *Celtic:* "Nobody has heard the *Titanic* for about two hours."

96 It was 2:40 when the *Carpathia* first sighted the green light from No. 2 boat; it was 4:10 when she picked up the first boat and learned that the *Titanic* had foundered. The last of the moaning cries had just died away then.

97 Captain Rostron took the survivors aboard, boatload by boatload. He was ready for them, but only a small minority of them required much medical attention. Bride's feet were twisted and frozen; others were suffering from exposure; one died, and seven were dead when taken from the boats, and were buried at sea.

98 It was then that the fleet of racing ships learned they were too late; the *Parisian* heard the weak signals of *MPA,* the *Carpathia,* report the death of the *Titanic.* It was then—or soon afterward, when her radio operator put on his ear-phones—that the *Californian,* the ship that had been within sight as the *Titanic* was sinking, first learned of the disaster.

99 And it was then, in all its white-green majesty, that the *Titanic's* survivors saw the iceberg, tinted with the sunrise, floating idly, pack-ice jammed about its base, other bergs heaving slowly nearby on the blue breast of the sea.

IV

100 But it was not until later that the world knew, for wireless then was not what wireless is today, and garbled messages had nourished a hope that all of the *Titanic's*

company were safe. Not until Monday evening, when
P. A. S. Franklin, Vice-President of the International
Mercantile Marine Company, received relayed messages
in New York that left little hope, did the full extent of
the disaster begin to be known. Partial and garbled lists
of the survivors; rumors of heroism and cowardice; stories spun out of newspaper imagination, based on a few
bare facts and many false reports, misled the world, ter-
rified and frightened it. It was not until Thursday night,
when the *Carpathia* steamed into the North River, that
the full truth was pieced together.

[101]   Flashlights flared on the black river when the *Carpathia* stood up to her dock. Tugs nosed about her;
shunted her toward Pier 54. Thirty thousand people
jammed the streets; ambulances and stretchers stood on
the pier; coroners and physicians waited.

[102]   In mid-stream the Cunarder dropped over the *Titanic's* lifeboats; then she headed toward the dock. Beneath the customs letters on the pier stood relatives of
the 711 survivors, relatives of the missing—hoping
against hope. The *Carpathia* cast her lines ashore; steve-
dores looped them over bollards. The dense throngs
stood quiet as the first survivor stepped down the gang-
way. The woman half-staggered—led by customs guards
—beneath her letter. A "low wailing" moan came from
the crowd; fell, grew in volume, and dropped again.

[103]   Thus ended the maiden voyage of the *Titanic*. The
lifeboats brought to New York by the *Carpathia,* a few
deck chairs and gratings awash in the ice-field off the
Grand Banks 800 miles from shore, were all that was
left of the world's greatest ship.

v

[104]   The aftermath of weeping and regret, of recriminations and investigations, dragged on for weeks. Charges
and countercharges were hurled about; the White Star
line was bitterly criticized; Ismay was denounced on the
floor of the Senate as a coward, but was defended by

those who had been with him on the sinking *Titanic* and by the Board of Trade investigation in England.

105   It was not until weeks later, when the hastily convened Senate investigation in the United States and the Board of Trade report in England had been completed, that the whole story was told. The Senate investigating committee, under the chairmanship of Senator Smith, who was attacked in both the American and British press as a "backwoods politician," brought out numerous pertinent * facts, though its proceedings verged at times on the farcical.* Senator Smith was ridiculed for his lack of knowledge of the sea when he asked witnesses, "Of what is an iceberg composed?" and "Did any of the passengers take refuge in the water-tight compartments?" The Senator seemed particularly interested in the marital status of Fleet, the lookout, who was saved. Fleet, puzzled, growled aside, "Wot questions they're arskin' me!"

106   The report of Lord Mersey, Wreck Commissioner in the British Board of Trade's investigation, was tersely damning.

107   The *Titanic* had carried boats enough for 1,178 persons, only one-third of her capacity. Her sixteen boats and four collapsibles had saved but 711 persons; 400 people had needlessly lost their lives. The boats had been but partly loaded; officers in charge of launching them had been afraid the falls would break or the boats buckle under their rated loads; boat crews had been slow in reaching their stations; launching arrangements were confused because no boat drill had been held; passengers were loaded into the boats haphazardly because no boat assignments had been made.

108   But that was not all. Lord Mersey found that sufficient warnings of ice on the steamer track had reached the *Titanic,* that her speed of 22 knots was "excessive under the circumstances," that "in view of the high speed at which the vessel was running it is not considered that the lookout was sufficient," and that her master made "a very grievous mistake"—but should not be

blamed for negligence. Captain Rostron of the *Carpathia* was highly praised. "He did the very best that could be done." The *Californian* was damned. The testimony of her master, officers, and crew showed that she was not, at the most, more than nineteen miles away from the sinking *Titanic* and probably no more than five to ten miles distant. She had seen the *Titanic's* lights; she had seen the rockets; she had not received the CQD calls because her radio operator was asleep. She had attempted to get in communication with the ship she had sighted by flashing a light, but vainly.

109   "The night was clear," reported Lord Mersey, "and the sea was smooth. When she first saw the rockets the *Californian* could have pushed through the ice to the open water without any serious risk and so have come to the assistance of the *Titanic*. Had she done so she might have saved many if not all of the lives that were lost.

110   "She made no attempt."

ANALYSIS

Baldwin must have decided early in organizing this essay that one of the hazards of reporting a past event, and especially one so sensational as this, is the mass of conflicting reports. What actually did happen? Can hearings and court testimony re-create an event? Very likely not, so Baldwin breaks his essay carefully.

He chooses the past tense for part one. He begins with the day of the maiden voyage, April 10, and takes this part up to 11:40 P.M., April 14. These facts are ascertainable: the ship's design, the passenger list, the course it set, the messages it sent and received, the warnings it should have heeded, and so forth. Baldwin is reporting fact.

The second part is mainly imaginative writing, or at best it is the piecing together of survivors' testimony added to Baldwin's knowledge of ships. How accurate are the details is a question Baldwin assumes we will not ask. He wisely shifts into the present tense. He wants us to feel we are there, *as though* it happened this way.

Parts three, four, and five revert to the past tense: what happened in and around the twenty boats launched, how the *Carpathia* brought 711 survivors to New York harbor, what the aftermath of recriminations and investigations revealed.

This is a long essay. These divisions help the reader immeasurably to sift his impressions of the description Baldwin gives him. It is not the only method he could have used. He might have written it from the viewpoint of one survivor (J. Bruce Ismay, chairman and managing director of the White Star line, for example). He could have used the Board of Trade investigation in England as his point of departure. But Baldwin, like James Ramsey Ullman, chooses a chronological description. His subject is the *Titanic,* just as Ullman's is Kilimanjaro. Put the subject into action, make the description come alive, give the reader names, dates, places, build the description toward a climax, or at least a firm conclusion—these seem to be the principles by which both authors operate. The reader must decide their effectiveness.

Questions on Content

1. Why did her builders think the *Titanic* was unsinkable?
2. Why did the *Californian* not hear the *Titanic's* SOS? Had they been in communication earlier in the evening?
3. Who, according to Baldwin's account of the sinking, was to blame for this accident? Explain.
4. What significant facts come to light through the investigations which followed the sinking?

Add to your vocabulary: perfunctory, pertinent, farcical.

Questions on Technique

1. To what purpose does Baldwin list all the proper nouns in paragraph six? How do they add to the impact of the story? Does it help to know the names of the crew members, such as Bride, Phillips, Smith, and the others?

2. Explain the effectiveness of Baldwin's timed "reports" in part two. Why should time play such an important role here?

3. Part two is filled with dialogue some of which Baldwin could only imagine. Does it sound credible to you? Would you have eliminated it entirely? Parts of it?

4. Why quote the words of the hymns sung that night aboard the *Titanic?* Is there irony ° in the name of the ship as well?

5. Part three is relatively calm, well-ordered description. Why does Baldwin not try to heighten the action here as he does in part two?

6. The docking of the *Carpathia* could be an occasion for elaborate description. Why should Baldwin choose to be so concise in this section?

7. What effect does he seek, in part five, by singling out Senator Smith and Lord Mersey from among all the charges and counter-charges after the disaster?

8. Discuss your reaction to Baldwin's last sentence (note that it is a one-sentence paragraph) ?

Suggestions for Writing

1. What experiences have you had with boats? Describe in 400 words your first attempt at rowing, a canoe trip, a boat you made yourself, a journey on a raft, a visit to a shipyard, an ocean journey.

2. Search your memory for a past occasion when you were involved in an experience that demanded quick thinking. Describe in five or six paragraphs the thoughts that passed through your mind as well as the situation itself.

3. Stretch your imagination. You are on the New York dock when the *Carpathia* comes into harbor with the *Titanic* survivors. Describe your impressions.

4. The *Titanic* disaster would not have happened if. . . . Describe in 400 words an unhappy experience of your own and show that *if* certain things had been done (precautions taken, decisions made, etc.) the whole experience would have been far different.

5. Describe in 400 words an experience in which irony plays a part as it does in the loss of the *Titanic.*

irony: See Glossary.

6. People react differently to an emergency. Describe an emergency in such a way that attention is centered on the different reactions of individuals to the same circumstances. You may have witnessed, for instance, a hurricane or tornado, a fire, an accident, an emergency plane landing.

PART TWO

EXPOSITION

If you have studied Part One, you have seen through a variety of models that descriptive writing tells us what a person or a thing or an experience looks like, sounds like, feels like. Our senses become attuned to the writer's by means of his word pictures. We share James Ramsey Ullman's exhilaration on Kilimanjaro, for example, because his descriptive prose tells us just how the altitude affects a human being, how the scree makes climbing difficult, what hazards one encounters in a snow field. We *see* the dragonflies Edwin Way Teale describes because he knows their history, their habits, and their anatomy. John Steinbeck tries to make us *feel* the slow pace and the dogged determination of a turtle crossing a highway. Clear sensory impressions ° are at the base of successful descriptive writing.

Expository prose does not, by any definition, avoid description, not any more than description can always remain pure and never encroach on the kind of writing we call narration. Ullman describes a mountain. His description is mainly concerned with the *what* of his subject. His narrating the events of the climb chronologically (*when* all this happened) is a secondary concern. Expository prose, on the other hand, is primarily concerned with the *why* or *how* of things. Description and narration are sometimes utilized, but only as secondary techniques, as supporting measures.

sensory impressions: See Glossary.

Appealing to our understanding rather than to our feelings, expository prose (as we use the term in this book) defines a word, explains a process, reports an incident, analyzes an idea, argues an opinion, defends an attitude, evaluates or judges an experience. You meet expository prose whenever you consult a dictionary or an encyclopedia, whenever you read an editorial, an analysis of current events, a book review, a scientific article, or a political argument.

The seven groups of expository models that follow are conveniently arranged for our inspection. Call them subdivisions of the larger term, if you wish. Call them methods of approach to the subject. But remember that they do not always exist in a wholly pure form. They are so grouped because the writer's *primary* intention is identifiable under the chapter in which he appears. We begin naturally with the most elementary forms of exposition, and move from there to reporting, analysis, argument, criticism, and finally the informal or personal essay. Each type of exposition will be explained as we come to it.

CHAPTER 3

Elementary exposition: definition

The purest form of definition is a dictionary entry. We have chosen two different dictionaries to illustrate the variety that can be achieved even in so standard a form of writing. These entries are followed by an encyclopedia definition of the same word. You will notice how much more complete this longer definition can be. When we ask each other, in conversation, "What do you mean by that?" or "How are you using that word?" we frequently need to explain usage. We have included in this chapter, therefore, an entry from a special kind of word-book, a dictionary of usage, which describes fine distinctions in the English language. Finally, we come to two attempts to define more difficult concepts, words that generally do not provoke agreement even when scholars explain them. Defining "railroad" or "library" is easier, you will agree, than defining "courage" or "beauty."

We will not deal with the models under this chapter as essays proper. They are all extracts from larger works and do not, therefore, interest us in terms of organization, style, and literary techniques. Definitions are, by their very nature, brief and utilitarian.

Let us pretend that you have never seen an opossum. How well does a dictionary do its job in showing us this animal through definition only?

Two Dictionary Entries

o·pos'sum (ŏ·pŏs'ŭm), *n.; pl.* -SUMS (-ŭmz). See PLURAL, *Note,* **3.** [Of Algonquian origin.] Any of a family (Didelphidae; esp., *Didelphis virginiana*) of American marsupials, chiefly nocturnal, largely arboreal, and almost omnivorous. When caught it feigns death.

Opossum (ŏpρ·sŭm). **1610.** [Amer. Indian name in Virginia.] **1.** General name of the small marsupial mammals of the American family *Didelphyidæ,* mostly arboreal, some (genus *Chironectes*) aquatic, of nocturnal habits, with an opposable thumb on the hind foot, and tail usu. prehensile; esp. *Didelphys virginiana,* the common opossum of the U.S. (Colloq. shortened to POSSUM, q.v.) **2.** Extended to various small or moderate-sized marsupials ; *esp.* the common name in Australia and Tasmania of those of the sub-family *Phalangistinæ,* more properly called Phalangers **1777.**
attrib. and *Comb.,* as o.·mouse, the Pygmy Flying Phalanger of Australia ; ·shrimp, a shrimp of the genus *Mysis* or family *Mysidæ,* so called from the brood-pouch in which the female carries her eggs.

ANALYSIS

The first entry, from Webster's dictionary, tells us several things. First, we learn the pronunciation, by means of diacritical markings. We need only to turn to the guide in the front of the dictionary to learn that the first vowel is pronounced like the "o" in "obey," the second like the "u" in "tub." The accent is on the sec-

nd syllable. The plural of the word is opossums, but
"*Note 3*" tells us that "especially in the language of
those who hunt and fish" the plural is sometimes "opossum." The bracketed information gives us etymological
history, that is, the origin or derivation of the word.
Here we know only its North American Indian source.
So far we have no verbal picture of the animal.

In two sentences, the opposum is classified. Alas, most
readers will need the dictionary to define the defining
words! We have here a model of conciseness, even of
whimsy,° for if you remove the parenthetical information you will discover the definition has a poetic ring.
But is this definition genuinely helpful? Not until we
inform ourselves that "marsupials" are animals which
carry their young in a pouch, that "arboreal" means in-
habiting trees, that "omnivorous" comes from the Latin
omnis (all) plus *vorare* (to eat greedily) and means this
animal will upset your garbage pail in search of food.
Adequate and accurate though it is, the definition is not
sufficient to *show* us fully what oppposums are like. If
we were not familiar with the common phrase, "playing
possum," we would not learn of it here.

Turning to an historical dictionary, we learn more
facts. Opossum first appeared in writing in 1610, most
likely among Virginian Indians whence it derives. The
colloquial usage has shortened it to possum. Following the suggestion "q. v."—an abbreviation for *quod
vide,* meaning, "which see"—we look up possum and
learn what Webster did not tell us: "to play possum"
means (in the United States) "to feign; to pretend illness." The *Oxford English Dictionary* also informs us
there are Australian opossums which should be called,
properly, phalangers, as they were named in 1777. And
further, there are combined uses of the word in "opos-
sum-mouse" and "opossum-shrimp." Your next door
neighbor might say that these two definitions still do not
sound like the animal he shot in his truck garden. Dictionaries, we remind ourselves, identify and distinguish
in a limited space all parts of speech.

For a fuller definition of this common noun, we turn
to a multi-volumed encyclopedia.

whimsy: See Glossary.

An Encyclopedia Entry

OPOSSUM, *oh PAHS um,* is the name for several kinds of small, primitive American animals related to the kangaroo. They have furry bodies and rather ratlike faces. Like other marsupials, the females have an external pouch in the skin of the abdomen. Here the 5 to 14 young are suckled for about two months after birth. The young are born before they have developed completely, and are smaller than honeybees.

Opossums are the only marsupials native to North America. The species range from Oregon to eastern New York, northward to Ontario, Canada, and southward to Patagonia in South America. In California, where they have been introduced, they are now common. Some opossum species of Central and South America are as small as mice, and sometimes travel north in bunches of bananas.

The best-known opossum is the *Virginia opossum.* When full-grown, it is larger than a cat. People in the South often bake its white flesh. They consider it a rare delicacy. This opossum has coarse, grayish-white hair; a piglike snout; large, naked ears; and a long, hairless, scaly tail by which it can hang from tree branches. Its claws and teeth are sharp. Opossums have 50 teeth, a greater number than any other North American mammal. Its tracks, in mud or dust, can be recognized easily because its toes are long and widely separated. Virginia opossums prowl at night. Hunting them is a favorite sport in the South.

When the young are newborn, they find their own way into the pouch. They come out when they are about two months old, but they still cling to their mother's back. They depend on her for several weeks more.

Opossums eat almost any kind of animal or vegetable food. When they are in danger, they lie motionless and pretend they are dead. From this habit we have taken the expression "playing possum."

Scientific Classification. Opossums make up the family *Didelphidae.* The Virginia opossum is genus *Didelphis,* species *virginiana.*   ROBERT T. HATT

See also ANIMAL (color picture, Central and South America [Water Opossum]); CUSCUS; YAPOK.

ANALYSIS

An encyclopedia is generally not interested in word derivations, although this one does provide pronunciations. By the time we reach the second sentence, we realize the difference between the dictionary's classifying definition and the encyclopedia's descriptive definition. "Furry bodies and a rather ratlike face" helps us to form a picture of what the opossum looks like. The comparison "smaller than honey bees" makes a strong impression. How can so tiny an animal survive in the mother's pouch? And does she move about for several weeks with five or six babies clinging to her back? This definition builds several more unusual images: the opossum hanging by its tail during the day, perhaps to sleep; prowling by night in search of food; playing dead when it knows it is in danger. In other words, the descriptive definition's chief function is not biological or etymological classification but illustrative embellishment.

A third kind of definition we might call comparative, or definition in terms of usage. It is almost always confined to linguistic ° problems.

An Entry in Fowler's MODERN ENGLISH USAGE

jargon is perhaps the most variously applied of a large number of words that are in different senses interchangeable, & under it the distinctions between them may be pointed out. The words are: *cant, dialect, gibberish, idiom, jargon, lingo, parlance, slang, vernacular.*

cant in current English means the insincere or parrotlike appeal to principles, religious, moral, political, or scientific, that the speaker does not believe in or act upon, or does not understand. It is best to restrict it to this definite use; but its earliest sense—special

linguistic: See Glossary.

vocabulary of the disreputable—is still used by philologists & in etymological discussions; & it means sometimes what is now more often expressed by *jargon* or *slang*, the special vocabulary of an art, profession, etc.

dialect is essentially local; *a d.* is the variety of a language that prevails in a district, with local peculiarities of vocabulary, pronunciation, & phrase.

gibberish is the name for unintelligible stuff: applied by exaggeration to a language unknown to the hearer (for which, as a familiar term, *lingo* is better), & to anything either too learnedly worded, or on the other hand too rudely expressed, for him to make out its meaning.

idiom is the method of expression characteristic of or peculiar to the native speakers of a language; i.e., it is racy or unaffected or natural English (or French etc.), especially so far as that happens not to coincide with the method of expression prevalent in other languages; & *an i.* is a particular example of such speech. An earlier sense, the same as that of *dialect,* still occurs sometimes. See also *idiom.*

jargon is talk that is considered both ugly-sounding & hard to understand: applied especially to (1) the sectional vocabulary of a science, art, class, sect, trade, or profession, full of technical terms (cf. *cant, slang*); (2) hybrid speech of different languages; (3) the use of long words, circumlocution, & other clumsiness.

lingo is a contemptuous name for any foreign language. It is sometimes used instead of jargon (1) & (2).

parlance, which means manner of speaking, has the peculiarity of possessing no significance of its own & being never used by itself; you can say That is dialect, That is slang, etc., but not That is parlance; *parlance* is always accompanied by an adjective or defining word or phrase, & that adjective, not *parlance,* gives the point: *in golfing* or *nautical parlance, in the parlance of the literary critics,* etc.

slang is the diction that results from the favourite

game among the young & lively of playing with words & renaming things & actions; some invent new words, or mutilate or misapply the old, for the pleasure of novelty, & others catch up such words for the pleasure of being in the fashion; many slang words & phrases perish, a few establish themselves; in either case, during probation they are accounted unfit for literary use. *S.* is also used in the sense of *jargon* (1), & with two distinctions: in general it expresses less dislike & imputation of ugliness than *jargon;* & it is naturally commoner about sporting vocabularies (*golf s.* etc.) than *jargon,* because many of the terms used in sports are slang in the main sense also.

vernacular describes the words that have been familiar to us as long as we can remember, the homely part of the language, in contrast with the terms that we have consciously acquired. *The vernacular* was formerly common, & is still occasional, for English as opposed to any foreign language; & by an unessential limitation, it is often applied specially to rustic speech & confused with *dialect.*

H. W. Fowler, *A Dictionary of Modern English Usage,* Oxford University Press, Oxford, England, 1926, pp. 307–08. Copyright 1956. Reprinted by permission of the Clarendon Press.

ANALYSIS

Is it legitimate to define one word in terms of another? When fine distinctions are what is sought, yes. Fowler's lexicon, published in England, has been an invaluable aid to writers for several decades. Margaret Nicholson's *Dictionary of American-English Usage* (Oxford Press, New York, 1957) is the American counterpart. Together they answer many questions on when a certain word is appropriate and when it is not. The words they choose to discuss are selective, of course. We cannot expect to find every word that troubles us in their pages.

The excerpt we have chosen may discuss several words new to your own vocabulary, like "parlance," "cant," or "vernacular." Several others—"jargon," "slang," "gibberish," "lingo"—are common to everyday speech. What Fowler is doing here is making distinctions that will help us to place these words in relation to each other and to choose exactly the right one when we are identifying speech we hear or read. Note that he does not give examples. This is a concise dictionary, as is Webster's *New Collegiate Dictionary.* Should he once begin illustration, there would be no end. He is trying, like Webster, to supply helpful explanations without wasting words. You will find it a challenge to apply illustrations of your own to these terms.

A fourth kind of definition is analytical or investigative. It searches *around* a subject. It offers tentative suggestions. It sometimes begins by eliminating what the word is not. It finds illustration helpful; and it often defines in terms of usage, or in terms of the author's particular viewpoint. The two following definitions—of jazz and of history—do not belong in a dictionary. They are explanations of what two words mean to these particular writers.

JOHN A. KOUWENHOVEN · *What Is Jazz?*

1   Let me begin by making clear that I am using the term jazz in its broadest significant application. There are circumstances in which it is important to define the term with considerable precision, as when you are involved in discussion with a disciple of one of the many cults, orthodox or progressive, which devote themselves to some particular subspecies of jazz. But in our present context we need to focus upon what all the subspecies (Dixieland, Be-bop, Swing, or Cool Jazz) have in common; in other words, we must neglect the by no means

"What is Jazz?" by John Kouwenhoven from "What's American about America?" From *Harper's Magazine,* July, 1956. Copyright 1956 by *Harper's Magazine.* Reprinted by permission of the author.

uninteresting qualities which differentiate one from another, since it is what they have in common which can tell us most about the civilization which produced them.

² There is no definition of jazz, academic or otherwise, which does not acknowledge that its essential ingredient is a particular kind of rhythm. Improvisation * is also frequently mentioned as an essential; but even if it were true that jazz always involves improvisation, that would not distinguish it from a good deal of Western European music of the past. It is the distinctive rhythm which differentiates all types of jazz from all other music and which gives to all of its types a basic family resemblance.

³ It is not easy to define that distinctive rhythm. Winthrop Sargeant has described it as the product of two superimposed devices: syncopation and polyrhythm, both of which have the effect of constantly upsetting rhythmical expectations. André Hodeir, in his recent analysis, *Jazz: Its Evolution and Essence,* speaks of "an unending alternation" of syncopations and of notes played *on* the beat, which "gives rise to a kind of expectation that is one of jazz's subtlest effects."

⁴ As you can readily hear, if you listen to any jazz performance (whether of the Louis Armstrong, Benny Goodman, or Charlie Parker variety), the rhythmical effect depends upon there being a clearly defined basic rhythmic pattern which enforces the expectations which are to be upset. That basic pattern is the $\frac{4}{4}$ or $\frac{2}{4}$ beat which underlies all jazz. Hence the importance of the percussive instruments in jazz: the drums, the guitar or banjo, the bull fiddle, the piano. Hence too the insistent thump, thump, thump, thump which is so boring when you only half-hear jazz—either because you are too far away, across the lake or in the next room, or simply because you will not listen attentively. But hence also the delight, the subtle effects, which good jazz provides as the melodic phrases evade, anticipate, and return to, and then again evade the steady basic four-beat pulse which persists, implicitly * or explicitly,* throughout the performance.

5 In other words, the structure of a jazz performance is, like that of the New York skyline, a tension of cross-purposes. In jazz at its characteristic best, each player seems to be—and has the sense of being—on his own. Each goes his own way, inventing rhythmic and melodic patterns which, superficially, seem to have as little relevance to one another as the United Nations building does to the Empire State. And yet the outcome is a dazzlingly precise creative unity.

6 In jazz that unity of effect is, of course, the result of the very thing which each of the players is flouting: namely, the basic 4/4 beat—that simple rhythmic gridiron of identical and infinitely extendible units which holds the performance together. As Louis Armstrong once wrote, you would expect that if every man in a band "had his own way and could play as he wanted, all you would get would be a lot of jumbled up, crazy noise." But, as he goes on to say, that does not happen, because the players know "by ear and sheer musical instinct" just when to leave the underlying pattern and when to get back on it.

CARL BECKER · *What Is History?*

1 Once upon a time, long, long ago, I learned how to reduce a fraction to its lowest terms. Whether I could still perform that operation is uncertain; but the discipline involved in early training had its uses, since it taught me that in order to understand the essential nature of anything it is well to strip it of all superficial and irrelevant * accretions *—in short, to reduce it to its lowest terms. That operation I now venture, with some ap-

"What Is History?" from "Everyman His Own Historian" by Carl Becker. Reprinted from *The American Historical Review*, January 1932. Copyright 1932 by The American Historical Review. Reprinted by permission of the publisher.

prehension and all due apologies, to perform on the subject of history.

2 I ought first of all to explain that when I use the term history I mean knowledge of history. No doubt throughout all past time there actually occurred a series of events which, whether we know what it was or not, constitutes history in some ultimate sense. Nevertheless, much the greater part of these events we can know nothing about, not even that they occurred; many of them we can know only imperfectly; and even the few events that we think we know for sure we can never be absolutely certain of, since we can never revive them, never observe or test them directly. The event itself once occured, but as an actual event it has disappeared; so that in dealing with it the only objective reality we can observe or test is some material trace which the event has left—usually a written document. With these traces of vanished events, these documents, we must be content since they are all we have; from them we infer what the event was, we affirm that it is a fact that the event was so and so. We do not say "Lincoln is assassinated"; we say "it is a fact that Lincoln was assassinated." The event *was,* but is no longer; it is only the affirmed fact about the event that *is,* that persists, and will persist until we discover that our affirmation is wrong or inadequate. Let us then admit that there are two histories: the actual series of events that once occurred; and the ideal series that we affirm and hold in memory. The first is absolute and unchanged—it was what it was whatever we do or say about it; the second is relative, always changing in response to the increase or refinement of knowledge. The two series correspond more or less; it is our aim to make the correspondence as exact as possible; but the actual series of events exists for us only in terms of the ideal series which we affirm and hold in memory. This is why I am forced to identify history with knowledge of history. For all practical purposes history is, for us and for the time being, what we know it to be.

3 It is history in this sense that I wish to reduce to its

lowest terms. In order to do that I need a very simple
definition. I once read that "History is the knowledge
of events that have occurred in the past." That is a simple definition, but not simple enough. It contains three
words that require examination. The first is knowledge.
Knowledge is a formidable word. I always think of
knowledge as something that is stored up in the *Encyclopædia Britannica* or the *Summa Theologica;* ° something difficult to acquire, something at all events that I
have not. Resenting a definition that denies me the title
of historian, I therefore ask what is most essential to
knowledge. Well, memory, I should think (and I mean
memory in the broad sense, the memory of events in-
ferred as well as the memory of events observed) ; other
things are necessary too, but memory is fundamental:
without memory no knowledge. So our definition becomes, "History is the memory of events that have occurred in the past." But events—the word carries an implication of something grand, like the taking of the
Bastille or the Spanish-American War. An occurrence
need not be spectacular to be an event. If I drive a
motor car down the crooked streets of Ithaca, that is an
event—something done; if the traffic cop bawls me out,
that is an event—something said; if I have evil thoughts
of him for so doing, that is an event—something
thought. In truth anything done, said, or thought is an
event, important or not as may turn out. But since we
do not ordinarily speak without thinking, at least in
some rudimentary way, and since the psychologists tell
us that we cannot think without speaking, or at least not
without having anticipatory vibrations in the larynx,
we may well combine thought events and speech events
under one term; and so our definition becomes, "History
is the memory of things said and done in the past." But
the past—the word is both misleading and unnecessary:

Summa Theologica: a work of Thomas Aquinas, the greatest sys-
tematizer of Catholic thought. It was written in 1266–73 in Italy
with the intention of exploring in question-and-answer form the
fundamental doctrines of Christian theology.

misleading, because the past, used in connection with history, seems to imply the distant past, as if history ceased before we were born; unnecessary, because after all everything said or done is already in the past as soon as it is said or done. Therefore I will omit that word, and our definition becomes, "History is the memory of things said or done." This is a definition that reduces history to its lowest terms, and yet includes everything that is essential to understanding what it really is.

ANALYSIS

John Kouwenhoven begins his definition by emphasizing an essential ingredient in any explanation of what is jazz—"a particular kind of rhythm." He is, however, quick to say that that rhythm is not easy to define. Does it help to tell us that "two superimposed devices: syncopation and polyrhythm" make jazz? This definition, like "an omnivorous, nocturnal marsupial" drives us farther into the dictionary. So Kouwenhoven says the basic rhythm pattern is $\frac{4}{4}$ or $\frac{2}{4}$. But must we not know musical annotation to understand that he means "four beats to the measure" or "two beats to the measure"? He helps by saying that the percussive or rhythm instruments—the "thump, thump, thump, thump"—accentuate this basic rhythm and we infer that jazz is a melodic phrase of infinite variation built on a continuous, unchanging rhythm pattern. Have we come any closer to a useful, simple definition? Can you take the analysis farther, improve these distinctions?

Carl Becker begins his difficult task "with some apprehension and all due apologies." He is attempting to define a word that has many uses. He limits it at once to mean knowledge of the past and not merely *all* that has happened in the past. He explains that past events are what we know them to be, the "ideal series" of events built up from records, usually written, of actual events that once occurred. But the word "knowledge" gives him trouble. After further consideration, he changes it to "memory" of the past. And then he is unhappy with "past." He substitutes "things said or done." Only now does he have "a definition that reduces history to its lowest terms." And it is admittedly a tentative definition which one scholar, Carl Becker, is satisfied with. Where would you begin, in your definition of history, to differ with Becker? What are the many specialized meanings of history? What is non-history?

Add to your vocabulary: improvisation, implicitly, explicitly, irrelevant, accretions.

Suggestions for Writing

1. Without referring to a dictionary, write a definition of three of these words, giving their basic meaning, and their common present-day usage: drama, supermarket, church, comic strip, highbrow, egghead, skindiving, wrestling, watercolor, barbecue.

2. Write an essay on the problem of distinguishing between the words in one of the following groups:
    a. attraction, infatuation, love.
    b. advertisement, commercial, propaganda.
    c. insult, slander, libel.
    d. compromise, appeasement, capitulation.

3. Fowler defined "jargon" in terms of "slang," "dialect," "lingo," and other words. He does not mention "colloquialisms," "journalese," or "gobbledygook" (also called "officialese") . Define and explain how they are related to jargon.

4. Attempt in an essay of 300 words a more complex, analytical definition of one of these words: democracy, conservatism, geography, censorship, comedy, literature, emotion, knowledge, faith, economics.

5. Develop one of these topics by definition:
    a. The best use of leisure.
    b. The need for going to college.
    c. The pleasures of reading.
    d. The joy of listening to music.
    e. The habit of watching television.
    f. The hypnosis of watching a film.

CHAPTER 4

Elementary exposition: process

A second, more complex method of definition we might call explanation of a process. Other words for it that come to mind are "structure" and "mechanism." These essays tell us in more detail, while at the same time defining, what is involved in a series of interrelated activities. We could seek, for example, a definition of "osmosis" or "chlorophyll," but would what we found answer the larger question of how plants grow? More than likely not. The concise definition of a single term is not sufficient. We need to combine several technical terms. We need to illustrate by example or precedent or even by anecdote. We need to expand the subject of plant growth to include problems of soil, fertilization, light, and seasonal change. The botanist would explain the subject in one way, the nurseryman another. The three essays in this group happen to be written by scientists. We are *not* suggesting that "process," "structure," or "mechanism" are only scientific terms. This kind of extended definition could as easily apply to oil painting, cooking, theories of language development, furniture manufacture, or dog training.

THOMAS HENRY HUXLEY · *The Method of Scientific Investigation*

In 1855, Professor Huxley began in England a series of lectures which he delivered to workingmen to see what he could do to educate "those hard-handed fellows who live among facts." His success was instantaneous. Many people posed as workingmen in order to hear him explain in simple language what scientific research and experiment were about. Huxley was a medical doctor, as well as a marine biologist and a scientific investigator without rival. To his students at St. Thomas' Hospital, London, he talked in technical terms. For the public at large he devoted careful energy to "translating" scientific principles into everyday examples and illustrations.

The passage which follows is an excerpt from Huxley's lectures in 1862 on Charles Darwin's theory of evolution. One listener was so impressed with Huxley's clarity of mind that he took shorthand notes and published them with the lecturer's permission. Darwin read them and is reported to have been immensely pleased. He saw that Huxley was able to lead his listener to words like "induction," "deduction," and "hypothesis" ° and persuade him that they are not frightening terms but rather apparatus he uses everyday in his thinking. What is more, Huxley never debased science in order to popularize it. He respected its complexity, but he argued that the principles behind scientific investigation can be understood by the layman with "a sort of special apprenticeship to the craft."

We can call this kind of writing extended definition or explanation of a process. How does it differ from the definition of opossum or jargon? First, in length, obviously. Second, in method. And finally, in language. As you read Huxley, keep in mind that he is talking to

induction, deduction, hypothesis: See Glossary.

skeptical as well as uneducated workingmen. He must persuade as well as define. He is building one definition on top of another. He extracts his examples from daily life, from the "things" we all know; but his ultimate aim is the definition not of a "thing" (such as an opossum) but of a reasoning process. All these aspects of his brief essay contribute to the "extension" of his definition.

¹ The method of scientific investigation is nothing but the expression of the necessary mode ° of working of the human mind. It is simply the mode at which all phenomena are reasoned about, rendered precise and exact. There is no more difference, but there is just the same kind of difference, between the mental operations of a man of science and those of an ordinary person, as there is between the operations and methods of a baker or of a butcher weighing out his goods in common scales, and the operations of a chemist in performing a difficult and complex analysis by means of his balance and finely graduated weights. It is not that the action of the scales in the one case, and the balance in the other, differ in the principles of their construction or manner of working; but the beam ° of one is set on an infinitely finer axis than the other, and of course turns by the addition of a much smaller weight.

² You will understand this better, perhaps, if I give you some familiar example. You have all heard it repeated, I dare say, that men of science work by means of induction and deduction, and that by the help of these operations, they, in a sort of sense, wring from Nature certain other things, which are called natural laws, and causes, and that out of these, by some cunning skill of their own, they build up hypotheses and theories. And it is imagined by many, that the operations of the common mind can be by no means compared with these processes, and that they have to be acquired by a sort of special apprenticeship to the craft. To hear all these large

mode: meaning "method," as used here.
beam: the bar of a balance from which the scales hang.

words, you would think that the mind of a man of science must be constituted differently from that of his fellow men; but if you will not be frightened by terms, you will discover that you are quite wrong, and that all these terrible apparatus ° are being used by yourselves every day and every hour of your lives.

3   There is a well-known incident in one of Molière's plays,° where the author makes the hero express unbounded delight on being told that he had been talking prose during the whole of his life. In the same way, I trust that you will take comfort, and be delighted with yourselves, on the discovery that you have been acting on the principles of inductive and deductive philosophy during the same period. Probably there is not one here who has not in the course of the day had occasion to set in motion a complex train of reasoning, of the very same kind, though differing of course in degree, as that which a scientific man goes through in tracing the causes of natural phenomena.

4   A very trivial circumstance will serve to exemplify this. Suppose you go into a fruiterer's shop, wanting an apple—you take up one, and on biting it, you find it is sour; you look at it, and see that it is hard and green. You take up another one and that too is hard, green, and sour. The shopman offers you a third; but, before biting it, you examine it, and find that it is hard and green, and you immediately say that you will not have it, as it must be sour, like those that you have already tried.

5   Nothing can be more simple than that, you think; but if you will take the trouble to analyse and trace out into its logical elements what has been done by the mind, you will be greatly surprised. In the first place you have performed the operation of induction. You found that, in two experiences, hardness and greenness

apparatus: Both "apparatus" and "apparatuses" are acceptable
    plurals.
one of Molière's plays: *Le Bourgeois Gentilhomme* (1670) , Act II,
    Scene 6. The hero is M. Jourdain. a rich tradesman.

in apples went together with sourness. It was so in the first case, and it was confirmed by the second. True, it is a very small basis, but still it is enough to make an induction from; you generalize the facts, and you expect to find sourness in apples where you get hardness and greenness. You found upon that a general law that all hard and green apples are sour; and that, so far as it goes, is a perfect induction. Well, having got your natural law in this way, when you are offered another apple which you find is hard and green, you say, "All hard and green apples are sour; this apple is hard and green, therefore this apple is sour." That train of reasoning is what logicians call a syllogism,° and has all its various parts and terms—its major premiss,° its minor premiss, and its conclusion. And, by the help of further reasoning, which, if drawn out, would have to be exhibited in two or three other syllogisms, you arrive at your final determination, "I will not have that apple." So that, you see, you have, in the first place, established a law by induction, and upon that you have founded a deduction, and reasoned out the special particular case. Well now, suppose, having got your conclusion of the law, that at some time afterwards, you are discussing the qualities of apples with a friend: you will say to him, "It is a very curious thing, but I find that all hard and green apples are sour!" Your friend says to you, "But how do you know that?" You at once reply, "Oh, because I have tried them over and over again, and have always found them to be so." Well, if we were talking science instead of common sense, we should call that an experimental verification. And, if still opposed, you go further, and say, "I have heard from the people in Somersetshire and Devonshire,° where a large number of apples are grown, that they have observed the same thing. It is also found to be the case in Normandy,° and in North America. In short, I find it to be the universal experience of man-

---

syllogism: See Glossary.   premiss: also spelled "premise."
Somersetshire and Devonshire: counties in southwest England.
Normandy: a region in northern France.

kind wherever attention has been directed to the subject." Whereupon, your friend, unless he is a very unreasonable man, agrees with you, and is convinced that you are quite right in the conclusion you have drawn. He believes, although perhaps he does not know he believes it, that the more extensive verifications are—that the more frequently experiments have been made, and results of the same kind arrived at—that the more varied the conditions under which the same results are attained, the more certain is the ultimate conclusion, and he disputes the question no further. He sees that the experiment has been tried under all sorts of conditions, as to time, place, and people, with the same result; and he says with you, therefore, that the law you have laid down must be a good one, and he must believe it.

6 In science we do the same thing—the philosopher exercises precisely the same faculties, though in a much more delicate manner. In scientific inquiry it becomes a matter of duty to expose a supposed law to every possible kind of verification, and to take care, moreover, that this is done intentionally, and not left to a mere accident, as in the case of the apples. And in science, as in common life, our confidence in a law is in exact proportion to the absence of variation in the result of our experimental verifications. For instance, if you let go your grasp of an article you may have in your hand, it will immediately fall to the ground. That is a very common verification of one of the best established laws of nature—that of gravitation. The method by which men of science establish the existence of that law is exactly the same as that by which we have established the trivial proposition about the sourness of hard and green apples. But we believe it in such an extensive, thorough, and unhesitating manner because the universal experience of mankind verifies it, and we can verify it ourselves at any time; and that is the strongest possible foundation on which any natural law can rest.

7 So much, then, by way of proof that the method of establishing laws in science is exactly the same as that

pursued in common life. Let us now turn to another matter (though really it is but another phase of the same question), and that is, the method by which, from the relations of certain phenomena, we prove that some stand in the position of causes toward the others.

⁸ I want to put the case clearly before you, and I will therefore show you what I mean by another familiar example. I will suppose that one of you, on coming down in the morning to the parlor of your house, finds that a teapot and some spoons which had been left in the room on the previous evening are gone—the window is open, and you observe the mark of a dirty hand on the window-frame, and perhaps, in addition to that, you notice the impress of a hobnailed shoe on the gravel outside. All these phenomena have struck your attention instantly, and before two seconds have passed you say, "Oh, somebody has broken open the window, entered the room, and run off with the spoons and the teapot!" That speech is out of your mouth in a moment. And you will probably add, "I know there has; I am quite sure of it!" You mean to say exactly what you know; but in reality you are giving expression to what is, in all essential particulars, an hypothesis. You do not *know* it at all; it is nothing but an hypothesis rapidly framed in your own mind. And it is an hypothesis founded on a long train of inductions and deductions.

⁹ What are those inductions and deductions, and how have you got at this hypothesis? You have observed in the first place, that the window is open; but by a train of reasoning involving many inductions and deductions, you have probably arrived long before at the general law—and a very good one it is—that windows do not open of themselves; and you therefore conclude that something has opened the window. A second general law that you have arrived at in the same way is, that teapots and spoons do not go out of a window spontaneously, and you are satisfied that, as they are not now where you left them, they have been removed. In the third place, you look at the marks on the window-sill, and the shoe-

marks outside, and you say that in all previous experience the former kind of mark has never been produced by anything else but the hand of a human being; and the same experience shows that no other animal but man at present wears shoes with hobnails in them such as would produce the marks in the gravel. I do not know, even if we could discover any of those "missing links" ° that are talked about, that they would help us to any other conclusion! At any rate the law which states our present experience is strong enough for my present purpose. You next reach the conclusion that, as these kinds of marks have not been left by any other animal than man, or are liable to be formed in any other way than by a man's hand and shoe, the marks in question have been formed by a man in that way. You have, further, a general law, founded on observation and experience, and that, too, is I am sorry to say, a very universal and unimpeachable * one—that some men are thieves; and you assume at once from all these premises—and that is what constitutes your hypothesis—that the man who made the marks outside and on the window-sill, opened the window, got into the room, and stole your teapot and spoons. You have now arrived at a *vera causa*—you have assumed a cause which, it is plain, is competent to produce all the phenomena you have observed. You can explain all these phenomena only by the hypothesis of a thief. But that is a hypothetical conclusion, of the justice of which you have no absolute proof at all; it is only rendered highly probable by a series of inductive and deductive reasonings.

¹⁰ I suppose your first action, assuming that you are a man of ordinary common sense, and that you have established this hypothesis to your own satisfaction, will very likely be to go off for the police, and set them on the track of the burglar, with the view to the recovery of

"missing links": In the study of man's evolution from lower types of animals, a "missing-link" in the evolutionary chain was hypothesized; that is, a form of animal between the anthropoid ape and man was believed to have existed.

your property. But just as you are starting with this object, some person comes in, and on learning what you are about, says, "My good friend, you are going on a great deal too fast. How do you know that the man who really made the marks took the spoons? It might have been a monkey that took them, and the man may have merely looked in afterwards." You would probably reply, "Well, that is all very well, but you see it is contrary to all experience of the way teapots and spoons are abstracted; so that, at any rate, your hypothesis is less probable than mine." While you are talking the thing over in this way, another friend arrives, one of the good kind of people that I was talking of a little while ago. And he might say, "Oh, my dear sir, you are certainly going on a great deal too fast. You are most presumptuous.* You admit that all these occurrences took place when you were fast asleep, at a time when you could not possibly have known anything about what was taking place. How do you know that the laws of Nature are not suspended during the night? It may be that there has been some kind of supernatural interference in this case." In point of fact, he declares that your hypothesis is one of which you cannot at all demonstrate the truth, and that you are by no means sure that the laws of Nature are the same when you are asleep as when you are awake.

¹¹ Well, now, you cannot at the moment answer that kind of reasoning. You feel that your worthy friend has you somewhat at a disadvantage. You will feel perfectly convinced in your own mind, however, that you are quite right, and you say to him, "My good friend, I can only be guided by the natural probabilities of the case, and if you will be kind enough to stand aside and permit me to pass, I will go and fetch the police." Well, we will suppose that your journey is successful, and that by good luck you meet with a policeman; that eventually the burglar is found with your property on his person, and the marks correspond to his hand and to his boots. Probably any jury would consider those facts a very good

experimental verification of your hypothesis, touching the cause of the abnormal phenomena observed in your parlor, and would act accordingly.

12   Now, in this supposititious * case, I have taken phenomena of a very common kind, in order that you might see what are the different steps in an ordinary process of reasoning, if you will only take the trouble to analyse it carefully. All the operations I have described, you will see, are involved in the mind of any man of sense in leading him to a conclusion as to the course he should take in order to make good a robbery and punish the offender. I say that you are led, in that case, to your conclusion by exactly the same train of reasoning as that which a man of science pursues when he is endeavoring to discover the origin and laws of the most occult phenomena.° The process is, and always must be, the same; and precisely the same mode of reasoning was employed by Newton ° and Laplace ° in their endeavors to discover and define the causes of the movements of the heavenly bodies, as you, with your own common sense, would employ to detect a burglar. The only difference is, that the nature of the inquiry being more abstruse,* every step has to be most carefully watched, so that there may not be a single crack or flaw in your hypothesis. A flaw or crack in many of the hypotheses of daily life may be of little or no moment as affecting the general correctness of the conclusions at which we may arrive; but, in a scientific inquiry, a fallacy, great or small, is always of importance, and is sure to be in the long run constantly productive of mischievous if not fatal results.

13   Do not allow yourselves to be misled by the common notion that an hypothesis is untrustworthy simply be-

occult phenomena: as Huxley uses it here, phenomena not apparent on mere inspection but discoverable by experimentation.

Newton: Sir Isaac (1642–1727), British scientist, mathematician, and philosopher, who formulated and proved the law of gravity.

Laplace: Pierre Simon, Marquis de (1749–1827), French astronomer and mathematician, famous for his theory, called the "nebular hypothesis," of the formulation of the planetary systems.

cause it is an hypothesis. It is often urged, in respect to some scientific conclusion, that, after all, it is only an hypothesis. But what more have we to guide us in nine-tenths of the most important affairs of daily life than hypotheses, and often very ill-based ones? So that in science, where the evidence of an hypothesis is subjected to the most rigid examination, we may rightly pursue the same course. You may have hypotheses, and hypotheses. A man may say, if he likes, that the moon is made of green cheese: that is an hypothesis. But another man, who has devoted a great deal of time and attention to the subject, and availed himself of the most powerful telescopes and the results of the observations of others, declares that in his opinion it is probably composed of materials very similar to those of which our own earth is made up: and that is also only an hypothesis. But I need not tell you that there is an enormous difference in the value of the two hypotheses. That one which is based on sound scientific knowledge is sure to have a corresponding value; and that which is a mere hasty random guess is likely to have but little value. Every great step in our progress in discovering causes has been made in exactly the same way as that which I have detailed to you. A person observing the occurrence of certain facts and phenomena asks, naturally enough, what process, what kind of operation known to occur in Nature, applied to the particular case, will unravel and explain the mystery? Hence you have the scientific hypothesis; and its value will be proportionate to the care and completeness with which its basis had been tested and verified. It is in these matters as in the commonest affairs of practical life; the guess of the fool will be folly, while the guess of the wise man will contain wisdom. In all cases, you see that the value of the result depends on the patience and faithfulness with which the investigator applies to his hypothesis every possible kind of verification.

ANALYSIS

Huxley's paragraphs are closely knit exposition. Even though we are reading here only an excerpt from one lecture, we will profit from watching how carefully Huxley takes his listener by the hand, as it were, and guides him into understanding four terms: induction, deduction, natural law, and hypothesis. Taken together, they explain the method of scientific investigation.

Paragraphs 1–3 serve as introduction. The scientist's mind, Huxley tells us, is no different from his fellow man's in *kind*. His methods of investigation differ only in *degree*. Or to put it another way, the butcher and the chemist share the same kind of mental operations, but their scales differ in minuteness of measure. What are these kinds of mental operations? Paragraphs 4–5 show us by simple examples how we reason inductively and deductively. Paragraph 6 introduces the idea of experimental verification and how, after enough evidence has been gathered, we establish a natural law. Paragraph 7 leads us to the fourth and most difficult term, hypothesis: "the method by which, from the relations of certain phenomena, we prove that some [laws] stand in the position of causes toward the others." Paragraphs 8–11 explain, by means of a complex but still homely example, the way in which induction, deduction, and natural laws are connected to a hypothesis. Paragraphs 12–13 discuss, in a general way, why science cannot do without hypotheses any more than we, in our daily lives, can do without them in reaching conclusions. In case we miss his original point (that science differs only in *degree*), Huxley repeats himself: The value of a scientific hypothesis "will be proportionate to the care and completeness with which its basis [has] been tested and verified."

This essay, we can agree, goes beyond the province of a dictionary or an encyclopedia in defining a process. We said earlier that it differs from a definition of opossum in length, method, and language. The length here is an obvious necessity. Hypothesis is best defined in terms of induction and deduction. Huxley proceeds by carefully arranged steps. The method is logical and illustrative. When one step is clear, he moves on to the more complicated idea, and each idea is *seen* in terms of a visual example. The language is concise (as we expect a definition to be) but it is also informal. Huxley talks to his listeners in the second person: "You will understand this better, perhaps, if I give you some familiar example," or "Well, now, you cannot at the moment answer that kind of reasoning." He imagines conversations we would hold with friends. He raises questions for us to answer. He chides us not to be misled. In a word, he *shows* us how we think, what those thought processes are called, and how they are related to the scientific method. Huxley's prose is a model of extended definition.

Questions on Content

1. What is a syllogism as Huxley defines it? How is it connected with inductive reasoning?
2. In a short paragraph, explain Huxley's example of deductive reasoning.
3. Why is experimental verification necessary to the establishing of a natural law?
4. Why is a "flaw or crack" in a scientific hypothesis of much greater consequence than in many of the hypotheses of daily life?

Add to your vocabulary: unimpeachable, presumptuous, supposititious, abstruse.

Questions on Technique

1. Huxley's sense of organization is most admirable here. In what way is the whole essay an extension and elaboration of his opening paragraph?
2. What other examples might he have used to demonstrate inductive reasoning? Would additional examples have improved the essay?
3. If Huxley were not talking to an audience but writing for a popular weekly on this subject, what changes in his technique might he make? in his examples?

Suggestions for Writing

1. Select three or four illustrations of inductive reasoning from your own experience and in a paragraph on each tell how they led you to forming syllogisms. For

example, you took violin lessons for one year with little success; you tried the trumpet for another year with even less success; your father now suggests he purchase a piano. You reason this way: I cannot learn to play a musical instrument. The piano is a musical instrument. Therefore, I cannot learn to play the piano. What would your father say to this kind of reasoning? Would he suggest more "experimental verification"?

2. In paragraph 11, Huxley mentions the "natural probabilities" of a case, that is, what we cannot demonstrate as the truth but what we want to persuade ourselves to accept as the truth. Write an essay of 350 words in which you discuss an experience where you wanted to accept the "natural probability" although you knew you could not prove it.

3. Write a brief account of an experiment you have performed in a science laboratory in which you were seeking proof inductively.

4. Huxley is loath to believe the moon is made of green cheese. With a small amount of research, write an essay explaining what we do know about the surface of the moon.

E. G. F. SAUER · *Celestial Navigation by Birds*

Thomas Huxley would have been enchanted by the essay that follows. It is at once a definition, a report on experimental verification, and a hypothesis reached by inductive reasoning.° For many years Professor Sauer has been interested in birds and their behavior patterns. As a student and teacher in Germany, he has made systematic study of their migratory habits. In 1957–1958, he spent a year in South-West Africa studying European migratory birds within their winter quarters. Some of his

hypothesis . . . inductive reasoning: See Glossary.

"Celestial Navigation by Birds" by E. G. F. Sauer from *Scientific American,* August 1958, © 1958 by Scientific American, Inc. Reprinted by permission of the publisher.

observations are the basis for this brief account of one problem which has long fascinated him: how European warblers find their way from northern Europe to Africa and back again.

It is unlikely that Sauer is writing for the "hard-handed workingman," as was Huxley, but it is worth noting that in spite of the authority of his words his prose is simple, direct, and nontechnical. The average layman can share his enthusiasm and his knowledge. As definition, the essay makes quite clear what celestial navigation entails. As a report on experimental verification, it lists three distinct sets of controls Sauer and his wife used to gather data. As a demonstration of a hypothesis, it sets out to show why Sauer's theory that the warbler flies by the stars is very likely true. As with all good scientists, Sauer is not insisting that we accept his point of view. There is less persuasion in his voice than in Huxley's; there is somewhat more formality in his sentences. But of what exposition needs above all—accuracy and clarity—there is plenty.

[1] In spring and summer the songbirds known as the warblers are familiar residents in the countries throughout Europe. City dwellers know them well, for the small, gray birds find a home to their liking in the shrubs and hedges of gardens and small parks. During the spring breeding season the air is filled with their loud, melodic singing as each male establishes a small territory for himself in noisy battle with a rival. Once the claims are decided, the truculence * and the songs subside; the birds proceed to mate and to raise their young. In late summer they feed amicably on elderberries and blackberries and they flit about in peace among the bushes. Then in August the birds begin to grow restless; their migratory instinct stirs. Suddenly, in one night, the whole resident population of one species is off and away. The next morning the bushes are filled with a new lot of warblers that have flown in from more northern areas; they stay for a few days and then they too fly on to the south. Through the weeks of September and October there is a

continuous coming and going of hordes of the migrating warblers. Gradually the number passing through diminishes. The species called the garden warblers disappears first, then the whitethroats, after them the lesser whitethroats, and finally the blackcaps.

2 Where do they go? Ornithologists ° know exactly where the warblers go, for they have banded these birds for many years and followed them to their winter homes. With the exception of some blackcaps, these warblers travel to various parts of Africa. Some of them migrate as far as from Scandinavia to the southern part of Africa—a distance of seven thousand miles and more. In the spring the birds migrate back to the same place that they left in the fall.

3 Most remarkable of all is that each bird finds its own way to its destination! The warblers do not follow a leader or make the journey as a group; they navigate individually. And young birds making their first migration reach their goal as surely as the experienced travelers. Somehow, purely by instinct, the warblers know exactly how to set their course.

4 The navigation powers of birds have fascinated investigators for more than a century. By now there is a large literature of well-documented testimony to their amazing performances. The late Werner Rüppell of Germany, one of the leading experimenters on bird migration, found that starlings taken from their nests near Berlin and carried away to all points of the compass would find their way back to their nesting places from as far as 1,250 miles away. The Manx ° Shearwater, a sea bird, has astonished investigators with still more spectacular feats; one shearwater, taken from the west coast of England by G. V. T. Matthews and flown by plane to Boston, was back in its English nest in 12 days, having winged its own way 3,067 miles across the unknown Atlantic. The North American golden plover migrates each fall from its breeding grounds along the

ornithologists: zoologists who deal with birds.
Manx: of the Isle of Man, in the Irish sea off northwest England.

west coast of Alaska to its winter home in the Hawaiian Islands. This bird, lacking webbed feet, cannot rest on the water as waterfowl do; it must fly on steadily for several weeks to reach its destination over thousands of miles of ocean. If it wandered only slightly off course, it would become lost and exhausted in the vast Pacific, but it finds its way unerringly to Hawaii.

⁵ Until recently attempts to explain the incredible navigation feats of birds were almost entirely a matter of speculation [see "The Navigation of Birds," by Donald R. Griffin, *Scientific American,* December, 1948]. Various theorists proposed that the birds were guided by the earth's magnetic field, by the Coriolis force ° arising from the earth's rotation, by landmarks, and so on. But more and more ornithologists have been driven to the conclusion that birds must rely mainly on celestial * navigation—the sun by day, the constellations by night.

⁶ The idea that birds are guided by the sun was suggested as long as half a century ago, but it was not taken seriously until the early 1950's, when experimenters began to turn up some interesting evidence. Gustav Kramer in Germany and G. V. T. Matthews in England discovered independently that homing pigeons and wild birds can use the sun as a compass and that they possess a "time sense" which allows them to take account of the sun's motion across the sky. Other zoologists have confirmed these findings. It has now been proved, in fact, that our warblers can orient * themselves by the sun.

⁷ But the warblers fly mainly at night. What sort of system do they use to steer their course in their nocturnal * migrations nearly halfway around the globe? Several years ago the author and his wife started a system-

Coriolis force: named for the French engineer and mathematician, G. C. Coriolis, in 1835. "Because of the earth's rotation, an object moving horizontally relative to the earth's surface appears to be acted on by a force tending to deflect it to the right in the northern hemisphere, to the left in the southern hemisphere. The apparent, or inertia, force is known as the Coriolis force or as the deflecting or deviating force of the earth's rotation." [*Encyclopædia Britannica,* 1958, Vol XV, p. 851.]

atic laboratory study of this question by means of specially designed cages in our aviary ° at Freiburg.

8 We had already seen laboratory proof of the stirring
of the migratory instinct in these small world-travelers
and of a seasonal time sense that governed this urge. We
had hatched and raised warblers in completely closed,
soundproof chambers where they lived in the illusion
of eternal summer, year in and year out. Yet, although
they seemed to have no outward cues of the yearly
rhythm of nature, in the autumn the birds would begin
to flit restlessly from branch to branch or flutter continually over their perches, night after wakeful night.
They kept this up for many weeks—about the length
of time it would have taken them to fly to Africa. Then
they went back to sleeping again at night. In the spring,
about the time that warblers migrate back from Africa
to their European homes, our birds again had a spell of
restless, wakeful nights. It was as if they had an inner
clock which told them when the time had come to take
wing for distant parts.

9 To explore the orientation question we now placed
warblers in a cage with a glass opening at the top, so
that they could see part of the sky (but nothing else of
their surroundings). At the season of migration the
birds would begin to flutter and, peculiarly enough,
each would take up a position pointing in a particular
geographic direction, like the needle of a compass. Even
when we tried to turn the birds away by rotating their
ring-shaped perch, they stubbornly turned back to the
preferred direction. The direction in each case was characteristic of the species: the garden warblers, the whitethroats, and the blackcaps all pointed toward the southwest, the lesser whitethroats toward the southeast (that
is, in the fall; in the spring these directions were reversed). Now these are precisely the directions in which
the respective species start their migrations from central
Europe to Africa! The lesser whitethroats start southeastward, flying across the Balkans, and then turn south

aviary: a house or enclosure in which birds are kept.

up the Nile Valley; the other species all take off south-westward and fly to Africa by way of Spain and Gibraltar.

[10] Experienced or inexperienced, the birds invariably took up the appropriate direction of flight in the cage. How did they know the direction? Seemingly the only clue available to them was the starry night sky overhead. To explore this theory further we now put them through a series of tests. We found that when the stars were hidden by thick clouds, the birds became completely disoriented. They were likewise confused when only diffuse * and strongly polarized light came through their skylight. To adopt and keep to a definite direction they needed a look at the starry sky. Indeed, the birds watched the sky so intently that shooting stars made them change their direction for a short time.

[11] For still more rigidly controlled experiments we proceeded to test the birds in a cage placed in a planetarium: ° that is, with a dome showing an artificial replica of the natural starry sky. Again, when the dome was merely illuminated with diffuse light (showing no stars), the warblers were unable to choose a preferred direction. But when the planetarium sky matched the local night sky, the birds took up the proper direction just as if they were seeing the natural sky, but now adjusted to the artificial planetarium directions.

[12] Now our artificial dome permitted us to shift the stars and constellations about. By changing the north-south declination (height) of the stars we could change the apparent geographical latitude, making the birds believe that they were farther south or north than they actually were. Similarly by shifting the sky in the east-west direction we might mislead the birds about their position in longitude. How would they behave under these circumstances?

[13] To illustrate the results I shall describe some experi-

planetarium: an optical device which projects a representation of the heavens upon a dome through the use of many stereopticons in motion.

ments with a lesser whitethroat warbler. Recall that the lesser whitethroat normally first travels southeastward across the Balkans and then turns due south, flying along the Nile to its winter home in the region of the Nile headwaters. In our experiments it turned out that as long as the planetarium sky was adjusted to the latitudes of 50 to 40 degrees north, this bird took up the expected flight position facing southeast. But as we shifted the sky, simulating * more southerly latitudes, the bird tended to turn more and more toward the southern direction, until, at the latitude of 15 degrees, it set its course due south!

14   In other words, this lesser whitethroat, which had spent all its life in a cage and never traveled under a natural sky, let alone migrated to Africa, still displayed an inborn agility to use the guidance of the stars to follow the usual route of its species, adjusting its direction nicely at each given latitude. Earlier investigators had supposed that these birds used landmarks to find their route: for example, that the coastline at the eastern end of the Mediterranean was the cue which told them to turn south. But our experiments proved that the birds are able to do it only by the stars.

15   Now let us see what happened when we shifted the planetarium sky to change the longitude, or, corresponding to it, the time. One night, while the lesser whitethroat was flapping its wings and heading in the southeast direction, we suddenly presented the bird with a sky shifted to the configuration five hours and 10 minutes advanced to the local time; in other words, the apparent geographical position of the cage then corresponded to a point 77.5 degrees eastward in longitude at this particular time. The bird at once showed that it was deeply disturbed. It looked excitedly at the unfamiliar sky and for almost a full minute stood irresolutely. Then it suddenly turned and took wing in the westward direction. According to the sky, its position at the moment corresponded to a point near Lake Balkhash in Siberia; the bird, to correct its displacement, was

heading directly toward the usual migration starting point in Europe.

[16] As we reduced its displacement, the bird shifted its heading more and more from due west toward the south. When the displacement was only an hour, corresponding to a position near Vienna, the lesser whitethroat headed south; when the canopy of stars was restored to the correct configuration at our locality for the season and time of night, the bird took up the normal heading toward the southeast.

[17] This behavior, confirmed by experiments with other birds, leaves no doubt that the warblers have a remarkable hereditary mechanism for orienting themselves by the stars—a detailed image of the starry configuration of the sky coupled with a precise time sense which relates the heavenly canopy to the geography of the earth at every time and season. At their very first glimpse of the sky the birds automatically know the right direction. Without benefit of previous experience, with no cue except the stars, the birds are able to locate themselves in time and space and to find their way to their destined homes.

[18] To be sure, the warblers do not have to rely solely on the constellations. In daytime they can guide themselves by the position of the sun. On cloudy nights they get some guidance from mountain ranges, coastlines, and river courses gleaming in the pale night shine. Only in almost total darkness, when thick clouds utterly hide the sky, are the birds in trouble: they circle helplessly and often are drawn to lighthouses.

[19] We are going on to study the warblers' orientation system in more detail, systematically removing constellations or stars from our planetarium sky one by one to see if we can reduce the guidance cues to a basic pattern. One very interesting puzzle is the fact that the birds must somehow be able to make adjustments to astronomical evolution, for in the course of time the pattern of constellations in the sky is slowly but constantly

changing. Even more difficult to explain is the mystery of how the birds ever came to rely on celestial navigation and to develop their skill in the first place. We know that the warblers are not the only creatures possessing this gift: other birds, insects, crabs, and spiders have been found by experiment to be capable of guiding themselves by the sun. But there are many other guidance mechanisms and signposts available on earth. What evolutionary process was it that endowed these animals with the highly sophisticated ability to read the stars?

20 Whatever the answer, we cannot help marveling at the wondrous celestial instinct of the warblers. When fall comes, the little garden warbler, weighing barely three quarters of an ounce, sets off one night on an unbelievable journey. All alone, never in the collective security of a flock, it wings its solitary way southwestward over Germany, France, and Spain, and then swings south to its distant goal in southern Africa. It flies on unerringly, covering a hundred miles and more in a single night, never once stopping in its course, certain of its goal. When drifted by heavy sidewinds, the bird navigates back to its primary course in the next calm night. In the spring it takes off again and northward retraces its path to its nesting place in a European thicket— there to give birth to a new generation of little warblers which will grow up, without being taught, with the selfsame capacity to follow the same route across the continents and oceans by the map of the stars.

ANALYSIS

Sauer's opening paragraph is a pleasantly oblique approach to his main subject—how birds navigate. He tells us here and in the next three paragraphs when they migrate, how far, and under what circumstances. In paragraph 5, he readily disposes of the old explanations of how they did it. Paragraph 6 is the actual beginning of his extended definition of celestial navigation. But "celestial" means "of the sky." Shall we learn about the birds' dependence on the sun as well as the stars? Paragraph 6 narrows the subject. Zoologists, we hear, have confirmed the "time sense" that allows birds "to take account of the sun's motion across the sky." The warblers, however, fly by night. They must possess a special sense to fly by the stars. With paragraph 8, Sauer begins his inductive reasoning. His experiments included completely closed chambers, glass-topped cages, and a planetarium with an artificial dome. The description of these experiments constitutes paragraphs 8–19, at which point Sauer stops short on a question he cannot answer: "What evolutionary process was it that endowed these birds and animals with the ability to read the stars?" The essay concludes gracefully with a paragraph that matches his opening. A bird weighing barely three quarters of an ounce sets off on an unbelievable journey. . . .

Sauer could have chosen several other ways of organizing his essay. He might have eliminated his general introduction and enlarged paragraph 5. Once the various theories were established, he could have set up his own to disprove them. Or he might have broken the essay into two parts: birds that orient themselves by the sun (Kramer's and Matthews' experiments) and the warblers' night flights (his own experiments). What does he gain by the organization as it stands? Far greater reader interest, surely. His essay is more than definition. It conveys much of the awe Sauer feels from his own discoveries. It is filled with specific fact, but it can also convey enthusiasm: "We are going on to study the warblers' orientation system in more detail"; "One very interesting puzzle"; "Even more difficult to explain." Compared with Huxley's, Sauer's essay is a more elaborate definition of a process.

Questions on Content

1. How do ornithologists keep track of bird flights?
2. What theories other than celestial navigation have been suggested to explain how birds fly from one continent to another?
3. How did Sauer employ a planetarium to test warblers?
4. Do warblers fly *only* by means of the stars? Explain.

5. What details about his "systematic laboratory study" does the author include? Would you have him tell us more about his aviary?

Add to your vocabulary: truculence, celestial, orient, nocturnal, diffuse, simulating.

Questions on Technique

1. Sauer cites other scientists—Rüppell, Matthews, Kramer—on the subject of navigation by birds. What does he add to his essay by doing so?
2. Paragraphs 15 and 16 may not be completely clear to a layman who does not understand Sauer's explanation. How would you rewrite them?
3. Sauer tells us nothing about the anatomy of the warbler, yet it is a bird that can fly thousands of miles in migration. Why do you suppose Sauer never discusses the warbler itself?

Suggestions for Writing

1. Choose an animal or bird you have observed closely. Define its distinguishing habits, that is, those peculiar to its species.
2. Using Sauer's method of reaching a hypothesis (birds navigate by the stars) by inductive reasoning (the laboratory experiments), write an essay of about 500 words on a belief you hold and the reasons for holding it.
3. Write an explanation of how fish swim, or snakes crawl, or bats see in the dark. Make the process or mechanism your subject matter.
4. We all, at one time or another, enjoy collecting things. Describe in six or seven paragraphs a collection you made in terms of the *variations* you discovered and how you classified them—coins, butterflies, rocks, stamps, buttons, and so forth.

ARTHUR C. CLARKE · *The Earth and Its Neighbors*

This third example of elementary exposition is the most ambitious. It not only defines solar system, atmosphere, and gravity (the three main subjects of these paragraphs), but it relates all three to space flight. Arthur C. Clarke has been writing on these subjects for many years, in both fiction and nonfiction. He is well known in his native England for an early book, Interplanetary Flight *(1950), and in both England and America for his more recent* The Challenge of the Spaceship *(1959). Since our magazines and daily papers are frequently full of news about missiles, satellites, and space travel, it is good to encounter a scientist who can explain simply the nature of our solar system and the problems man will have to solve before he can move through it.*

Clarke begins with elementary facts. As you read this chapter from The Exploration of Space, *you will discover that it breaks easily into two parts. He wishes first to demonstrate the immensity of space. He does it by a reduction scale, by analogy (a kind of comparison), and by drawings. The second half of the essay (beginning with paragraph 13) discusses atmosphere and gravity by defining them, by analyzing what they mean to space flight, and again by providing a convenient analogy Clarke wants us to* understand *as thoroughly as possible without calling upon a vocabulary familiar only to astronomers and physicists.*

His achievement is considerable. This is expository writing that proceeds step by step (as does Huxley's). It explains clearly and imaginatively (as does Sauer's).

"The Earth and Its Neighbors" from *The Exploration of Space* by Arthur C. Clarke, Harper & Bros. Copyright 1951, © 1959 by Arthur Charles Clarke. Reprinted, with drawings adapted from original, by permission of the publishers.

*And, what is more, it moves toward a concluding para-
graph which raises the main issues for the succeeding
chapters of his book. Once we understand the nature of
"the earth and its neighbors," we will be ready to consider the two conditions any space traveler must surmount.*

> Beneath, the tides of day and night
> With flame and darkness ridge
> The void, as low as where this earth
> Spins like a fretful midge.
> D. G. ROSSETTI—*The Blessèd Damozel*

1   The first difficulty one encounters in trying to envisage
interplanetary flight is that of scale. The distances involved are so enormous, so much greater than those we
meet in everyday life, that at first they are quite meaningless. However, this is something that (with practice)
can be fairly easily overcome.

2   There are still primitive peoples to whom a hundred
miles is an inconceivably great distance—yet there are also
men who think nothing of traveling ten thousand miles
in a few days. As speeds of transport have increased, so
our sense of distance has altered. Australia can never be
as remote to us as it was to our grandfathers. In the same
way, one's mental attitude can adapt itself to deal with
interplanetary distances, even if the mind can never
really envisage them. (And, after all, can the mind *really*
envisage a thousand miles?)

3   The first step in this "familiarization procedure" is
the scale model. To begin with, let us concentrate on
Earth and Moon alone, ignoring the other planets. We
will take a scale on which a man would still be visible
to the naked eye, our reduction factor being 1,000 to 1.
The Earth is now a sphere 8 miles in diameter, and 240
miles away is another sphere, the Moon, 2 miles across.
On this scale, a human being would be a little less than
a twelfth of an inch high, the speed of the fastest aircraft ° would be under a mile an hour, and that of a V-2

fastest aircraft: Keep in mind that this essay was written in 1951.

rocket ° about three and a half miles an hour. The twelfth-of-an-inch-high man contemplating the gulf between Earth and Moon is thus in much the same position as an intelligent ant trying to picture the size of England.

4 To bring in the planets, we must alter the scale again, making the man sink far below visibility. With a reduction of a million-fold, the Earth is now 40 feet in diameter, the Moon 10 feet across and a quarter of a mile away. The Sun is 93 miles away and almost a mile across; 36 and 67 miles from it, respectively, circle Mercury and Venus. Mercury is 15 feet across, Venus 38—a little smaller than the Earth. Beyond the Earth's orbit is Mars, 20 feet in diameter and 140 miles from the Sun. It is accompanied by two tiny satellites, ° only about half an inch across.

5 Outwards from Mars is a great gulf, empty save for thousands of minor planets or "asteroids," few of which on this scale are much larger than grains of sand. We have to travel 483 miles from the Sun—340 beyond Mars—before we meet Jupiter, the largest of all the planets. In our model he would be over 400 feet in diameter, with eleven satellites ranging in size from 15 feet to a few inches across.

6 You may feel that our model is getting somewhat unwieldy despite our drastic reduction of a million-to-one, but we are still nowhere near the limits of the Sun's empire. There are four more planets to come—Saturn (diameter 350 feet); Uranus (150 feet); Neptune (160 feet); and Pluto (20 feet). And Pluto is 3,700 miles from the Sun. . . .

7 This model of our Solar System shows very clearly the *emptiness* of space, and the difficulty of representing on the same scale both the sizes of the planets and the distances between them. If we reduced the Earth to the size of a table-tennis ball, its orbit would still be half a

V-2 rocket: a long-range ballistic missile developed by the Germans before World War II and used by them against Great Britain in 1940.

satellite: a small body which revolves round a planet.

mile across, and Pluto would be ten miles from the Sun.
8   A pictorial attempt to show the planets, their satellites,
and their orbits to the correct scale is given in Figure 1.

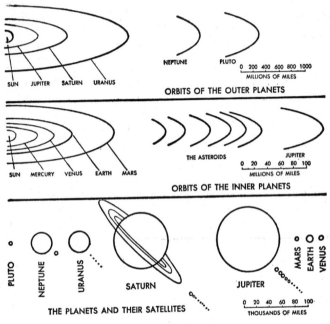

Figure 1. The Solar System

Even in the most "magnified" of the diagrams, however,
it is not possible to represent the smaller satellites accurately.

Three other points remain to be mentioned before
our picture of the Solar System is complete. In the first
place, it is not a stationary affair. All the planets are
moving, and in the same direction round the Sun. The
innermost planet, Mercury, takes only 88 days to complete one revolution, while Pluto takes 248 years—so
that astronomers will have to wait until A.D. 2178 before

it returns to the part of the sky where it was discovered in 1930. This increase in period from Mercury to Pluto is not merely due to the greater distances which the outer planets have to travel. They also move more slowly. Mercury is moving in its orbit at 107,000 m.p.h., the Earth at a more modest 68,000, and Pluto at a mere 10,000 m.p.h.

¹⁰ The second important point is that almost all the planets lie in or very near the same plane, so that the Solar System is virtually "flat." There are exceptions to this rule, the worst being Pluto, whose orbit is inclined at an angle of 17 degrees to that of the Earth's, but on the whole it is fairly well obeyed—and it certainly simplifies the problem of interplanetary navigation.

¹¹ Finally, the shapes of the orbits. They are very nearly circular, with the Sun at the center. Only Mercury, Mars, and—once again—Pluto depart seriously from this rule, their orbits being appreciably elliptical. That of Pluto, in fact, is so eccentric * that it can sometimes come closer to the Sun than does Neptune.

¹² This, then, is the family of planets of which our world is a rather junior member. Despite its size, it forms a virtually isolated system in space, owing to the remoteness of even the nearest stars. With perfect precision, age after age, the planets swing in their orbits round the Sun—for they are moving in an almost total vacuum, beyond the reach of friction or any force which might check their speed.

¹³ The airlessness of space must have seemed an insuperable * barrier to interplanetary voyages in the days when it was first realized that the atmosphere extends only a little way from the Earth. Today we know better— for if there was any appreciable amount of matter in space, it would not be possible to reach the speeds which are required for journeys to other worlds. However, this would be rather a theoretical consideration, since those worlds themselves would long ago have ceased to exist: the resistance to their motion would have made them spiral inwards until they dropped into the Sun.

14 We must now return to Earth, which for a long time to come will be the starting point for all our voyages, and consider what obstacles we will have to overcome if we wish to leave it.

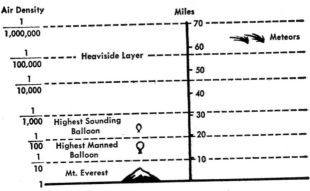

Figure 2. The Earth's Atmosphere

15 As we have already mentioned, the atmosphere is both a help and a hindrance. We cannot live if the pressure of the surrounding air falls below about one-half of its sea-level value, and most men would be practically incapacitated well before this figure was reached. As we ascend from the Earth's surface, the pressure and density of the air fall steadily, and in Figure 2 an attempt has been made to show this on the correct scale. The greatest height at which men can live permanently is three and a half miles, and this requires a long period of adaptation.

16 The absence of atmosphere does not, of course, merely affect men, but also machines. Airplanes—whether propelled by airscrews or jets—are air-burning devices just as much as men are, the difference being that in the human engine the combustion is gentler and the conversion of energy to power rather more subtle. In addition, aircraft require the atmosphere for support: wings and airscrews would both be useless in a vacuum. These

factors set a limit to the height at which conventional aircraft can ever operate. That limit is between 10 and 15 miles—or, roughly speaking, where the air pressure is more than one-twentieth of its sea-level value.

[17] Balloons can function at considerably greater altitudes—up to 25 miles if only carrying very light instruments—but presently they too reach a level where the surrounding air is little denser than the hydrogen in the envelope, and so can give them no more buoyancy. Until the advent of the giant rocket, no object made by man had ever risen above this level—with the single exception of the shells from the Paris gun (usually misnamed "Big Bertha") in the 1914 War. These had a peak altitude of 30 miles, and, if the gun could have been fired vertically, would have reached a height of over 40 miles.

[18] The atmosphere, however, does not come to an end at the level where balloons will rise no further: indeed, it never comes to an end at all, but dwindles with distance as a musical note dies away with time, until at last there is no means of detecting its presence. Fifty miles up there is still enough to play a very important rôle in our modern lives, for here the tenuous * gases are ionized ° to form the reflecting layer (the ionosphere or Heaviside layer) which makes long-distance radio communication possible and provides many of the strange noises which occasionally intrude upon our listening. Around this level most of the meteors which come racing into the atmosphere at speeds of 100,000 m.p.h. or more meet their doom, for at these velocities even the ionosphere can produce tremendous frictional resistance.

[19] The last indication we have of the atmosphere's presence is given by the aurora, whose ghostly beams and curtains of light we seldom see in southern latitudes, but which are common enough near the magnetic poles. The aurora is produced by electrical discharges very similar to those in neon signs, and its outermost streamers extend to heights of six hundred miles. Well below this

ionized: separated or changed into ions, which are electrically charged atoms, radicals, or molecules.

altitude, however, we are in a vacuum better than any that can be produced in the laboratory.

20   It might be thought that, because the atmosphere is so relatively shallow, it could be ignored as far as interplanetary flight is concerned. This is not the case: as we shall see later, it sets a limit to the speed we can develop near the Earth's surface on the way into space and —much more important—it offers a means of making a safe landing on the return.

21   This thin blanket of air, without which life as we know it would be impossible, is held tightly to the Earth by the force of gravity. If gravity were weaker by a factor of four or five, the atmosphere would have escaped into space—as has happened in the case of the Moon. So we can be thankful for gravity in this respect, even though when we contemplate the task of leaving the Earth we may wish it had a much smaller value.

22   Of all natural forces, gravity is the most universal and it dominates any discussion of space-flight. Here on the Earth's surface we can never escape from its influence, and its value is practically constant over the whole of the planet. With increasing altitude it slowly diminishes, though so slowly that even at the greatest height yet reached by rocket (250 miles)° it still has 90 per cent of its value at sea level. As the distance from the Earth lengthens into the thousands of miles, the reduction becomes substantial: twelve thousand miles up, a one-pound weight would weigh only an ounce. It follows, therefore, that the further away one goes from the Earth the easier it is to go onwards. (A practical example of the saying that nothing succeeds like success.) As far as gravity is concerned, leaving the Earth is rather like climbing a hill which at first is very steep but later becomes more and more gentle until finally it is almost perfectly flat. Yet it is never quite flat: the Earth's gravitational pull extends throughout the universe, even if for

greatest height yet reached by rocket (250 miles) : Since this essay was written, both American and Russian rockets have attained heights well in excess of 250 miles.

almost all purposes it can be ignored after a distance of a million miles or so.

23   This picture of gravity as producing a hill, up which we have to climb to get away from the Earth, is a very useful one, and we will employ it again later. In the meantime, Figure 3 will give some visual idea of the way

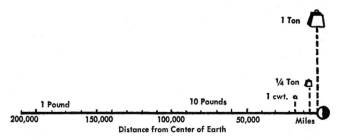

Figure 3. The Reduction of Gravity with Distance

in which gravity falls off with distance—and should help to dispel the surprisingly common impression that it simply finishes when one is still quite close to the Earth.

24   If we ever hope to build spaceships, therefore, we must bear in mind two fundamental points. In the first place, any method of propulsion which depends on the atmosphere will be useless. And secondly, even if we have a device which can produce thrust in an airless vacuum, our ship must be provided with enough energy to fight its way outwards for thousands of miles against the pull of Earth's gravity.

25   The first condition is easily fulfilled. It is the second —the energy problem—which is by far the more serious: yet even that can be solved without invoking any new and fundamental discoveries. We do not have to wait until someone produces "anti-gravity" before we can travel to the planets: the means is already at hand. It is the rocket.

ANALYSIS

Clarke does not waste space on introductory remarks. With the first sentence we plunge into the problem of how to describe the solar system in terms we can manage. Astronomical distances are immense. Can the mind *really* envisage a thousand miles, he asks. If not, what can we do with the distance of 93,000,000 miles between Earth and Sun? Clarke proposes a three-step "familiarization procedure."

First, reduce all sizes to scale: "We will take a scale on which a man would still be visible to the naked eye, our reduction factor being 1,000 to 1." Second, provide a useful analogy: "The twelfth-of-an-inch-high man contemplating the gulf between Earth and Moon is thus in much the same position as an intelligent ant trying to picture the size of England." Third, diagram the information: "A pictorial attempt to show the planets, their satellites, and their orbits to the correct scale is given in Figure 1." We can hardly ask more of Clarke than this three-fold explanation. He most likely agrees, for in paragraph 12 he says, "This, then, is the family of planets of which our world is a rather junior member." With these elementary facts in mind, Clarke moves into the more complex concepts of atmosphere and gravity.

He repeats his method in the second half of the essay. Figure 2 makes the relationship between height and density visually clear. Paragraphs 15–19 describe in words what happens as we soar upwards into the atmosphere. Paragraph 22 provides a second useful analogy: "As far as gravity is concerned, leaving the Earth is rather like climbing a hill which at first is very steep but later becomes more and more gentle until finally it is almost perfectly flat." With nice precision, Clarke moves toward his final point: in building spaceships, we will have to surmount two problems, thrust and energy.

Note that Clarke does *not* assume that we are ready to understand the mechanics of producing thrust in an airless vacuum or the way in which a rocket solves the energy problem. His subject is the earth and its neighbors. By explaining the solar system and how it works, by defining atmosphere and gravitational pull, he is preparing us to approach the more difficult concepts of thrust and energy. This, then, is another use of definition: the clarifying of one idea or process in order to build up our knowledge. Man proceeds by nature from the simple to the complex.

Questions on Content

1. Jupiter is the largest of the major planets, Pluto is the farthest from the Sun. What else does Clarke tell us about Pluto?
2. How does Clarke try to show us the *emptiness* of space?
3. How is the atmosphere both a help and a hindrance to space travel?
4. Why does gravity "dominate any discussion of space flight"?
5. How far out in space does the gravitational pull extend?

Add to your vocabulary: eccentric, insuperable, tenuous.

Questions on Technique

1. Why should Clarke want to begin this scientific essay with a quotation from a nineteenth-century poem? What is "a fretful midge"? Does it describe what you think of as this earth?
2. Some readers might object to the abruptness of the opening paragraph of this essay. How would you write it? Do you think the essay ought to begin with the subject of space travel rather than distances?
3. Figure 3 is, perhaps, not the easiest kind of diagram to read. How would you improve it?

Suggestions for Writing

1. In 500 words, rewrite Clarke's description of the solar system *without* using either his reduction scale or his diagrams.
2. Clarke writes only three paragraphs on the subject of gravity. Enlarge his discussion.
3. Using a standard encyclopedia, gather some pertinent facts about the Sun and then organize them into a

definition of this star. Use analogies and a reduction to scale if you wish.

4. Search your memory for examples from your own experience of how the word "distance" (or some other word like "tall" or "smart" or "big") changed its meaning as you grew older. Write an essay of 400–500 words on this subject, using such details, perhaps, as walking to grade school, hikes at camp, bicycle trips, driving your family's car, the summer vacations.

CHAPTER 5

Reports and analyses

As we pick up our morning paper, just before breakfast, we ask one thing of the prose we read: conciseness. Reporters know that. When they file a story, they aim to tell us what happened, where, at what time, to whom. The first paragraph of a news report attracts our attention and gives us basic facts. "A young New Weston housewife," we might read, "was slightly injured yesterday when her car plunged through a guard rail on the South Street Bridge and landed upside down on the New York Central and New Haven Railroad tracks. The accident occurred at 5:20 P.M., as Mrs. Florence Burkhardt, 32, of 115 Elm Road, was returning from her bookkeeper's job at the New Weston Savings and Loan Association."

As the account continues (we have already decided whether we want to go on reading), the reporter will naturally fill in the details: how she sustained only slight injuries, what caused the accident, who called the police, what hospital she was taken to, when railroad traffic was resumed. It is unlikely that he will pause to comment on women drivers, the epidemic of South Street traffic accidents, or the need for another railroad bridge. We might call this kind of writing "routine reporting," the prose we use to give the news. "News" means "recent events." Last week's news reports perish quickly. They are not models we need to imitate, serviceable though the prose may be.

Yet this section of the book is labeled "reports and

analyses" and the account of Mrs. Burkhardt's accident is clearly expository prose. Are there, perhaps, various kinds of "reports"? Does the reporter ever have an opportunity to embellish a story, to write for the sake of writing, to make words "come alive" rather than just "service" the facts? Do some reports come close to being analyses? Are some analyses designed to inform us of certain facts ("report" on a situation or case study or committee report) before they establish opinions, arrive at conclusions? The answer to all these questions is yes. Reports and analyses can be stimulating reading. They can demand just as vibrant vocabulary and careful organization as descriptive essays. The five models that follow will demonstrate this third kind of exposition.

We begin with a brief but delightful example by a reporter who loves words. McCandlish Phillips, writing for the New York *Times*, knows how to make a vocabulary fit a situation. He has a sense of humor, as well as a sense of whimsy.° He also has a keen eye. Given a routine news assignment (a jeweler moves to larger quarters), he meets routine with imagination. Watch how he conveys all the basic facts, but in a somewhat leisurely order, if one can be said to be leisurely in a 364-word report.

McCANDLISH PHILLIPS · *Winston Moves $35,000,000 Gems*

1 An armored truck moved quickly through the steel-gray emptiness of Fifth Avenue not much after dawn yesterday, leaving wet slashes in the snow. Inside, guards stood watch on two foot lockers.

2 Within the lockers lay a wondrous miscellany—emeralds, rubies, sapphires, and diamonds in motionless

whimsy: See Glossary.

"Winston Moves $35,000,000 Gems" by McCandlish Phillips from the New York *Times*, March 23, 1960. © 1960 by The New York Times Company. Reprinted by permission of the publishers.

galaxies. Harry Winston, Inc., was moving $35,000,000 in jewels to new quarters.

3 This was the third of four trips in a supposedly theft-proof vehicle that normally carries a less precious commodity—money in bulk.

4 Mr. Winston was taking his estimable cargo from his old converted town house at 7 East Fifty-first Street to a new place on the southwest corner of Fifth Avenue and Fifty-Sixth Street.

5 With $35,000,000 in jewels to transfer, this could be about the longest five-block distance in the world. The figure was Mr. Winston's obliging stab at the wholesale value of his wares.

6 His approximation of the number of stones involved had a satisfying ring. "Millions," he said with an airy distaste for precision.

7 The first two trips were made Monday morning; the last two yesterday.

8 The transfer could have been made in a single run, but that was too rich a proposition even for Brink's Inc., which was insured for a mere $10,000,000 a load.

9 With a sapphire the size of a duck's egg and diamonds as big as lumps of sugar involved, the voyage was a little disappointing. It seemed somehow as if roses should have been strewn in the way.

10 Instead, four black trunks with moldering leather handles were set in the foyer of the old building. The hasps on each were secured with lead seals and a sort of wasp's nest of knots.

11 A few minutes later, in a driving snow, two of the trunks were pushed into the truck. Men in plain clothes were posted at both ends of the block. Eight others, unseen, watched from secret vantages. They remained until the truck returned for the last two trunks.

12 Four uniformed men climbed into the canary yellow interior of the truck, which followed a radio car up the avenue, ignoring traffic lights.

13 At the new place the trunks were stored in a shelfless whitewashed vault the size of a vestibule.

ANALYSIS

Phillips has several facts to convey: who is moving what, from where to where, when. He could, it is true, tell us all this in one paragraph. He wisely avoids doing it, not even mentioning Harry Winston, Inc. in the opening sentences. (The headline, of course, has already met this demand, and Phillips feels free to "entice" us into his "story.") What we do not expect from a news report we happily find here: atmosphere. The streets have a "steel-gray" emptiness. The wet snow is "slashed" by the tires. The jewels are like "duck's eggs" and "lumps of sugar." The four black trunks "with moldering leather handles" are tied "with a sort of wasp's nest of knots." They are placed in the "canary yellow interior of the truck" and then stored in a "shelfless whitewashed vault the size of a vestibule." He uses a surprising amount of color and imagery ° for so brief an account.

What other verbal delights do we find? Before we are told anything so crass as the value of these stones, Phillips indulges in a sentence right out of the *Arabian Nights*: "Within the lockers lay a wondrous miscellany —emeralds, rubies, sapphires, and diamonds in motionless galaxies." Who of us has seen a *trunkful* of jewels? But were we to see them, would not "galaxy" be the exact word to describe them—the Milky Way in precious stones? And what of their value? Mr. Winston gives an "obliging stab" at their worth. Jewels are priceless, is the implication. The transfer is insured "for a mere $10,000,000 a load." The vehicle "normally carries a less precious commodity—money in bulk." Phillips' whimsy finally creeps in: "It seemed somehow as if roses should have been strewn in the way." Winston, we like to think, would have approved.

Now it is apparent that Phillips could not treat all assignments this way. A meeting of the UN Assembly, a political rally, a school board decision all require another vocabulary. Yet the good reporter will make his prose work for him whenever he can. He will not merely *tell* us a fact (order the details, that is) when he can

imagery: See Glossary.

show us (that is, make us feel what is happening) . When Phillips reported, on another occasion, the arrival of a political candidate at an airport, he wrote: "The eager Bostonians did everything but resolve themselves into formations to spell out 'WELCOME.' Four bands boomed out marches, usually in consecutive order, but sometimes in clashing coincidence." These details contribute graphic description to what might otherwise be routine facts. They form an image in our mind's eye and thus bring color to expository writing. When you read the newspapers tomorrow or listen to a news commentator on radio or television, watch for these little flourishes of style. They are not difficult to imitate.

Suggestions for Writing

1. Stretch your imagination. Your hometown has built a new high school. It is moving day. The trucks have taken all the heavy furniture, but the students have volunteered to move the rest. Report the occasion in less than 500 words.

2. Using Phillips' technique, describe an ordinary occasion in an unusual way. For example, a senior prom as seen by a visitor from the Near East, a football game as witnessed by someone who has never watched football, a Hallowe'en parade as seen by a four-year old child, a musical recital as listened to by a father who dislikes music.

3. Take a simple incident from your own life: going to camp, visiting Chicago, playing in a championship game, seeing live theater for the first time. Report it with this in mind: your reader wants to know what happened, but he also wants to share the feelings you experienced. Do *not* use the first person.

4. Prepare an account of about 400 words of an event— social, athletic, musical—that took place last month in your school. Tell your reader *all* the basic facts in as direct a way as you can.

WILLIAM L. LAURENCE · *Dawn over Zero*

McCandlish Phillips deals with a relatively unimportant incident. In the report that follows, William L. Laurence recounts a most important occasion. Where Phillips could afford to embellish, Laurence has to restrain himself forcibly. He does not always succeed. The experience he witnessed transcends the power of words. Not that he was unprepared to do it justice. Scientist, lecturer, and journalist, Laurence has won two Pulitzer prizes among other awards. For over thirty years he has been writing for the New York Times; *since 1956 he has been the science editor. In 1959 he published* Men and Atoms. *He was trained, therefore, to capture this occasion in words as well as to understand the scope of the undertaking.*

You will observe that Laurence incorporates both of these tasks—reporting and analyzing—in his prose. The journalist is relating all the facts; the scientist cannot resist commenting. But taken as a whole, this essay is a factual account. Paragraphs 6–27 are, in essence, a long count-down. We hear names, dates, places. We know what will take place at 5:30 A.M. It is not suspense he strives for. But the tension of waiting is there, nevertheless. Paragraphs 24–27 cannot move fast enough. Laurence has built his essay with this effect in mind. But he achieves other effects, as well. First let us read this remarkable report.

1 The Atomic Age began at exactly 5:30 mountain war time on the morning of July 16, 1945, on a stretch of semi-desert land about fifty air-line miles from Alamogordo, New Mexico, just a few minutes before the dawn of a new day on that part of the earth. At that great moment in history, ranking with the moment when man first put fire to work for him, the vast energy locked within the heart of the atoms of matter was released for the first time in a burst of flame such as had never before been seen on this planet, illuminating earth and sky, for a brief span that seemed eternal, with the light of many super-suns.

2   The elemental flame, first fire ever made on earth that did not have its origin in the sun, came from the explosion of the first atomic bomb. It was a full-dress rehearsal preparatory to dropping the bomb over Hiroshima and Nagasaki—and other Japanese military targets, had Japan refused to accept the Potsdam Declaration ° for her surrender.

3   The rehearsal marked the climax in the penultimate ° act of one of the greatest dramas in our history and the history of civilized man—a drama in which our scientists, under the direction of the Army Corps of Engineers, were working against time to create an atomic bomb ahead of our German enemy. The collapse of Germany marked the end of the first act of this drama. The successful completion of our task, in the greatest challenge by man to nature so far, brought down the curtain on the second act. The grand finale came three weeks afterward in the skies over Japan, with a swift descent of the curtain on the greatest war in history.

4   The atomic flash in New Mexico came as a great affirmation to the prodigious * labors of our scientists during the past four years. It came as the affirmative answer to the until then unanswered question: "Will it work?"

5   With the flash came a delayed roll of mighty thunder, heard, just as the flash was seen, for hundreds of miles. The roar echoed and reverberated from the distant hills and the Sierra Oscuro range near by, sounding as though it came from some supramundane ° source as well as from

Potsdam Declaration: issued at Potsdam, Germany, July 26, 1945, outlining the terms under which Japan would be allowed to surrender to the Allied Forces.

penultimate: next to last.   supramundane: above the earth.

the bowels of the earth. The hills said yes and the mountains chimed in yes. It was as if the earth had spoken and the suddenly iridescent * clouds and sky had joined in one affirmative answer. Atomic energy—yes. It was like the grand finale of a mighty symphony of the elements, fascinating and terrifying, uplifting and crushing, ominous, devastating, full of great promise and great forebodings.

6   I watched the birth of the era of atomic power from the slope of a hill in the desert land of New Mexico, on the northwestern corner of Alamogordo Air Base, about 125 miles southeast of Albuquerque. The hill, named Compania Hill for the occasion, was twenty miles to the northwest of Zero, the code name given to the spot chosen for the atomic bomb test. The area embracing Zero and Compania Hill, twenty-four miles long and eighteen miles wide, had the code name Trinity.

7   I joined a caravan of three buses, three automobiles, and a truck carrying radio equipment at 11 P.M. on Sunday, July 15, at Albuquerque. There were about ninety of us in that strange caravan, traveling silently and in the utmost secrecy through the night on probably as unusual an adventure as any in our day. With the exception of myself the caravan consisted of scientists from the highly secret atomic bomb research and development center in the mesas and canyons of New Mexico, twenty-five miles northwest of Santa Fe, where we solved the secret of translating the fabulous energy of the atom into the mightiest weapon ever made by man. It was from there that the caravan set out at 5:30 that Sunday afternoon for its destination, 212 miles to the south.

8   The caravan wound its way slowly over the tortuous roads overlooking the precipitous canyons of northern New Mexico, passing through Espagnola, Santa Fe, and Bernalillo, arriving at Albuquerque at about 10 P.M. Here it was joined by Sir James Chadwick, who won the Nobel prize and knighthood for his discovery of the neutron, the key that unlocks the atom; Professor Ernest O. Lawrence of the University of California, master atom-

smasher, who won the Nobel prize for his discovery of the cyclotron; Professor Edwin M. McMillan, also of the University of California, one of the discoverers of plutonium, the new atomic energy element; and several others from the atomic bomb center, who, like me, had arrived during the afternoon.

9   The night was dark with black clouds, and not a star could be seen. Occasionally a bolt of lightning would rend the sky and reveal for an instant the flat semi-desert landscape, rich with historic lore of past adventure. We rolled along on U. S. Highway 85, running between Albuquerque and El Paso, through sleeping ancient Spanish-American towns, their windows dark, their streets deserted—towns with music in their names, Los Lunas, Belen, Bernardo, Alamillo, Socorro, San Antonio. At San Antonio we turned east and crossed "the bridge on the Rio Grande with the detour in the middle of it." From there we traveled ten and one half miles eastward on U. S. Highway 380, and then turned south on a specially built dirt road, running for twenty-five miles to the base camp at Trinity.

10   The end of our trail was reached after we had covered about five and one fifth miles on the dirt road. Here we saw the first signs of life since leaving Albuquerque about three hours earlier, a line of silent men dressed in helmets. A little farther on, a detachment of military police examined our special credentials. We got out of the buses and looked around us. The night was still pitch-black save for an occasional flash of lightning in the eastern sky, outlining for a brief instant the Sierra Oscuro Range directly ahead of us. We were in the middle of the New Mexico desert, miles away from nowhere, with hardly a sign of life, not even a blinking light on the distant horizon. This was to be our caravansary °until the zero hour.

11   From a distance to the southeast the beam of a searchlight probed the clouds. This gave us our first sense of

caravansary: a kind of inn, in the Near East, where caravans rest at night.

orientation. The bomb-test site, Zero, was a little to the left of the searchlight beam, twenty miles away. With the darkness and the waiting in the chill of the desert, the tension became almost unendurable.

12 We gathered in a circle to listen to directions on what we were to do at the time of the test, directions read aloud by the light of a flashlight:

13 At a short signal of the siren at minus five minutes to zero, "all personnel whose duties did not specifically require otherwise" were to prepare "a suitable place to lie down on." At a long signal of the sirens at minus two minutes to zero, "all personnel whose duties did not specifically require otherwise" were to "lie prone on the ground immediately, the face and eyes directed toward the ground and with the head away from Zero." "Do not watch for the flash directly," the directions read, "but turn over after it has occurred and watch the cloud. Stay on the ground until the blast wave has passed (two minutes). At two short blasts of the siren, indicating the passing of all hazard from light and blast, all personnel will prepare to leave as soon as possible.

14 "The hazard from blast is reduced by lying down on the ground in such a manner that flying rocks, glass, and other objects do not intervene between the source of blast and the individual. Open all car windows.

15 "The hazard from light injury to eyes is reduced by shielding the closed eyes with the bended arms and lying face down on the ground. If the first flash is viewed, a 'blind spot' may prevent your seeing the rest of the show.

16 "The hazard from ultraviolet light injuries to the skin is best overcome by wearing long trousers and shirts with long sleeves."

17 David Dow, assistant to the scientific director of the Atomic Bomb Development Center, handed each of us a flat piece of colored glass such as is used by arc welders to shield their eyes. Dr. Edward Teller of George Washington University cautioned us against sunburn. Someone produced sunburn lotion and passed it around. It was an eerie sight to see a number of our highest-ranking sci-

entists seriously rubbing sunburn lotion on their faces and hands in the pitch-blackness of the night, twenty miles away from the expected flash. These were the men who, more than anybody else, knew the potentialities of atomic energy on the loose. It gave one an inkling of their confidence in their handiwork.

[18] The bomb was set on a structural steel tower one hundred feet high. Ten miles away to the southwest was the base camp. This was G.H.Q. for the scientific high command, of which Professor Kenneth T. Bainbridge of Harvard University was field commander. Here were erected barracks to serve as living-quarters for the scientists, a mess hall, a commissary, a post exchange, and other buildings. Here the vanguard of the atomists, headed by Professor J. R. Oppenheimer of the University of California, scientific director of the Atomic Bomb Project, lived like soldiers at the front, supervising the enormously complicated details involved in the epoch-making tests.

[19] Here early that Sunday afternoon gathered Major General Leslie R. Groves, commander in chief of the Atomic Bomb Project; Brigadier General T. F. Farrell, hero of World War I, General Grove's deputy; Professor Enrico Fermi, Nobel prize winner and one of the leaders in the project; President James Bryant Conant of Harvard; Dr. Vannevar Bush, director of the Office of Scientific Research and Development; Dean Richard C. Tolman of the California Institute of Technology; Professor R. F. Bacher of Cornell; Colonel Stafford L. Warren, University of Rochester radiologist; and about a hundred and fifty other leaders in the atomic bomb program.

[20] At the Base Camp was a dry, abandoned reservoir, about five hundred feet square, surrounded by a mound of earth about eight feet high. Within this mound bulldozers dug a series of slit trenches, each about three feet deep, seven feet wide, and twenty-five feet long. At a command over the radio at zero minus one minute all observers at Base Camp lay down in their assigned

trenches, "face and eyes directed toward the ground and with the head away from Zero." But most of us on Compania Hill remained on our feet.

21   Three other posts had been established, south, north, and west of Zero, each at a distance of 10,000 yards (5.7 miles). These were known, respectively, as South-10,000, North-10,000, and West-10,000, or S-10, N-10, and W-10. Here the shelters were much more elaborate—wooden structures, their walls reinforced by cement, buried under a massive layer of earth.

22   S-10 was the control center. Here Professor Oppenheimer, as scientific commander in chief, and his field commander, Professor Bainbridge, issued orders and synchronized the activities of the other sites. Here the signal was given and a complex of mechanisms was set in motion that resulted in the greatest burst of energy ever released by man on earth up to that time. No switch was pulled, no button pressed, to light this first cosmic fire on this planet.

23   At forty-five seconds to zero, set for 5:30 o'clock, young Dr. Joseph L. McKibben of the University of California, at a signal from Professor Bainbridge, activated a master robot that set off a series of other robots, until, at last, strategically spaced electrons moved to the proper place at the proper split second.

24   Forty-five seconds passed and the moment was zero.

25   Meanwhile at our observation post on Compania Hill the atmosphere had grown tenser as the zero hour approached. We had spent the first part of our stay eating an early morning picnic breakfast that we had taken along with us. It had grown cold in the desert, and many of us, lightly clad, shivered. Occasionally a drizzle came down, and the intermittent flashes of lightning made us turn apprehensive glances toward Zero. We had had some disturbing reports that the test might be called off because of the weather. The radio we had brought with us for communication with Base Camp kept going out of order, and when we had finally repaired it some blatant *

band would drown out the news we wanted to hear. We knew there were two specially equipped B-29 Super-fortresses high overhead to make observations and recordings in the upper atmosphere, but we could neither see nor hear them. We kept gazing through the blackness.

²⁶ Suddenly, at 5:29.50, as we stood huddled around our radio, we heard a voice ringing through the darkness, sounding as though it had come from above the clouds: "Zero minus ten seconds!" A green flare flashed out through the clouds, descended slowly, opened, grew dim, and vanished into the darkness.

²⁷ The voice from the clouds boomed out again: "Zero minus three seconds!" Another green flare came down. Silence reigned over the desert. We kept moving in small groups in the direction of Zero. From the east came the first faint signs of dawn.

²⁸ And just at that instant there rose from the bowels of the earth a light not of this world, the light of many suns in one. It was a sunrise such as the world had never seen, a great green super-sun climbing in a fraction of a second to a height of more than eight thousand feet, rising ever higher until it touched the clouds, lighting up earth and sky all around with a dazzling luminosity.

²⁹ Up it went, a great ball of fire about a mile in diameter, changing colors as it kept shooting upward, from deep purple to orange, expanding, growing bigger, rising as it expanded, an elemental force freed from its bonds after being chained for billions of years. For a fleeting instant the color was unearthly green, such as one sees only in the corona of the sun during a total eclipse. It was as though the earth had opened and the skies had split. One felt as though one were present at the moment of creation when God said: "Let there be light."

³⁰ To another observer, Professor George B. Kistiakowsky of Harvard, the spectacle was "the nearest thing to doomsday that one could possibly imagine." "I am sure,"

he said, "that at the end of the world—in the last milli-second of the earth's existence—the last man will see what we have just seen!"

31 A great cloud rose from the ground and followed the trail of the great sun. At first it was a giant column, which soon took the shape of a supramundane mush-room. For a fleeting instant it took the form of the Statue of Liberty magnified many times. Up it went, higher, higher, a giant mountain born in a few seconds instead of millions of years, quivering convulsively. It touched the multicolored clouds, pushed its summit through them, kept rising until it reached a height of 41,000 feet, 12,000 feet higher than the earth's highest mountain.

32 All through this very short but extremely long time-interval not a sound was heard. I could see the silhou-ettes of human forms motionless in little groups, like desert plants in the dark. The newborn mountain in the distance, a giant among the pygmies of the Sierra Oscuro Range, stood leaning at an angle against the clouds, a vibrant volcano spouting fire to the sky.

33 Then out of the great silence came a mighty thun-der. For a brief interval the phenomena we had seen as light repeated themselves in terms of sound. It was the blast from thousands of blockbusters going off simulta-neously at one spot. The thunder reverberated all through the desert, bounced back and forth from the Sierra Oscuro, echo upon echo. The ground trembled under our feet as in an earthquake. A wave of hot wind was felt by many of us just before the blast had warned us of its coming.

34 The big boom came about one hundred seconds after the great flash—the first cry of a newborn world. It brought the silent, motionless silhouettes to life, gave them a voice. A loud cry filled the air. The little groups that had hitherto stood rooted to the earth like desert plants broke into a dance—the rhythm of primitive man dancing at one of his fire festivals at the coming of spring. They clapped their hands as they leaped from

the ground—earthbound man symbolizing the birth of a
new force that for the first time gives man means to free
himself from the gravitional pull of the earth that holds
him down.

³⁵   The dance of the primitive man lasted but a few
seconds, during which an evolutionary period of about
10,000 years had been telescoped. Primitive man was
metamorphosed * into modern man—shaking hands, slapping his fellow on the back, all laughing like happy
children.

³⁶   The sun was just rising above the horizon as our
caravan started on its way back to Albuquerque and Los
Alamos. We looked at it through our dark lenses to compare it with what we had seen.

³⁷   "The sun can't hold a candle to it!" one of us remarked.

ANALYSIS

What problems faced Laurence when he came to assemble the facts and write this essay? He had observed
history in the making. How was he to treat the event?
First, the good reporter would tell us what happened
(how foolish that question sounds here, but nonetheless
we do want to know), where it happened, when, and
who witnessed it. Laurence does all this conscientiously.
He names the scientists and the military men; he identifies them; he locates Compania Hill and Zero; he keeps
a chronological order; he gives us distances and heights
in accurate numbers. Second, he *shows* us what he saw:
the night of July 16 was "dark with black clouds," the
desert was cold and the men shivered, a "green flare
flashed out through the clouds." Then came the great explosion. Paragraphs 28–33 are pure description. Awesome it must have been. Laurence wants us to hear it as
well as see it. Third, he feels he must comment on this
monumental occasion, if only briefly. He begins his essay with these comments (paragraphs 1–4). He concludes
with a few more (paragraphs 34–35). They round out
his report.

A highly critical reader might suggest to Laurence that

he mars this essay by what he writes in paragraph 5, and where he places it, as well. Let us look closely at the opening of the report. The topic sentence ° is almost a pronouncement, but considering the subject it is what we need and expect. The rest of this first paragraph is written in the same key. An historical event of prime importance took place on July 16, 1945. Laurence does not underrate it. Paragraph 4 ends with the question which American scientists must have asked hundreds of times in the months before this experiment: "Will it work?" Since the reader knows at this stage in the essay that it did, indeed, work, one wonders if paragraph 5 is not anticipating (even spoiling) Laurence's "climax" (paragraphs 28–29) and at the same time indulging in a kind of ornate prose which does not match the rest of the essay. This is a minor point, to be sure. It is one questionable paragraph in a memorable record. But place paragraph 5 next to paragraphs 28–29. Are not the latter two more forcefully written (the string of adjectives in paragraph 5 is particularly unconvincing)? Is not the "climax" (paragraphs 28–29) the point at which the reader is ready, even breathless, for a description of the mighty flash, the reverberating thunder? You will want to answer these questions for yourself.

Questions on Content

1. Where did this first atomic explosion take place? Describe the area.
2. What instructions were given to the witnesses?
3. Was the bomb *dropped?* What does Laurence say about its detonation?
4. What did the explosion look like? Describe what followed the flash.

Add to your vocabulary: penultimate, prodigious, iridescent, blatant, metamorphosed.

Questions on Technique

1. Why should Laurence want to give us the names of so many men associated with this experiment, paragraphs 8 and 19, for example?

topic sentence: See Glossary.

2. Why does he devote four paragraphs to the directions on what the observers were to do at the time of the test?

3. This essay uses very little technical jargon such as Army talk or scientific terms. What does Laurence gain by avoiding it?

4. In paragraphs 34–35, Laurence compares his colleagues to primitive man dancing. Why is this comparison particularly apt here?

5. What effect does Laurence achieve with his last paragraph? Why is the cliché,° "can't hold a candle to it," so apt at this point in the essay?

Suggestions for Writing

1. Read Laurence's essay carefully, then rewrite it in the third person in 600–800 words as though your report were going to be part of an objective historical article.

2. Using any of the details of the essay you wish, reorganize and rewrite Laurence's report in 700 words.

3. With a little research, write an essay of 600 words on what happened in Hiroshima, Japan, on August 6, 1945. John Hersey's essay "Hiroshima" (*New Yorker,* August 31, 1946, and subsequently in book form) is a moving reportorial account of that event.

4. From your own experience, choose an event of some consequence to you. Discuss the importance of what happened and then the details surrounding it, choosing details which will illustrate *why* this event was significant. For example, you wanted for several reasons to make a journey on your own. One day you finally boarded a train or bus for X city. Or, you always wanted to take part in a play because (a) you like the theater, (b) you admire actors, (c) you need self-assurance. Then came the day you were selected for a role in the school play.

cliché: See Glossary.

WOLFGANG LANGEWIESCHE · *The Revolution in*
Small Plane Flying

"But I know very little about flying," you will say,
"and care even less about small planes. What has this
man Langewiesche to tell me that I can understand?"

A great deal, and Langewiesche is a man to listen to.
Frederick Lewis Allen, onetime editor of Harper's, called
him "one of the ablest expository writers using the English language in our time." Langewiesche is in love with
airplanes. He knows their history, their anatomy, and
their performance under all sorts of conditions. He has
been flying since he was a student of sociology at the
University of Chicago in the early 1930's. A pilot li-
censed on land and sea planes, on helicopters and
gliders, he has flown over many continents and oceans.
What is more, though he did not come to the United
States from Germany until 1929, he has been writing
about his adventures in a kind of idiomatic English
that one expects only from the native-born, and seldom
finds. I'll Take the High Road (1939) does for the Piper
Cub days what Lee Strout White does for the Model T.
A Flier's World (1951) describes the scientific, technolog-
ical, and human problems of flying, a kind of technical
manual for the layman. In fact, Langewiesche has written
for technical magazines as well as Harper's for years.

In this brief essay, Langewiesche demonstrates how
easy it is for a reporter to slip over into expository analysis, especially when he is so well-informed. His main
task here is to introduce us to the "new" small plane.
Why has it caused a revolution in flying? How did it
succeed? His approach is ingenious. For the first eighteen
paragraphs of this essay, Langewiesche contrasts the new

planes with the old. No need to guess which comes off the better. Then for fourteen paragraphs we confront economic and utilitarian aspects of these new planes. The last third of the essay raises some problems to come.

We have past, present, future, nicely dovetailed. It is a means of organization which he manipulates easily, and in which he is never constricted. His ultra-relaxed style—full of colloquialisms,° clever comparisons, the simplest of explanations—keeps us entertained while we are being informed. This is painless learning. It is reporting with more than a little analysis.

¹ A lot has happened to the small airplane since you last looked. It has become amazingly easy to fly. The war-trained pilot would not recognize flying now: it is hardly an art any more. Even those who learned after the war (in a big wave, mostly on the GI bill °) still learned on airplanes of the prewar type and carried away a picture of intricacy and peril that no longer covers the facts.

² The big change came only about seven years ago. It was more than mere "product-improvement"—sound-proofing, vibration-proofing, this or that new "feature." It was a shift to a new design formula, and it changed the very nature of the beast. And with this change has come an amazing boom in private flying. For the first time, after thirty years of trying, the small airplane really *sells*—and how!—and it sells not to a small circle of professional pilots and air-taxi operators and to sportsmen, but to the general public. The aerial automobile is here.

³ What is this new formula? A combination of three things: new landing gear, new controls, new means of aerial pathfinding. The new landing gear you can plainly see. The airplane used to sit on the ground with

colloquialisms: See Glossary.
GI bill: The original bill for World War II veterans contained three major benefits: guaranteed and insured loans; education and training; and readjustment allowances for unemployment.

its nose high, like a dog baying at the moon. Now it sits level, like an automobile. The third wheel (which turns like a castor) used to be under the tail. Now it is under the nose. The simple switch-around makes a profound difference.

4 On the old gear, the airplane was a nasty ground-vehicle. Landing was a delicate operation. You had to let the airplane sink to the ground in a nose-high attitude so that it would touch on all three wheels at once. This was the famous "three-point landing." If you touched front-wheels-first, the airplane would nose up and balloon back into the air. This was called a bounce. From it the airplane then came down, a few seconds later, to hit the ground again front-wheels-first and balloon off again—and so on. Each bounce was a little steeper, each ground-contact a little harder, with an increasing chance of cracking up. A pilot therefore had to learn not only how to three-point the airplane—difficult in itself—but also what to do in case he had failed to three-point: how to catch it on the top of a bounce with stick and throttle and let it down gently.

5 And bouncing was not the only wrong thing the airplane wanted to do. Once on the ground and rolling, it wanted to curve off to one side or the other and act like a dog chasing his tail. This was called a ground loop. If you let this happen, it tilted up sidewise and cracked up. So, at the moment of touchdown, the most critical part of the flight only began—fighting with rudder and brakes to keep the run straight. And that was not all. The airplane could also "drag a wing" or go up on its nose, or flip over on its back—all these tricks arising from the nature of the landing gear. And against each of those tricks, too, the pilot had to have a quick, well-practiced counter-trick for instant use.

6 And that's still not all. The difficult nature of the landing fed back into the landing *approach*. You can land three-point only at one speed—the slowest at which the airplane is capable of flying. Hence your approach glide also had to be slow. This meant you could not

maneuver at will. If you were a little too high, you could not simply nose down a little: you would have picked up excess speed, which would then have prevented you from landing. You would have "floated" just above the runway, unable to get down, until the excess speed had faded out. A clumsy pilot could use up a quarter-mile of airport just floating, and then set down and roll into the fence! Yet if you *didn't* nose down during the approach, you could, with a small misjudgment of your gliding angle, arrive over the edge of the airport with 200 feet of altitude and "overshoot" the whole field! Or again, in trying to avoid these errors, you could fall into their opposites: instead of overshooting, you could "undershoot"; instead of floating you might "pancake."

7 All this is now wiped out. With the new gear, you can slobber it on anyhow, it makes no difference: there is no bounce. The moment the wheels touch the ground, the airplane assumes a level, no-lift attitude and clings to the ground. What's more, it wants to run straight, more or less. Even if you don't steer it at all, it will not ground loop. It acts about like an automobile. And you can put the brakes on as hard as you please: you can't nose over! This ease of ground-handling feeds back into the landing approach. If you find yourself a little high, you *can* afford to glide a little steeper. If this makes you a little fast, you set the airplane down anyway and put on the brakes. To the Old Timer, a first-landing on the "tricycle" gear is a sort of joke. Just at the moment you are all set to start working, it's all over. The short cut makes you giggle.

8 The ease of landing now feeds back into all one's flying. On the old gear, flight was one of those things that are "easy to get, hard to get rid of." The last thing was always the hardest and your best chance of tearing up the ship. Now, if there is anything fit to land on, you are confident of your ability to land on it. In the old days, instructors preached: "A flight is not over until the airplane has stopped." Now, the flight is practically over when you first see the airport in the distance. And there

are plenty of airports. This induces tranquillity of spirit where there used to be tension.

9   The second item in the new formula is something you can't see. You can only feel it as you turn the airplane right or left. It is a mechanical linkage in the airplane's control system. It mechanizes a lot of work the pilot used to have to do by skill and feel. In flying an airplane, your feet rest on two rudder pedals which swing the airplane's nose right and left. Your hand is on a wheel which banks and unbanks the airplane. In the old airplane, the handwork had to be co-ordinated with the footwork—so much turn of the wheel, so much pressure on one or the other pedal, and this in just the right proportions, with right timing. If your co-ordination was poor, the airplane would skid and side-slip and fish-tail. In extreme cases, bad co-ordination could put you into a tailspin.

10   Just to turn right or left with an airplane was therefore really an art. The practice of turns used up practically all the training time that didn't go into approaches and landings. You did steep turns and shallow turns, gliding turns and climbing turns. You picked a road and did "S" turns across it. You picked two barns as pylons ° and did figure eights around them, not to mention the Lazy Eight, the Wing-over, and the Chandelle.° All this, essentially, to learn proper co-ordination of the controls.

11   "Can't you *feel* it?" the instructor would say. "You're using too much rudder."

12   And despite all the practice, many pilots were poor at co-ordination. The main cause of fatal accidents in flying was "loss of control in a turn."

13   All *that* is now mostly wiped out—both the learning task, and the danger factor. The co-ordination between stick and rudder has turned out to be mathematically calculable: it is not really a matter of feel, but a me-

pylons: posts or towers marking a prescribed course of flight.
Chandelle: an abrupt climbing turn, approximately to a stall.

chanical relationship. A mechanical linkage between the two controls can imitate it. Most small airplanes now have such a linkage (out of sight, in their innards) and co-ordinate themselves. Others accomplish much the same thing through an extra-long tail with an extra-big vertical fin on it. You can fly them with your feet on the floor, except during take-off and landing and violent maneuvers.

14   The theoretical simplicity of flying has suddenly begun to be a fact. You fly an airplane as you ride a bicycle: If you want to turn, you bank—and it comes around all by itself; if you level the wings again, it flies straight. With this simplicity, there drops away much of the training problems; also much risk: the mechanical co-ordination doesn't get tense and doesn't make the mistakes that lead to loss of control. Now you cruise with two fingers on the wheel.

15   The third item in the new formula is electronic navigation. You no longer rely on map reading, and you can no longer get lost. It used to be normal, almost required, for a pilot to get lost at least once or twice, and it was a terrifying experience. You could not ask anybody. To do that, you had first to find an airport; to do that, you had to know where you were. So you were being carried away by a relentless monster, and steadily getting lower on fuel, and you knew that in the end you would come down willy-nilly.

16   One way to keep from getting lost was to follow "the iron compass"—the railroad. But suppose you followed the wrong branch? So you learned to trust your real compass. You drew a straight line on the map, with a mark every ten miles; you learned to keep track of time, to make notes. In bad weather you flew with your thumb on the map, moving it forward as you went, so as not to lose your place.

17   All *that* is now wiped out. The United States (and much of the rest of the world) is dotted with radio lighthouses, called Omni-Directional Range Stations, which

send out a directional radio signal—a signal which is slightly different in each direction. Aboard the airplane, a special receiver interprets these signals. To find out where you are you twirl a dial until a needle centers; you then read off a scale: "I am now north of the Woodstown Omni." Next you tune in on another Omni station—say, Centerville—and read: "I am now west of Centerville Omni." You look at the map; you run your finger north from Woodstown and west from Centerville: where the two lines cross, that's where you are. It's simple. You are always on a known and numbered track (in fact, always on the crossing of two tracks), and though the tracks are only radio beams and might seem insubstantial, they soon become as real as if they were numbered highways. Many pilots now fly with maps that show no terrain features at all. They navigate by radio only, and keep the great American landscape for a pet.

18 Thus the new-formula airplane dissolves, in three big hunks, most of the difficulty of flying: approach-and-landing; co-ordination and the turn; navigation. Beyond these three, there never was anything really difficult. The law still requires forty hours of training for a private pilot's license, but the difference is that more time can now be spent teaching the practical use of the machine in actual cross-country flight: the use of the radio, the logic and courtesies of air traffic, the judgment of weather. The license means more. In the old days, the holder of a brand-new private license was fit at best to take his girl on a local sight-seeing hop. Now he is ready to start *using* the airplane. A friend of mine runs a small flying school in Massachusetts. He says: "Anybody who gets a private license here can rent any of my airplanes the next day and fly it to California, if he likes."

19 The new formula has changed not only the technique of piloting, but also the whole style of the small airplane, its sociology and economics. Under the old formula, the way to make an airplane easy to fly was to make it slow and light, with big wings and a small en-

gine. This is also the best way to make it cheap—and manufacturers struggled to bring the small airplane within reach of people who buy second cars or small motorboats. The highest development of this type was the famous Piper Cub. It cruised at 70, landed at 30. It carried fuel for 180 miles.

[20] It had two seats. It cost less than $2,000. It was so light and slow it made the air feel thick, like mashed potatoes. But it was a "real airplane," representative of all the airplanes of its era, from the *Spirit of St. Louis* to the DC3. That is, it gave you every opportunity to make every mistake you might make on those other airplanes: On a Cub you could bounce, ground loop, overshoot, undershoot, drag a wing, pancake, stall, spin, and get lost just as on any airplane. But because it was so light and slow, it did these things gently and gave you time to correct your errors. Hundreds of thousands of people learned to fly on it. It was in all respects a machine within the reach of the average man. Only—it didn't go very fast very far. It lacked utility.

[21] Under the new formula, small airplanes can be comparatively heavy, small-winged, high-powered, and still be easy to handle. The new airplanes cruise at 135, 150, 200 mph, land at 60. Almost all have four seats and carry ample luggage. The two-seat airplane has almost faded out. The non-stop range is 600 to 1,200 miles. The public handles these lively machines without trouble because they don't bounce or ground loop, are self-coordinating, and have electronic means of orientation. And the new machine is of course much more useful. At 150 mph, flying direct from where you are to where you want to go, you can beat airliners that fly 300 mph but *don't* go exactly where you want to go, don't go when you are ready, and don't go straight.

[22] The new machine is also much more expensive: $15,000 to $20,000 is today "medium-priced." Miraculously, this has not stopped sales. On the contrary. The industry has discovered that expensive airplanes are easier to sell than cheap ones. Even a cheap airplane is

too expensive for the man who has no practical use for
it. Even an expensive airplane pays its way for the man
who has a lot of business traveling to do. Almost all airplanes now are sold to companies or otherwise hooked
onto a business expense account, and the elegant word
to use is "executive airplanes" for the smaller ones,
"corporation airplanes" for the multi-engined ones.

[23] So the new airplane has brought out a new type of
owner and pilot. All through the 'thirties and again in
the first postwar decade, most pilots were young, and
flew mostly for the needs of their souls; or else by way of
training for a professional flying career. Or both. Now,
the typical private airplane owner is over forty, an executive, stabilized by a wife, children, home, country
club, and job. He flies because he likes to fly—"You can't
sell an airplane to anybody who isn't crazy about flying,"
says a dealer—but he expects utility. He wants to go in
a hurry, with comfort and privacy, and to get home for
the weekend.

[24] This means a different style of flying. "Buzzing" has
stopped. So has the emphasis on skill. Almost nobody
does a Chandelle any more. On the new airplanes, anybody can fly well enough, and the duffer can land almost as short as the maestro. The practice of simulated
emergencies has stopped: the simulated forced landings,
intentional spins, steep turns, power stalls. Some of this
practice, we know now, was more dangerous than the
emergencies it was supposed to prepare for. The new
pilot is more like the average American driver. His technique is unambitious but he is safe, perhaps for that
very reason. He doesn't try anything funny. He has an
airplane that can really go places and so he goes, more
or less straight, at a high, efficient, altitude, in long hops.
That is the safest kind of flying there is.

[25] Now, it is the non-flying public that lags behind the
times. Most people now think about the small airplane
in terms that would have been approximately correct in
1939—as a sport, ranging somewhere between sports-

car racing and mountain climbing. You *can* afford it, and it might be a lot of fun, but . . . That the small airplane has a practical use, that it is in fact a business machine, is not yet understood. Yet for every businessman who now uses an airplane, ten others could use it equally well. They just haven't heard.

[26] One reason is that the airplane makes its poorest showing in a region which still dominates the world of print and radio—along the Northeastern Seaboard, and especially New York. The weather there is often bad; the Alleghenies reach into the clouds and seal that section off from the rest of the country. The big airline fields don't make the private flier welcome. They are surrounded by special high-density air traffic zones in which special regulations apply. Other available fields often have poor facilities, are hard to reach from town, and unattractive. At the same time, New York and Washington have good airline service to all parts of the country. So the private airplane is less needed and can't compete so well.

[27] Toward the West and South, all those values change. The country is mostly flat, distances are great, and public transport is poor, especially crosswise to each region's main line of travel. The weather gets progressively drier. Partly for this reason, the Rocky Mountains are not the Great Wall you'd think they'd be. Toward the South, too, the weather gets clearer. In most of the U. S., unflyable weather is fairly rare, and of short duration.

[28] The psychological climate also improves away from the Northeast. Cities realize what solid-gold traffic the small airplane brings. Chicago, Cleveland, Milwaukee, Memphis offer the private flier a downtown landing strip at the waterfront. Many other cities have special fields devoted mostly or entirely to private traffic, well-equipped and attractive and close to town. Just for example, Shreveport, New Orleans, St. Paul, Seattle, Atlanta, Oklahoma City. In Phoenix or San Francisco, you taxi up to a magnificent terminal building purely for private ships.

[29] But of all this, the general public sees little. The airline passenger's eye cannot distinguish the many landing strips on farms and ranches, at resorts, near oil wells and construction jobs or high up in the National Forests. He sometimes sees the private fleet but only as a flock of gay-colored birds that sit at the other side of the field. He calls them all "Piper Cubs" or "sports jobs." To the layman, a $25,000 machine is almost indistinguishable from the $2,500 trainer. A $75,000 airplane can look ridiculous when it taxies among the $3-million airliners. Here comes a little boy, people feel, just *playing* airplane.

[30] It's a sort of secret world. Gone are the days of the leather jacket and the silver lapel-wings. In a hotel dining room, only a pilot's ear can tell, from the conversation at the next table, that those people have flown in from Texas in a Cessna. For that matter, there is very little to say about a machine which, like the airplane in the American West, just simply *works*. The flier today has fewer adventures per hour, and many fewer per mile, than the motorist.

[31] The statistics of private flying are also deceptive. There are about 35,000 private airplanes in heavy business use. Most of them are four-seat or more, and of the new formula. Another 35,000 small airplanes are used for training, for crop-dusting, and for pleasure. Many of them fly very little; most of them are two-seaters and survivors from the old formula. The total number is not much more than we had ten years ago, and they are involved in a disproportionate number of accidents.°

[32] What does not show is the striking rise in value, activity, and seriousness of economic purpose, compared with ten years ago. Roughly speaking, the small airplane now goes twice as fast, carries twice as many people, and flies twice as many hours per year as it used to. It almost

---

° Partly because of these old planes, private flying is still hazardous. The Cornell-Guggenheim Aviation Safety Center recently reported that 778 lives were lost in 4,800 accidents to 70,000 private and business aircraft in 1959.—*The Editors, Harper's Magazine.*

never flies for the sake of flying, but almost always on business, or at least for the sake of transporting persons. The total increase in activity is therefore staggering. In hours flown, or airplane miles flown, private aviation is now the heaviest user of the American air space. The oil industry alone now owns more multi-engined airplanes than the airlines do. In passenger-miles flown, of course, the airlines still dwarf everything.

³³ The amazing thing in all this is the "cultural lag." Mechanically-linked controls are the oldest thing in heavier-than-air aviation. They were used by the Wright brothers in their first airplane. The level landing, anti-bounce undercarriage also was used by many pioneers. Later, these solutions were forgotten in the effort to save weight, to get more performance, and to solve pesky practical problems such as, for instance, how to land and taxi cross-wind. They were re-synthesized in the middle 'thirties by a brilliant man, Fred E. Weick, into some airplanes that were perfect specimens of the new formula. It took the small-plane industry almost twenty years to switch solidly to the new formula.

³⁴ Why? Inertia * maybe; but also—the customer did not want his airplane easy to fly. People flew airplanes mostly for the purpose of becoming a pilot—or of *being* a pilot. What was the point of flying an airplane that needed no co-ordination, that would not bounce, and on which you could not demonstrate spin-recoveries to a government inspector? Bureaucracy * helped by restricting the licenses of those who learned on the easy-fly airplanes. So they were indeed not really quite pilots.

³⁵ At the same time, the small airplane itself also lags behind. Even now, it is only half as docile,* safe, and useful as it could well be, using only the technical means available. The small airplane still has no brake—in flight, that is. And therefore, the approach-and-landing is still, even on the new landing gear, a maneuver requiring more skill than anything the auto driver has to do. In a car, you can go down a hill of any steepness with any

desired slowness. In an airplane, you can't. The angle at which you descend still affects your speed. You therefore still cannot simply and effortlessly steer your airplane down to a spot and set it down on it with precision. It's still a maneuver requiring logic and planning. But jet liners and jet fighters now have flight-brakes; sail planes have long had means of killing altitude without picking up speed, and the small airplane will have them too.

[36] The airplane still lacks the secret quality which makes a car so easy to drive—the tendency to go straight unless *commanded* to turn. You have to *make* a car turn by considerable force on the wheel; to keep it turning, you have to keep holding the wheel deflected; and the moment you release the wheel, the car straightens out. The airplane now has the same stability *on the ground,* but not yet in the air. In flight, the airplane always wants to go into a turn, unprovoked by the pilot, to one side or the other. And it won't come out of itself: if allowed its head, it goes into a descending spiral. So, to fly straight, the pilot must nudge the airplane every few seconds by small but positive actions on the controls. If he looks down at his map a little too long, he will, on looking up, find himself in a banked turn, nose-down.

[37] This is the Why and How behind that famous 29,000-foot spiral dive of an airliner over the Atlantic, last year. It is also the reason why "blind" flight, *i.e.,* flight through clouds, is a problem. And in all flight it puts a great work load on the pilot. But you can build into an airplane the same self-straightening tendency an automobile has. Such airplanes have already been demonstrated. Only the need for this quality is not yet recognized: the lag again.

[38] The small airplane's greatest handicap is the weather. It's not really a skill problem, but one of utility. When the weather gets too bad, the small airplane simply has to sit on the ground and wait. In some respects, the weather problem has become worse. In today's faster airplanes, you can no longer sneak through by hedge-hopping, *i.e.,* flying low along a railroad track

or highway: obstructions would show up too suddenly.
And the faster airplane can't turn so sharply. Also, a
terrible new danger has risen—the television tower that
stands in some unexpected place, spidery and almost invisible.

39 The only way to beat the weather is the airline way,
flying blind *through* the clouds or to the top of them.
Pioneers among private fliers are now doing this. But it
requires a professional level of skill, much special equipment, and a special license. What's so hard about it is
not the primary task—to keep the airplane on its course
and to know where you are—but secondary problems.
It's the lag once more. Blind flight is legal only under
air traffic control. Controllers' instructions are given to
the pilot in rapid speech over a rather low-fi radio. They
are often hard to hear correctly, and even harder to
grasp.

40 Someday, the ground will issue orders through some
"read-out" device on the airplane's panel—red and green
lights, arrows, etc., which will tell the pilot to "hold" or
go, climb or descend, take this course or that. When this
comes, flying *through* the weather will be as easy as following the signs and traffic lights through a strange city.
To make it come requires no new invention, but merely
the use of existing art: "merely" a nation-wide, multi-
billion-dollar system of electronic devices. It is a problem of government rather than of science.

41 The air traffic problem exists only because of a lag
in government action. Fortunately, it's a problem the
private ship has in common with the airliner and the
military. It is aviation's most pressing problem, and will
certainly be solved. Once it is solved, not only will we
fly almost regardless of weather, but there will be plenty
of air space for everybody. The air only *seems* crowded
—because our present control techniques are so wasteful
of air space. Figuratively speaking, we are allowing only
one automobile per city block, because we have not yet
invented the traffic light, the stop sign, the white line.

The real traffic-carrying capacity of the air is unlimited, for all practical purposes of this century.

42 And so, fantastic as it sounds, it's now in the bag that soon—another twenty years?—the airplane will be not only the fastest private means of transport, but also the safest, the most weatherproof, and the most effortless to handle.

ANALYSIS

It would be difficult to disagree with Langewiesche's opening sentence. We have not, frankly, looked at the small plane very closely. The Piper Cub is familiar because it is parked near the little hangars on the "amateur" airfields outside our hometowns. The Viscount turbo-props and the Boeing jetliners are more likely to be the planes we know from use. But Langewiesche will have us "looking" before this essay is completed. His topic sentence ° comes at the end of the second paragraph. He is determined to prove that any one of his readers now and in the future will find flying the new small planes easy and enjoyable. Langewiesche is thoroughly convinced by his own arguments. This conviction is refreshing in a report that could otherwise be routine.

How shall he explain the three improved elements of the "new formula": landing gear, controls, and pathfinding? By comparison. One paragraph barrel rolls into the next: "And bouncing was not the only thing wrong," "And that's still not all," "All this is now wiped out," "All *that* is now mostly wiped out." Paragraph 18—the reader is there before he knows it—begins with a convincing "Thus the new-formula airplane dissolves, in three big hunks, most of the difficulty of flying." Langewiesche is not above using the colloquial ° "hunks" in the middle of a discussion on how modern inventions have taken the risk out of small plane flying.

Beginning with paragraph 19 Langewiesche gets down to basic facts. Who owns these new planes? How much do they cost? Where are they used? Langewiesche has enticed us into the air, as it were, before he gives us the

topic sentence: See Glossary.   colloquial: See Glossary.

brute facts. If a medium-priced plane costs \$15,000–\$20,000, shall we read further? Indeed, yes. Langewiesche is always optimistic about the future. "It is the non-flying public that lags behind the times," he tells us, in paragraph 25. Why? He tells us that, too. He is still on that subject at the close of paragraph 34.

The last eight paragraphs are more expository analysis than reporting. Langewiesche gives us his explanation of why "the small airplane itself also lags behind." The whole subject of blind flight might well, you say, belong in another essay. It is surely more complicated than he makes it sound. But that is exactly his point. These eight paragraphs are tied to his title (and to the topic sentence of paragraph 2) by this one main problem of the future: how to beat the weather. We need " 'merely' a nation-wide, multi-billion-dollar system of electronic devices." *That* is the complex subject he does not raise. The blind flight *is* part of the revolution now at hand. Langewiesche's concluding paragraph is as difficult to disagree with as his opening sentence. His last twenty-five words are a prediction and a summing-up. He makes no claims which he did not substantiate in the clearest expository prose.

Questions on Content

1. Describe flying an old-model small plane. How does Langewiesche use these terms: ground loop, landing approach, undershoot, pancake, tailspin?
2. In what specific ways have the new small planes caused a "revolution"?
3. Why are small private planes of more use in the West and South than in the East?
4. Why are the statistics of private flying deceptive?
5. Why is blind flight legal only under air traffic control?

Add to your vocabulary: inertia, bureaucracy, docile.

Questions on Technique

1. In the midst of fairly technical explanation, Langewiesche is often extremely informal in his style. For example, a ground loop is "like a dog chasing his tail" (paragraph 5). The new tricycle landing gear is a short cut that "makes you giggle" (paragraph 7). What

other examples can you find? Why do you suppose he uses informal diction ° to describe scientific material?

2. How does Langewiesche explain the Omni-Directional Range Station? Could he make this explanation more visual and thus clearer? How?

3. In what sense does Langewiesche use the term "cultural lag"? In what way does it involve our government as well as the customer and the plane?

4. This essay is written with an emphasis on the second person: "A lot has happened . . . since *you* last looked." What effect does Langewiesche want to achieve? Would you prefer to read this information in a straight technical report? Why?

Suggestions for Writing

1. Using the facts Langewiesche gives us, rewrite this essay in 500 words as though your report on the new small plane were to appear in a weekly news magazine.

2. Using an informal style, describe a landing you are making in an old-model light plane.

3. You are taking your first trip on a large commercial plane or steamship. "Report" it to a friend in a letter of 350–500 words.

4. Write a report on the compact automobiles, comparing them to the larger models. Or discuss the influx of foreign cars in the American market.

5. In 600 words, report on a "revolution" you know at first hand: the changes in athletic rules, "cool" jazz as opposed to Dixieland bands or swing, abstract painting, improvements in stage equipment, what television can do that radio could never have achieved, new trends in the movies.

diction: See Glossary.

DARRELL HUFF · *How to Lie with Statistics*

"How-to" books have been popular for many years and may well continue to be, for the "do-it-yourself" craze shows no signs of abating. As a contributor to Pop-ular Science, Darrell Huff has done his share in explain-ing how to pave your yard, install plastic counter tops, judge used power tools, and build an abacus. He has been an editor of Liberty, Look, *and* Better Homes and Gardens. *He is now a partner in Cavedale Craftsmen, an organization that prepares how-to-do-it articles for mag-azines and instruction manuals for manufacturers.*

In 1950, Huff published in Harper's *an article on statistics which proved so popular that four years later he expanded it into a book with the same title. It is said that his interest in statistical analysis began with a course in college. One wonders, however, when he began analyzing analyses. In "How to Lie with Statistics," Huff does not intend to report to us specific facts. What he does wish to demonstrate is how analysis experts can lead us to any conclusions they desire. The first para-graph is all he needs for a springboard. He is bemused and annoyed by distorted reasoning. He is particularly annoyed by the ease with which statistics can be used to bolster distorted conclusions. Thomas Huxley defined the inductive method of thinking as "assemblying the facts." Huff warns us that* interpreting *the facts is the "higher" grade of reasoning and that we must be wary of whose analysis we are reading. What statistics mean depends on the director of the survey.*

If, by chance, you feel statistical analysis is a tech-nique that the twentieth century has inflated, alas, un-wisely, consider this remark in the mid-nineteenth century by Benjamin Disraeli, Queen Victoria's prime minister: "There are three kinds of lies: lies, damned lies, and statistics."

1   "The average Yaleman, Class of '24," *Time* magazine reported last year ° after reading something in the New York *Sun,* a newspaper published in those days, "makes $25,111 a year."

2   Well, good for him!

3   But, come to think of it, what does this improbably precise and salubrious * figure mean? Is it, as it appears to be, evidence that if you send your boy to Yale you won't have to work in your old age and neither will he? Is this average a mean ° or is it a median? ° What kind of sample is it based on? You could lump one Texas oilman with two hundred hungry free-lance * writers and report *their* average income as $25,000-odd a year. The arithmetic is impeccable,* the figure is convincingly precise, and the amount of meaning there is in it you could put in your eye.

4   In just such ways is the secret language of statistics, so appealing in a fact-minded culture, being used to sensationalize, inflate, confuse, and over-simplify. Statistical terms are necessary in reporting the mass data of social and economic trends, business conditions, "opinion" polls, this year's census. But without writers who use the words with honesty and understanding and readers who know what they mean, the result can only be semantic ° nonsense.

5   In popular writing on scientific research, the abused statistic is almost crowding out the picture of the white-jacketed hero laboring overtime without time-and-a-half in an ill-lit laboratory. Like the "little dash of powder, little pot of paint," statistics are making many an im-

last year: that is, 1949.   mean: the arithmetic average.
median: the middle number in a sequence of numbers. If five men
    earn $2, $4, $7, $8, and $9, respectively, the *mean* wage is $6 (the
    total divided by five) ; the *median* wage is $7.
semantic: pertaining to signification or meaning.

portant fact "look like what she ain't." Here are some of the ways it is done.

⁶ *The sample with the built-in bias.* Our Yale men—or Yalemen, as they say in the Time-Life building—belong to this flourishing group. The exaggerated estimate of their income is not based on all members of the class nor on a random or representative sample of them. At least two interesting categories of 1924-model Yale men have been excluded.

⁷ First there are those whose present addresses are unknown to their classmates. Wouldn't you bet that these lost sheep are earning less than the boys from prominent families and the others who can be handily reached from a Wall Street office?

⁸ There are those who chucked the questionnaire into the nearest wastebasket. Maybe they didn't answer because they were not making enough money to brag about. Like the fellow who found a note clipped to his first pay check suggesting that he consider the amount of his salary confidential: "Don't worry," he told the boss. "I'm just as ashamed of it as you are."

⁹ Omitted from our sample then are just the two groups most likely to depress the average. The $25,111 figure is beginning to account for itself. It may indeed be a true figure for those of the Class of '24 whose addresses are known and who are willing to stand up and tell how much they earn. But even that requires a possibly dangerous assumption that the gentlemen are telling the truth.

¹⁰ To be dependable to any useful degree at all, a sampling study must use a representative sample (which can lead to trouble too) or a truly random one. If *all* the Class of '24 is included, that's all right. If every tenth name on a complete list is used, that is all right too, and so is drawing an adequate number of names out of a hat. The test is this: Does every name in the group have an equal chance to be in the sample?

¹¹ You'll recall that ignoring this requirement was

what produced the *Literary Digest's*° famed fiasco. When names for polling were taken only from telephone books and subscription lists, people who did not have telephones or *Literary Digest* subscriptions had no chance to be in the sample. They possibly did not mind this underprivilege a bit, but their absence was in the end very hard on the magazine that relied on the figures.

12 This leads to a moral: You can prove about anything you want to by letting your sample bias itself. As a consumer of statistical data—a reader, for example, of a news magazine—remember that no statistical conclusion can rise above the quality of the sample it is based upon. In the absence of information about the procedures behind it, you are not warranted in giving any credence at all to the result.

13 *The truncated,* or gee-whiz, graph.* If you want to show some statistical information quickly and clearly, draw a picture of it. Graphic presentation is the thing today. If you don't mind misleading the hasty looker, or if you quite clearly *want* to deceive him, you can save some space by chopping the bottom off many kinds of graphs.

14 Suppose you are showing the upward trend of national income month by month for a year. The total rise, as in one recent year, is 7 per cent, as shown in the graph on p. 219. That is clear enough. Anybody can see that the trend is slightly upward. You are showing a 7 per cent increase and that is exactly what it looks like.

Literary Digest: a popular magazine, begun in 1890. In the presidential campaign of 1936, a *Digest* poll showed the Republican candidate Landon as winning over the Democratic candidate Roosevelt. This error (Roosevelt carried all states except Maine and Vermont) was responsible in large part for the magazine's suspension of publication and merging with *Time* in 1938.

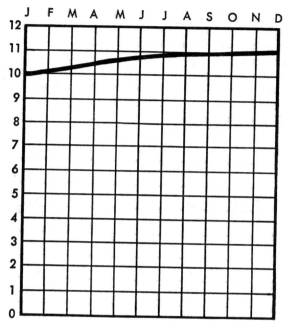

¹⁵ But it lacks schmaltz.° So you chop off the bottom, this way:

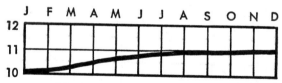

The figures are the same. It is the same graph and nothing has been falsified—except the impression that it gives. Anyone looking at it can just feel prosperity throbbing in the arteries of the country. It is a subtler equivalent of editing "National income rose 7 per cent" into ". . . climbed a whopping 7 per cent."

¹⁶ It is vastly more effective, however, because of that illusion of objectivity.

schmaltz: As Huff uses it, it means "kick."

17 *The souped-up graph.* Sometimes truncating is not enough. The trifling rise in something or other still looks almost as insignificant as it is. You can make that 7 per cent look livelier than 100 per cent ordinarily does. Simply change the proportion between the ordinate and the abscissa.° There's no rule against it, and it does give your graph a prettier shape.

18 But it exaggerates, to say the least, something awful:

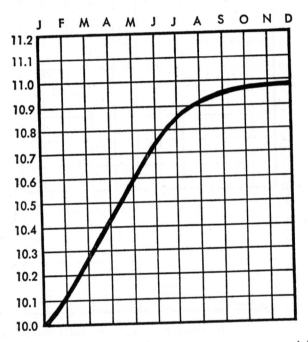

19 *The well-chosen average.* I live near a country neighborhood for which I can report an average income of $15,000. I could also report it as $3,500.

the ordinate and the abscissa: In Huff's graph, the horizontal markings (J, F, M, A, etc., standing for the months of the year) are the axis of abscissa; the vertical figures (0–12 in the first graph, 10.0–11.2 in the "souped-up" graph) are the axis of the ordinate.

20 If I should want to sell real estate hereabouts to people having a high snobbery content, the first figure would be handy. The second figure, however, is the one to use in an argument against raising taxes, or the local bus fare.

21 Both are legitimate averages, legally arrived at. Yet it is obvious that at least one of them must be as misleading as an out-and-out lie. The $15,000-figure is a mean, the arithmetic average of the incomes of all the families in the community. The smaller figure is a median; it might be called the income of the average family in the group. It indicates that half the families have less than $3,500 a year and half have more.

22 Here is where some of the confusion about averages comes from. Many human characteristics have the grace to fall into what is called the "normal" distribution. If you draw a picture of it, you get a curve that is shaped like a bell. Mean and median fall at about the same point, so it doesn't make very much difference which you use.

23 But some things refuse to follow this neat curve. Income is one of them. Incomes for most large areas will range from under $1,000 a year to upward of $50,000. Almost everybody will be under $10,000, way over on the left-hand side of that curve.

24 One of the things that made the income figure for the "average Yaleman" meaningless is that we are not told whether it is a mean or a median. It is not that one type of average is invariably better than the other; it depends upon what you are talking about. But neither gives you any real information—and either may be highly misleading—unless you know which of those kinds of average it is.

25 In the country neighborhood I mentioned, almost everyone has less than the average—the mean, that is—of $15,000. These people are all small farmers, except for a trio of millionaire week-enders who bring up the mean enormously.

26 You can be pretty sure that when an income average

is given in the form of a mean nearly everybody has less than that.

27 *The insignificant difference or the elusive error.* Your two children Peter and Linda (we might as well give them modish names while we're about it) take intelligence tests. Peter's I.Q., you learn, is 98 and Linda's is 101. Aha! Linda is your brighter child.

28 Is she? An intelligence test is, or purports to be, a sampling of intellect. An I.Q., like other products of sampling, is a figure with a statistical error, which expresses the precision or reliability of the figure. The size of this probable error can be calculated. For their test the makers of the much-used Revised Stanford-Binet have found it to be about 3 per cent. So Peter's indicated I.Q. of 98 really means only that there is an even chance that it falls between 95 and 101. There is an equal probability that it falls somewhere else—below 95 or above 101. Similarly, Linda's has no better than a fifty-fifty chance of being within the fairly sizeable range of 98 to 104.

29 You can work out some comparisons from that. One is that there is rather better than one chance in four that Peter, with his lower I.Q. rating, is really at least three points smarter than Linda. A statistician doesn't like to consider a difference significant unless you can hand him odds a lot longer than that.

30 Ignoring the error in a sampling study leads to all kinds of silly conclusions. There are magazine editors to whom readership surveys are gospel; with a 40 per cent readership reported for one article and a 35 per cent for another, they demand more like the first. I've seen even smaller differences given tremendous weight, because statistics are a mystery and numbers are impressive. The same thing goes for market surveys and so-called public-opinion polls. The rule is that you cannot make a valid ***** comparison between two such figures unless you know the deviations.° And unless the difference between the

deviations: straying from the standard.

figures is many times greater than the probable error of each, you have only a guess that the one appearing greater really is

[31] Otherwise you are like the man choosing a camp site from a report of mean temperature alone. One place in California with a mean annual temperature of 61 is San Nicolas Island on the south coast, where it always stays in the comfortable range between 47 and 87. Another with a mean of 61 is in the inland desert, where the thermometer hops around from 15 to 104. The deviation from the mean marks the difference, and you can freeze or roast if you ignore it.

[32] *The one-dimensional picture.* Suppose you have just two or three figures to compare—say the average weekly wage of carpenters in the United States and another country. The sums might be $60 and $30. An ordinary bar chart makes the difference graphic. [See following.]

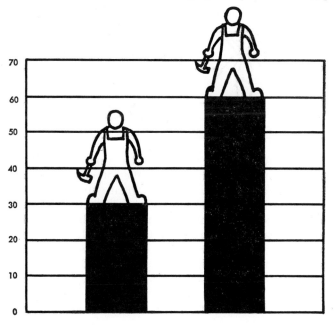

That is an honest picture. It looks good for American carpenters, but perhaps it does not have quite the oomph you are after. Can't you make that difference appear overwhelming and at the same time give it what I am afraid is known as eye-appeal? Of course you can. Following tradition, you represent these sums by pictures of money bags. If the $30 bag is one inch high, you draw the $60 bag two inches high. That's in proportion, isn't it?

³³ The catch is, of course, that the American's money bag, being twice as tall as that of the $30 man, covers an area on your page four times as great. And since your two-dimensional picture represents an object that would in fact have three dimensions, the money bags actually would differ much more than that. The volumes of any two similar solids vary as the cubes of their heights. If the unfortunate foreigner's bag holds $30 worth of dimes, the American's would hold not $60 but a neat $240.

³⁴ You didn't say that, though, did you? And you can't

be blamed, you're only doing it the way practically everybody else does.

35 *The ever-impressive decimal.* For a spurious * air of precision that will lend all kinds of weight to the most disreputable statistics, consider the decimal.

36 Ask a hundred citizens how many hours they slept last night. Come out with a total of, say, 7.813. Your data are far from precise to begin with. Most people will miss their guess by fifteen minutes or more and some will recall five sleepless minutes as half a night of tossing insomnia.

37 But go ahead, do your arithmetic, announce that people sleep an average of 7.813 hours a night. You will sound as if you knew precisely what you are talking about. If you were foolish enough to say 7.8 (or "almost 8") hours it would sound like what it was—an approximation.

38 *The semiattached figure.* If you can't prove what you want to prove, demonstrate something else and pretend that they are the same thing. In the daze that follows the collision of statistics with the human mind, hardly anybody will notice the difference. The semiattached figure is a durable device guaranteed to stand you in good stead. It always has.

39 If you can't prove that your nostrum ° cures colds, publish a sworn laboratory report that the stuff killed 31,108 germs in a test tube in eleven seconds. There may be no connection at all between assorted germs in a test tube and the whatever-it-is that produces colds, but people aren't going to reason that sharply, especially while sniffling.

40 *The unwarranted assumption, or* post hoc ° *rides again.* The interrelation of cause and effect, so often

nostrum: a quack medicine.
post hoc: short for *post hoc, ergo propter hoc,* meaning in Latin "after this, therefore because of it" and designating an error in logic: taking for a cause of something that which is merely earlier in time.

obscure anyway, can be most neatly hidden in statistical data.

41 Somebody once went to a good deal of trouble to find out if cigarette smokers make lower college grades than nonsmokers. They did. This naturally pleased many people, and they made much of it.

42 The unwarranted assumption, of course, was that smoking had produced dull minds. It seemed vaguely reasonable on the face of it, so it was quite widely accepted. But it really proved nothing of the sort, any more than it proved that poor grades drive students to the solace of tobacco. Maybe the relationship worked in one direction, maybe in the other. And maybe all this is only an indication that the sociable sort of fellow who is likely to take his books less than seriously is also likely to sit around and smoke many cigarettes.

43 Permitting statistical treatment to befog causal relationships is little better than superstition. It is like the conviction among the people of the Hebrides ° that body lice produce good health. Observation over the centuries had taught them that people in good health had lice and sick people often did not. *Ergo,* lice made a man healthy. Everybody should have them.

44 Scantier evidence, treated statistically at the expense of common sense, has made many a medical fortune and many a medical article in magazines, including professional ones. More sophisticated observers finally got things straightened out in the Hebrides. As it turned out, almost everybody in those circles had lice most of the time. But when a man took a fever (quite possibly carried to him by those same lice) and his body became hot, the lice left.

45 Here you have cause and effect not only reversed but intermingled.

46 There you have a primer in some ways to use statistics to deceive. A well-wrapped statistic is better than

Hebrides: islands in the Atlantic Ocean west of Scotland.

Hitler's ° "big lie": it misleads, yet it can't be pinned onto you.

47 Is this little list altogether too much like a manual for swindlers? Perhaps I can justify it in the manner of the retired burglar whose published reminiscences amounted to a graduate course in how to pick a lock and muffle a footfall: The crooks already know these tricks. Honest men must learn them in self-defense.

ANALYSIS

Huff's essay explains itself. He organizes in the simplest fashion: a brief introduction, nine examples (some with drawings), and an extremely brief conclusion. He is assured that his reader will find his categories clear and his reasoning just. Wisely, we think, he does not linger on his initial statistic about the Yale men, but varies the kind of pronouncements of which he, as analyst, has grown to be skeptical.

What's more he does not "explode" obviously gross exaggerations. That would be too easy; for example, Abraham Lincoln's prediction that the U.S. population would reach 230,689,914 in 1930 or Mark Twain's tongue-in-cheek demonstration that, according to statistics, we can expect the lower Mississippi River to be only a mile and three-quarters long by the year 2616. The strength of this essay lies in its *ordinary* statistical examples and its straightforward discounting of them. Peter's and Linda's I.Q.: how many times have you heard of this unquestioned faith in numbers? The well-chosen average: how often have you wondered whether grades in school measure what they are supposed to measure? We do not need to look only at the ad-men for our examples. Everyone of us is guilty of accepting data and trends and polls without questioning them closely enough.

Hitler: Adolf Hitler (1889–1945?), Nazi leader and dictator of Germany, 1933–1945. In his book *Mein Kampf* he declared that ". . . the great masses of the people . . . will more easily fall victims to a great lie than to a small one." Because he practiced this technique in his propaganda during World War II his name has become associated with the "big lie."

Finally, Huff calls his essay "How to Lie with Statistics." Do not be fooled by his title. He is writing on a serious subject. In order not to sound moralizing, he has reversed his approach. His examples show us how the easy lie is achieved. You might think he speaks here as though (see his last paragraph) he were writing a manual for swindlers. Not at all. "Honest men must learn [these tricks] in self-defense," he tells us. He is not attacking statistics. He respects honest data honestly interpreted. But "semantic nonsense" is another matter. Observe, then, how skillfully Huff analyzes nonsense. His conclusions are brief because his analysis is so convincing.

Questions on Content

1. How does Huff distinguish between a *random* sample and a *representative* sample? What does he mean by "letting your sample bias itself"?
2. How can you create an "illusion of objectivity" and at the same time distort meaning (paragraphs 13–16)?
3. How does "ignoring the error in a sampling study lead to all kinds of silly conclusions" (paragraph 30)? Why is "deviation" an important component of a sampling?
4. How can statistics be used "to befog causal relationships" (paragraphs 40–44)?

Add to your vocabulary: salubrious, free-lance, impeccable, truncated, valid, deviations, spurious.

Questions on Technique

1. Huff devotes very little space to introducing his subject. What advantage does he gain by beginning abruptly with his illustrations?
2. Huff breaks his essay into nine distinct divisions or examples. What difficulties might he have encountered by trying to run them all together, as, for example, Wolfgang Langewiesche does in grouping his arguments?
3. Consider the language of this essay. How is it adapted to the subject matter? Why does he use so many short sentences?
4. How do the graphs and drawings help the author demonstrate his thesis?

Suggestions for Writing

1. Take any one of Huff's nine categories and enlarge his discussion by citing more examples. Perhaps you can incorporate the advertisements in your favorite magazines. In what ways are you being persuaded to buy this or try that?
2. The last chapter of Huff's book is called "How to Talk Back to Statistics." Subheadings in this chapter read: "Who Says So?" "How Does He Know?" "What's Missing?" "Did Somebody Change the Subject?" and "Does It Make Sense?" Write an essay of 600 words that considers some or all of these questions on a pronouncement that *you* question.
3. Write an essay of 500 words in which you demonstrate how statistics which you have helped to assemble (in a survey, a science laboratory, an opinion poll) were handled honestly and *did* prove something of value.
4. Write a "how-to" analysis on a subject of particular interest to you: how to sail, how to develop film, how to make ceramics, how to teach dancing. Do not simply give information; analyze the special problems involved.

DEREK COLVILLE · *British and American Schools*

Derek Colville served in the RAF for six years during World War II and took his degrees in English literature at the University of Durham (England) and Washington University (St. Louis). He taught at the University of Toronto and Yale, and now teaches English at the University of California. He is well-qualified, then, to make this comparative analysis of British and American schools. He writes as though in explanation of a fact that has impressed him—"astonished" is the word he uses

"British and American Schools" by Derek Colville from *Harper's Magazine,* October 1957. Copyright by Harper & Bros. 1957. Reprinted by permission of the author.

—*over the years: "that in education the English-speaking nations have had so little to give each other." His essay is an attempt to cite particular reasons why.*

We say "comparative analysis." We must qualify the method slightly as Colville employs it. As an Englishman writing for an American magazine, he does not feel it necessary to outline in detail the American school and college system. The second half of this comparison can be assumed, implied. From time to time, he makes quick reference to certain aspects of the American school system, but he avoids a point by point analysis. In fact he admits that the two systems "cannot be simply compared as wholes."

To the casual reader it may seem, then, that Colville's essay is mistitled, that he is talking most of the time about British institutions. But this is not a simple factual report of how British youth is educated and the changes the future will bring. Each detail he cites implies an American counterpart, and they all point toward his concluding paragraph: "American schools . . . must achieve the means of satisfactory basic training." As you read Colville, take note of how subtly he is saying what it is in British education that would strengthen our school systems. It is not a "simple and pedestrian conclusion" as he modestly calls it. This essay is a good model of writing which is one quarter reporting, one half analysis, and one final quarter argument.

[1] "The class was keen and intelligent," said the visiting professor from England. "They were excited by the poems we read, and they had insight. They talked more readily than classes do at home. It was a delightful teaching experience. But when I asked them to write on those same poems they were lost. Their papers were appalling. They couldn't plan, construct, find words for their meaning, or even punctuate and spell. It was a shattering anticlimax."

[2] That class took place at a well-known Southern university, and the visitor's comments have a significance

more than pedagogical. For this professor was about to return to England. Whatever suggestions he had for American education would reach only English ears.

³ The case dramatizes an astonishing fact—that in education the English-speaking nations have had so little to give each other. In spite of the impressive exchange programs, the fellowships, the years spent across the Atlantic by Britons and Americans, little direct attempt has been made to answer—or even put—certain questions: What does American (or British) education offer which the other lacks? What are the main differences? What can each country learn from them for its own use? As an Englishman teaching in an American college, I find it tempting to try to indicate where some answers might lie.

⁴ What is British education? It is not, as some Britons fondly imagine, a program producing through sheer efficiency vast numbers of polished people. In fact, Americans might well look more closely at the "polish" hastily assumed by a few British educated visitors to this country, before they allow themselves to be intimidated * by it. British education does not justify any condescension, or—something common in American universities—a mixture of envy and admiration at an idea of its sophistication. For the two systems, while having things to give each other, cannot be simply compared as wholes, because their objects are quite different.

⁵ That of the British school system is to train most children to use their language and simple mathematics, and to gain a general idea of the past and present forms of the world well enough to earn their living in manual trades, or the simpler office jobs—and to think responsibly and independently: it is not always reached. The system also produces a tiny minority for university training. It is—perhaps ironically in a welfare state—a patrician * system selecting a small intellectual aristocracy through a kind of obstacle race with increasingly difficult obstacles.

⁶ The American ideal, on the other hand, is democratic

throughout—higher education for many—perhaps, some day, for most. Now this is immensely desirable. Britain does not reject it—her schools and universities are crammed—but she has neither the physical facilities nor money to make it a serious goal. British insurance companies do not advertise schemes to make money available for Johnnie to go to college. Their assumption—if they ever thought about it—would be that Johnnie will probably not go to college at all, and if he does it will only be because he is particularly gifted in a special field: then his expenses will be paid by the government, his local district, his college, or all three.

7   Apart from these general differences, an outline of the British system reveals special ones which are potentially useful.

8   The English child must by law attend school at five. At the so-called secondary (grade) schools he studies basic subjects—typically English, arithmetic, and general knowledge. He is drilled repeatedly—even tiresomely— in their main processes. At ten or eleven, he takes an examination to determine his fitness for grammar (high) school. About one in three will so advance—and here is the first great selection. Those not chosen continue basic subjects at grade school until they leave at fifteen.

9   Those chosen for high school immediately broaden their subject range to eight or so. My own program was: English language and literature, history (British and European), French, Latin or German, mathematics, physics, and biology or chemistry. Here is the same insistence on thoroughness: I have heard one German word flung back and forth between schoolmaster and schoolboy for twenty minutes to get the pronunciation right. After five years of high school study (at sixteen or seventeen), the English youth takes a further national examination. Armed with its results, about 80 per cent of the students leave high school and apply for their first jobs. The rest remain at high school a further two years, studying four subjects, two intensively. Usually they work entirely in humanities or entirely in science. Then,

when the student is eighteen or nineteen, he takes still another national examination, by which he may get a place at a university, and, if he does well, some kind of scholarship.

10   Some will not be offered a place, and some, who cannot pay their own way, will not win enough financial help to take one. Probably no more than one British schoolboy out of forty really attains his chance to reach university, and the proportion of the population completing a degree is by American standards fabulously small—perhaps 1½ per cent or 2 per cent. (There are only fifteen universities in England, and most are small to American eyes.)

11   This process continues at the university. The student concentrates on one subject for three years. The formal demands of lectures and other regimentation * are slight and the humanities student in particular, apart from sessions with his tutor, is left to his own resources. This affects students variously. Some put themselves under a discipline far stricter than any that could be enforced by the university. My own group of friends chose a hilarious round of sport and pleasure which could only be described as the broadest education by osmosis. Because of sound—and compulsory—grounding at school, this is not as dangerous as it sounds, though it must be made up for by two months of desperate note-making and cramming. For finally all students face a considerable examination at the end of their three years. It usually lasts ten days or so—a three-hour paper a day—and covers their whole field. In English, for instance, one takes, on successive days, three-hour papers in the literature of each century ("literature" being considered poetry, prose, and drama) , as well as in Shakespeare, literary criticism, Anglo-Saxon,° and Middle English.°

12   These examinations are, inevitably, competitive and selective. They are marked by staff of other universities

Anglo-Saxon: more commonly, Old English, spoken from about 450–1100.

Middle English: spoken from about 1100–1500.

who do not know the writers, and the results are classified as First, various kinds of Second, Third, and lower. For any kind of serious academic future, or the best civil-service jobs, a First or a good Second is necessary. Postgraduate degrees in Britain have never been necessary even for university teachers, although they are coming to be: they are purely research degrees.

13 It is clearly difficult to make valid comparison between this and the American system. It would be misleading, for instance, to compare an American with a British freshman, because the latter is a survivor in an elite group. Valid comparisons are possible, but not at the same level: an English university student would have a good deal in common with an American graduate student doing the course work for his Ph.D. New British graduates coming to the United States, I found, can successfully use their undergraduate training for the Ph.D. course exams here.

14 This British system is not at all ideal. Its defects are obvious ones. Its soullessness is reflected in its excessive dependence on examinations: two examples of this suffice. The idea of charting the whole of a child's future course on the basis of an examination taken at the age of ten or eleven is indefensible, even repugnant.* Thousands of British children of late development but immense potentiality (the two are not, as the system assumes, incompatible *) must so far have been deprived of the advanced education they deserve. The enraged parent whose offspring has failed to get into high school has become a stock figure in England, and often he has justice on his side.

15 This same unimaginative use of examinations is ubiquitous.* I had a university friend who could have become a dedicated and inspiring teacher, who got a Third in his Finals in French through a combination of nervousness, worry, and illness. The one task he was most admirably fitted to do in life—university teaching of French literature—became forever beyond his reach, though the quality of his entire three years' work at the

university had never been excelled. Fortunately he was a man of means and was able to start all over again in German. One could compile a long list of great intellects whose university examination results were remarkably mediocre: it would include Wordsworth, Matthew Arnold, Ruskin, and Cardinal Newman.

[16] This soulless inflexibility extends to British university life itself. Life at residential universities is bounded by a crust of traditional formality which intimidates, not helps, the ordinary student. It is quite immovable. My undergraduate years began after six years in the RAF. All my fellow freshmen were veterans; there were several ex-Majors and an ex-Colonel of nearly forty. But the gates of the college were closed at 10:00 P.M., and being out after eleven was a serious offense. This was not an attempt to chasten us; the rules had been made for eighteen-year-olds, and the force of tradition was inviolable.

[17] Perhaps the reason why the British undergraduate is so resourceful in his common rooms ° and debating halls, so alive and inquiring in his friends' rooms in the small hours, is that restrictions force him to turn to his own kind. By American standards, the faculty are an immense distance away, and their remoteness is symbolized by their "high table" with its wines and superior food, as opposed to the students' "low table" in the college dining halls.

[18] Similarly, the English university can gain much from the idea of a classroom in which the students do most of the talking. It is amazing to come to America and see lecturer after lecturer ask for questions and be inundated * with them. It is a dangerous tactic for a speaker in Britain, for he knows he faces the risk of a strained and deadening silence. The ideal "Be seen and not heard" is an unconscious part of the average English student, and his seminars are usually not general discussions, but the formal reading of a paper with com-

common rooms: in English colleges, rooms for reading, after-dinner coffee, meetings, and the like.

ments by the professor. The British university has much to learn from America of the value of informality and close contact between student and teacher. The American ideal is farther from the cloister,° but it is nearer life.

19 Many facets of American education are in fact more closely related to real life than their equivalents are in Britain. The interest in them is public and general rather than private and specialized. American students, with their summer jobs, are never far from the ordinary processes of life—a healthy trend only in its infancy in England, and then forced by financial need. Needing money, I worked as a café cashier in England in 1947. Even so recently, it was amusing to be regarded as an eccentric whose novel method of summer diversion was to be humored because of a university background.

20 There are, however, values in British education which Americans might usefully survey. The schooling has both coherence and concentration. It is a part of a larger unified system, in which one self-contained stage leads to another, yet a majority of students can drop out at any one and be adequately grounded, not only for work, but for the ordinary responsibilities of life—thinking and writing clearly and logically, voting, and so on.

21 By "concentration" I mean that a few basic subjects, early in school life, are consistently stressed, while no attempt is made to provide the esoteric * optional subjects—from home economics to cheer leading—which some American schools are said to provide. Perhaps I overstress compulsory fundamentals, since my own work is in English, where their need is most obvious. The British system does prove that children of twelve, and even ten, can be taught to express their thoughts simply and accurately, to do so in the most reasonable and connected order, and to support and illustrate their comments. But every American college teacher who deals with freshmen of eighteen and nineteen has to devote considerable time to this elementary goal.

cloister: a place of religious seclusion.

[22] This is a frightening comparison, but there are reasons for it.

[23] Great variation in quality of schools and colleges, as in America, is not a problem in Britain, where universities must be chartered by the government before they can grant degrees, and schools are under the direction of local boards responsible to a central education ministry. This is not necessarily an argument for federalizing education here: the geography of Britain makes central control natural. In fact, schools have been relatively standard in quality for years in Britain.

[24] There seems to be a need in America for some kind of qualitative standard for schools. For instance, Yale now finds it necessary, in selecting students for admission, to have a classification system with symbols standing for a whole range between schools of recognized stature, and those of which almost nothing is known.

[25] The comparative thoroughness of British schools is partly a matter of working hours. In New Haven—and Connecticut is a relatively literate state—the public high schools near Yale, which I am told are typical, commonly pour out hundreds of students at two o'clock in the afternoon. This is an hour when the British schoolboy has hardly begun his long afternoon session, after which he faces hours of homework to be thoroughly tested the next day.

[26] If such comparisons are invidious,* they still need making, for it is not enough to dismiss the matter by talk of overcrowding. Most countries face postwar problems of school overcrowding. Moreover, this difference between the two countries in academic working expectation shows even in university examinations. As I write of the ten three-hour examinations at English universities—a thirty-hour total session covering three years' work —Yale has just replaced its two-hour exams (in each of five subjects, covering one semester's or four months' work) by three-hour ones, and the *Yale Daily News* records that both students and faculty are seriously worried by the problem of fatigue.

27   This is not the place to discuss progressive education. I merely record that British schooling generally concentrates conservatively on basic techniques. Progressive or "child-centered" education is a postwar development confined largely to English "Infant" schools for tiny children. At all subsequent stages, the question of traditional *versus* progressive education hardly arises. Faced with the choice of whether a biology class should learn, say, to dissect a fish or should first, à la Dewey,° connect fish with their own lives by an afternoon's fishing—as has happened in the U.S.A.—British educators would simply take the position that dissecting was a useful technique to master, and, with so much else to be learned, left no time for the other.

28   Indeed, when I think of my "grade school" years in England—and it was only in the 'thirties!—I am amused to reflect how much certain of their aspects, factually recounted, must suggest a Dickens novel to present American ears. When I was eight or so, we were given weekly arithmetic tests in preparation for the examination two years later, which would grant or forbid us high school careers. School began at eight-thirty, but we were encouraged to begin earlier (more overtime!) and some of my schoolmates were so intimidated that they would come at six o'clock in the morning. While we worked, the headmaster would move along unceasingly behind the rows of seats, slapping us with great vigor if we made a mistake or were in process of making one. At ten-thirty he took the papers away, and came back in the afternoon to work through the problems with us. We got a cut with the cane for each one wrong.

29   This is hardly the ideal method, though it is fair to add that I am now, while execrable * in general mathematics, both quick and accurate in arithmetic! This kind of punishment has rightly gone in both countries, but

Dewey: John Dewey (1859–1952), American philosopher and educator, father of the Progressive School movement in education.

here in America it seems to have taken away with it an insistence on fundamentals, which has remained in Britain despite an emancipated discipline.

30 The directions which British experience might usefully suggest to America are deceptively simple—a united system, leading logically to the university yet able to produce literate—and even thinking—people at any stage. This involves, of course, something which sounds foolishly idealistic—higher, and uniform, school standards in the various states—but it is not as Utopian * as it may sound. Higher standards in basic subjects might well replace time and money spent on less central optional ones. Experimentation might still be encouraged without allowing it to replace teaching—and even drilling—in fundamentals. Less "progressive" education; more time spent in school; more homework given as an imperative task. And even, possibly, federal aid used *effectively* to bring backward school areas to the required standard, and some federally administered examinations in basic subjects. After all, certain educational matters —Rhodes scholarships, foundation grants, the draft exemption examinations, the Graduate Record tests for postgraduate work—have all been handled successfully on a national basis.

31 Federalism in education is worth consideration. There is a large measure of federal control in British education, even where it might be thought most dangerous—in the university. Most Americans are surprised to learn that British universities are government-subsidized, and, since they are repeatedly assured by the press that this inevitably means government control of thought, they are also shocked. Yet thought in British universities is certainly as free as in American. How is this achieved? The money for the universities' use is dispensed by a committee composed of academic members of the universities themselves. These men, being interested above all in seeing academic freedom preserved, and being of all shades of political opinion, manage to

apportion money between various institutions according to their needs and to their general satisfaction, with no strings attached.

32 There are certain signs that America is in fact moving toward an enlightened federalism in education. The Morse-Clark bill,° which came before the Senate this year, would provide 50,000 scholarships for high school graduates to attend college, the awards being made on the results of competitive examination. This may be regarded as an admirable adaptation of part of the rigorously competitive British system, without the latter's drawbacks. But the high aims of this American program will not materialize unless the high schools can guarantee to equip those 50,000 gifted students with the fundamentals with which to gain the absolute maximum from college.

33 To return to our visiting professor's opening remark, the stranger who surveys American education at present senses a kind of tragedy. He cannot avoid the impression, as he looks round the country, that the warmth and idealism of the mass of its people, the intelligence and curiosity of its students, deserve better than they have.

34 Even the naïveté of some American students compels the visitor's admiration. It implies an honest and fresh curiosity, and a naïvely curious student would often be worth his weight in gold amidst the precocious sophistication of many a British freshman class. The American college freshman today is, in the largest sense, better educational material than his British opposite. The American boy has more to know, has a greater desire to know it, and is more influential once he finds out—unless the defects in his schooling have prematurely blunted his self-confidence. His naturalness and ease enable him to draw out the restrained faculty member (it is this way round, and not *vice versa,* and this is often necessary). He will give his own most intimate poetic attempts to his professor with less hesitation than many a British under-

The Morse-Clark bill: It failed to pass the Senate.

graduate will have in greeting his professor in the street.
[35] He can often, mercifully, survive bad grounding and struggle through to an articulate self-reliance. And given enough well-grounded students, the American college can provide an education remarkably adapted to the individual interests of the good one: all he needs to fill his place in a world increasingly dependent on his being an educated man is there for the taking. But these custom-tailored chances cannot materialize for those who, however bright, lack grounding.

[36] This adaptability of the American college, and the individual treatment and incentives it offers the deserving student, are important both for the college and for schools as well. Broadly speaking, the individual chances mentioned above (like the Scholar of the House program at Yale, which leaves good students free from all formal requirements to pursue their own work for a year) are the prizes only for a combination of intelligence and solid grounding. How many more could grasp them if part of their early college career did not have to be sacrificed to remedying omissions in their schooling? The colleges cry out for the bright student; the red carpet awaits him, and opens up to him a career of great contribution. But whatever the causes, some schools at least, far from providing and encouraging such potential students, seem, judging by results, to have retarded their development.

[37] The conclusion can hardly be avoided: American schools (mostly grade and high, but even some private schools) *must* achieve the means of satisfactory basic training. They must spend more time on more central subjects. They must do thoroughly the grinding work of inculcating * basic facts and logical principles. I am almost ashamed at having reached so simple and pedestrian ° a conclusion. But it cannot be overstressed: it must be done at any cost, even that of accepting some central control. If we look after the schools, the colleges will look after themselves.

pedestrian: commonplace, dull.

ANALYSIS

What is British education? Colville raises the question in paragraph 4 and spends most of the essay answering it. Note, however, how he pauses to make quick comparisons. Paragraph 6 begins "The American ideal, on the other hand. . . ." Paragraph 13 admits that "it would be misleading, for instance, to compare an American with a British freshman." Paragraphs 17–20 mention American standards, facets of American education, or "values in British education which Americans might usefully survey." "Here in America" and "to American ears" interrupt his discussion of the British system. His conclusion (paragraphs 30–37) does not surprise us, consequently. It answers the unstated question of "what is wrong with American schools." It returns to the visiting professor's remarks (paragraphs 1–2) for good reasons. "We deserve better than we have" is an opinion Colville wants to document. The words "grounding," "basic training," "central subjects" keep recurring here. We are prepared to believe, by the clarity and the facts of his earlier paragraphs, that British schools indeed have something to offer us in educational theory.

What facts does Colville employ to bring us to this opinion? Paragraphs 8–9 should impress all of us who have expected or expect uninterrupted education from grade school through college. Even if we can meet the expense, do we earn this right academically in America, we might ask ourselves. Paragraphs 25–28 are a great contrast in thoroughness of preparation, working hours, kinds of examinations. Paragraph 31 raises the issue of federal support and how Britain manages it. We can say, fairly, that Colville is not prejudiced, that he is not attempting to "sell" us his own country's methods, that he is always willing to point out the many weaknesses in the British system. This method of organization works well for him as a result. He keeps an open mind, but he knows from experience that *certain* aspects of the system by which he was educated could improve our own schools. Part of the force of this analysis is Colville's willingness to tell us why. He is not satisfied with simple fact, comparison, or contrast. In as concise a way as possible, he discusses the reasons. It is this desire to explain *why* and *how* (what we said earlier all good expository prose does) that gives Colville's essay stature and conviction.

Questions on Content

1. Would you call the British educational system "democratic"? What elimination examinations do British students take, beginning at age ten or eleven?
2. What defects in the British system does Colville note?
3. How does the teaching of compulsory fundamentals in British schools compare with American methods? What advantages does he see in the British system?
4. Why does Colville believe "federalism in education" (paragraph 31) worth consideration?
5. What conclusion regarding the needs of American schools can "hardly be avoided"?

Add to your vocabulary: intimidated, patrician, regimentation, repugnant, incompatible, ubiquitous, inundated, cloister, esoteric, invidious, execrable, Utopian, inculcating, pedestrian.

Questions on Technique

1. One way of organizing this essay would have been a point-by point analysis. Would it, do you think, have brought more clarity to Colville's argument?
2. Paragraph 3 raises three questions. Where does Colville try to answer them in the rest of the essay?
3. Paragraph 37 states a firm conclusion. Does Colville anticipate this conclusion by discussing it elsewhere in the essay?
4. How could more illustrative anecdotes improve this essay? Where would you like to see them used?

Suggestions for Writing

1. Write an essay of 400 words in which you discuss only the "teaching of basic fundamentals" as you remember them. How were you "drilled" in mathematics or foreign languages? How much writing did you do? How many hours of homework was a normal evening's assignment?
2. Take all the facts Colville gives us on British education and write an essay which points out why some

elements of this system would not work in American schools.

3. In 500 words, write an article called "How to Improve American Schools," or be more specific and call it "The Fault Lies in the Students, Perhaps?" Your reader is an intelligent layman who needs to be informed of facts as well as of your opinions.

4. Do some research in newspapers and magazines of the last several years on the subject of scholarships for college study. What kind of aid is available: federal, institutional (the colleges themselves), industrial, foundational? Write a 600-word report that could be read to your class to inform them of your findings.

5. Write an essay in which you make use of comparative analysis. You might compare high school education today with that of your parents' day. Or you might compare the advantages of growing up in the country to growing up in the city.

CHAPTER 6

Argument and persuasion

We are confronted daily with the kind of expository writing we call argument and persuasion. In letters, newspapers, magazines, and brochures, we are urged to share this opinion or believe that point of view. The radio and television commercials coax us to try the large economy size. Political speeches beseech us to vote for the only obviously qualified candidate. Organized propaganda aims at spreading particular doctrines or information. Loosely defined, argument and persuasion are the type of prose which communicates opinions with the desire to convince the reader to accept them as just and true.

A finer distinction may be made between the two terms. Argument is the kind of writing which seeks to win assent to a belief or opinion. Persuasion goes one step further and enlists arguments in order to accomplish some proposed action. You will understand that it is not always easy to distinguish these two types of prose because they are so closely allied. You have seen how reports and analyses merge on occasion. You will also discover in the five models which follow that once the arguments are established, persuasive action is implied or anticipated if not directly sought.

Perhaps the simplest statement of argument is in the editorial, and so we begin there with a brief model. In *Science,* a weekly magazine published by the American Association for the Advancement of Science, Joseph

Turner, an assistant editor, demonstrates how good expository argument presents propositions, in this case three. We call these statements propositions because they are what the writer *proposes* to prove. They are not fact; they are debatable opinions. Two of these propositions Turner calls "extremes." He seeks to convince us of the validity of calling the third proposition an intelligent mean or middle ground.

JOSEPH TURNER · *Between Two Extremes*

[1] With science supporting an ever-expanding military technology, many people in this country are wondering to what extent American scientists should assume responsibility for the uses to which the government puts their discoveries and talents. It has always been possible, of course, to speak of pure research, just as it has always been possible, we suppose, to speak of the pure act of sitting down to a meal and consuming it with impeccable table manners. But any piece of behavior can acquire moral properties, given the appropriate circumstances— even eating one's fill, as when the roast is small and the company large.

[2] One view of the scientist's responsibility for the social consequences of scientific truths is that this responsibility ends with the scientist's willingness to do work directly or indirectly for the government, including work on weapons. According to this view, being a good scientist no more gives one special privileges in determining national policy than being a good information clerk at an airport entitles one to select destinations for travelers. The area of special competence of scientists lies in the discovery of technical facts; decisions of public policy rest with elected or appointed public officials.

"Between Two Extremes" reprinted with a minor change from an editorial by Joseph Turner in *Science*, vol. 131, p. 1013 (1960), with permission of the journal.

³ An opposite opinion concerning the obligations of scientists holds that scientists should consider the possible consequences of any piece of research before it is begun, and if the research is judged more a threat to the country, or humanity at large, than a benefit, they should refuse their services. A man cannot delegate to a superior the responsibility for the moral consequences of his acts, the second view claims. To be sure, to predict future applications of new discoveries calls more for the talents of a prophet than for those of a scientist. No one now knows to what uses, or abuses, the fall of parity ° in physics may some day prove amenable.* But somewhere along the line, basic research becomes applied research, and forecasts about the uses of discoveries become something more than anybody's guess.

⁴ Between the two opposing positions lies a third position which holds that at least some scientists, although they fear the dangers posed by a further increase in military power, have the duty to work on projects that the government deems necessary, but that scientists also have the duty to state their opinions on matters lying outside science. If this is the age of specialization, so this argument runs, it is also the age of specialists working together on teams. Public officials should have the final word, but any attempt to understand the full range of consequences—military, political, economic, and moral— of new advances in research, requires the views of the men who understand those advances best.

⁵ It is this third position that expresses our own con-

---

fall of parity: In 1957, Professor Tsung Dao Lee of Columbia University and Chen Nin Yang of the Institute for Advanced Study at Princeton received the Nobel prize in physics for "their penetrating investigation of the so-called parity laws which has led to important discoveries regarding elementary particles." Their contribution to physical research destroyed for all time what had long been called the "Principles of Conservation of Parity" according to which "space possessed a well-balanced quality of symmetry in which every existing object was balanced by a corresponding mirror image that had to respond to the same law of nature." (See New York *Times,* November 1, 1957.)

victions, and that seems to express the convictions of most of the persons in this country who are presently concerned with these problems—although, admittedly, agreement on general principles does not necessarily imply agreement on particular cases. The first position errs because, pushed to its conclusion, it turns the citizen's obligations to the state into despotism; while the second position errs because, if pushed, it turns the moral integrity * of the individual into anarchy. The third position seeks the mean ° between the scientist's assuming too little responsibility for the consequences of his research and his assuming too much responsibility.

ANALYSIS

We should keep in mind that Turner's audience, in this magazine editorial, is composed chiefly of practising scientists. He does not need to fill in details. In fact, most editorials assume that the reader is informed, alert, and ready to hear the argument. Space is limited.

Turner states his case concisely. Paragraph 1 announces the question: to what extent should American scientists assume responsibility for governmental use of their talents and discoveries. He gives us no elaborating instances; he cites no agencies, projects, or scientists by name. His editorial is concerned with principle only. Three points of view are presented in three succeeding paragraphs: (a) scientists are responsible only for the discovery of technical facts, not for decisions of public policy; (b) scientists are responsible for the moral consequences of an applied use of their technical discoveries; they should refuse their services if they foresee a threat; and (c) at least some scientists have the duty both to work on governmental projects and to share in understanding the full range of consequences. In brief, Turner has the scientist face no responsibility, full responsibility, or a shared responsibility with public officials. In paragraph 5 he tells us—convinces us?—why the third or mean position is the wisest solution.

the mean: midway between two extremes.

This editorial is a bare outline of an argument, yet it illustrates neatly the presentation of propositions and the manner in which argument takes a decided stand, a specific point of view when alternatives are offered. There is no opportunity here to adduce facts or the opinion of authorities, as we shall observe in other models. Turner is not so much *proving* here as he is stating basic reasoning. The reasoning, he would wish us to believe, is sound.

Add to your vocabulary: amenable, integrity.

Suggestions for Writing

1. Mr. Turner's editorial suggests a major problem facing the world today, that of coping intelligently with the great and dangerous scientific advances now irretrievably part of our civilization. While man advances scientifically, he remains morally and psychologically the same confused human being he has always been. For example, at a time when science has made it impossible for any nation to survive a major war, many nations are vigorously strengthening their military forces. In an essay of 500 words, state your opinion of what mankind must do to save itself from the dangers of scientific advancement.

2. Choose another subject and imitate in 400 words Turner's structure paragraph by paragraph: statement of subject, three propositions, your opinion which of the three is wisest. You might choose to write about compulsory military training, College Board examinations, learning foreign languages, or summer work.

3. Write a 350-word editorial for your school paper on a current school issue of general interest to all students. Take a firm stand in stating your beliefs.

4. In a 400-word essay, criticize an editorial you have clipped from a recent newspaper. Discuss the method of organization the writer uses, his language, his power of convincing you (or not convincing you, as the case may be). How would you improve his argument?

PHILIP WYLIE · *Science Has Spoiled My Supper*

Unlike Turner's editorial, in which three propositions are considered, Philip Wylie's essay deals with one main argument. He announces it boldly in his title. He restates it in his second paragraph. He makes us feel the subject has long been simmering and that now it has come to a boil. Anyone who has read Wylie's Generation of Vipers *(1942) knows how relentlessly he can pursue an argument, how severely he can complain of the weaknesses he finds in American manners and morals. This essay is out of that same mold.*

Mr. Wylie has had a varied writing career, on the staff of the New Yorker, *in Hollywood, on newspapers, and in publishing houses. He is so well known for frank expression of his negative opinions that his method has come to be called, jestingly, veneration of gripers. And an effective method it is, specific in its attack, full of bite, uncompromising in its conclusions. By the time you finish reading Wylie's argument, you will probably agree he has cause for anger.*

¹ I am a fan for Science. My education is scientific and I have, in one field, contributed a monograph to a scientific journal. Science, to my mind, is applied honesty, the one reliable means we have to find out truth. That is why, when error is committed in the name of Science, I feel the way a man would if his favorite uncle had taken to drink.

² Over the years, I have come to feel that way about what science has done to food. I agree that America can set as good a table as any nation in the world. I agree that our food is nutritious and that the diet of most of us is well-balanced. What America eats is handsomely

packaged; it is usually clean and pure; it is excellently preserved. The only trouble with it is this: year by year it grows less good to eat. It appeals increasingly to the eye. But who eats with his eyes? Almost everything used to taste better when I was a kid. For quite a long time I thought that observation was merely another index of advancing age. But some years ago I married a girl whose mother is an expert cook of the kind called "old-fashioned." This gifted woman's daughter (my wife) was taught her mother's venerable skills. The mother lives in the country and still plants an old-fashioned garden. She still buys dairy products from the neighbors and, in so far as possible, she uses the same materials her mother and grandmother did—to prepare meals that are superior. They are just as good, in this Year of Grace, as I recall them from my courtship. After eating for a while at the table of my mother-in-law, it is sad to go back to eating with my friends—even the alleged "good cooks" among them. And it is a gruesome experience to have meals at the best big-city restaurants.

³ Take cheese, for instance. Here and there, in big cities, small stores and delicatessens specialize in cheese. At such places, one can buy at least some of the first-rate cheeses that we used to eat—such as those we had with pie and in macaroni. The latter were sharp but not too sharp. They were a little crumbly. We called them American cheeses, or even rat cheese; actually, they were Cheddars.° Long ago, this cheese began to be supplanted by a material called "cheese foods." Some cheese foods and "processed" cheese are fairly edible; but not one comes within miles of the old kinds—for flavor.

⁴ A grocer used to be very fussy about his cheese. Cheddar was made and sold by hundreds of little factories. Representatives of the factories had particular customers, and cheese was prepared by hand to suit the grocers, who knew precisely what their patrons wanted in rat cheese, pie cheese, American, and other cheeses. Some

Cheddars: smooth-textured cheeses originally made at Cheddar, England, but now made extensively in the United States as well.

liked them sharper, some liked them yellower; some liked anise seeds in cheese, or caraway.

5   What happened? Science—or what is called science—stepped in. The old-fashioned cheeses didn't ship well enough. They crumbled, became moldy, dried out. "Scientific" tests disclosed that a great majority of the people will buy a less-good-tasting cheese if that's all they can get. "Scientific marketing" then took effect. Its motto is "Give the people the least quality they'll stand for." In food, as in many other things, the "scientific marketers" regard quality as secondary so long as they can sell most persons anyhow; what they are after is "durability" or "shippability."

6   It is not possible to make the very best cheese in vast quantities at a low average cost. "Scientific sampling" got in its statistically nasty work. It was found that the largest number of people will buy something that is bland and rather tasteless. Those who prefer a product of a pronounced and individualistic flavor have a variety of preferences. Nobody is altogether pleased by bland foodstuff, in other words; but nobody is very violently put off. The result is that a "reason" has been found for turning out zillions of packages of something that will "do" for nearly all and isn't even imagined to be superlatively good by a single soul!

7   Economics entered. It is possible to turn out in quantity a bland, impersonal, practically imperishable substance more or less resembling, say, cheese—at lower cost than cheese. Chain groceries shut out the independent stores and "standardization" became a principal means of cutting costs.

8   Imitations also came into the cheese business. There are American duplications of most of the celebrated European cheeses, mass-produced and cheaper by far than the imports. They would cause European food-lovers to gag or guffaw—but generally the imitations are all that's available in the supermarkets. People buy them and eat them.

9   Perhaps you don't like cheese—so the fact that decent

cheese is hardly ever served in America any more, or used in cooking, doesn't matter to you. Well, take bread. There has been (and still is) something of a hullabaloo about bread. In fact, in the last few years, a few big bakeries have taken to making a fairly good imitation of real bread. It costs much more than what is nowadays called bread, but it is edible. Most persons, however, now eat as "bread" a substance so full of chemicals and so barren of cereals that it approaches a synthetic.*

10   Most bakers are interested mainly in how a loaf of bread looks. They are concerned with how little stuff they can put in it—to get how much money. They are deeply interested in using chemicals that will keep bread from molding, make it seem "fresh" for the longest possible time, and so render it marketable and shippable. They have been at this monkeyshine for a generation. Today a loaf of "bread" looks deceptively real; but it is made from heaven knows what and it resembles, as food, a solidified bubble bath. Some months ago I bought a loaf of the stuff and, experimentally, began pressing it together, like an accordion. With a little effort, I squeezed the whole loaf to a length of about one inch!

11   Yesterday, at the home of my mother-in-law, I ate with country-churned butter and home-canned wild strawberry jam several slices of actual bread, the same thing we used to have every day at home. People who have eaten actual bread will know what I mean. They will know that the material commonly called bread is not even related to real bread, except in name.

12   For years, I couldn't figure out what had happened to vegetables. I knew, of course, that most vegetables, to be enjoyed in their full deliciousness, must be picked fresh and cooked at once. I knew that vegetables cannot be overcooked and remain even edible, in the best sense. They cannot stand on the stove. That set of facts makes it impossible, of course, for any American restaurant— or, indeed, any city-dweller separated from supply by more than a few hours—to have decent fresh vegetables. The Parisians manage by getting their vegetables picked

at dawn and rushed in farmers' carts to market, where no middleman or marketman delays produce on its way to the pot.

13 Our vegetables, however, come to us through a long chain of command. There are merchants of several sorts —wholesalers before the retailers, commission men, and so on—with the result that what were once edible products become, in transit, mere wilted leaves and withered tubers.*

14 Homes and restaurants do what they can with this stuff—which my mother-in-law would discard on the spot. I have long thought that the famed blindfold test for cigarettes should be applied to city vegetables. For I am sure that if you puréed * them and ate them blindfolded, you couldn't tell the beans from the peas, the turnips from the squash, the Brussels sprouts from the broccoli.

15 It is only lately that I have found how much science has had to do with this reduction of noble victuals to pottage. Here the science of genetics ° is involved. Agronomists and the like have taken to breeding all sorts of vegetables and fruits—changing their original nature. This sounds wonderful and often is insane. For the scientists have not as a rule taken any interest whatsoever in the taste of the things they've tampered with!

16 What they've done is to develop "improved" strains of things for every purpose but eating. They work out, say, peas that will ripen all at once. The farmer can then harvest his peas and thresh them and be done with them. It is extremely profitable because it is efficient. What matter if such peas taste like boiled paper wads?

17 Geneticists have gone crazy over such "opportunities." They've developed string beans that are straight instead of curved, and all one length. This makes them easier to pack in cans, even if, when eating them, you can't tell them from tender string. Ripening time and identity of

genetics: the branch of biology dealing with heredity and variation among related organisms. As an applied science it deals with the fundamentals of plant and animal breeding.

size and shape are, nowadays, more important in carrots than the fact that they taste like carrots. Personally, I don't care if they hybridize ° onions till they are as big as your head and come up through the snow; but, in doing so, they are producing onions that only vaguely and feebly remind you of onions. We are getting some varieties, in fact, that have less flavor than the water off last week's leeks.* Yet, if people don't eat onions because they taste like onions, what in the name of Luther Burbank ° do they eat them for?

18 The women's magazines are about one third dedicated to clothes, one third to mild comment on sex, and the other third to recipes and pictures of handsome salads, desserts, and main courses. "Institutes" exist to experiment and tell housewives how to cook attractive meals and how to turn leftovers into works of art. The food thus pictured looks like famous paintings of still life. The only trouble is it's tasteless. It leaves appetite unquenched and merely serves to stave off famine.

19 I wonder if this blandness of our diet doesn't explain why so many of us are overweight and even dangerously so. When things had flavor, we knew what we were eating all the while—and it satisfied us. A teaspoonful of my mother-in-law's wild strawberry jam will not just provide a gastronome's ° ecstasy: it will entirely satisfy your jam desire. But, of the average tinned or glass-packed strawberry jam, you need half a cupful to get the idea of what you're eating. A slice of my mother-in-law's apple pie will satiate * you far better than a whole bakery pie.

20 That thought is worthy of investigation—of genuine scientific investigation. It is merely a hypothesis,° so far, and my own. But people—and their ancestors—have been eating according to flavor for upwards of a billion

hybridize: to interbreed.
Luther Burbank: United States naturalist (1849–1926) who produced a number of new species of plants.
gastronome: an epicure, a man who knows and enjoys good food.
hypothesis: a proposition assumed as a premise in an argument.

years. The need to satisfy the sense of taste may be innate * and important. When food is merely a pretty cascade of viands, with the texture of boiled cardboard and the flavor of library paste, it may be the instinct of *genus homo* ° to go on eating in the unconscious hope of finally satisfying the ageless craving of the frustrated taste buds. In the days when good-tasting food was the rule in the American home, obesity * wasn't such a national curse.

²¹   How can you feel you've eaten if you haven't tasted, and fully enjoyed tasting? Why (since science is ever so ready to answer the beck and call of mankind) don't people who want to reduce merely give up eating and get the nourishment they must have in measured doses shot into their arms at hospitals? One ready answer to that question suggests that my theory of overeating is sound: people like to taste! In eating, they try to satisfy that like. The scientific war against deliciousness has been stepped up enormously in the last decade. Some infernal * genius found a way to make biscuit batter keep. Housewives began to buy this premixed stuff. It saved work, of course. But any normally intelligent person can learn, in a short period, how to prepare superb baking powder biscuits. I can make better biscuits, myself, than can be made from patent batters. Yet soon after this fiasco * became an American staple, it was discovered that a half-baked substitute for all sorts of breads, pastries, rolls, and the like could be mass-manufactured, frozen—and sold for polishing off in the home oven. None of these two-stage creations is as good as even a fair sample of the thing it imitates. A man of taste, who had eaten one of my wife's cinnamon buns, might use the premixed sort to throw at starlings—but not to eat! Cake mixes, too, come ready-prepared—like cement and not much better-tasting compared with true cake.

²²   It is, however, "deep-freezing" that has really rung down the curtain on American cookery. Nothing is improved by the process. I have yet to taste a deep-frozen

genus homo: anthropologically speaking, man is genus *Homo,* family *Hominidae,* class *Mammalia.*

victual that measures up, in flavor, to the fresh, unfrosted original. And most foods, cooked or uncooked, are destroyed in the deep freeze for all people of sense and sensibility. Vegetables with crisp and crackling texture emerge as mush, slippery and stringy as hair nets simmered in Vaseline. The essential oils that make peas peas—and cabbage cabbage—must undergo fission and fusion in freezers. Anyhow, they vanish. Some meats turn to leather. Others to wood pulp. Everything, pretty much, tastes like the mosses of tundra,° dug up in midwinter. Even the appearance changes, often-times. Handsome comestibles you put down in the summer come out looking very much like the corpses of woolly mammoths ° recovered from the last Ice Age.

²³ Of course, all this scientific "food handling" tends to save money. It certainly preserves food longer. It reduces work at home. But these facts, and especially the last, imply that the first purpose of living is to avoid work—at home, anyhow.

²⁴ Without thinking, we are making an important confession about ourselves as a nation. We are abandoning quality—even, to some extent, the quality of people. The "best" is becoming too good for us. We are suckling ourselves on machine-made mediocrity. It is bad for our souls, our minds, and our digestion. It is the way our wiser and calmer forebears fed, not people, but hogs: as much as possible and as fast as possible, with no standard of quality.

²⁵ The Germans say, *"Mann ist was er isst*—Man is what he eats." If this be true, the people of the U.S.A. are well on their way to becoming a faceless mob of mediocrities, of robots. And if we apply to other attributes the criteria we apply these days to appetite, that is what would happen! We would not want bright children any more; we'd merely want them to look bright—and get through school fast. We wouldn't be interested in

tundra: one of the vast, nearly level treeless plains of the arctic regions of Europe, Asia, and North America.
mammoths: large, extinct species of elephant.

beautiful women—just a good paint job. And we'd be
opposed to the most precious quality of man: his in-
dividuality, his differentness from the mob.

26   There are some people—sociologists and psychologists
among them—who say that is exactly what we Americans
are doing, are becoming. Mass man, they say, is on the
increase. Conformity, standardization, similarity—all on
a cheap and vulgar level—are replacing the great American ideas of colorful liberty and dignified individualism.
If this is so, the process may well begin, like most human behavior, in the home—in those homes where a
good meal has been replaced by something-to-eat-in-a-
hurry. By something not very good to eat, prepared by a
mother without very much to do, for a family that doesn't
feel it amounts to much anyhow.

27   I call, here, for rebellion.

ANALYSIS

American food is losing its flavor—this is Wylie's argument. How does he set out to "prove" his proposition?
He uses three examples: cheese, bread, vegetables. And
wisely he speaks of each from personal experience. He
does not settle for principles alone. He has specific ob-
jections. Using his mother-in-law's table as the ideal
standard, he employs strong contrasts. On one side are
properly-aged cheeses, home-baked bread, freshly-picked
vegetables. He admires equally his mother-in-law's country-churned butter and home-canned wild strawberry
jam. On the other side are "improved processes," "scientific marketing," "greater shippability," and "premixed
or deep-frozen products." The results, he assures us, are
devastating: cheeses that strike him as bland and tasteless, bread that is mostly air, vegetables that resemble
cooked cardboard. He makes few concessions to geneticists and cooking institutes. Why, he asks, must we continue to eat this tasteless fare?

With this main argument "proved," Wylie moves
(paragraph 19) to a corollary argument, that is, an additional inference from his chief proposition. Are we, he
asks, overeating because we cannot taste what we eat?

Has food become fodder, stuffing, pre-mixed, ready-prepared substitutes? Does deep-freezing lead directly to dieting? He is quite serious when he says (paragraph 20) that this theory is worthy of genuine scientific investigation.

Wylie suggests a second corollary (paragraph 25) : if man is what he eats, we are well on our way "to becoming a faceless mob of mediocrities, of robots." Science has not only ruined our suppers and our waistlines, it has made mass man's vulgar level the standard. If we accept the "commonest low denominator" in foodstuffs, something-to-eat-in-a-hurry, we will, in time, accept it throughout our civilization. By paragraph 26, Wylie is almost ready to begin another essay on mobocracy, mass rule, and assembly-line thinking. His main argument has gathered momentum. His last, one-sentence paragraph cuts it off. He is not ready to propose, or at least not here, how the rebellion shall begin. His essay is a fine model of argument. He does not, in the rhetorical sense, directly relate his proofs to a proposed action. Argument stops short of persuasion.

Questions on Content

1. What are the differences Wylie cites between old-fashioned Cheddars and the modern processed cheese foods?
2. What does Wylie mean by the terms "scientific marketing" and "scientific sampling"? Be specific.
3. Why can we not find fresh vegetables in our markets?
4. What "opportunities" have geneticists taken "advantage" of?
5. What are Wylie's specific complaints about deep freezing?

Add to your vocabulary: synthetic, tubers, puréed, genetics, hybridize, leeks, satiate, hypothesis, innate, obesity, infernal, fiasco. How do you distinguish between pottage, victuals, viands, and comestibles?

Questions on Technique

1. Wylie's mother-in-law plays a significant role in this essay. How would you describe it?
2. How does Wylie describe bread? What experiment

did he try with a whole loaf? Why is this a visually effective detail of his argument?
3. In paragraph 16, he says peas today taste like "boiled paper wads." This is an apt simile.° What other similes can you find in this essay?
4. Wylie could have ended this essay with paragraph 18. What do paragraphs 19–27 add to the enlargement of the main argument? Do the first eighteen paragraphs warrant this enlargement?

Suggestions for Writing

1. Take Wylie's last paragraph as a springboard for a 500-word essay. Tell us how *you* would conduct the rebellion against tasteless food. Perhaps you wish to call your essay "It Won't Happen in My House."
2. Write an essay in which you reverse all of Wylie's arguments. Call it "Science Has Improved My Supper."
3. Let us imagine that Wylie wished to end his essay with paragraph 18, but he needed more proof to "fatten" his argument. What could you add? Homogenized milk, oleomargarine, dried potatoes, TV dinners, frozen soups, heat-'n-serve everything? Write a 500-word letter to Mr. Wylie describing these examples or others.
4. Write an essay of about 500 words called "We Don't Have Time for It Anymore." Use as your subject one or two of these aspects of so-called modern civilization: the drip-dry clothes which are supposed to need no ironing, Shakespeare's plays as cut for television, super-highways that avoid the countryside, condensed novels, and so forth.
5. Defend this statement in 500 words: "Standardization is nothing to fear; mass man will not wreck our country." You might begin with the improved phonographs and recordings as examples.

simile: See Glossary.

DAVID L. COHN · *Moonlight and Poison Ivy*

As a social historian, David L. Cohn wrote on a wide variety of subjects: race relations, international trade, tariff policy, the American automobile, and, like Philip Wylie, the manners and morals of the American people. Though born in Greenville, Mississippi, he lived for many years in New Orleans where, as a retired business-man, he wrote of his travels and observations. One of the aspects of our society which most appalled Cohn is our self-delusion. He had frequently written on the ease with which we, as a people, sell ourselves false ideas and ideals. Again like Wylie, Cohn was harshly critical of the gloss of our luxuries, the immaturity of our behavior, the search we are making for the easy way.

The essay that follows is argument based on a premise indirectly stated in the title. This title, you will discover, is more subtle than it sounds. As you read Cohn's essay, keep in mind that he is talking not only of a "sweet and sour" or "white and black" attitude toward love and marriage. He mentions, in paragraph 13, the "dealers in reality." What is this reality we will not face? Why are American "attitudes toward marriage . . . crippling, if not fatal, to the central relationship in men's lives"?

I

1 There is little doubt that our attitudes toward marriage, stemming as they must from our attitudes toward life and living, are crippling, if not fatal, to the central relationship in men's lives. If we tell the young that life is easy, when it is hard; that it is kind, when it is replete with cruel ironies; that all is to be had for the asking, when every blessing must be paid for singly or doubly; that it is a succession of high moments, when most of it is pedestrian; that it is "romantic," in the sense of affording high adventure, when its glory lies in man's struggle against forces he cannot even comprehend; that bigness is greatness and success is achievement—if we teach all these things, then not only is youth corroded, corrupted, and misled, while its well-springs are poisoned at the source, but the revulsion when it comes is, and must be, shattering.

²   Yet this is what we do tell the young; what they are told every day by many magazines, the movies, the radio, and national advertisers. It is, apparently, what we believe, or affect to believe. It is also false, it does not square with human experience, and it is disastrous to marriage.

³   More and more, American marriage is coming to be a detour to divorce. The divorce rate alone does not fully illuminate the whole shabby matrimonial scene since it reflects only those cases of discord that are made public, but it is an index to private failure become national failure on a huge scale.

⁴   Of what significance are miracles of production, our hard work and ingenious gadgets, our cluttered catalogue of things sensible and nonsensical that make up our so-called high standard of living, if millions of men and women take little or no joy in each other; if the house vanishes, the family breaks up, the home is transient? * For what does the ordinary man strive if not for a wife, a home, children, permanence of tenure * and affection under one roof? And if these prove to be but an illusion, if the husband becomes an alimony payer, the father a stranger to his children, the seeker for permanency a wanderer, is not ours a matrimonial anarchy? *

⁵   Why should such anarchy prevail? There is no easy answer to this question. Investigators attribute it to money troubles, friction with in-laws, poor housing, the increasing financial independence of women. These play their part, but some of its causes lie in our national character and attitudes. Marriage and divorce are what they are, to a large degree, because we are what we have become.

⁶ American marriage is dangerously weakened at its inception because of our preference for moonlight and poison ivy—the lies elders tell the young about marriage, and the hourly elaboration of these lies, cunningly persuasive, by many magazines, the radio, the movies, national advertisers. It is rarely portrayed for what it is: a difficult and demanding exercise in human relationships; a partnership, not without austerity,* in which losses as well as profits are shared; an undertaking dynastic * as well as individual. More common—vulgarly and infantilely—marriage is portrayed as a gumdrop heaven: soft, gooey, and oh, so sweet.

⁷ It is, of course, a heaven of huge dimensions—not for us a one-room, walk-up Nirvana °—so that the couple attaining it must move about in a Cadillac with a sliding top, and are showered with completely furnished cottages, tickets for trips to Bermuda, whole wardrobes by Christian Dior,° television sets, memberships in a country club, and two foam rubber clouds; all delicately scented with Elizabeth Arden's Blue Grass perfume. The country that invented the airplane and the drive-in movie is certainly not going to cling to yesterday's antiquated model of marriage.

⁸ We are not content, therefore, to marry for reasons that have always moved most people elsewhere. It is not enough that marriage is desirable as a division of labor; that a man wants a woman to run his house and the woman wants a house to run. We scorn the fact that monogamic marriage ° was born of race experience, the trial-and-error method of centuries having demonstrated that, for most of us, it is the best way for a man and woman to live together and to transmit property through inheritance. We find it repulsive that marriage is no "It must be fate"

Nirvana: a Sanskrit word meaning, as Cohn uses it, "oblivious to care or pain."

Christian Dior: one of Paris' most famous dress designers, now deceased.

monogamic marriage: the marriage of one woman to one man, the opposite of polygamy, which allows man to take several wives at one time.

relationship dreamed up by a bored faun who missed his train at Indianapolis.

9 Nor are we content, even, that marriage should proceed from love as other men have known it, for this would be to recognize the emotion for what it, in part, is: bitter-sweet, subtly demanding, frequently tempestuous, and capable of vanishing for no apparent reason. It is intolerable to us who dread the tenuous * as primitive men dread the evil eye, that love's life might hang upon threads so gossamer * as the cadence of a voice, the clasp of hands, the looks of eyes, the word said, the word unsaid. We find it unbearable that love demands constant replenishing and care; as much care indeed as one gives to one's car. But we do not, for these reasons, reject romantic love in marriage. Allegedly we marry for no other reason. We have created our own moonlight and poison ivy image of love and marriage: a handsome couple, forever fair and young, perpetually embracing on the moon-misty shores of a Cythera ° that the map reveals to be Deaf Smith County, Texas.

10 So, too, we say "Love is blind." We mean thereby that the lover sees no imperfections or incompatibilities in the beloved, and love's blindness, therefore, will ensure forever love and marriage. Since this is palpably * false, and is indeed anti-romantic, lending to the one or the other a wooden perfection suitable for a department store dummy but not for flesh and blood, whose living wonder is its mixture of elements, it follows that when, some morning at the breakfast table, the shuttered eye sees once more, all is disillusion.

11 Other peoples, wiser perhaps than we, if less "romantic," give another interpretation to the same phrase. Love is blind, they say, because the lover consciously closes his eyes to the beloved's failings, content that the good outweighs the bad. These are not our optics,° how-

Cythera: a small island off Greece, famous as a sanctuary of Venus, goddess of love.

These are not our optics: We do not look [at love] this way.

ever, since in love we prefer the straight line irresolute, the rounded curve wavy. It is, moreover, a mature point of view that we find shocking because we invariably associate love with immaturity. Hence Hollywood grandmothers are condemned to go on playing ingénue roles, and Hollywood lovers, with arteries of '98, are forever Princeton '41.

¹² We do not want to look at life steadily and whole, seeing that it is noble and ignoble, generous and mean, beautiful and ugly, cleanly and filthy, melancholy and joyous; compounded of pain as well as happiness; its gold inextricably * mingled with baser metals. Not for us the concept that symmetry ° derives from asymmetry; or that, in the words of William Blake,° "There is a strange disproportion in beauty."

¹³ Powerful agencies disseminate * our deadly notion of marriage as a tinsel heaven on earth, often to the muted music of woodwinds blown by those quaint people known as parents. For every dealer in reality who languishes for lack of trade, there are a thousand dealers in illusion besieged by anxious customers. Yet they did not invent the moonlight and poison ivy concept of love and marriage. They merely exploit what is in our minds.

II

¹⁴ High among our illusions affecting love, marriage, and much else—a natural child of moonlight and poison ivy—is the installment plan mentality. It dictates that you do not have to do anything, or become anything, if you can wangle the small down payment on what you want; the rest "just a few cents a day."

¹⁵ Do you want to marry a rich, handsome young man with (as the magazines put it) "lean flanks" and "strong teeth," the better to eat you, mah chile? It's easy. Simply use Princess Mafou's Face Powder. At your next dinner

symmetry: regularity of form or arrangement.
William Blake: English poet and artist (1757–1827) .

party three men, dead ringers for Winthrop Rockefeller,° will trample one another in the rush to marry you.

16   Suppose you have no face. Do not be discouraged. Hands will do the trick as well; or eyelashes, fingernails, hair. There was the girl who could not bring her man to gaff until she discovered Beautress (pronounced Bow-tress). "My date with Bill that night," runs the ad, "found me confident in the new-found glamor of my sparkling Beautress lovely hair . . . His cheek touched its new alluring softness while we danced . . . My heart stood still when he murmured: 'Dream Girl, that gorgeous hair rates a bridal veil.' "

17   They were married in a rented submarine, spent their honeymoon at the Stork Club,° occasionally left their martinis to pick up a peck of emeralds at Cartier's,° and because of the housing shortage are now roughing it in a twenty-room hut at Palm Springs.° They are deliriously happy and will always be in a state of delirium. For when Bill occasionally looks grumpy, his Dream Girl orders a "festive walnut cake," chockful of genuine Shasta Brand Walnuts. "Imagine getting kissed for your cake!" says the ad.

18   This being the case, why should any woman burden herself with such old-fashioned backbreaking loads as brains, charm, literacy, efficiency, or resemblance to the human race? She can get her man with a shampoo and keep him with walnuts. Go to your favorite drugstore tomorrow, buy yourself a bottle of the American Dream in the new economy size, shake well before using, and live luxuriously ever afterward.

19   If you can read the ads, it is not unlikely that you can read a book, although the strain will be greater. There are dozens of books telling you how to handle every question of love and marriage in this happy world

Winthrop Rockefeller: one of the five grandsons of the famous John D. Rockefeller, American capitalist and philanthropist.
Stork Club: a well-known nightclub in New York City.
Cartier's: the Paris and New York jewelry shop.
Palm Springs: a fashionable California resort.

rapidly becoming free of dandruff. It is as simple as finding the recipe for lemon pie in Fannie Farmer. Why, then, be concerned with understanding and patience? Why listen to the shy counsel of the shy heart when the ready-made answer to your perplexities is at hand just as the biscuit mix is on your pantry shelf, leaving little to do except heat and serve?

20 Whence our feverish search for the easy way; our obsession with the opiate * dream? Is it that we have no faith except in the infallibility of machinery and so stand incredulous and shaken when the airplane falls? Has ours become a culture from the periphery of the eyelids outward, lacking inner content? Are we, despite our physical energy, an intellectually lazy people, satisfied to take shadow for substance, package for contents, and black or white for truth because we are too lethargic * to search out the nuances ° where truth, ever elusive, lies? Has some malign enchantment unfitted us to face life as it is, so that its essence escapes us and we face eventual destruction from within or from without? Is the high point of our civilization reached when a radio announcer screams to a nation enthralled, "That's right, Mrs. Deffenbaugh!" while $20,000 worth of things, including a houseboat and a wall can-opener, drop into the lap of the lucky winner?

21 Better marriage relations in this country await an extensive revaluation of our attitude toward life and living. If our values are shabby and our attitudes adolescent, how can American marriage, made in our image, be anything but a monumental failure?

ANALYSIS

Let us go at once to the heart of this essay. Cohn states his argument clearly in the first two paragraphs. Our mass media—radio, magazines, movies (and he would now add television)—misrepresent life by oversimplifying it. Alas, we accept this false picture as true. This glossing-

nuances: shades of difference; subtle variations.

over of complexities, some of them unpleasant, Cohn argues, is disastrous to marriage. Here is what we can call the basic premise of this essay, the main argument to be proved.

Now what does Cohn mean by "moonlight and poison ivy"? He very possibly uses the phrase in several ways. First, it suggests romantic illusion (the gooey dream world we think of as "love") and unhappy, decidedly unromantic disillusion (the brutal awakening that leads to divorce). This reading of the title is "white and black." Love is all moonlight; marriage, we are amazed to discover, is poison.

A second reading of the title is suggested in paragraph 6 and is developed in the succeeding five paragraphs. It differs markedly from the first. Americans have convinced themselves that love and marriage are and forever will be uninterrupted bliss, life on foam rubber clouds, a perpetual embrace on "the moon-misty shores of a Cythera." They will not read the map. They refuse to know Deaf Smith County, Texas, Cohn's way of naming reality, or the truth, or whatever you wish to call the awakening from the dream.

A third reading comes from paragraph 12. It is the whole point of Cohn's argument. Love and marriage are both moonlight *and* poison ivy. Cohn says it in no less than seven different ways—"noble and ignoble, generous and mean. . . ." When, he asks (paragraph 13), will we listen to the "dealer in reality" and turn off the "muted music of woodwinds"? This third reading is harsh acceptance of fact. Do we, perhaps, not want to admit life is dross *and* gold, chaff *and* wheat? The second half of Cohn's essay answers that question.

We can call this second half "proof" of his argument. If you feel Cohn is exaggerating, take the last issue of a national woman's magazine and read *every* advertisement. You will multiply the "shampoo and walnuts" cure-alls tenfold. Read the best seller lists or search your bookshops. Cohn has only begun to document his theme. What he is arguing here is, in a sense, an extension of the last paragraphs of Philip Wylie's essay on "scientific advancement." Both writers raise questions we must answer for ourselves. They do not leave us in any doubt how they feel.

Questions on Content

1. Cohn ends his first paragraph: ". . . the revulsion when it comes is, and must be, shattering." What "revulsion" is he talking about?
2. How does he describe our "gumdrop heaven"?
3. Paragraphs 10–11 discuss the phrase "love is blind" from two viewpoints. What are they?
4. What does Cohn mean by "installment plan mentality"?
5. What point is he making with his "shampoo and walnuts" examples? Does he exaggerate?

Add to your vocabulary: transient, tenure, anarchy, austerity, dynastic, tenuous, palpably, inextricably, symmetry, disseminate, opiate, lethargic, nuances. What are gossamer threads?

Questions on Technique

1. The opening paragraph of this essay contains an exceedingly long second sentence. Would you have written it this way? Why?
2. What effect does Cohn seek with phrases like "soft, gooey, and oh, so sweet"? Where else does he use them?
3. In paragraphs 15–17, Cohn uses sarcasm ° effectively. What other examples can you find in this essay?
4. Why bring Mrs. Deffenbaugh into paragraph 20? What is Cohn's point in using this illustration?

Suggestions for Writing

1. Cohn speaks of face powder, shampoo, and walnuts by their brand name. Using several national magazines as sources for advertisements, write a 500-word essay elaborating the claims Cohn argues are fostering an installment plan mentality in America.
2. You may well disagree with Cohn on American youth's attitude toward love and marriage. Your generation may be far more realistic than this essay suggests. Establish your argument and carry it through with proof in about 600 words.
3. Take one of the many slogans we call clichés,° and disprove it with examples from your experience. You might call your essay "Haste Does Not Always Make

sarcasm: See Glossary.   cliché: See Glossary.

Waste," "A Stitch in Time Doesn't Always Save Nine,"
or "A Word to the Wise is Not Sufficient."
4. Write a 600-word essay which begins "Not all of us
search for the easy way." Make your argument and
proof as personal as possible.
5. Write an essay in which you give your own formula
for a happy marriage, basing your ideas in part on
married couples you have known. What concessions
and compromises must both husband and wife be prepared to make?

RICHARD L. NEUBERGER
and HARLEY B. MARKHAM · *Outdoor Advertising:*
Two Points of View

*We mentioned earlier in this book that argument
and persuasion are closely allied. As the Cohn and Wylie
essays demonstrate, argument tries to make us believe
what the author believes, to share his opinion, to join
with him in his enthusiasms or his complaint. Persuasion
does all of this, and proposes a certain action or actions
as well. We have all heard debaters raise their voices to
convince us that we must give up smoking or enlist in
the drive against slums or fight the construction of a
new highway. We hear politicians persuade listeners to
vote the liberal or the conservative ticket. The mails are
full of letters and brochures which urge one to buy more
insurance, to subscribe to a new book club, to assist the
Community Players in a benefit performance. All of
these "arguments plus" are persuasion.*

*As a member of the Senate Public Works Committee,
Senator Richard L. Neuberger proposed a bill "to provide Federal assistance in the control of signboards along
the 41,000 miles of our new Interstate Highway." In
1957 the proposal was defeated. That same year the
Saturday* Review *invited the Senator from Oregon to
debate the issue, in their pages, with Harley B. Mark-*

ham. Mr. Markham has worked in advertising for more than thirty years and has served as chairman of the Outdoor Advertising Association of America. You will discover very quickly, in reading these essays, that Neuberger and Markham hold diametrically different points of view. You are asked to take sides. Notice also that you are being persuaded here by a heightened style. These are emotional appeals. Neuberger and Markham are moved by their own "oratory." They use more than reason to convince us.

RICHARD L. NEUBERGER · *What Is America For?*

1 When I was a schoolboy in my native state of Oregon, my favorite song was "America the Beautiful." At the age of forty-four it was my unhappy lot, however, to sit at a green-felt conference table while my colleagues of the Senate Public Works Committee voted down my bill to provide Federal assistance in the control of signboards along the 41,000 miles of our new Interstate Highway system. "America the Beautiful" did not fare very well that afternoon in the Senate Office Building. A well-organized billboard lobby had licked it. The vote in committee was seven to six.

2 The greatest advertising bonanza in history has thus come to the men who dominate the signboard industry. The publishers of a newspaper or magazine, as well as the operators of TV and radio stations, must risk heavy investments to give their media some value to advertisers. They must buy tons of costly paper, purchase or lease huge printing presses, erect elaborate studios and transmitting equipment, hire editors and photographers and entertainers, and finally often distribute their product

"What Is America For?" by Richard L. Neuberger from *Saturday Review*, November 9, 1957. Copyright by Saturday Review Inc. Reprinted by permission of publishers.

from door to door or through the mails. No such burden falls on what is euphemistically ° known as the "outdoor advertising industry." It will have its media ready-made, after the American motoring public spends $33 billion to construct a vast network of roads linking every major metropolitan area in the land.

³   Futhermore, the signboard proprietors hold enslaved a captive audience. Readers can avoid the advertisements in this issue of the *Saturday Review*. I need not read the displays in the *Washington Post* or *Pendleton East-Oregonian*. But the motorist must look at the signboards along U. S. 30 or else prepare to meet his Maker. Indeed, among the relatively modest expenses of the billboard industry lurks the pay of skilled road engineers, who craftily locate the sprawling twenty-four foot sheets where the driver's eye cannot possibly shun these signs as he wheels his sedan around a curve or over the crest of a hill. They are purposely situated to be within his normal sweep of vision.

⁴   The threadbare case for outdoor advertising is exposed by the flimsy arguments advanced in support of allowing our roadsides to be defaced for private profit. In testimony before the Senate Public Works Committee these arguments fitted into three principal categories:

1. State's rights
2. Highway safety
3. Free enterprise

⁵   My wife and I know how hollow and hypocritical is the trite shibboleth ° of "state's rights" with respect to this particular issue. As members of the Oregon State Legislature, we tried to secure anti-billboard legislation at the state level. There we were told that such matters were more properly the concern of cities, counties, and local zoning authorities. We also were advised, of course, that keeping highways free of billboards by law would be a first step in "Sovietizing" America. Although the

euphemistically: substituting a mild word for a harsh or blunt one.
shibboleth: a pet phrase of a party or a sect.

signboard operators raised the cry of "state's rights" to defeat my bill in the U. S. Senate, there is no record of the industry ever having supported effective regulation or control in any of the forty-eight states.

6 Then, in its presentation before our committee, the outdoor advertising colossus * claimed that its gaudy picket fence of signs would keep motorists from falling asleep at the wheel. The insult implicit in this claim is that the senses of the average American have been so deadened by raucous * sales messages that he needs the stimulus of whiskey, gasoline, and soft-drink ads in order to break the monotony of rivers, fields, and groves of ever-green or alder trees! Two main roads connect the teeming Washington and Baltimore citadels of population— U. S. 1 and the Washington-Baltimore Freeway. U. S. 1 is a verdant * billboard jungle. Signs sprout along it like undergrowth in the Matto Grosso.° The Freeway has been protected—thus far—from mutilation. It is my understanding that the Freeway, in addition to affording an infinitely more pleasant pilgrimage between the two cities, actually is safer than its sign-plastered sister route. Certainly, no statistics uphold the thesis of the companies that the billboards flanking U. S. 1 are a safe contrast to the dangerous monotony of the Freeway.

7 The free-enterprise argument of the signboard companies implies that they have an inherent right under our Constitution to plaster with signs any road built with public funds. If this is an inalienable American privilege, why should not other advertisers set up their material at the Government Printing Office or hang posters from Federal courthouses? And what of the right of Conrad Hilton ° to install a guest wing at the Pentagon Building?

8 One of the most effective claims of the outdoor advertisers was that rigid control of signs would work a grim hardship on small business along the roads—motels,

Matto Grosso: a state in southwestern Brazil, also spelled Mato Grosso.

Conrad Hilton: prominent international hotel owner.

hotels, garages, restaurants. Ex-Senator Scott Lucas, one of the leading spokesmen for the advertisers, even referred ominously to an adverse impact on the entire U. S. economy because of the $25 billion spent by families touring our highways. This, of course, implies that people traveling a sign-free road will not buy fuel for their cars, food for their stomachs, or seek shelter at night! I have always thought the warning voiced by Mr. Lucas was exactly contrary to facts. For example, there are three places in the world where tourist expenditures comprise a major source of income—Switzerland, Hawaii, and Alaska. All these realms are virtually free of billboards. Indeed, such protection of the alpine and tropical countrysides actually may stimulate the flow of wayfarers' dollars, pounds, or francs.

[9] One of our most authoritative witnesses was Bertram D. Tallamy, appointed recently by President Eisenhower to be Federal Highway Administrator. He will have charge of the great new interstate road program. In his home state of New York, Mr. Tallamy supervised the 432-mile Thruway from New York City to Buffalo. Signs on the Thruway are restricted to neat, standardized panels which indicate the distance to a general "Service Area" or the fact that a gas station and coffee shop are one mile away. These signs are in precisely the same pattern as those which herald distance, speed limits, directions, or curves. Actual commercial or brand advertising, as such, is forbidden. Two or three times I asked Mr. Tallamy if roadside business had suffered as a result of these controls on signs and billboards. He always answered in the negative.

[10] Despite so categorical a reply from a famous highway engineer with actual experience in this domain, the outdoor advertising companies insisted—right up to the hour that my bill was narrowly defeated in committee— that restrictions on billboards would seal the fate of small entrepreneurs ° pumping gas, serving food, or pat-

entrepreneurs: owners or managers of a business, as Neuberger uses the word.

ting down beds beside the roads. Yet, if our highways are made more attractive to the eye, will not a larger number of nomads set out upon them with their families—and will not these people need all the commodities and services offered along the way?

[11] With one breath the outdoor advertisers try to hide behind the backs of small, locally owned roadside facilities by mourning that these places will suffer in patronage if signs are controlled. But with their next gasp the advertising firms insist that the ugly signs are not those erected in the interest of the mighty national brand-name corporations but, rather, the on-the-premises signs heralding restaurants, motels, etc.

[12] Regardless of the equity of this claim, it is academic. The new interstate highways are, by law, to be breached by only limited-access conduits of travel for reasons of safety. Motels and filling stations cannot hem in the interstate roads because such direct intrusion would be illegal. These accommodations will be clustered principally around the interchanges—near the widely scattered clover-leaf turnoffs. My bill, for co-operative Federal-state regulation of signs, would allow a limited number of signs at the interchanges but—to all practical purposes—not in the open countryside.

[13] Such concessions have never budged the big outdoor advertisers. Their appetite for plastering our nation's roadsides is insatiable.* What if Mount Hood is shut off or a thicket of lush cedars barricaded? Who cares? The so-called self-policing imposed by the industry is largely confined to areas where signs do not have a high media value, anyway. The tiger vows not to eat carrots!

[14] Said ex-Senator Lucas: "This country was built on economics, not beauty." Perhaps this explains why, only 150 years after Lewis and Clark ° were first to span what is now our nation, we have made such awesome depredations * upon so many of our natural resources.

[15] The tremendous hardwood forests of the Lake States

Lewis and Clark: Meriwether Lewis and William Clark were joint commanders of an expedition to Oregon in 1804–06.

are all but gone. We wiped out 60 million bison so fast that President Theodore Roosevelt had trouble finding a few hundred to save as museum and zoo pieces. Count-less passenger pigeons were slaughtered to the last bird. In my home state of Oregon, greatest of the timber states, one sawmill community after another has cut itself out of logs. "Only God can grow a tree," wrote John Muir,[a] "but only Uncle Sam can save a tree." But what if Uncle Sam gets into the hands of people who are indifferent to the pollution of rivers, to the wholesale shooting for sport of herds of elk and caribou, to the systematic de-struction of the few grizzlies left in the Rockies and Bit-terroots,[o] to the draining of marshes where migratory waterfowl must find sanctuary, to the choking off of Chinook salmon [o] runs which seek the remote head-waters to spawn, to the commercializing of the last hand-ful of upland wilderness solitudes—yes, and callous, too, to the need for preserving the scenic majesty along our $33 billion investment in interstate highways?

16 Is that what we want in America?

HARLEY B. MARKHAM • *What's the Shouting About?*

1 The current attack on "billboards" is intensely emo-tional in origin and is being waged with complete dis-regard of facts, logic, and economics. Satirical cartoons and poems, biting editorials, clarion * Senatorial ora-tions, and other militant speeches make lively reading

John Muir: United States naturalist, explorer, and writer (1838–1914).

Bitterroots: a range of the Rocky Mountains on the boundary be-tween Idaho and Montana.

Chinook salmon: largest of the Pacific salmon, also called king or quinnat salmon.

"What's the Shouting About?" by Harley B. Markham from *Saturday Re-view*, November 9, 1957. Copyright by Saturday Review Inc. Reprinted by permission of publishers.

and listening. They have all but drowned out the voices of outdoor advertising men and advertisers as they ask: "Where are these 'billboard canyons' you say blot out your views of mountains, fields, and rivers?"

² The truth is that they don't exist. Actually, standardized outdoor advertising—call them "billboards" if you will—is a socially conscious, legitimate, and useful business which makes substantial contributions to the economic and social welfare of our country.

³ I am proud to be in the outdoor advertising business, and so are all my colleagues. For generations outdoor advertising has been a medium of proved effectiveness, an integral part of a growing America. Standardized outdoor advertising displays have a colorful heritage as part of Americana.° As a popular art form they have won recognition by museums and other art authorities throughout the country. They are just as much a part of the American scene as baseball or the neighborhood drugstore—and they have just as much right to exist. Most important of all, they have helped build many great names of American industry: Coca-Cola, General Motors, Wrigley, Standard Oil, Ford, and many others.

⁴ Standardized outdoor advertising is represented by the Outdoor Advertising Association of America, Inc., which had its origin more than sixty-five years ago. There are 776 member companies in the Association, doing business in more than 15,000 communities. Their annual volume is about $200 million, which is more than 90 per cent of the total volume of standardized outdoor advertising. These member companies operate standardized poster panels and painted bulletins on land which they own or lease for the purpose, as distinguished from miscellaneous signs.

⁵ This distinction is important. Nine times out of ten, when our critics charge that "billboards deface the countryside," we have found that they are not talking about

---

Americana: books, documents, maps and so forth relating to the history and development of America. Markham uses the term loosely.

our standardized displays at all, but about other kinds of signs for which our industry is in no way responsible.

⁶   Like all good citizens and good neighbors, we recognize and accept our public and social responsibilities. Our policies are in the public interest. Our Association members voluntarily pledge adherence to a strict code of practices imposing high ethical standards upon our industry. For instance, this code says: *"We share the public interest in natural scenic beauty, parks, and historical monuments. We do not erect our advertising displays in such areas."*

⁷   That is plain enough and it means just what it says. We want to keep America beautiful, too. Here are other provisions of our self-imposed code to insure operations in the public interest: *"We believe in and support zoning based on sound community planning."*

⁸   Many communities have adopted zoning standards and restrictions for such purposes as to distinguish between business and commercial areas and those which are residential in character. We agree that reasonable restrictions affecting business and commercial practices are desirable in any well-planned community. We, therefore, pledge full support of sound zoning, and are willing to be treated under zoning just like any other business. *"We place outdoor advertising displays only upon property we own or lease for that purpose."*

⁹   Critics who would legislate us out of business either don't know or ignore the issue of proper and lawful land use—the fact that private property rights are involved because our displays are always located on private land owned or leased by us—never on highway rights of way. And these same critics who scream that "billboards" are despoiling scenic beauty also conveniently ignore the fact that more than 85 per cent of all standardized outdoor displays are in strictly urban areas zoned for business.

¹⁰   *"We locate our structures with discretion and good taste with respect to frequency and concentration."*

¹¹   Again playing fast and loose with the facts, some

critics would have the public believe that "billboards" are placed indiscriminately * along virtually every inch of highway, thus creating so-called "billboard canyons" or "ribbon slums." Nothing could be further from the truth. As businessmen we are deeply interested in the orderly growth of the communities where we operate. We recognize the need for discretion and good taste in developing business and industrial areas. Accordingly, we locate outdoor displays in a manner which will promote the business interests of the community, and at the same time preserve attractive features.

12   The term "ribbon slums" has been used to describe heavy concentrations of business and the signs of varied size and shape advertising them. They are for the most part "on premise" signs advertising goods and services available on the premises. They may not be pleasing to some people, but from another viewpoint they represent one way of doing business in a highly competitive area. Thus, "ribbon slums" exist because the people in the area permit them. If a remedy is needed or desired, it lies in proper zoning at the local level.

13   *"We only display outdoor advertising which is truthful in every respect, and in accordance with high moral standards."*

14   Our medium has been praised by objective authorities as the "cleanest" of all advertising media with respect to accuracy, truthfulness, and good taste. We intend to keep it that way.

15   *"We actively and continuously support worthy public causes through our contributions of outdoor advertising displays."*

16   For generations the standardized outdoor advertising industry has *every month* contributed a substantial portion of its facilities as a public service in support of worthy causes for the good of the community, state, and nation. These contributions average about $1.7 million worth of outdoor advertising space annually. Typical of the many causes supported by our Association members

are Community Chests, Red Cross, Cancer Society, Religion in American Life, March of Dimes, Mental Health, Traffic Safety, and many others.

[17]   We are proud of our record. It is shocking to have misinformed or malicious critics slander us with the charge that outdoor advertising displays create a traffic safety hazard and are a factor in causing accidents. But we are glad to note, however, that even some of the most reckless and irresponsible of critics are dropping that line, because when challenged they have been unable to muster a single fact to support the charge, not from insurance companies, traffic authorities, or anybody else. On the contrary, a scientific test conducted at Iowa State College said in part: "Numerous signs in the driver's field of vision in no way influenced efficiency at the wheel adversely, and in fact seemed beneficial by about 10 per cent."

[18]   Much of the argument against outdoor advertising is on esthetic * grounds: "Outdoor advertising is ugly, a highway blight, marring beautiful scenery." We admit that it's not easy to win an argument solely on esthetics. That's because art and esthetics are subjective; opinions, not facts, and not always informed opinions at that. It's all a matter of personal viewpoint and taste. The picture that hangs proudly in the Louvre as a great work of art is just a blob of paint to some people.

[19]   As for our poster panels and painted bulletins—well, we try to make them as attractive as we can. They are simple and functional. A few years ago we retained Raymond Loewy, the noted industrial designer, to develop a new standard panel. More than half of the panels being rebuilt each year are now Loewy designed.

[20]   Prize-winning artists such as Howard Scott, Raymond Savinac, and Norman Rockwell illustrate our advertising copy. Their work is judged annually in national competition by leading art authorities. Outdoor advertising art has been praised for its simplicity of design, directness, and symbolism.

[21]   These are some of the facts about our business, as

distinguished from fancy. We don't pretend to be perfect. Like any other business, we have our problems and we make mistakes. But on the whole we think we have a pretty good record. We ask for no special treatment. All we ask is the same fair treatment accorded any other legitimate business. We regard our outdoor advertising structures as business installations, just as much so as the garage or store.

[22] The charge has been made that a so-called "billboard lobby," working against the public interest, was responsible for the defeat of proposed federal legislation which would have discriminated against outdoor advertising. That charge is ridiculous. As citizens and businessmen we did present the honest facts of our case, a right granted to every American citizen. Even Senator Neuberger, sponsor of the bill against our medium, recognized at the Senate Subcommittee hearings that our industry representatives had every right to protect their business.

[23] With respect to all the punitive legislation proposed against us, we'd like to make one point clear. We have no intention or desire of exploiting the Interstate Highway system in rural areas. In keeping with the policies set forth in our code, the only place we want to be, or have any right to be, is in business or industrial areas or where business is appropriate. We are a business. We create business. We belong with business.

[24] Americans are a fair-minded people. We have every confidence that when they have the facts—all the facts—they will join us in demanding: What's all the shouting about?

ANALYSIS

Neuberger is angry. He asks what America is for. His question needs interpretation as well as answering. At first glance, it asks what America is in favor of, what it supports. But his title also poses the questions: What is happening to our countryside? What will be the fate of our roads and hills? Shall our greenery go the way of our bison? Is America for the people or for private profit?

Having lost his fight to pass a bill in the Senate, Neuberger is understandably irritated, and he concludes his article with a woefully pessimistic diagnosis. How does he reach his last question: "Is that what we want in America?"

He devotes most of his essay to "exploring the flimsy arguments" of his opponents. For our convenience, he lists them in paragraph 4. Paragraphs 5–11 try to demolish them. While you are judging for yourself the efficiency of his attack, do not fail to note the emotionally charged words and phrases he uses to sway our feelings: "the threadbare case," "hollow and hypocritical," "the outdoor advertising colossus," "gaudy picket fence of signs," "raucous sales messages," "greatest advertising bonanza in history," and others. This heightened language aims at inciting us to write our senators to protest this defacement of public highways.

Paragraph 15 uses analogies ° to emphasize further what dangerous precedents we have set in the past, what foolish waste he sees us now contemplating. Ex-Senator Lucas says, "This country was built on economics, not beauty." Neuberger argues that hardwood forests, marshes, streams, shorelines are of both economic *and* esthetic concerns. The body of this essay attacks the economic interests of a billboard lobby. Neuberger's positive arguments are conservation of beauty and natural resources. We *must,* he says, preserve our public lands.

Harley B. Markham takes the defensive in this debate. His opening sentence disapproves of emotional arguments. By the end of the second paragraph we know we are listening to a man who will defend a "socially conscious, legitimate, and useful business" in a business-like way. He centers his essay around six excerpts from the code of the Outdoor Advertising Association of America. He elaborates his defense in terms of these excerpts. For the most part it is a well-reasoned defense, assuming that we understand at the outset that esthetic matters— the preservation of beauty—are not of first importance. In paragraph 22, Markham bluntly states "our industry representatives [have] every right to protect their business."

analogies: See Glossary.

But if Neuberger is generous with his emotionally-charged words and phrases, so is Markham with his emotional reasoning. Experienced debaters will call some of his sentences *non sequiturs,* by which they mean inferences or conclusions not necessarily derived from the premise or original argument. Consider just a few:

Paragraph 3: [Billboards] are just as much a part of the American scene as baseball or the neighborhood drugstore—and they have just as much right to exist."

Paragraph 14: "Our medium has been praised by objective authorities as the 'cleanest' of all advertising media with respect to accuracy, truthfulness, and good taste."

Paragraph 18: "The picture that hangs proudly in the Louvre as a great work of art is just a blob of paint to some people."

Paragraph 19: "A few years ago we retained Raymond Loewy, the noted industrial designer, to develop a new standard panel."

Paragraph 20: "Prize-winning artists such as Howard Scott, Raymond Savinac, and Norman Rockwell illustrate our advertising copy."

Paragraph 21: "We don't pretend to be perfect. Like any other business, we have our problems and we make mistakes."

Paragraph 24: "Americans are fair-minded people. We have every confidence that when they have the facts—all the facts—they will join us in demanding: What's all the shouting about?"

Persuasion frequently uses this argument-by-association technique. Markham combines his reasonable point of view—a business has a right to defend its existence—with people and things he doubtless feels most of his readers recognize, understand, and approve of: baseball, the corner drugstore, the "cleanest," Raymond Loewy, prize-winning artists, business problems, fair-minded Americans. The whole of paragraph 16 is argument-by-association. Like Neuberger, Markham hopes you will answer his final question as he wishes you to.

What is your choice?

Questions on Content

1. Why does Neuberger call the veto of his bill the "greatest advertising bonanza in history"?
2. How does Neuberger attack the argument of "free enterprise"? Why does he use Switzerland, Alaska, and Hawaii as examples?
3. Why was Bertram D. Tallamy an "authoritative witness"?
4. In what way does the code of practices, as Markham excerpts it, prevent the abuses Neuberger claims are being made? Does Markham offer proof?
5. What are "ribbon slums"? How does Markham distinguish between "standardized outdoor advertising" and "on-premise signs"? Is this distinction vital to the argument?

Add to your vocabulary: euphemistically, shibboleth, colossus, raucous, verdant, insatiable, depredations, clarion, indiscriminately, esthetic. What is a "categorical reply" (Neuberger, paragraph 10)? What is "punitive legislation" (Markham, paragraph 23)?

Questions on Technique

1. Neuberger cites the song "America the Beautiful" in his first paragraph. How does he use it as a theme throughout his essay?
2. What is your opinion of the argument in this sentence in paragraph 7 of Neuberger's essay: "And what of the right of Conrad Hilton to install a guest wing at the Pentagon Building?"
3. What does Neuberger mean by this phrase (paragraph 13): "The tiger vows not to eat carrots!"? How else might he have expressed the same idea?
4. Is this sentence of Markham's (paragraph 11) self-contradictory: "We locate outdoor displays in a manner which will promote the business interests of a community, and at the same time preserve attractive features."? Why?
5. Why should Markham want to use the figures he employs in paragraph 4 or the names of companies he cites in paragraph 3?

Suggestions for Writing

1. Select what you think are the strongest and weakest arguments from either Neuberger's or Markham's essay and write a 300-word essay on why you think as you do in the light of their primary subject: "Outdoor Advertising on our Interstate Highways."
2. Write an essay of 600 words on the subject "Outdoor Advertising in My Hometown."
3. Prepare one side of a debate on a current school issue. Outline your arguments. Plan a persuasive conclusion which will move your listeners to action. Now write, in 300-400 words, a summary of what you are going to say.
4. How well can you write argument or persuasion?

     a. Answer your best friend on an argument which you oppose and he favors.

     b. Answer an editorial in a recent newspaper. Do it as a letter to the editor.

     c. Convince your parents, in a 500-word essay, that you are old enough to be allowed to drive the family car or travel alone or attend college in another section of the United States, or do some other thing they are reluctant to allow.

     d. Defend yourself against an accusation.

     e. Attack a new regulation of which you disapprove.

CHAPTER 7

The critical essay: society

After inspecting four groups of essays under the familiar rhetorical headings—definition, process, report, and argument—we turn now to two somewhat freer forms of expository writing: the critical essay and the informal essay. These essays observe, judge, and review. They are as much concerned with *why* and *how* as those in the preceding chapters in Part Two. However, they are less, shall we say, insistent, less urgent, less determined to convey a specific body of facts, to record a certain event, to exhort us to believe or to act.

The informal essayist, as we shall discover, rarely adheres to an explicit pattern of logic. He does not always report events in chronological order. He does not set forth arguments in series, though he may hold firmly to debatable points of view. The critical essayist, likewise, feels freer to talk "around" a subject. That is not to suggest he is writing disorganized prose. Instead of analyzing a subject, he illuminates it. In place of propounding an idea, he explores it. Critical writing can give us new insight into a work of art or a problem in linguistics ° or a political issue. It can set us to thinking by raising questions, citing parallels, recalling history. It is a kind of elaboration, an intellectual exercise. The ends are sometimes persuasion, more often perceptive judgment and tentative conclusion.

linguistics: See Glossary.

ERIC SEVAREID · *The Dark of the Moon*

Eric Sevareid's essay is a good introduction to social criticism. For years he worked for the Minneapolis Star, *the Paris* Herald-Tribune, *and the United Press in Paris. He is now known internationally as CBS correspondent and reporter of world affairs. In print and on the air he has been commenting on history in the making. Here he discusses current affairs which concern all of us, but note that what he has to say has no resemblance to a news report. He is not dealing in facts, figures, dates, or places. He uses no statistics, proves nothing. Yet he takes as his subject "front-page talk." One aspect of social criticism is just this method of discussing an issue in general terms.*

¹ This, thank goodness, is the first warm and balmy night of the year in these parts; the first frogs are singing. Altogether this is hardly the night for whispering sweet sentiments about the reciprocal trade act, the extension thereof. But since we are confined, by tradition, to the contemplation of public themes and issues, let us contemplate the moon. The lovely and luminous * moon has become a public issue. For quite a few thousand years it was a private issue; it figured in purely bilateral ° negotiations between lovers, in the incantations of jungle witch doctors and Indian corn planters. Poets from attic windows issued the statements about the moon, and they made better reading than the mimeographed handouts now being issued by assistant secretaries of defense.

² The moon was always measured in terms of hope and reassurance and the heart pangs of youth on such a night as this; it is now measured in terms of mileage and foot-

bilateral: two-sided.

"Dark of the Moon" by Eric Sevareid from *The Reporter*, April 17, 1958. © by the Reporter Magazine Company. Reprinted by permission of the publishers and author.

pounds of rocket thrust. Children sent sharp, sweet wishes to the moon; now they dream of blunt-nosed missiles.

3   There must come a time, in every generation, when those who are older secretly get off the train of progress, willing to walk back to where they came from, if they can find the way. We're afraid we're getting off now. Cheer, if you wish, the first general or Ph.D. who splatters something ° on the kindly face of the moon. We shall grieve for him, for ourself, for the young lovers and poets and dreamers to come, because the ancient moon will never be the same again. Therefore, we suspect, the heart of man will never be the same.

4   We find it very easy to wait for the first photographs of the other side of the moon, for we have not yet seen the other side of Lake Louise or the Blue Ridge peak that shows through the cabin window.

5   We find ourself quite undisturbed about the front-page talk of "controlling the earth from the moon," because we do not believe it. If neither men nor gadgets nor both combined can control the earth from the earth, we fail to see how they will do so from the moon.

6   It is exciting talk, indeed, the talk of man's advance toward space. But one little step in man's advance toward man—that, we think, would be truly exciting. Let those who wish try to discover the composition of a lunar crater; we would settle for discovering the true mind of a Russian commissar or the inner heart of a delinquent child.

7   There is, after all, another side—a dark side—to the human spirit, too. Men have hardly begun to explore these regions; and it is going to be a very great pity if we advance upon the bright side of the moon with the dark side of ourselves, if the cargo in the first rockets to reach there consists of fear and chauvinism ° and suspicion. Surely we ought to have our credentials in order, our hands very clean, and perhaps a prayer for forgiveness

splatters something: The Russian multistage rocket Lunik ii hit the moon on September 13, 1959.

chauvinism: over-zealous patriotism or devotion to a cause.

on our lips as we prepare to open the ancient vault of the shining moon.

ANALYSIS

In spite of his lighthearted opening paragraph, Sevareid is wholly serious. Not frightened, not pessimistic, he is nevertheless wary. He expresses this caution with a simple image. "We're afraid we're getting off [the train of progress] now," he says, using the editorial "we." Shall we take him at his word? Is Sevareid turning his back on the future? Would he like to call off all exploration of outer space, bring back the satellites man has put in orbit, close down Cape Canaveral—all to keep the "lovely and luminous moon" a "private issue" for lovers and poets? No, not exactly that. We will still have a luminous moon on "the first warm and balmy night" of every year. But Sevareid is troubled.

The dark side of the human spirit troubles him far more than the dark side of the moon entices our scientists. Consider his simple sentence (paragraph 7): "Men have hardly begun to explore these [dark] regions." How many past attempts that implies! Sophocles, Shakespeare, Goethe, Mann, to name only creative artists; the prophets of the Bible, and the founders of modern psychiatry; lawmakers and judges of every century; philosophers and scientists—all of this combined knowledge, some of it 5,000 years old, has only begun to answer the ancient question: what is man? If we were wholly rational creatures, we would need no disarmament conferences, we could disband the United Nations, we should have no fear of "fear and chauvinism and suspicion." But man has always been victim of his own emotions, singly, in groups, in nations. We might ask Sevareid: Must we wait for man to become perfect before we take another giant step in science? Has not man always tried the impossible and called it progress? Shall we stop him now?

Questions on Content

1. What does Sevareid mean when he says, "We find ourself quite undisturbed about the front-page talk of 'controlling the earth from the moon,' because we do not believe it"?
2. Explain what Sevareid means by his comparison between discovering the composition of a lunar crater and understanding the inner heart of a delinquent child.

Add to your vocabulary: luminous, bilateral, chauvinism.

Questions on Technique

1. Why is the phrase "purely bilateral negotiations between lovers" so apt where it is used (paragraph 1)?
2. What use does Sevareid make of Lake Louise, a Blue Ridge peak, a Russian commissar, and a delinquent child in this essay? What have they to do with space exploration?

Suggestions for Writing

1. Answer Sevareid's essay from the point of view of your generation. Call your essay "Space Travel and How American Youth Feel About It."
2. Using Sevareid's method (talking "around" a subject), discuss a matter of general interest in your school *and* your own feelings about it. You might write on athletics, extra-curricular organizations, the school cafeteria, or homework.
3. Choose one of the following subjects and write two 300-word contrasting essays, one on the optimistic side and one on the pessimistic:
    a. Increasing college enrollments
    b. Super-highways
    c. Super-markets
    d. The movies
    e. Automation
4. Write an essay comparing the attitudes toward scientific "progress" expressed in Philip Wylie's "Science Has Spoiled My Supper" and in Sevareid's essay.

C. P. SNOW · *The Future of Man*

Eric Sevareid's essay is an easy bridge to C. P. Snow's. Snow, too, is concerned about the future, how science is molding it, how man is facing it. As social critic, he writes from a more academic background than Sevareid. He is both a scientist and a novelist. Since the early 1930's, he has been writing in England a series of novels under the general title Strangers and Brothers. The Masters (1951) *and* The Affair (1960) *have sold widely in the United States. For many years he was also a physicist, college administrator, and Civil Service Commissioner. Recently he has travelled widely and has written much on the effect of organized science on our culture, what new problems future growth will bring, where moral responsibility lies.*

When this essay appeared in the Nation *in 1958, it was followed by an equally forceful article called "The Man of the Future," written by Philip Siekevitz, a biochemist. The* Nation *gave the two essays the joint title "Science and Hope." Snow's contribution is all of that: hope in face of overwhelming scientific discoveries, in face of the devastating destruction of the past. He talks here about man's fate, as individuals, as nations, as a race.*

[1]   Auschwitz and Hiroshima.° We have seen all that; in some of it we have acquiesced * or helped. No wonder we

Auschwitz and Hiroshima: In World War II, the Germans maintained a concentration camp in Auschwitz, in southern Poland. Approximately 4,000,000 inmates, mostly Jews, were put to death here. Auschwitz is the German spelling for the Polish name, Oswiecim. On August 8, 1945, an American B-29 dropped an atomic bomb on the city of Hiroshima, Japan, killing directly or indirectly 75,000–80,000 persons and destroying approximately 70,000 buildings.

"The Future of Man" by C. P. Snow from *The Nation*, September 13, 1958. © 1958 Nation Associates, Inc. Reprinted by permission of publisher.

are morally guilty. Men like ourselves have done such things—and at the same time men like ourselves, sometimes the same men who have taken a hand in the horrors, have been showing more concern for the unlucky round them than has ever been shown by a large society in human history. That is the moral paradox ° in which we have to live.

² It is wrong to try to domesticate the horrors. The mass slaughter of the concentration camps was both the most awful and the most degrading set of actions that men have done so far. This set of actions was ordered and controlled by abnormally wicked men, if you like, but down the line the orders were carried out by thousands of people like the rest of us, civil servants, soldiers, engineers, all brought up in an advanced Western and Christian society. While it was people not like the rest of us but a great deal better, people who for imagination and morality, not to speak of intellect, stand among the finest of our race, people like Einstein, Niels Bohr, and Franck,° who got caught up in the tangle of events which led to Hiroshima and Nagasaki.° The dropping of those bombs was of a lesser order of wickedness from what was done at Auschwitz. But Western man ought not to forget that he did it; Eastern man certainly won't.

³ At the same time we ought not to forget what there is to our credit. Some kinds of optimism about man's nature are dangerous—but so are some kinds of pessimism. Think of the care the Swedes and the Danes are taking of their old and poor, or of prisoners, or of social misfits. Nothing like that has been done at any period or in any place until our lifetime. We can congratulate ourselves in Britain, too. The Scandinavians have not made anything like a perfect society. In some ways we have not got

paradox: See Glossary.

Einstein, Niels Bohr, and Franck: Albert Einstein (1879–1955), German-born American physicist and mathematician; Niels Bohr (1885–), Danish physicist; James Franck (1882–) German-born American physical chemist.

Nagasaki: The second military use of an atomic bomb was over Nagasaki, Japan, on August 9, 1945.

as near to it as they have. But we have both made a better shot at it than anyone before us.

4   Britain is a much fairer and a much kinder society than the one I was born into in 1905. It may seem sentimental to have consciences troubled about capital punishment, about removing one life when Western man has recently eliminated twenty million: yet it is a sign of moral sensitivity. So is the attempt, however grudging, to treat women as though they were equal human beings. So is the feeling behind the Wolfenden Report.° So is the conviction—so urgent in the United States—that children have a special right to happiness.

5   Some of these feelings may lead to practical follies (I believe that the American one is making a mess of their education), but that is not the point. They are signs of a development of something very rare in the world up to now, which one might call moral kindness. I have no doubt that in Scandinavia, England, some, though not all, of the United States, and perhaps three or four other countries in the West, the amount of fairness, tolerance, and effective kindness within the society would seem astonishing to any nineteenth-century man.

6   It would also seem astonishing to any nineteenth-century man how much we know. There is probably no one now alive as clever as Clerk Maxwell or Gauss; ° but thousands of people know more than Clerk Maxwell or Gauss, and understand more of those parts of the world that they spent their lives trying to understand. Put those two down, or even greater men, such as Newton and Archimedes,° in front of what is now understood—and

Wolfenden Report: Sir John Wolfenden, Vice-Chancellor of Reading University, England, headed a committee which prepared a report for Parliament in 1957 on public law and private morals.

Maxwell or Gauss: James Clerk Maxwell (1831–1879), British physicist; Karl Friedrich Gauss (1777–1855), German mathematician.

Newton and Archimedes: Sir Issac Newton (1642–1727), British scientist who formulated the law of gravity; Archimedes (287?–212 B.C.), Greek mathematician who discovered the principles of specific gravity and of the lever.

they would think it wonderful. So it is, and we can take pride and joy in it. It will go on; the search to understand is one of the most human things about us. Compared with our ancestors, there are some trivial physical differences. We are a good deal taller and heavier, we live much longer. But above all, we know more.

7   All this it would be reasonable to call progress, so long as we don't expect of progress more than it can give. In each of our individual lives there is, of course, something beyond human help. Each of us has to live part of his life alone: and he has to die alone. That part of our experience is right outside of time and history, and progress has no meaning there. In this sense, the individual condition is tragic. But that is no excuse for not doing our best with the social condition.

8   To think otherwise, to take refuge in facile * despair, has been the characteristic intellectual treachery of our day. It is shoddy. We have to face the individual condition: for good and evil, for pettiness and the occasional dash of grandeur, we have to know what men are capable of: and then we can't contract out. For we are part, not only of the privileged North European–British American enclave ° of progress, but of another progress which is altering the whole world.

9   I mean something brutally simple. Most people in Asia still haven't enough to eat: but they have a bit more than before. Most people in Asia are still dying before their time (on the average, Indians live less than half as long as Englishmen) : but they are living longer than before. Is *that* progress? This is not a subject to be superior or refined or ingenious about, and the answer is: *of course it is.*

10   It is because Western man has grown too far away from that elemental progress that we can't get on terms with most of the human race. Through luck we got in first with the scientific-industrial revolution; as a result, our lives became, on the average, healthier, longer, more

enclave: a tract or territory enclosed within foreign territory.

comfortable to an extent that had never been imagined; it doesn't become us to tell our Chinese and Indian friends that that kind of progress is not worth having.

¹¹ We know what it is like to live among the shops, the cars, the radios, of Leicester and Orebro and Des Moines.° We know what it is like to ask the point of it all, and to feel the Swedish sadness or the American disappointment or the English Welfare State ° discontent. But the Chinese and Indians would like the chance of being well-fed enough to ask what is the point of it all. They are in search of what Leicester, Orebro and Des Moines take for granted: food, extra years of life, modest comforts. When they have got these things, they are willing to put up with a dash of the Swedish sadness or American disappointment. And their determination to get them is likely in the next thirty years to prove the strongest social force on earth.

¹² Will they get them? Will the social conditions everywhere reach within foreseeable time something like the standard of the privileged Western enclave? There is no technical reason why not. If it does, the level of moral kindness will go up in parallel. These ought to be realistic hopes. There seems only one fatality that might destroy them. That is, it goes without saying, an H-bomb war.

¹³ No one can pretend that it is not possible. For myself, I think that it won't happen even though we have seen how good and conscientious men have become responsible for horrors, even though two atomic bombs have been dropped already, and by Western man. But I still think, partly as a guess, partly as a calculation, that we shall escape the H-bomb war—just as I think we shall

Leicester and Orebro and Des Moines: cities in England, Sweden, and the United States, respectively.

English Welfare State: the term applied to the English social revolution which, in the last twenty years, has brought to a country which is ostensibly a monarchy such reforms as tight central governmental controls, nationalized railroads and health service, social security measures, and the like.

escape the longer-term danger of Malthusian ° over-population.

14   It may easily be that I am letting hope run away with me about the H-bomb war. Some of the wisest disagree with me. Let us imagine that they are right and that the H-bombs go off. Is that going to be the end? I find it difficult to believe. In England a lot of us would be dead, our children with us. A lot of Americans and Russians would also be killed outright. No one knows how many would die afterwards through effects of radiation. But I don't believe that men have at present the resources to destroy the race.

15   If that is so, and if after an H-bomb war a viable ° fraction of the world population were left untouched (my guess is that it would be a large fraction, at least two-thirds) , then we should all be amazed how soon hope of progress took possession again. The human species is biologically a very tough one, and tough in a sense no animal species can be, through its intelligence, its organization of knowledge, the capacity of its members not to be totally bound within the rapacious * self. After the most hideous H-bomb war, the inhabitants of Africa and India and South America would have the strength of those qualities to build on. The material and scientific gap, left through the devastation of the West and Russia, would be filled up at a speed not flattering to Western or Russian self-esteem. What would the moral scar be?

16   I think we can already answer that question, for we too have, as I said at the beginning, witnessed horrors and assisted at them. Most of us don't live constantly in the presence of Hiroshima and Auschwitz: the memory doesn't prevent us getting morally concerned about the fate of one murderer or cross because a lonely and im-

Malthusian: Thomas Malthus (1766–1834) , British political economist, contended that population, since it increased faster than the means of subsistence, should be checked by social and moral restraints.
viable: capable of living.

poverished old man doesn't have enough calls from the District Visitor.°

17 It would be just the same if the Northern hemisphere became more or less destroyed. Men elsewhere would not live under that shadow; they would be busy with their own societies. If those societies were less fair and morally sensitive than ours is now, they would soon catch up. Within a bizarrely short interval, after hundreds of millions of people had been incinerated by H-bombs, men in countries unaffected would be passionately debating capital punishment. It sounds mad, but it is the kind of madness which makes human beings as tough as they are, and as capable of behaving better than they have so far behaved.

18 So there remains a sort of difficult hope. As long as men continue to be men, individual man will perceive the same darkness about his solitary condition as any of us does now. But he will also feel occasional intimations * that his own life is not the only one. In the midst of his egotisms, pettiness, power-seekings, and perhaps the horrors these may cause, he will intermittently * stretch a little beyond himself. That little, added to the intelligence and growing knowledge of the species, will be enough to make his societies more decent, to use the social forces for what, in the long sight of history, are good ends.

19 None of it will be easy. As individuals, each of us is almost untouched by this progress. It is no comfort to remember how short human history is. As individuals, that seems just an irony.° But as a race, we have scarcely begun to live.

ANALYSIS

Snow discusses several major aspects of man's nature in this essay, and he does it with sufficient elaboration to

District Visitor: a person who does parochial work in a district under a clergyman's direction.
irony: See Glossary.

let us digest what is on his mind. It might help us to list his main points:

1. Man has shown to his fellow men extreme cruelty at one moment in history and great kindness at another. This is the moral paradox or contradiction we must face (paragraphs 1–5).
2. We have extended our knowledge greatly in the last several centuries (paragraph 6).
3. The individual condition (a single life) is tragic and fleeting, but the social condition (the race as a whole) is improving (paragraphs 7–11).

Up to this point, you may feel that Snow is unusually optimistic about the future. As a scientist, he can foresee the day when we will have enough food for all mankind, though it may take several decades. He recognizes what we call "progress" in our modest comforts, our extra years of life. But the shadow is always there. He defines it in his fourth point.

4. Man has also invented the means of blowing himself up, namely the H-bomb (paragraph 12).

The rest of his essay is devoted to two questions which naturally arise when the H-bomb is mentioned: Will we use it, and if we do, will mankind survive in sufficient numbers to propagate the race? The burden of his reply to both questions is as optimistic as the first half of this essay. Are we surprised? Not if we caught the conviction of his seventh paragraph. Individual man is weak, Snow admits, but collectively mankind is indestructible. He re-states this feeling in paragraphs 17–19, calling it "a sort of difficult hope." Do you agree?

Questions on Content

1. What does Snow mean by "the privileged North European-British American enclave of progress" (paragraph 8)?
2. How do Leicester, Orebro, and Des Moines differ from towns in India (paragraph 11)?
3. When Snow says (paragraph 14), "I don't believe that men have at present the resources to destroy the race," does he offer proof?

Add to your vocabulary: acquiesced, facile, enclave, viable, rapacious, intimations, intermittently.

Questions on Technique

1. Why are Auschwitz and Hiroshima effective words with which to open this essay?
2. What effect does Snow achieve with his many references to proper names: Einstein, Bohr, Franck, Newton, and so forth? Does he lose some of that effect if we do not know his local references, such as the Wolfenden Report and the District Visitor?
3. How does he substantiate his theory that mankind will survive even an H-bomb war?

Suggestions for Writing

1. If you have read Eric Sevareid's essay, "The Dark of the Moon," reread Snow's paragraph 18. Does Snow unknowingly answer Sevareid's statement (in his last paragraph) that "it is going to be a very great pity if we advance upon the bright side of the moon with the dark side of ourselves"? Write a 500-word essay on these two authors' use of "individual man" and "mankind." Incorporate as many of your own opinions as you wish.
2. Write an essay of 400–600 words on the subject "The World I [We] Face." Do not write a simple description or a projection of your plans. Talk of the problems you know you will have to face and how you expect to surmount them.
3. Stretch your imagination. Write a 500-word essay on what a visitor from the Far East might find remarkable in your hometown. Consider such things you take for granted as new houses everywhere, stores fully stocked, cars in profusion, the average man's health and diet, our luxuries, our pastimes.
4. Do some research. In the fifteen years since the atomic bomb was dropped on Hiroshima, that city has undergone great rebuilding. When did it begin? How was it financed? What memorials have been erected? Reread paragraph 15 of Snow's article before you begin an essay on "Hiroshima and the Hope of Progress."
5. Write a comparison between Snow's attitude toward science and Eric Sevareid's.

CHAPTER 8

The critical essay: literature

For centuries, men have been discussing the creative imagination in expository prose. The shelves of commentaries—books, pamphlets, articles—on Shakespeare's work, for example, would astound the average theatergoer who simply enjoys the plays on stage, to say nothing of how Shakespeare would react were he to return today. We call this kind of exposition literary criticism.

You have been engaged in writing literary criticism longer than you think. Its simplest form is the book review. Perhaps you reported on your first book orally, telling the class what you read and how the story "turned out." When you came to writing reports, you realized that summarizing the plot was not enough if you wished to give your own views of the work. Good newspaper critics, especially in the Sunday supplements, also do more than summarize. They describe the contents of a new work and judge its worth, telling us *why* it is good or bad, *how* it succeeds or fails.

We include no book reviews among the three models of literary criticism for one obvious reason: you know and have experienced this kind of writing. Let us look, instead, at three critical essays which do more than review the first appearance of a book or survey the contents in a general way. Like the two social critics, Eric Sevareid and C. P. Snow, these writers talk "around" their subject. They illuminate and explore. J. B. Priestley investigates the characters of Macbeth and his wife. He makes no attempt to review the whole play. John Ciardi gives close attention to one poem in order to discuss the nature of poetry and Robert Frost's genius. Lord Conesford, a harsh critic indeed, berates our use of the English language. His essay is concerned with semantics,° rather than with literature. These three models offer a variety of methods of literary criticism. We will begin with the shortest of the three selections.

J. B. PRIESTLEY · Macbeth: *An Afterword*

Literary criticism is never a substitute for the work of art itself. You might argue that neither is reading Macbeth *a substitute for seeing it produced. True, but we must make a concession somewhere to the few opportunities many of us have to hear Shakespeare's poetry on the stage. Priestley assumes, in this essay, that we have at least* read *the play. He does not discuss the plot. He does not identify Duncan or Banquo. He never mentions Macduff. He speaks of the witches as though we all were aware of their prophecies. Priestley makes these assumptions in order to get at what he thinks is the heart of the play: ambition leading to violence. He can best discuss this theme through the main characters. What conclusion Priestley draws about the nature of mankind in general is directly related to his treatment of Macbeth and his queen.*

In 1960 Priestley published a lengthy critical study called Literature and Western Man. *The New York* Times *reviewer commented above all on the gusto with which Priestley wrote, the "sense of personal engagement with great books" which one feels in his presence. Since Priestley is a novelist and playwright as well as a critic, one is not surprised to find him bringing us close to the imaginative power that pervades a work of art. He is clearly in awe of this creature Macbeth. Watch how he transmits that feeling of wonder, and then of terror.*

semantics: See Glossary.

Like *Hamlet, King Lear,* and *Othello, Macbeth* was produced during what is generally called the third or tragic period of Shakespeare's life as a dramatist. It was a time when his stupendous powers were at their height, but when some inward conflict made him intensely aware of the contrast in our life between good and evil, light and dark, reasonable and peaceful order and chaotic violence. Some division in himself enabled him to give the fullest expression to these contrasts in hundreds of lines that haunt the mind like great tragic music. The world we discover in these tragedies is a terrible one.

2   Indeed, we might say that in *Macbeth,* a tragedy of tremendous power, Hell is let loose. Notice how much of it seems to take place at night, to be intimately concerned with darkness: it is a drama in black, edged with the crimson of spilled blood. Our old actors were very superstitious, and one of their superstitions, which I can remember myself, was that it was very unlucky to produce *Macbeth,* as if the presence of the play attracted to the theater various accidents and misfortunes. This is probably only another tribute to its astonishing power as a piece of literature.

3   To this day, after knowing the play for fifty years, some of its speeches make me feel my hair is standing on end. Macbeth himself is one of the great poets among Shakespeare's characters, for in line after line, speech after speech, he says wonderful things. And the fact that Shakespeare gives him such things to say, of a power and insight and poetry unmatched by any other character in the drama, proves definitely, to my mind, that Shakespeare saw it as Macbeth's play and nobody else's, not even Lady Macbeth's. The play is about what happens to Macbeth when ambition and the promptings of evil (represented by the witches) overcome the reluctance of an imaginative man—and Macbeth is essentially an imaginative man—to embark on a course of violent and criminal actions.

4   Many criminals, especially murderers, are people without imagination. They commit murder because other

people, their victims, do not seem to them to be real persons like themselves but mere obstacles to be got out of the way. They are so unimaginative and strongly self-centered that they, alone, really exist in a world of robots, dummies, shadows. Strictly speaking, such criminals are so far removed from ordinary personal and social relationships that they are mad. They do not defy their consciences because they have no consciences to defy.

⁵ But Macbeth is not one of these dreary criminal lunatics. He is an imaginative man, of unusual courage and ability, as Shakespeare makes us realize when Macbeth is first discussed, in Scene 2, Act I. (These opening scenes are always very informative and important in Shakespeare). But there is some weakness, some fatal flaw, in his character. We are made to realize this as soon as he enters and speaks his very first line: "So foul and fair a day I have not seen." This revealing line is spoken within hearing of the witches, who are aware of this flaw in his character. It suggests that already, in the hour of his triumph as a victorious general, there is in him some strange and dangerous confusion, bringing together and mingling what is "foul" and what is "fair." And notice that in this scene Banquo, a straightforward man, merely expresses a natural disgust for the witches, whereas Macbeth is fascinated by their prophecies, urging them to tell him more. There is more than impatient ambition here—though there is that too, and Shakespeare is always suspicious of such ambition—for behind it there is this fatal flaw, this inability to keep a strict watch along the border between good and evil, a weakness of the central and all-important conscience.

⁶ We do not know, however, how far Macbeth would have gone (for we soon discover that he cannot help recoiling in disgust and horror from criminal acts) if it had not been for his wife. It is she who encourages him by every feminine device, from wifely sympathy to artful scorn of what she calls his cowardice. Had his wife been an ordinary tenderhearted woman, instead of being so ambitious, ruthless, callous,* then we feel that his career

of crime—and that is what it is—would probably have been checked at the outset. But instead of pulling him out of it, she thrusts him further into it. Yet she is not really stronger than he is, for when he has reaped the full and terrible harvest of his crimes, she is no longer his partner, steeling his will, but a mere wreck of a woman, out of her mind.

7 What are we to make of this? It is all very difficult. My own view is that Shakespeare, beginning with the witches, felt so strongly impelled to hurry us into this atmosphere of darkness, evil, and doom, that he had to omit a scene that we need very badly. This scene, which would have had to be chiefly played between Macbeth and his wife, would have shown us what kind of relationship existed between them before any crime was committed or even considered. Lacking such a scene, and with it any knowledge of what their normal relationship was, we cannot help being puzzled by the character of Lady Macbeth. Why did she urge him on so relentlessly? And why, having shown herself to be far more ruthless than he was, does she break down so soon, leaving him alone to face the consequences of his actions?

8 This bewilderment explains something that always happens when this play is produced. In spite of the fact that she breaks down and then disappears from the play before it is over, the part of Lady Macbeth, with its many powerful speeches and highly dramatic situations, is always assumed by actresses, producers, directors, and critics, to be a very fine part, a magnificent gift from Shakespeare to any leading actress able to play tragedy. Yet it is my experience that whenever the part is actually played, no matter how gifted the particular actress may be, the more intelligent drama critics always express some disappointment, as if something in the part had escaped the actress. But in my view it is Shakespeare and not the actresses who must be blamed. The part is, in fact, not a fine part, the character of Lady Macbeth not having been solidly established and not having been soundly

welded into the action of the play. She is indeed its chief weakness.

⁹ We can only guess at what Shakespeare had in mind. Certainly he needed some character, entirely in Macbeth's confidence and determined to egg him on, in order to show us that he was not all criminal, that he had scruples * and terrible doubts, that he was very much a divided man. A wife would seem to be the best possible person to play this character. She could talk to Macbeth as nobody else could, playing confidently upon his feelings. And it is true that a very feminine woman, devoted to her husband and his career and ruthlessly ambitious both for herself and him, might overcome his doubts and scruples better than anybody else could. (There is a bad tradition in the theater that Lady Macbeth should be played as a commanding and rather masculine type of woman, but it is much better, truer to life, if she is seen to be a rather small, dainty, very feminine type, as pretty and soft but as cunning and ruthless as a cat.) But that he should have such a wife, instead of the more usual kind ready to protect him from his worse self, is simply bad luck for Macbeth, and true tragedy should be outside mere bad luck. Unless, of course, one argues that it is the fatal flaw in Macbeth that led him to fall in love with and then marry a woman like Lady Macbeth, a woman who, when the time came, would strengthen his darker, criminal side.

¹⁰ To be as utterly ruthless and callous as she appears to be at first, when she is ready to do things her husband shrinks from doing, means that Lady Macbeth has had to suppress all her natural womanly feelings. But she can only do this up to a point, and when one crime follows another and there is no end to the bloodshed and horror, the suppressed half of her takes its revenge by striking at her very sanity, finally taking her out of reality altogether. And by this time, as we discover, Macbeth has almost ceased to care whether she is mad or sane, living or dead, for no personal relationship means anything to

him any longer, existing as he does in a kind of Hell where there are no such relationships, where nothing now has any real meaning.

11 Macbeth's great speech, one of the greatest in all dramatic literature, which follows the news of the Queen's death, offers us the key to the whole tragedy:

> She should have died hereafter;
> There would have been a time for such a word.
> Tomorrow, and tomorrow, and tomorrow,
> Creeps in this petty pace from day to day
> To the last syllable of recorded time,
> And all our yesterdays have lighted fools
> The way to dusty death. Out, out, brief candle!
> Life's but a walking shadow, a poor player
> That struts and frets his hour upon the stage
> And then is heard no more. It is a tale
> Told by an idiot, full of sound and fury,
> Signifying nothing.

Now much earlier, in Scene 3, Act II, after Duncan's death has been discovered and Macbeth is pretending to be as astonished and as much shaken as the others, we can find in Macbeth's speech on his re-entrance a curious foretaste of his final despair:

> Had I but died an hour before this chance,
> I had lived a blessed time; for, from this instant,
> There's nothing serious in mortality.
> All is but toys; renown and grace is dead;
> The wine of life is drawn, and the mere lees *
> Is left this vault to brag of.

He is largely pretending, yet there is something in him, some defeated goodness, that is already beginning to feel that "the wine of life is drawn."

12 Nor is Macbeth alone in this, for a little later in the play, at the beginning of Scene 2, Act III, Lady Macbeth, left alone for a moment, speaks to herself in this vein:

> Naught's had, all's spent,
> Where our desire is got without content.
> 'Tis safer to be that which we destroy
> Than by destruction dwell in doubtful joy.

And very soon she will begin destroying herself, losing her wits in the attempt to lose a world no longer endurable.

13 As these two destroy life in others, they also destroy the life in themselves. Macbeth the murderer is slowly murdering Macbeth. And being an imaginative man, not without some goodness in him, he knows this, and has known it from the moment he committed his first crime. Whatever is good, cherishing life, expands it, adds form and rich color to it, gives it bloom and flavor. But evil, despising and hating life, contracts it, diminishes and bleaches it, makes it formless and meaningless in the end. Macbeth's famous speech shows us the defeat of goodness, the triumph of evil, in its terrible vision of a dusty nothingness and an endless idiocy.

14 We must not imagine that these ideas of good and evil only apply to life in Scotland in the eleventh century or in England early in the seventeenth century. They apply with equal force to our life here and now. Indeed, when reading about the more murderous types of American gangsters, I have often felt that their kind of life lacked precisely those qualities that stupid people imagined it to have: namely, excitement, zest, enthusiasm. They seemed to live in that stale, dead atmosphere which we find in Macbeth's last despairing vision of existence. The evil to which they had given themselves had cut them off from everything that expands and enhances, colors and flavors life.

15 "Methought I heard a voice cry 'Sleep no more.' Macbeth does murder sleep." Yes, and soon, before he has done, he has murdered honor and friendship, murdered all possibility of innocent pleasure and joy, murdered love and all satisfying human relationships. And his tragedy is that from first to last he is terribly aware of what he is losing, for he is neither a madman nor a dumb brute, as so many murderers are, but a man who might have been great and good but for that fatal flaw in his nature. Through that crack in his conscience, as the witches perceived, the destructive forces of evil would invade his

soul, giving him a crown that no longer meant anything, in a darkening ruin of a life on which the sun would never rise again.

ANALYSIS

Priestley has three theories about this tragedy. First, it is "Macbeth's play and nobody else's." Second, Lady Macbeth is its chief weakness. Third, "as these two [characters] destroy life in others, they also destroy the life in themselves." This "defeated goodness" is seen early in the play and comes to its climax in Macbeth's famous "Tomorrow, and tomorrow" speech in Act V. Priestley does not debate or argue these theories. He merely expounds them as a means of getting closer to the power of the play. He feels his theory on Lady Macbeth might help to illuminate a difficult role. He feels, also, that if we take Macbeth's "Tomorrow, and tomorrow" speech as "the key to the whole tragedy" we will see more clearly "the triumph of evil" as Shakespeare wanted us to see it. This is what we mean by talking "around" a subject. Priestley calls his essay an "afterword." We might call it "thoughts on the nature of evil."

Each reader will react to Priestley's criticism according to his own knowledge of and enthusiasm for the play. It is hard for any critic to strike a common ground; he must adhere to his own ideas and hope they will fall among sympathetic readers. Lady Macbeth is one of the cruxes, or perplexing difficulties, of this play. Priestley's explanation of the problem is intriguing. Is her role badly written? Is playing her on stage a trap, not a gift, for a fine actress? Should she be feminine and wily rather than brash and masculine? If your answer to these questions is yes, have you then a better understanding of the complexity of this role?

We might say to Priestley that Lady Macbeth is a foil for Macbeth; that is to say, she is "sacrificed" early in the play to give Macbeth a warning of "which way madness lies." When Shakespeare takes her "out of reality altogether," is not Macbeth's insensitivity (if we can call it that) to her death a frightening aspect of the hero and of what is to follow? In paragraph 13, Priestley writes that "evil . . . makes [life] formless and meaningless in the end." To Macbeth, his wife's death is meaningless. In time, his own will seem the same. Had Shakespeare enlarged the role of Lady Macbeth, she might have dominated too much of the play. She might have been harder to "sacrifice." One is reminded of Mercutio (in *Romeo and Juliet*) and Julius Caesar in somewhat the same positions; they dominated the stage when they were on it. If this is "Macbeth's play and nobody else's," might not Shakespeare have been unwilling to run the risk of Macbeth's losing it?

These counter-arguments are only another way of talking "around" this perplexing but fascinating subject. Literary criticism is not so much interested in settling an issue as in raising intelligent questions. Interpretation is often tentative. What is your reaction to the play? to what Priestley writes? to this example of critical method?

Questions on Content

1. What other plays belong in Shakespeare's third or tragic period?
2. What does Priestley have to say about criminals and imagination? How does Macbeth, through his work or deeds, show that he is an "imaginative man"?
3. What kind of scene or scenes does Priestley think *Macbeth* lacks in explanation of the Macbeth/Lady Macbeth relationship?
4. What does Priestley mean when he says (paragraph 13) "Macbeth the murderer is slowly murdering Macbeth"?

Add to your vocabulary: callous, scruples, lees.

Questions on Technique

1. Priestley could easily have begun this essay with a consideration of the chronological order of events in this play. Why do you suppose he chose not to?
2. How does Priestley develop the "foul and fair" aspect of Macbeth's character after first discussing it in paragraph 5?
3. Interpret Lady Macbeth's lines: " 'Tis safer to be that which we destroy/Than by destruction dwell in doubtful joy." How does Priestley relate these lines to Macbeth's lines in the "Tomorrow, and tomorrow" speech?

4. Priestley gives his essay a neat introduction (two paragraphs) and conclusion (two paragraphs). How does he divide the remaining paragraphs; that is, what chief subjects does he discuss? Could you suggest a better balance?

Suggestions for Writing

1. In a 400-word essay, defend Lady Macbeth's role as one which is soundly welded to the action of the whole play.
2. Write a 500-word essay on the witches and their contribution to the sense of horror in this play.
3. Choose another Shakespeare play with which you are familiar. Discuss in 400 words the hero's or heroine's role. Is it the dominant one of the play or are there other main roles? Is any role in the play difficult to cast?
4. If you disagree with Priestley on any of the points of his argument, write a "Reply to Priestley" giving reasons for your disagreement.
5. Write a critical essay on a serious film or play you have seen recently or a good novel you have read. Discuss in 500 words the major theme in this work of art; that is, the "point" or the "meaning" of the film or novel (such as the theme of *Macbeth* being ambition leading to violence and death).

JOHN CIARDI · *Robert Frost: The Way to the Poem*

John Ciardi is Professor of English in Rutgers University, poetry editor of the Saturday Review, *and director of the Bread Loaf (Vermont) Writers' Conference. But his creative energies go into his poetry.* Homeward to America *(1940) was his first volume to be published;* 39 Poems *(1959) his seventh. As teacher and lecturer,*

"Robert Frost: The Way to the Poem" by John Ciardi from *Saturday Review*, April 12, 1958. Copyright © 1958 by Saturday Review Inc. Reprinted by permission of publishers.

Ciardi has long been sharing with his students the pleasures of poetry, the zest that goes into writing it and that can, equally, go into reading it. "Creative reading" we could call it.

In the essay that follows, Ciardi demonstrates what we mean by a close reading of a poem. He takes Frost's quatrains apart, but he also puts them back together again so that we are left with a poem analyzed, not a mere prose paraphrase. Ciardi believes that if we do no more than "message hunt" (that is, turn the poetry into a prose statement that makes a convenient moral or a final examination answer), we close our eyes and ears to beauty. The intelligent reading of a poem illuminates all its facets: the rhythm, the rhyme scheme, the words, the meaning.

In discussing the words of Frost's poem, Ciardi uses three terms which may need definition: simile, metaphor, and symbol. A simile compares a thing or character, with the words like *or* as, *to something of a different kind or character; for example, she was as happy as a lark, or, my love is like a red, red rose, or, his smile is like a dagger in my heart. A metaphor compares one thing or character, without the words* like *or* as, *to another, generally of dissimilar kind or character; for example, A mighty fortress is our God, or, Death is a cordial old and rare. A symbol, on the other hand, is the object, character, or quality which is a sign of, or which stands for, or suggests, something other than itself by reason of relationship, convention, or association; for example, the fox is a symbol of craftiness, purple is the symbol of rank or authority, a white flag is the symbol of surrender.*

STOPPING BY WOODS ON A SNOWY EVENING

by Robert Frost

Whose woods these are I think I know.
His house is in the village though;
He will not see me stopping here
To watch his woods fill up with snow

> My little horse must think it queer
> To stop without a farmhouse near
> Between the woods and frozen lake
> The darkest evening of the year.
>
> He gives his harness bells a shake
> To ask if there is some mistake.
> The only other sound's the sweep
> Of easy wind and downy flake.
>
> The woods are lovely, dark and deep.
> But I have promises to keep,
> And miles to go before I sleep,
> And miles to go before I sleep.*

¹   The School System has much to say these days of the virtue of reading widely, and not enough about the virtues of reading less but in depth. There are any number of reading lists for poetry, but there is not enough talk about individual poems. Poetry, finally, is one poem at a time. To read any one poem carefully is the ideal preparation for reading another. Only a poem can illustrate how poetry works.

²   Above, therefore, is a poem—one of the master lyrics of the English language, and almost certainly the best-known poem by an American poet. What happens in it? —which is to say, not *what* does it mean, but *how* does it mean? How does it go about being a human reenactment of a human experience? The author—perhaps the thousandth reader would need to be told—is Robert Frost.

³   Even the TV audience can see that this poem begins as a seemingly-simple narration of a seemingly-simple incident but ends by suggesting meanings far beyond anything specifically referred to in the narrative. And even readers with only the most casual interest in poetry might be made to note the additional fact that, though the poem suggests those larger meanings, it is very careful never to abandon its pretense to being simple narration.

There is duplicity ° at work. The poet pretends to be talking about one thing, and all the while he is talking about many others.

4   Many readers are forever unable to accept the poet's essential duplicity. It is almost safe to say that a poem is never about what it seems to be about. As much could be said of the proverb. The bird in the hand, the rolling stone, the stitch in time never (except by an artful double-deception) intend any sort of statement about birds, stones, or sewing. The incident of this poem, one must conclude, is at root a metaphor.°

5   Duplicity aside, this poem's movement from the specific to the general illustrates one of the basic formulas of all poetry. Such a grand poem as Arnold's "Dover Beach" and such lesser, though unfortunately better known, poems as Longfellow's "The Village Blacksmith" and Holmes's "The Chambered Nautilus" are built on the same progression. In these three poems, however, the generalization is markedly set apart from the specific narration, and even seems additional to the telling rather than intrinsic ° to it. It is this sense of division one has in mind in speaking of "a tacked-on moral."

6   There is nothing wrong-in-itself with a tacked-on moral. Frost, in fact, makes excellent use of the device at times. In this poem, however, Frost is careful to let the whatever-the-moral-is grow out of the poem itself. When the action ends the poem ends. There is no epilogue and no explanation. Everything pretends to be about the narrated incident. And that pretense sets the basic tone of the poem's performance of itself.

7   The dramatic force of that performance is best observable, I believe, as a progression in three scenes.

8   In scene one, which coincides with stanza one, a man —a New England man—is driving his sleigh somewhere at night. It is snowing, and as the man passes a dark patch

duplicity: deception, pretending to be or do one thing when actually being or doing another.
metaphor: See Glossary.
intrinsic: belonging to a thing by its very nature.

of woods he stops to watch the snow descend into the darkness. We know, moreover, that the man is familiar with these parts (he knows who owns the woods and where the owner lives), and we know that no one has seen him stop. As scene one forms itself in the theater of the mind's-eye, therefore, it serves to establish some as yet unspecified relation between the man and the woods.

⁹ It is necessary, however, to stop here for a long parenthesis: Even so simple an opening statement raises any number of questions. It is impossible to address all the questions that rise from the poem stanza by stanza, but two that arise from stanza one illustrate the sort of thing one might well ask of the poem detail by detail.

¹⁰ Why, for example, does the man not say what errand he is ⊕n? What is the force of leaving the errand generalized? He might just as well have told us that he was going to the general store, or returning from it with a jug of molasses he had promised to bring Aunt Harriet and two suits of long underwear he had promised to bring the hired man. Frost, moreover, can handle homely detail to great effect. He preferred to leave his motive generalized. Why?

¹¹ And why, on the other hand, does he say so much about knowing the absent owner of the woods and where he lives? Is it simply that one set of details happened-in whereas another did not? To speak of things "happening-in" is to assault the integrity * of a poem. Poetry cannot be discussed meaningfully unless one can assume that everything in the poem—every last comma and variant spelling—is in it by the poet's specific act of choice. Only bad poets allow into their poems what is haphazard or cheaply chosen.

¹² The errand, I will venture a bit brashly for lack of space, is left generalized in order the more aptly to suggest *any* errand in life and, therefore, life itself. The owner is there because he is one of the forces of the poem. Let it do to say that the force he represents is the village of mankind (that village at the edge of winter) from which the poet finds himself separated (has separated

himself?) in his moment by the woods (and to which, he recalls finally, he has promises to keep). The owner is he-who-lives-in-his-village-house, thereby locked away from the poet's awareness of the-time-the-snow-tells as it engulfs and obliterates the world the village man allows himself to believe he "owns." Thus, the owner is a representative of an order of reality from which the poet has divided himself for the moment, though to a certain extent he ends by reuniting with it. Scene one, therefore, establishes not only a relation between the man and the woods, but the fact that the man's relation begins with his separation (though momentarily) from mankind.

13 End parenthesis one, begin parenthesis two.

14 Still considering the first scene as a kind of dramatic performance of forces, one must note that the poet has meticulously * matched the simplicity of his language to the pretended simplicity of the narrative. Clearly, the man stopped because the beauty of the scene moved him, but he neither tells us that the scene is beautiful nor that he is moved. A bad writer, always ready to overdo, might have written: "The vastness gripped me, filling my spirit with the slow steady sinking of the snow's crystalline perfection into the glimmerless profundities of the hushed primeval wood." Frost's avoidance of such a spate ° illustrates two principles of good writing. The first, he has stated himself in "The Mowing": "Anything *more* than the truth would have seemed too weak" (italics mine). Understatement ° is one of the basic sources of power in English poetry. The second principle is to let the action speak for itself. A good novelist does not tell us that a given character is good or bad (at least not since the passing of the Dickens tradition): he shows us the character in action and then, watching him, we know. Poetry, too, has fictional obligations: even when the characters are ideas and metaphors rather than people, they must be *characterized in action.* A poem does not *talk about* ideas; it *enacts* them. The force of the poem's performance, in fact, is precisely to act out (and thereby to make us act

spate: an excessive quantity.   understatement: See Glossary.

out emphatically, that is, to *feel out,* that is, to *identify with*) the speaker and why he stopped. The man is the principal actor in this little "drama of why" and in scene one he is the only character, though as noted, he is somehow related to the absent power.

15 End second parenthesis.

16 In scene two (stanzas two and three) a *foil* is introduced. In fiction and drama, a foil is a character who "plays against" a more important character. By presenting a different point of view or an opposed set of motives, the foil moves the more important character to react in ways that might not have found expression without such opposition. The more important character is thus more fully revealed—to the reader and to himself. The foil here is the horse.

17 The horse forces the question. Why did the man stop? Until it occurs to him that his "little horse must think it queer" he had not asked himself for reasons. He had simply stopped. But the man finds himself faced with the question he imagines the horse to be asking: what *is* there to stop for out there in the cold, away from bin and stall (house and village and mankind?) and all that any self-respecting beast could value on such a night? In sensing that other view, the man is forced to examine his own more deeply.

18 In stanza two the question arises only as a feeling within the man. In stanza three, however (still scene two), the horse acts. He gives his harness bells a shake. "What's wrong?" he seems to say. "What are we waiting for?"

19 By now, obviously, the horse—without losing its identity as horse—has also become a symbol.° A symbol is something that stands for something else. Whatever that something else may be, it certainly begins as that order of life that does not understand why a man stops in the wintry middle of nowhere to watch the snow come down. (Can one fail to sense by now that the dark and the snow-

symbol: See Glossary.

fall symbolize a death-wish, however momentary, *i.e.*, that hunger for final rest and surrender that a man may feel, but not a beast?)

²⁰ So by the end of scene two the performance has given dramatic force to three elements that work upon the man. There is his relation to the world of the owner. There is his relation to the brute world of the horse. And there is that third presence of the unownable world, the movement of the all-engulfing snow across all the orders of life, the man's, the owner's, and the horse's—with the difference that the man knows of that second dark-within-the-dark of which the horse cannot, and the owner will not, know.

²¹ The man ends scene two with all these forces working upon him simultaneously. He feels himself moved to a decision. And he feels a last call from the darkness: "the sweep/Of easy wind and downy flake." It would be so easy and so downy to go into the woods and let himself be covered over.

²² But scene three (stanza four) produces a fourth force. This fourth force can be given many names. It is certainly better, in fact, to give it many names than to attempt to limit it to one. It is social obligation, or personal commitment,* or duty, or just the realization that a man cannot indulge a mood forever. All of these and more. But, finally, he has a simple decision to make. He may go into the woods and let the darkness and the snow swallow him from the world of beast and man. Or he must move on. And unless he is going to stop here forever, it is time to remember that he has a long way to go and that he had best be getting there. (So there is something to be said for the horse, too.)

²³ Then and only then, his question driven more and more deeply into himself by these cross-forces, does the man venture a comment on what attracted him "The woods are lovely, dark and deep." His mood lingers over the thought of that lovely dark-and-deep (as do the very syllables in which he phrases the thought), but the final decision is to put off the mood and move on. He has his

man's way to go and his man's obligations to tend to before he can yield. He has miles to go before his sleep. He repeats that thought and the performance ends.

24 But why the repetition? The first time Frost says "And miles to go before I sleep," there can be little doubt that the primary meaning is: "I have a long way to go before I get to bed tonight." The second time he says it, however, "miles to go" and "sleep" are suddenly transformed into symbols. What are those "something-elses" the symbols stand for? Hundreds of people have tried to ask Mr. Frost that question and he has always turned it away. He has turned it away *because he cannot answer it.* He could answer some part of it. But some part is not enough.

25 For a symbol is like a rock dropped into a pool: it sends out ripples in all directions, and the ripples are in motion. Who can say where the last ripple disappears? One may have a sense that he knows the approximate center point of the ripples, the point at which the stone struck the water. Yet even then he has trouble marking it surely. How does one make a mark on water? Oh very well—the center point of that second "miles to go" is probably approximately in the neighborhood of being close to meaning, perhaps, "the road of life"; and the second "before I sleep" is maybe that close to meaning "before I take my final rest," the rest in darkness that seemed so temptingly dark-and-deep for the moment of the mood. But the ripples continue to move and the light to change on the water, and the longer one watches the more changes he sees. Such shifting-and-being-at-the-same-instant is of the very sparkle and life of poetry. One experiences it as one experiences life, for everytime he looks at an experience he sees something new, and he sees it change as he watches it. And that sense of continuity in fluidity is one of the primary kinds of knowledge, one of man's basic ways of knowing, and one that only the arts can teach, poetry foremost among them.

26 Frost himself certainly did not ask what that repeated last line meant. It came to him and he received it. He

"felt right" about it. And what he "felt right" about was in no sense a "meaning" that, say, an essay could apprehend,* but an act of experience that could be fully presented only by the dramatic enactment of forces which is the performance of the poem.

27 Now look at the poem in another way. Did Frost know what he was going to do when he began? Considering the poem simply as an act of skill, as a piece of juggling, one cannot fail to respond to the magnificent turn at the end where, with one flip, seven of the simplest words in the language suddenly dazzle full of never-ending waves of thought and feeling. Or, more precisely, of felt-thought. Certainly an equivalent stunt by a juggler —could there be an equivalent—would bring the house down. Was it to cap his performance with that grand stunt that Frost wrote the poem?

28 Far from it. The obvious fact is that *Frost could not have known he was going to write those lines until he wrote them.* Then a second fact must be registered: *he wrote them because, for the fun of it, he had got himself into trouble.*

29 Frost, like every good poet, began by playing a game with himself. The most usual way of writing a four line stanza with four feet to the line is to rhyme the third line with the first, and the fourth line with the second. Even that much rhyme is so difficult in English that many poets and almost all of the anonymous ballad makers do not bother to rhyme the first and third lines at all, settling for two rhymes in four lines as good enough. For English is a rhyme-poor language. In Italian and in French, for example, so many words end with the same sounds that rhyming is relatively easy—so easy that many modern French and Italian poets do not bother to rhyme at all. English, being a more agglomerate ° language, has far more final sounds, hence fewer of them rhyme. When an Italian poet writes a line ending with "vita" (life) he has literally hundreds of rhyme choices available. When an

---

agglomerate: literally, collected into a cluster or mass. As Ciardi uses the word, it means mixed or blended.

English poet writes "life" at the end of a line he can summon "strife, wife, knife, fife, rife," and then he is in trouble. Now "life-strife" and "life-rife" and "life-wife" seem to offer a combination of possible ideas that can be related by more than just the rhyme. Inevitably, therefore, the poets have had to work and rework these combinations until the sparkle has gone out of them. The reader is normally tired of such rhyme-led associations. When he encounters "life-strife" he is certainly entitled to suspect that the poet did not really want to say "strife" —that had there been in English such a word as, say, "hife," meaning "infinite peace and harmony," the poet would as gladly have used that word instead of "strife." Thus, the reader feels that the writing is haphazard, that the rhyme is making the poet say things he does not really feel, and which, therefore, the reader does not feel except as boredom. One likes to see the rhymes fall into place, but he must end with the belief that it is the poet who is deciding what is said and not the rhyme scheme that is forcing the saying.

30   So rhyme is a kind of game, and an especially difficult one in English. As in every game, the fun of the rhyme is to set one's difficulties high and then to meet them skillfully. As Frost himself once defined freedom, it consists of "moving easy in harness."

31   In "Stopping by Woods on a Snowy Evening" Frost took a long chance. He decided to rhyme not two lines in each stanza, but three. Not even Frost could have sustained that much rhyme in a long poem (as Dante,° for example, with the advantage of writing in Italian, sustained triple rhyme for thousands of lines in "The Divine Comedy"). Frost would have known instantly, therefore, when he took the original chance, that he was going to write a short poem. He would have had that much foretaste of it.

32   So the first stanza emerged rhymed a-a-b-a. And with the sure sense that this was to be a short poem, Frost decided to take an additional chance and to redouble: in

Dante: Dante Alighieri (1265–1321), Italian poet.

English three rhymes in four lines is more than enough; there is no need to rhyme the fourth line. For the fun of it, however, Frost set himself to pick up that loose rhyme and to weave it into the pattern, thereby accepting the all but impossible burden of quadruple rhyme.

33   The miracle is that it worked. Despite the enormous freight of rhyme, the poem not only came out as a neat pattern, but managed to do so with no sense of strain. Every word and every rhyme falls into place as naturally and as inevitably as if there were no rhyme restricting the poet's choices.

34   That ease-in-difficulty is certainly inseparable from the success of the poem's performance. One watches the skill-man juggle three balls, then four, then five, and every addition makes the trick more wonderful. But unless he makes the hard trick seem as easy as an easy trick, then all is lost.

35   The real point, however, is not only that Frost took on a hard rhyme-trick and made it seem easy. It is rather as if the juggler, carried away, had tossed up one more ball than he could really handle, and then amazed himself by actually handling it. So with the real triumph of this poem. Frost could not have known what a stunning effect his repetition of the last line was going to produce. He could not even know he was going to repeat the line. He simply found himself up against a difficulty he almost certainly had not foreseen and he had to improvise to meet it. For in picking up the rhyme from the third line of stanza one and carrying it over into stanza two, he had created an endless chain-link form within which each stanza left a hook sticking out for the next stanza to hang on. So by stanza four, feeling the poem rounding to its end, Frost had to do something about that extra rhyme.

36   He might have tucked it back into a third line rhyming with the *know-though-snow* of stanza one. He could thus have rounded the poem out to the mathematical symmetry ° of using each rhyme four times. But though

symmetry: regularity of form or arrangement.

such a device might be defensible in theory, a rhyme repeated after eleven lines is so far from its original rhyme
sound that its feeling as rhyme must certainly be lost.
And what good is theory if the reader is not moved by
the writing?

[37]   It must have been in some such quandary ° that the
final repetition suggested itself—a suggestion born of the
very difficulties the poet had let himself in for. So there
is that point beyond mere ease in handling a hard thing,
the point at which the very difficulty offers the poet the
opportunity to do better than he knew he could. What,
aside from having that happen to oneself, could be more
self-delighting than to participate in its happening by
one's reader-identification with the poem?

[38]   And by now a further point will have suggested itself:
that the human-insight of the poem and the technical-
ities of its poetic artifice ° are inseparable. Each feeds
the other. That interplay is the poem's meaning, a matter not of WHAT DOES IT MEAN, for no one can ever say
entirely what a good poem means, but of HOW DOES IT
MEAN, a process one can come much closer to discussing.

[39]   There is a necessary epilogue. Mr. Frost has often
discussed this poem on the platform, or more usually in
the course of a long-evening-after a talk. Time and again
I have heard him say that he just wrote it off, that it just
came to him, and that he set it down as it came.

[40]   Once at Bread Loaf,° however, I heard him add one
very essential piece to the discussion of how it "just
came." One night, he said, he had sat down after supper
to work at a long piece of blank verse. The piece never
worked out, but Mr. Frost found himself so absorbed in
it that, when next he looked up, dawn was at his window.
He rose, crossed to the window, stood looking out for a
few minutes, and *then* it was that "Stopping by Woods"

quandary: a state of perplexity or doubt.
artifice: workmanship, construction.
Bread Loaf: a small community on Bread Loaf Mountain near
     Middlebury, Vermont, where the Bread Loaf School of English
     holds summer classes.

suddenly "just came," so that all he had to do was cross the room and write it down.

41   Robert Frost is the sort of artist who hides his traces. I know of no Frost worksheets anywhere. If someone has raided his wastebasket in secret, it is possible that such worksheets exist somewhere, but Frost would not willingly allow anything but the finished product to leave him. Almost certainly, therefore, no one will ever know what was in that piece of unsuccessful blank verse he had been working at with such concentration, but I for one would stake my life that could that worksheet be uncovered, it would be found to contain the germinal * stuff of "Stopping by Woods"; that what was a-simmer in him all night without finding its proper form, suddenly, when he let his still-occupied mind look away, came at him from a different direction, offered itself in a different form, and that finding that form exactly right the impulse proceeded to marry itself to the new shape in one of the most miraculous performances of English lyricism.

42   And that, too—whether or not one can accept so hypothetical a discussion—is part of HOW the poem means. It means that marriage to the perfect form, the poem's shapen declaration of itself, its moment's monument fixed beyond all possibility of change. And thus, finally, in every truly good poem, "How does it mean?" must always be answered "Triumphantly." Whatever the poem "is about," *how* it means is always how Genesis means: the word become a form, and the form become a thing, and—when the becoming is true—the thing become a part of the knowledge and experience of the race forever.

ANALYSIS

In his critical essay on *Macbeth,* J. B. Priestley discusses only one aspect of the play, the main characters. Ciardi moves carefully, line by line, through the whole of Frost's poem. The poem's brevity allows this close reading, and it would be both presumptuous and unnecessary to go over the ground Ciardi covers so well. But we might outline the essay in order to see how a critic uses a single poem to say something pertinent about the nature of poetry.

In rough outline form, "Robert Frost: The Way to the Poem" might look something like this:

I. The obvious meaning and larger meaning (paragraphs 2–7)
II. Reading line by line
    A. "Scene one" (paragraph 8)
        1. Questions to be answered (paragraphs 9–13)
        2. Notes to be made (paragraphs 14–15)
    B. "Scene two" (paragraphs 16–22)
    C. "Scene three" (paragraphs 23–26)
III. Looking at the poem in another way (paragraphs 27–37)
IV. The nature of poetry in general (paragraph 38)
V. Frost's writing of this poem (paragraphs 39–41)
VI. How a poem means (paragraph 42)

There are doubtless other ways of outlining this essay, but what is likely to be evident in any outline is Ciardi's steady moving forward toward an explanation of his basic distinction (announced in paragraph 38): not WHAT DOES A POEM MEAN? but HOW DOES A POEM MEAN? Ciardi could have called his essay "The Way into *a* Poem," for what he is trying to do is show us how to read, creatively, imaginatively, how to allow the *suggested* meanings of a poetic line to take flight, as it were.

He does not use the words "denotation" and "connotation" here, but he might have. Words first of all *denote* a meaning, that is, mark plainly or point out as distinctly as possible what the word stands for. For example, the *denotation* of the word "dog" is "a carnivorous domesticated mammal." But the word "dog" also *connotes* meanings, that is, suggests, implies, leads you further on to associated meanings. For example, *connotations* of the word "dog" are friendliness or watchfulness, rascality or ostentation or worry. Ciardi explains throughout this essay that poetry makes constant use of connotations, the meanings "around" a word.

This, then, is another kind of literary criticism. Ciardi takes a particular poem to show us poetic form in action.

He does not relate the poem to the body of Frost's work. We feel he could, however, easily go on from here to demonstrate with other poems *how* a poem means.

Questions on Content

1. How does Ciardi distinguish between a "tacked-on" moral and the "whatever-the-moral-is" growing out of the poem itself?
2. What is meant by a "foil," and how does Frost use one in this poem?
3. In what way did Frost get himself into trouble with the rhyme scheme of this poem? Why is the English language rhyme-poor in comparison with French and Italian?
4. In what way does Ciardi compare the juggler with the poet?
5. In paragraph 39, Ciardi says "there is a necessary epilogue"? What does the epilogue add to our knowledge of how a poet works?

Add to your vocabulary: intrinsic, integrity, meticulously, spate, commitment, apprehend, quandary, artifice, germinal.

Questions on Technique

1. This essay develops around one poem. Why do you think Ciardi chose to give us a specific example rather than talk in general terms about "how a poem means"?
2. Paragraphs 9–15 use the parenthetical technique, that is, interrupt the main argument to digress for a moment. Do you find this a good writing method? Why?
3. Why is Ciardi's discussion of Italian and French rhyming (paragraph 29) a good introduction to what he he has to say in the next eight paragraphs?

Suggestions for Writing

1. Imitate Ciardi's poetic criticism in 500 words. Choose one poem you have studied and show how the words, the rhyme, and the rhythm combine to delight the reader.
2. Write a 500-word critical essay on Robert Frost's po-

etry in more general terms: his homely subject matter or his use of dialogue or his attitude toward nature. You may choose another poet if you wish.

3. Write an analysis of one of your own poems, explaining how you happened to write it, why you chose the words and figures of speech you did.

4. Write an essay, in 600 words, discussing why the short story is more rewarding an art form for you than the short poem. Or reverse this argument.

5. If you like poetry and enjoy reading it, write an essay (500 words) explaining why you like it. If you dislike poetry, write an essay telling why you dislike it.

LORD CONESFORD · *You Americans Are Murdering the Language*

In a speech before the Authors' Club in London, Lord Conesford caused a sensation by his vigorous attack on what he called the "American pretentious illiteracy." The Saturday Evening Post *invited him, in 1957, to carry on this assault in their pages. This essay is the result. Lord Conesford would be offended if we prefaced his article with any further explanation of what he is about. He might reply, "I say exactly what I mean, in the clearest way I know how. That's the trouble with you Americans, you. . . ." But let him say it.*

1   As a lover of English I am appalled by the growth of illiteracy and the flood of gibberish.° I am determined to fight them. Those who think like me may be a minority, but we have many friends on both sides of the Atlantic. More than twenty years have passed since my friend Sir Alan Herbert wrote *What a Word* to rouse and encourage the warriors in this good cause. Since then, that cause has been greatly strengthened by Sir Ernest Gowers,

gibberish: foolish talk, unintelligible language.

whose book, *The Complete Plain Words,* is the most practical work on the subject. In the United States, too, though most Americans appear not to have noticed what is happening to their language, there are determined critics of "gobbledygook," an admirable word which they have invented to describe one of the things that we are fighting. In Canada, Mr. Vincent Massey has thrown himself into the fray in a recent university lecture on "Uncertain Sounds."

² There are three good reasons why we should fight for our language: The need for clarity of thought, the need to be understood, and the duty to enrich and not to injure the noblest language and the richest literary heritage in the world.

³ Clarity of thought is impossible without clarity of language. Never has clear thinking been more needed than today; never has the correct use of words been more neglected. Since language provides the essential tools of thought, you cannot have a clear thought unless you frame it in clear words. The woolly word betrays the muddled mind.

⁴ Secondly, the purpose of language is to convey the thought of the speaker or writer to another mind. It will not do so unless the thought is expressed with clarity and precision. Even that will not be enough if the language used is so verbose ° or repulsive that those addressed will not trouble to attend. Why should they? You insult your audience or your reader if you do not take the trouble to express yourself briefly and clearly. I say deliberately "take the trouble." It is, of course, much easier to be long-winded and vague. The great Pascal ° wrote in 1657: "I have made this letter longer than usual, because I lack the time to make it short."

⁵ Thirdly, if these are the requirements of language everywhere, a special duty is imposed on those who speak English. For we have the greatest lyric poetry in the world and a superb tradition of great writers in prose.

verbose: wordy.

Pascal: Blaise Pascal (1623–1662), French philosopher and scientist.

The man who corrupts our language is a poisoner of the wells of human thought and inspiration.

6   I intend to give examples of the barbarism, illiteracy, and decay that I am attacking. My primary concern is with the language used in my own country, but most of my examples will be American, since America is the principal culprit. I agree with Mr. Mencken ° that the English language and the American language are two streams of English. The two streams will certainly diverge,* but any development injurious to either will, I believe, injure both. Certainly American usage is bound to exert great influence on English everywhere on account of American numbers and the wide dissemination of American films. The fact that American usage is likely to prevail is not, as most Americans assume, a reason for not troubling whether that usage is good or bad—nor is there any reason for supposing that it must be good merely because it prevails. There is a Gresham's law ° in language as in economics. Bad currency once admitted will tend to drive the good out of circulation. The bilge of Hollywood will sink the language of Churchill and Lincoln.

7   Let me correct at the outset a common misunderstanding. Of course I recognize that language is a living and growing thing. I would not confine it in a straitjacket, fighting all innovation.* On the contrary, I glory in the fact that English is a versatile * and adaptable instrument, capable of meeting new needs and serving vigorous and inventive peoples. The question is not whether the English language shall grow. It is whether it shall grow in strength, beauty, and variety, or degenerate and decay and proliferate * in feeble gibberish.*

8   In enriching the language to meet new needs, slang can play an admirable part. Slang has this general char-

Mencken: H. L. Mencken (1880–1956) was well known during his lifetime for attacks on bad usage of the English language. His study, *The American Language* (1919, revised in 1936, two Supplements, 1945, 1948), is full of semantic analyses.

Gresham's law: named for Sir Thomas Gresham (1519?–1579), English financier and adviser to Henry VIII and Elizabeth I.

acteristic. Either it is not very good, in which case it is short-lived; or it is good and is found to serve a useful purpose, in which case it stays and enriches the language. It is to slang that we owe such excellent words as "mob" (from *mobile vulgus*), "bus," and many others. American slang has made an especially rich contribution, and shown characteristic vigor, inventiveness, and wit. Let me give some examples of good slang, most of them American in origin:

bamboozle	glad rags	killjoy
blurb	half-baked	racket
cold feet	hard-boiled	rubberneck
debunk	highbrow	stooge
double cross	hunch	stunt
gate-crash	joy ride	yes-man

Far from attacking American slang, I fear that it may soon be the only virile * part of American speech.

⁹ The test to be applied, when a new word is suggested or it is sought to give an old word a new meaning, is this: Does the change enrich the language? The easiest and silliest way in which to impoverish the language is to misuse a good existing word that conveys a clear and precise meaning and thereby to destroy that meaning and render the word useless. This is what Americans have done by using "alibi" when they mean "excuse." An alibi can never be an excuse, and an excuse can never be an alibi. A man pleads an alibi when he denies that he did an act and says that he could not have done it, since he was elsewhere (alibi) at the time. By an excuse, on the other hand, he admits the act, but says there was a good reason for it. The distinction should really not be too difficult for the ordinary intelligence to grasp. The misuse is a barbarism which has made the language poorer by depriving it of a once-useful word. It is like spoiling a chisel by using it as a screwdriver. It is linguistic murder.

¹⁰ Let me pass from American murder to American pretentious * illiteracy; from the destruction of an old word to the invention of a new word which clearly cannot bear

the meaning assigned to it. "Underprivileged" is the leading example. This word appears to be used as a synonym for "poor," a word which strikes many Americans as mildly improper, though I do not know whether they propose to rewrite the Beatitudes.° I have found in many conversations that, while they understand the criticism that the word "underprivileged" is pretentious,* they do not see immediately that it is illiterate, but it demonstrably is. A privilege is a special advantage which one person has over another or one class over another class. It is an inequality before the law. An underprivileged person must mean a person who has not enough privilege—a person, that is to say, who has not enough advantage over his neighbor. To pretend that you are in favor of equality before the law and then to use a word which complains that there is not enough inequality seems to me to exceed the stupidity limit.

11   Let me pass to a different criticism—the invention of inferior new words which then tend to supersede * better old ones. Consider what has happened to the word "move" and its derivatives. People used to say that a man was "moved" by anger or by love or by greed—or whatever it might be—to take some action or other, and what moved him was his "motive." Then somebody, rightly or wrongly, felt the need for "motivate." From that there proceeded the noun "motivation," and I have a horrible fear that some American will soon treat "motivation" itself as a verb, and we shall hear of people being "motivationed." Whether that horror occurs or not, I have already noticed in an American newspaper the question: "What are his motivations?" where not long ago the writer would have said, "What are his motives?" If "motivation" ousts "motive," does anyone doubt that the language will be the poorer?

12   The risk of this happening seems all the more obvious when I observe the strong tendency in America—except in headlines, and sometimes even there—to prefer

Beatitudes: declarations of blessedness pronounced by Christ in the Sermon on the Mount.

the long word to the short and to revel in the addition of unnecessary syllables. Formerly a person had an aim or object. Today, however, "objective" is rapidly superseding "object" in this sense. In America "transportation" has virtually ousted "transport." A comic example of the tendency came to my notice in one of the glossy American weeklies which can never say a simple thing like "Miss Blank is an actress," but think it very smart to say, "Miss Blank practises the Thespian art"—meaning the art of Thespis, the Greek poet. After a short time, "Thespian" had become "Thespianic," and the last time I saw the magazine, "Thespianic" had grown to "Thespianical." Heaven knows what later developments may have been.

¹³   The reader should also note what happened with "pack" (verb) and "package" (noun). They have been followed by "packaging," which is itself now threatened by "prepackaging"!

¹⁴   Other examples of the love of the long word are the use of "mentality" for mind; "proportion" or "percentage" for part; "ideology" for faith, doctrine, or belief; and "assignment" for task or job. Even when the use of some monosyllables seems unavoidable, the rule appears to be never to use one word if you can use three. How else can you account for "in short supply" instead of "scarce" and "at this time" instead of "now"?

¹⁵   A much more serious threat to the language is the deplorable American habit of destroying the simple, strong transitive verb ° by pointless additions of adverbial particles. One of the glories of the English language is its extraordinary wealth of monosyllables. It is true that the English language also shows amazing versatility in adding a preposition to the simple verb to give a variety of meanings. Consider, for example, what can be done with "take." We can take to people, take them

transitive verb: expressing an action directed upon an object; for example, she set the lamp on the table. *Set*, a transitive verb, takes an object, *lamp*. Intransitive verbs do not take objects; for example, we sat there for three hours.

up, take them down, take them off, or take them in. Consider, too, "play up," "knock out," "carry on," "keep off." The phrasal verb can thus enrich the language. But today there is a growing tendency to do the opposite—to make the language weaker by adding unnecessary particles, not to change the meaning which the verb would have without the particle, but merely for the sake of verbosity.

> And how can man die better
> Than facing fearful odds
> For the ashes of his fathers
> And the temples of his gods?

wrote Macaulay. Are you sure that "face up to" is better or stronger than "face"? Is it really better to "meet up with" a man than to meet him, to "visit with" friends than to visit them, to "study up on a subject" than to study it? "Soften up" is inferior to soften, "drown out" is inferior to drown, "lose out" is inferior to lose. You "pay off" an army when you discharge it, but to say that some policy has "paid off," when you simply mean that it has proved profitable, seems to me deplorable. Soon, I suppose, American parents will teach their children that "honesty pays off"!

16   I cannot understand how anybody with an eye and an ear for English can tolerate this scattering of feeble particles.

17   Let me pass to a pleasanter topic—the use of words so ambiguous ° as to cause confusion. A good example of this is the use of "breakdown" in the sense of "analysis," "subdivision," or "classification." This seems to me a foolish practice and many years ago I called public attention to the serious risk of misunderstanding. An official had spoken of "the breakdown of the European services of the B.B.C.," ° not meaning that those services had in fact broken down, but referring to the relative number of broadcasts to different countries. My warning was not heeded and I am now beginning to enjoy the fun. Ameri-

ambiguous: not clear in meaning; capable of being understood in two or more possible senses.
B.B.C.: British Broadcasting Corporation.

cans must not be surprised if a reference to "the population of the United States broken down by age and sex" makes us laugh.

[18] Another word which has become immensely popular among politicians, officials, and journalists is the adjective "over-all." In about nine cases out of ten, the word now bears no meaning whatever and can be omitted without affecting the sense in any way. In the tenth case, the meaning may be "total," "average," "overriding," "complete," or any one of several other things. I hope that some expert in business efficiency will make an estimate of the profit that would be derived by any business that simply prohibited the use of the word. The word would then be omitted wherever it had no meaning, and in the remaining cases the right word would be substituted.

[19] Twenty-two years ago Alan Herbert wrote: "There seems to be a notion that any British or American subject is entitled to take any noun or adjective, add '-ize' to it, and say 'I have made a new verb! What a good boy am I!'"

[20] This queer notion has led to some very odd results; none odder, perhaps, than "hospitalize," not meaning, as you would naturally suppose, "convert into a hospital," but "send to a hospital." "Hospitalize," as the literate know, is no more capable of meaning "send to a hospital" than "canalize" is of meaning "throw into a canal." But that will not deter people from writing nonsense. Meanwhile, I am still waiting to hear what happens to a hospitalized man when he is cured. Is he dehospitalized or homeized?

[21] It is not only by the addition of "-ize" to nouns and adjectives that some deplorable new verbs are being created. A man signs a letter with his name, and his signed name is his signature. It seems incredible that there should be people who wish to create a verb "to signature," but there are. There are probably people, as Alan Herbert has suggested, who regret that Shakespeare did not write: "Where the bee suctions, there suction I"—or perhaps they think that he did.

²² Snobbery, too, can produce some strange expressions. Our ratcatchers grew dissatisfied with their ancient and honorable name and became "rodent operatives." A rodent operative is presumably a workman with prominent front teeth in the habit of gnawing, or—more technically —with strong incisor but no canine teeth. In America, I gather from Mr. Mencken's book, the ratcatchers decided to be "exterminating engineers." I hope all this has brought them happiness.

²³ Some years ago I decided to compile an anthology of "bottlenecks." I started my collection by writing the following letter to *The Times* of London:

> In order to illustrate the progress (or whatever it is) of our language, I am compiling a brochure on bottlenecks. I shall accordingly be grateful for any significant additions to these examples from recent journalism:
>
> (1) "The biggest bottleneck in housing," meaning the worst, most constricting, and presumably narrowest bottleneck.
>
> (2) "Bottlenecks must be ironed out" (leading article in the daily press).
>
> (3) "Bottlenecks ahead" and "Bottleneck in bottles" (recent headlines).
>
> (4) "The economy of the Ruhr is bound to move within a vicious circle of interdependent bottlenecks."
>
> (5) "What is planned is actually a series of bottlenecks. The most drastic bottleneck is that of machine tools."
>
> (6) "One bottleneck . . . which is particularly far-reaching and decisive."

²⁴ My collection now includes, in addition to the gems already mentioned, bottlenecks described as human, vital, aggravated, supreme, overriding, and world-wide. I have read the patriotic call "Man the bottlenecks" and the poetic "Is a bottleneck approaching?" I do not know whether you have the same wealth of metaphorical bottlenecks in the United States.

²⁵ An equally absurd anthology could easily be com-

piled of "targets" and "ceilings," both of which are great
favorites with our officials. Any reader who would pursue
this fascinating subject further can consult *The Complete Plain Words* by Sir Ernest Gowers, already cited,
where he will find some superb examples. Two of my
favorites are these official statements:

> "The advisory committee did not apply for a general
> increase in the ceilings."
> "Any ceiling imposed under this rule may be in-
> creased or waived * if the contributor agrees."

[26] "Ceiling" means maximum prices in the first quotation and maximum benefits in the second. As Gowers
comments, "If one wants more headroom one does not
increase the ceiling, still less perform the curious operation of waiving it; one raises it."

[27] For real fun and games, however, you will not beat
the use of "literally" when what is meant is not literally
but metaphorically. A newspaper reported of one of our
high-court judges that "he literally died in harness," but
the earlier statement that throughout a debate "Mr. Glad-
stone had sat literally glued to the Treasury Bench" will
never be surpassed.

[28] Let me now turn to the strange American delusion
that the words "as of" can always be used before a date
as if they were a temporal preposition. Of course, you
can have a letter "of" a certain date. Further, if the letter was not, in fact, written on that date, but you wish it
to be treated as if it had been, you can describe the letter
as "as of" that date. The expression is, however, now
often used where there is no letter or other noun for the
words to qualify. That practice is wholly illiterate. An
additional illiteracy is introduced when the words "as
of" precede not a date, but the adverb "now." "As of
now" is a barbarism which only a love of illiteracy for its
own sake can explain. What is generally meant is "at
present."

[29] As Mencken and others have pointed out, the headline has had great influence on the use of words, and has

even modified their meaning. An amusing example is the word "bid," which most people now imagine means "attempt." One can see how this development came about. A bid at an auction, if accepted, becomes a contract and the goods fall to the bidder. In that sense the bid is an attempt to obtain the goods, but an essential intermediate step is the acceptance of the bid and consequent agreement. That really makes the headline "Wife Murder Bid" very funny. It implies that the husband offered to murder his wife and, if she had said yes, he would have done so. In the absence of her consent he would have abandoned the whole affair. I wonder.

³⁰ Is it possible to lay down any rules as a guide to good English? Attempts have been made from time to time, the best known, perhaps, being those of Fowler and Quiller-Couch.° Fowler advised the writer "to be direct, simple, brief, vigorous, and lucid." * He then gave some general rules as regards vocabulary, and the first three at any rate have been, I think, universally approved. They are:

"Prefer the familiar word to the farfetched.
"Prefer the concrete word to the abstract.
"Prefer the single word to the circumlocution."

³¹ Quiller-Couch added the excellent advice to use transitive verbs, to use them in the active voice,° and to use few adjectives, since by his use of the straight verb and his economy of adjectives you could tell whether a man's style was masculine or neuter.

³² Sir Ernest Gowers has reduced the essential rules to three—avoiding the superfluous * word, choosing the familiar, and choosing the concrete.

Fowler and Quiller-Couch: H. E. Fowler (1858–1933), English lexicographer and compiler of *A Dictionary of Modern English Usage* (1926), among other books; Sir Arthur Quiller-Couch (1863–1944), English author, editor of the *Oxford Book of English Verse*.

active voice: A verb in the active voice expresses an action performed *by* its subject (Jimmy broke the windowpane). A verb in the passive voice expresses an action performed *upon* its subject (The windowpane was broken by Jimmy).

³³ Matthew Arnold gave this advice: "Have something to say and say it as clearly as you can. That is the only secret of style."

³⁴ If I added anything, it would be this: Never forget that English is incomparably rich in monosyllables and that, if this wealth is used and the short words are made the backbone of speech and writing, they can give them simplicity, strength, and beauty. They will also provide the setting for such longer and more melodious words as may be needed or desired. This has always been known to great writers of English, in poetry and prose, in every age. This is also true of the great orators and men of action.

³⁵ You can improve almost any jargon ° by translating it into simple language, by saying, for example, "help after the war" instead of "assistance during the postwar period." Conversely you can ruin any great utterance by translating it into officialese. Nelson signaled at Trafalgar: "England expects that every man will do his duty."

³⁶ Alan Herbert's translation of that signal into official jargon is devastating satire because it is so little exaggerated.

³⁷ It runs: "England anticipates that with regard to the current emergency, personnel will duly implement their obligations in accordance with the functions allocated to their respective age groups."

³⁸ I ventured to take Sir Winston Churchill's famous declaration: "Give us the tools, and we shall finish the job" and to translate it into the jargon now in fashion: "Donate to us the implements and we shall finalize the assignment."

³⁹ No one knew the immense power and importance of the monosyllable better than Shakespeare. His sonnet "Shall I compare thee to a summer's day" has ninety-one monosyllables out of a total of 114 words, of which "possession" is the longest. Take again this tremendous speech of Lear:

jargon: gibberish; unintelligible language. See also page 135.

> Come, let's away to prison;
> We two alone will sing like birds i' the cage:
> When thou dost ask me blessing, I'll kneel down,
> And ask of thee forgiveness: so we'll live,
> And pray, and sing, and tell old tales, and laugh
> At gilded butterflies, and hear poor rogues
> Talk of court news; and we'll talk with them too,
> Who loses, and who wins; who's in, who' out;
> And take upon's the mystery of things,
> As if we were God's spies; and we'll wear out,
> In a wall'd prison, packs and sects of great ones
> That ebb and flow by the moon.

40 It is perhaps the greatest speech in all tragedy and uses the shortest words.

41 Of course Shakespeare occasionally revels in such long and magnificent words as "the multitudinous seas incarnadine," ° but look at the setting of short words in which he frames them:

> "No, this my hand will rather
> The multitudinous seas incarnadine
> Making the green one red."

Let me pass from poetry to prose, and from Shakespeare to Churchill. Let me quote a passage from what I believe to be the finest of all his speeches, his speech to the House of Commons on May 13, 1940, because it has exactly the qualities of great English utterance that I have tried to describe—the direct, short, simple words providing a perfect setting for the splendid rhythm and cadences of the longer:

> ". . . I would say to the House, as I said to those who have joined this Government: 'I have nothing to offer but blood, toil, tears, and sweat.'
> "We have before us an ordeal of the most grievous kind. We have before us many, many long months of struggle and of suffering. You ask: What is our policy? I will say: It is to wage war, by sea, land and air, with all our might and with all the strength that God can give us: to wage war against

ⁿcarnadine: to make pink, red, or crimson.

a monstrous tyranny, never surpassed in the dark, lamentable catalogue of human crime. That is our policy. You ask: What is our aim? I can answer in one word: Victory—victory at all costs, victory in spite of all terror, victory, however long and hard the road may be; for without victory, there is no survival."

[42] Lincoln's Gettysburg address has a perfection that defies quotation of an isolated passage. I would invite every reader who glories in its greatness to agree that the English language, there so splendidly employed, is worth saving from the corruption and ill-treatment with which it is now threatened and assailed.

ANALYSIS

Linguistics, descriptive and historical, is the science of language. Conesford is concerned with semantics, that is, how we use words and how words change in usage. On pages 135–137 of this book, we looked at an excerpt from H. E. Fowler's *Modern English Usage*. Conesford's essay discusses the same sort of problems which interested Fowler, but he talks of the corruption, decay, and dissolution that are threatening the English language more than of the finer distinctions of good usage. This critical essay has many of the attributes we found in the models of argument and persuasion.

Conesford cannot, of course, encompass a whole language in one essay, not even in a book. How does he develop his subject here? He devotes his first five paragraphs to saying why we should protect our language. In paragraph 6 he calls America the principal culprit in doing the opposite—"murdering the language." Paragraphs 7–8 might be designated a parenthetical note: American slang is healthy; its contributions to the growth of our language must be acknowledged.

We said earlier that a critical essayist frequently talks "around" a subject. Conesford is doing that here, by offering varied examples of how we Americans are impoverishing language. We could label the paragraphs in this way:

Murder: paragraph 9.
Pretentious illiteracy: paragraph 10.
Invention of inferior new words: paragraphs 11–14.
Destruction of transitive verbs by adding adverbial particles: paragraphs 15–16.
Ambiguity: paragraphs 17–29.

Conesford then takes a positive stance and suggests answers to his own question: Is it possible to lay down any rules as a guide to good English?

Fowler's rules: paragraph 30.
Quiller-Couch's rules: paragraph 31.
Sir Ernest Gowers' rules: paragraph 32.
Matthew Arnold's advice: paragraph 33.
Conesford's advice: paragraphs 34–38.
Shakespeare as ideal model: paragraphs 39–40.
Churchill as ideal model: paragraphs 41–42.

The result is a critical essay that is rich with suggestion. Conesford does not exhaust an idea or a group of examples. He touches on a bad habit or a failing in our speech and then moves on to another topic, or "different criticism," as he calls it. All of us can offer more examples of inferior new words, ambiguous expressions, and the like. We are, in a sense, adding unconsciously to Conesford's arguments as we think of these examples while we read. Conesford counts on that.

Questions on Content

1. What three good reasons does Conesford offer for urging us to "fight for our language"?
2. What does Conesford have to say about American films and their effect on language in England?
3. What does he mean by "pretentious illiteracy"?
4. What three rules does Fowler offer on the subject of vocabulary? What one suggestion would Conesford add?

Add to your vocabulary: verbose, diverge, innovation, versatile, proliferate, gibberish, virile, pretentious, supersede, ambiguous, waived, lucid, superfluous, jargon.

Questions on Technique

1. Conesford begins and ends this "attack" with positive rather than negative subjects: why we should fight for our language, and rules and examples of good speech. Explain why you think this is—or is not—a wise method of organization.
2. Paragraph 8 simply lists examples of American slang. Should Conesford have discussed them? Why?
3. Is his anthology of "bottlenecks" convincing argument against ambiguity? Why?
4. Could paragraphs 39–42 be dispensed with? If they were, would his "attack" be strengthened?
5. Do you see any danger in advising young writers to stick to short, simple words? Explain.

Suggestions for Writing

1. Take any one of the five groups of examples (paragraphs 9–29) and write a 400-word essay elaborating Conesford's argument with examples of your own.
2. Slang dates very fast. Write an essay of 500 words in which you discuss slang your parents used, slang you use now (which adults may have trouble understanding), and slang which you, perhaps, did not understand when you first heard it.
3. Is Hollywood alone to blame for spoiling our language? Write an essay of 500 words on the ways in which radio, television, and the movies affect our language. Be specific.
4. Take one or several examples of what you consider good writing in terms of diction, that is, the choice of the right word, and write a 400-word essay defending your selection(s).
5. Is it possible to become too dependent on slang? Write a brief essay based on specific examples showing why and how the overuse of slang may seriously handicap a young person.

CHAPTER 9

The informal essay

Two centuries ago, Dr. Samuel Johnson, the British author and lexicographer, defined the informal essay as "a loose sally of the mind; an irregular indigested piece; not a regular and orderly composition." The word "sally" is especially apt in this definition. It is a word with three distinct meanings: a rushing or bursting forth, as a sortie of the besieged upon the besiegers; an excursion off the usual track, a jaunt; and a flight of wit or fancy.

You will find no "sortie of troops upon the besiegers" in the five selections we have chosen for this last division of expository prose, though Robert Benchley's musings on Shakespeare could be described as an outburst of resentment. Flights of wit and excursions off the beaten track you will find. All five essays demonstrate quite clearly that the informal essayist follows no rigid set of rules. He begins with one subject and digresses into others at will. He indulges in irony and satire.° His humor is good-natured, sometimes eccentric. In a lighthearted, meandering, relaxed style he invites us to listen; he establishes a kind of friendship in a few dozen paragraphs. His argument, if there is one, is never forced. The issues are seldom crucial. To hold us against our will is the antithesis of his technique.

You may now be wondering if some of the selections under descriptive writing would not qualify, at least in part, for this division of exposition. Certainly James Thurber's "University Days" and Lee Strout White's

irony and satire: See Glossary.

"Farewell, My Lovely!" have some of this relaxed, digressive quality. (Both Thurber and E. B. White reappear in this group of informal essays.) Laurie Lee and Ruth McKenney have, in their reminiscences of childhood, more than enough lighthearted humor to qualify. As we have said elsewhere in this book, the types of writing frequently overlap. Pure description and pure exposition are rarities.

JAMES THURBER · *How to Name a Dog*

If you have read James Thurber's "University Days" on page 52 of this book, you will need no introduction to the wonderful world of whimsy ° he inhabits. The titles of his books alone tell us much about this great humorist: The Middle-Aged Man on the Flying Trapeze, My Life and Hard Times, The Seal in the Bedroom, Let Your Mind Alone. *The essay that follows is taken from a collection called* The Beast in Me and Other Animals. *Thurber loves dogs. "Probably no one man should have as many dogs in his life as I have had," he once wrote, "but there was more pleasure than distress in them for me." There is also pleasure for us in Thurber's informal essay on how, or perhaps it is how not, to name a dog.*

1 Every few months somebody writes me and asks if I will give him a name for his dog. Several of these correspondents in the past year have wanted to know if I would mind the use of my own name for their spaniels. Spaniel owners seem to have the notion that a person could sue for invasion of privacy or defamation * of character if his name is applied to a cocker without written permission, and one gentleman even insisted that we

whimsy: See Glossary.

conduct our correspondence in the matter through a notary public. I have a way of letting communications of this sort fall behind my roll-top desk, but it has recently occurred to me that this is an act of evasion, if not, indeed, of plain cowardice. I have therefore decided to come straight out with the simple truth that it is as hard for me to think up a name for a dog as it is for anybody else. The idea that I was an expert in the business is probably the outcome of a piece I wrote several years ago, incautiously revealing the fact that I have owned forty or more dogs in my life. This is true, but it is also deceptive. All but five or six of my dogs were disposed of when they were puppies, and I had not gone to the trouble of giving to these impermanent residents of my house any names at all except Hey, You! and Cut That Out! and Let Go!

² Names of dogs end up in 176th place in the list of things that amaze and fascinate me. Canine cognomens ° should be designed to impinge * on the ears of the dogs and not to amuse neighbors, tradespeople, and casual visitors. I remember a few dogs from the past with a faint but lingering pleasure: a farm hound named Rain, a roving Airedale named Marco Polo, a female bull terrier known as Stephanie Brody because she liked to jump from moving motor cars and second-story windows, and a Peke called Darien; ° but that's about all. The only animals whose naming demands concentration, hard work, and ingenuity are the seeing-eye dogs. They have to be given unusual names because passers-by like to call to seeing-eyers—"Here, Sport" or "Yuh, Rags" or "Don't take any wooden nickels, Rin Tin Tin." A blind man's dog with an ordinary name would continually be distracted from its work. A tyro ° at naming these dogs might make the mistake of picking Durocher or Teeftal-

cognomens: names.

Peke called Darien: When we read this pun, Thurber expects us to recall a line from Keats' "On First Looking into Chapman's Homer": "Silent, upon a peak in Darien." The Isthmus of Panama was formerly called the Isthmus of Darien.

tyro: a beginner or novice.

low. The former is too much like Rover and the latter could easily sound like "Here, fellow" to a dog.

[3] Speaking of puppies, as I was a while back, I feel that I should warn inexperienced dog owners who have discovered to their surprise and dismay a dozen puppies in a hall closet or under the floors of the barn, not to give them away. Sell them or keep them, but don't give them away. Sixty per cent of persons who are given a dog for nothing bring him back sooner or later and plump him into the reluctant and unprepared lap of his former owner. The people say that they are going to Florida and can't take the dog, or that he doesn't want to go; or they point out that he eats first editions or lace curtains or spinets, or that he doesn't see eye to eye with them in the matter of housebreaking, or that he makes disparaging remarks under his breath about their friends. Anyway, they bring him back and you are stuck with him—and maybe six others. But if you charge ten or even five dollars for pups, the new owners don't dare return them. They are afraid to ask for their money back because they believe you might think they are hard up and need the five or ten dollars. Futhermore, when a mischievous puppy is returned to its former owner it invariably behaves beautifully, and the person who brought it back is likely to be regarded as an imbecile or a dog hater or both.

[4] Names of dogs, to get back to our subject, have a range almost as wide as that of the violin. They run from such plain and simple names as Spot, Sport, Rex, Brownie, and Rover—all originated by small boys—to such effete and fancy appellations as Prince Rudolph Hertenberg Gratzheim of Darndorf-Putzelhorst, and Darling Mist o' Love III of Heather-Light-Holyrood—names originated by adults, all of whom in every other way, I am told, have made a normal adjustment to life. In addition to the plain and the fancy categories, there are the Cynical and the Coy.* Cynical names are given by people who do not like dogs too much. The most popular cynical names during the war were Mussolini, Tojo,

and Adolf.° I never have been able to get very far in my exploration of the minds of people who call their dogs Mussolini, Tojo, and Adolf, and I suspect the reason is that I am unable to associate with them long enough to examine what goes on in their heads. I nod, and I tell them the time of day, if they ask, and that is all. I never vote for them or ask them to have a drink. The great Coy category is perhaps the largest. The Coy people call their pets Bubbles and Boggles and Sparkles and Twinkles and Doodles and Puffy and Lovums and Sweetums and Itsy-Bitsy and Betsy-Bye-Bye and Sugarkins. I pass these dog owners at a dogtrot, wearing a horrible fixed grin.

5 There is a special subdivision of the Coys that is not quite so awful, but awful enough. These people, whom we will call the Wits, own two dogs, which they name Pitter and Patter, Willy and Nilly, Helter and Skelter, Namby and Pamby, Hugger and Mugger, Hokery and Pokery, and even Wishy and Washy, Ups and Daisy, Fitz and Startz, Fetch and Carrie, and Pro and Connie. Then there is the Cryptic * category. These people select names for some private reason or for no reason at all—except perhaps to arouse the visitor's curiosity, so that he will exclaim, "Why in the world do you call your dog *that?*" The Cryptics name their dogs October, Bennett's Aunt, Three Fifteen, Doc Knows, Tuesday, Home Fried, Opus 38, Ask Leslie, and Thanks for the Home Run, Emil. I make it a point simply to pat these unfortunate dogs on the head, ask no questions of their owners, and go about my business.

6 This article has degenerated into a piece that properly should be entitled "How Not to Name a Dog." I was afraid it would. It seems only fair to make up for this by confessing a few of the names I have given my own dogs, with the considerable help, if not, indeed, the insistence, of their mistress. Most of my dogs have been females,

Mussolini, Tojo, and Adolf: during World War II, the leaders of Italy, Japan, and Germany, respectively: Benito Mussolini, Hideki Tojo, and Adolf Hitler.

and they have answered, with apparent gladness, to such names as Jeannie, Tessa, Julie, and Sophie. Sophie is a black French poodle whose kennel name was Christabel, but she never answered to Christabel, which she considers as foolish a name for a dog as Pamela, Jennifer, Clarissa, Jacqueline, Guinevere, and Shelmerdene. Sophie is opposed, and I am also, to Ida, Cora, Blanche, and Myrtle.

7   About six years ago, when I was looking for a house to buy in Connecticut, I knocked on the front door of an attractive home whose owner, my real estate agent had told me, wanted to sell it and go back to Iowa to live. The lady agent who escorted me around had informed me that the owner of this place was a man named Strong, but a few minutes after arriving at the house, I was having a drink in the living room with Phil Stong,° for it was he. We went out into the yard after a while and I saw Mr. Stong's spaniel. I called to the dog and snapped my fingers but he seemed curiously embarrassed, like his master. "What's his name?" I asked the latter. He was cornered and there was no way out of it. "Thurber," he said, in a small frightened voice. Thurber and I shook hands, and he didn't seem to me any more depressed than any other spaniel I have met. He had, however, the expression of a bachelor on his way to a party he has tried in vain to get out of, and I think it must have been this cast of countenance that had reminded Mr. Stong of the dog I draw. The dog I draw is, to be sure, much larger than a spaniel and not so shaggy, but I confess, though I am not a spaniel man, that there are certain basic resemblances between my dog and all other dogs with long ears and troubled eyes.

8   The late Hendrik Van Loon ° was privy to the secret that the dog of my drawings was originally intended to

Phil Stong: American journalist and novelist (1899–   ), known for his novels dealing with life in rural Iowa, especially *State Fair* (1932).

Hendrik Van Loon: Dutch-born American journalist (1882–1945), author of numerous popular books on history and science.

look more like a bloodhound than anything else, but that he turned up by accident with legs too short to be an authentic member of this breed. This flaw was brought about by the fact that the dog was first drawn on a telephone memo pad which was not large enough to accommodate him. Mr. Van Loon labored under the unfortunate delusion that an actual bloodhound would fit as unobtrusively into the Van Loon living room as the drawn dog does in the pictures. He learned his mistake in a few weeks. He discovered that an actual bloodhound regards a residence as a series of men's rooms and that it is interested only in tracing things. Once, when Mr. Van Loon had been wandering around his yard for an hour or more, he called to his bloodhound and was dismayed when, instead of coming directly to him, the dog proceeded to follow every crisscross of the maze its master had made in wandering about. "That dog didn't care a darn about where I was," Mr. Van Loon told me. "All he was interested in was how I got there."

[9] Perhaps I should suggest at least one name for a dog, if only to justify the title of this piece. All right, then, what's the matter with Stong? It's a good name for a dog, short, firm, and effective. I recommend it to all those who have written to me for suggestions and to all those who may be at this very moment turning over in their minds the idea of asking my advice in this difficult and perplexing field of nomenclature.*

ANALYSIS

One has the feeling, after reading Thurber, that this author could write an essay on almost anything, given enough time and a reasonable subject. His style is the epitome of unpretentious eloquence. It is simple, direct, and exact. His criticisms of society, in his collected essays, are quietly penetrating; but they are seldom harsh. His drawings are expert caricature; ° but the original, honest and human, still shows beneath the exaggeration.

caricature: See Glossary.

In these nine paragraphs, Thurber covers a surprising amount of territory. He does not do it by following a logical structure: beginning, middle, and end. In fact, for at least one-third of this essay he does not stay close to his subject—how to name a dog—though all he writes here is about dogs. Is the willful digression, you might ask, a part of the informal essayist's technique? Certainly it is part of Thurber's. Paragraphs 3 and 8, and much of paragraph 7, could easily be removed. The disposal of a litter of puppies, Phil Stong's spaniel, and Hendrik Van Loon's bloodhound are not *directly* connected with his title. But they enrich this essay by virtue of being digressions. This is unhurried writing. It aims at entertaining rather than informing you. And besides, Thurber warns us that "it is as hard for [him] to think up a name for a dog as it is for anybody else," that "names of dogs end up in 176th place in the list of things that amaze and fascinate [him]."

But could Thurber be making a more subtle use of these digressions than trying to avoid writing on a subject which, so he says, and we do not believe him, he is ill-prepared to discuss? With paragraph 3, he might wish to divert our attention from dogs' names, for a moment, but he also might wish to let us know that he has learned from long experience about puppies' behavior. No matter what he says about naming dogs he is not a tyro at raising them. Paragraph 8 tells us, if we do not know it already, that Thurber has been drawing dogs with something less than accuracy but with great imagination. Paragraph 7 is an obvious foretaste of his delightful conclusion. The informal essayist can teach us new techniques, such as these digressions, if we look closely enough.

And what of the humor in this piece, you ask? It permeates every paragraph. You need no help in finding it.

Questions on Content

1. Why should Thurber have the reputation of being an expert at naming dogs?
2. How does he distinguish between names that are Coy, Cynical, and Cryptic?
3. What did Hendrik Van Loon learn, to his sorrow, about bloodhounds?

Add to your vocabulary: defamation, cognomen, impinge, tyro, coy, cryptic, nomenclature.

Questions on Technique

1. Paragraph 1 is written in a simple vocabulary. Paragraph 2 opens with an exaggerated statement, for humorous effect. What effect does Thurber seek with the next sentence: "Canine cognomens should be designed to impinge on the ears of the dogs. . . ."? Why does he not say, "Dogs should hear their names easily"?

2. Speaking of exaggeration, consider paragraph 4. Is Thurber's wild imagination at work here or does he wish his reader to take him literally?

3. What is your reaction to the first three sentences of paragraph 6? Do you think Thurber planned his essay with this "confession" in mind?

4. Note that paragraph 7 is an anecdote, a short narrative used to make a point. This use of narrative is common in informal essays. How does this narrative arouse interest?

5. How are paragraphs 7 and 8 related to each other? Notice the transition sentences.

Suggestions for Writing

1. Try your hand at the same subject, but call your essay "Dogs [Cats, Birds] I Have Known."

2. Most families have had a pet of some kind at some time. Write a 500-word essay on your family's pet or pets. Do not only describe the animals.

3. Write a 400-word essay on "What's in a Name?"

4. Informal essayists express their ideas and opinions on a great variety of subjects and frequently without much basic research. Try writing a 400-word essay on "I Hate Gardening," "I'm Glad to See Summer End," "On Baby-Sitting," "Telephone Calls," or "On Studying for Examinations."

ROBERT BENCHLEY · *Looking Shakespeare Over*

*We suggested, a page or two earlier, that James Thur-
ber could very likely write on anything. Robert Benchley
not only could but did. He was a humorist, drama critic,
magazine writer, and sometime motion-picture actor who
endeared himself to American audiences by his whimsical satire.° When his son, Nathaniel, came to edit an
anthology,* The Benchley Roundup *(1954), he said he
had to read from over a thousand previously published
pieces in order to select about ninety of the best, written
between 1915–1945. He urges us, in his preface to the
collection, to read the book "piecemeal rather than in
one lump—picked up and put down as though you were
waiting for a telephone call or for guests to arrive." Here
is one of the characteristics of the informal essay Dr.
Johnson included in his definition—the sudden sally of
the mind, fleeting, short-lived.*

*If we call Benchley's work social satire, we must put
the emphasis on the humorous side of his writing. Satire can be, like Jonathan Swift's, biting and scornful.
Benchley's never is. His subject is the average middle-
class American coping, or trying to cope, with the mechanical gadgets and the social predicaments of the
twentieth century. Nathaniel Benchley thinks his father's
humor cannot be analyzed. "It is sometimes mad," he
writes, "sometimes penetrating, and sometimes based on
nothing more than word associations, and the only generalization that can be made with any degree of certainty
is that it is different." The essay that follows will give
you a chance to judge for yourself.*

whimsical satire: See Glossary.

1   There was a time during the winter in New York when you couldn't walk a block without stepping on some actor or actress playing Shakespeare. They didn't all make money, but it got the author's name into the papers, and publicity never hurt anyone, let alone a writer who has been dead three hundred years and whose stuff isn't adaptable for the movies.

2   The only trouble with acting Shakespeare is the actors. It brings out the worst that is in them. A desire to read aloud the soliloquy (you know the one I mean) is one of the first symptoms a man has that he is going to be an actor. If ever I catch any of my little boys going out behind the barn to recite this speech, I will take them right away to a throat specialist and have their palates removed. One failure is enough in a family.

3   And then, too, the stuff that Will wrote, while all right to sit at home and read, does *not* lend itself to really snappy entertainment on the modern stage. It takes just about the best actor in the world to make it sound like anything more than a declamation by the young lady representing the Blue and the Gray on Memorial Day. I know that I run counter to many cultured minds in this matter, but I think that, if the truth were known, there are a whole lot more of us who twitch through two-thirds of a Shakespearean performance than the last census would lead one to believe. With a company consisting of one or two stars and the rest hams (which is a good liberal estimate) what can you expect? Even Shakespeare himself couldn't sit through it without reading the ads on the program a little.

4   But you can't blame the actor entirely. According to present standards of what constitutes dramatic action, most of Will's little dramas have about as much punch as a reading of a treasurer's report. To be expected to thrill over the dramatic situations incident to a large lady's dressing up as a boy and fooling her own husband, or to follow breathlessly a succession of scenes strung together like magic-lantern slides and each ending with a

perfectly corking rhymed couplet,° is more than ought to be asked of anyone who has, in the same season, seen *Loyalties* ° or any one of the real plays now running on Broadway.

⁵ It is hard to ask an actor to make an exit on a line like:

> "I am glad on't: I desire no more delight
> Than to be under sail and gone tonight"

without sounding like one of the characters in Palmer Cox's Brownies ° saying:

> "And thus it was the Brownie Band,
> Came tumbling into Slumberland."

⁶ That is why they always have to exit laughingly in a Shakespearean production. The author has provided them with such rotten exits. If they don't do something— laugh, cry, turn a handspring, or something—they are left flat in the middle of the stage with nothing to do but say, "Well, I must be going." In *The Merchant of Venice,* the characters are forced to keep up a running fire of false-sounding laughter to cover up the artificial nature of what they have just said:

> "At the park gate, and therefore haste away
> For we must measure twenty miles today.
> A-ha-ha-ha-ha-ha!" *(Off l.c.)* °

⁷ To hear Lorenzo and Gratiano ° walking off together you would have thought that Lorenzo had the finest line

rhymed couplet: Shakespeare writes in unrhymed iambic pentameter, that is, blank verse. He usually ends a scene with two rhymed lines, called a rhymed couplet.

Loyalties: a play (1922) by the English novelist and playwright John Galsworthy (1867–1933) .

Palmer Cox's Brownies: American illustrator and author (1840–1924) , well-known for a series of "Brownie" books for children.

Off l. c.: Exit left center.

Lorenzo and Gratiano: In *The Merchant of Venice,* Jessica, daughter of Shylock, elopes with the young man, Lorenzo. Gratiano is one of the friends of Antonio, merchant of Venice.

of funny stories in all Venice, so loud and constantly did they laugh, whereas, if the truth were known, it was simply done to save their own and Shakespeare's face. Now my contention is that any author who can't get his stuff over on the stage without making the actors do contortions, is not so good a playwright technically as Eugene Walter ° is. And now for the matter of comedy.

8   An actor, in order to get Shakespeare's comedy across, has got to roll his eyes, rub his stomach, kick his father in the seat, make his voice crack, and place his finger against the side of his nose. There is a great deal of talk about the vulgarity and slapstick humor of the movies. If the movies ever tried to put anything over as horsy and crass as the scene in which young Gobbo ° kids his blind father, or Falstaff ° hides in the laundry hamper, there would be sermons preached on it in pulpits all over the country. It is impossible for a good actor, as we know good actors today, to handle a Shakespearean low comedy part, for it demands mugging ° and tricks which no good actor would permit himself to do. If Shakespeare were alive today and writing comedy for the movies, he would be the headliner in the Mack Sennett ° studios. What he couldn't do with a cross-eyed man!

9   Another thing that has made the enjoyment of Shakespeare on the stage a precarious venture for this section of the theater-going public at least, is the thoroughness

Eugene Walter: American journalist (1874–1941), who began in 1901 to write a series of violent, melodramatic plays.

Gobbo: In *The Merchant of Venice*, Launcelot Gobbo, one of Shakespeare's great clowns, is the son of Old Gobbo, who is stone blind.

Falstaff: the most famous of all of Shakespeare's comic characters. In *The Merry Wives of Windsor* he hides in a laundry hamper in one scene. He also has a main role in *Henry IV, Parts I and II*.

mugging: making faces or grimacing, in the theatrical sense.

Mack Sennett: Hollywood movie director who in the years 1912–16 brought his specialized brand of slapstick comedy to perfection. His subjects were usually the Keystone cops, never-ending chases, bathing beauties, and custard pies in someone's face.

with which the schools have desiccated ° his works. In
The Merchant of Venice, for example, there was hardly
a line spoken which had not been so diagnosed by English teachers from the third grade up that it had lost
every vestige of freshness and grace which it may once
have had. Every time I changed schools, I ran into a
class which was just taking up *The Merchant of Venice.*
Consequently, I learned to hate every word of the play.
When Bassanio said:

> "Which makes her seat of Belmont Colchis' strand,
> And many Jasons come in quest of her" °

in my mind there followed a chorus of memories of
questions asked by Miss Mergatroid, Miss O'Shea, Miss
Twitchell, Mr. Henby, and Professor Greenally, such as:
"Now what did Shakespeare mean by 'Colchis' strand'?"
"Can anyone in the room tell me why Portia's lovers
were referred to as 'Jasons'?" "Robert Benchley, I wonder if you can leave off whispering to Harold Bemis long
enough to tell me what other Portia in history is mentioned in this passage?"

¹⁰   Perhaps that is the whole trouble with Shakespeare
anyway. Too many people have taken him up. If they
would let you alone, to read snatches from his plays now
and then when you wanted to, and *stop* reading when you
wanted to, it might not be so bad. But no! They must
ask you what he meant by this, and where the inflection
should come on that, and they must stand up in front of
scenery and let a lot of hams declaim at you while you
are supposed to murmur "Gorgeous!" and "How well he
knew human nature!" as if you couldn't go to Bartlett's
Quotations and get the meat of it in half the time. I
wouldn't be surprised, if things keep on as they are, if
Shakespeare began to lose his hold on people. I give him
ten centuries more at the outside.

desiccated: dried up.
Belmont Colchis' . . . Jasons: Jason was a hero of Greek legend who
led the Argonauts in quest of the Golden Fleece. He successfully
obtained it at Colchis.

ANALYSIS

Irreverent is the word for Benchley when he tackles subjects like "Opera Synopses," "How to Study International Finance," "Compiling an American Tragedy," or "Paul Revere's Ride." Shakespeare comes in for his share of the satire. It is not every critic who can call the great poet "Will" and complain that his plays are not "really snappy entertainment on the modern stage." Benchley can do it with a wisp of a smile that somehow comes through in all his writings. But his opening paragraphs are just the warm-up. He has three complaints to make and, for all his humor, he makes them seriously: Shakespeare's plays are a breathless succession of scenes strung together with incredible exit lines; Shakespeare's low comedy characters demand mugging and horseplay no respectable actor wants to permit himself to do; the treatment of Shakespeare in the schools makes it difficult to discover the freshness and grace the plays once had.

This is not the place to question the justice of Benchley's complaints. In fact, one of the intriguing aspects of this essay is the sudden veering from humor to seriousness and back again. Benchley gives himself away, of course, with his last lines—another ten centuries and Will's little dramas are going to lose their hold on the people! Satire is built on this making of the ridiculous statement with a straight face. Witness, for another example, Benchley's claim: "as if you couldn't go to Bartlett's *Quotations* and get the meat of it in half the time."

But all is not satire. Shakespeare's exit lines *are* frequently silly. Falstaff's hiding in the laundry hamper *is* "horsy and crass." Shakespeare *has* been desiccated—exactly the word for it—in some schoolrooms. Like George Bernard Shaw, who believed that he could tell his audience the deepest truths when he had them laughing, Benchley puts on a clown's face to speak his severest lines. This is informal writing with a twist. Nathaniel Benchley thought his father's work might be unique. Perhaps he is right.

Questions on Content

1. What specifically does Benchley find awkward about Shakespeare's exit lines?
2. How have the schools desiccated Shakespeare's works, according to Benchley?
3. What does he suggest as a proper way to read Shakespeare?

Add to your vocabulary: desiccated.

Questions on Technique

1. Benchley uses hyperbole ° in this essay; for example, "I will take [my boys] right away to a throat specialist and have their palates removed." Where else do you find examples of hyperbole?
2. What use does Benchley make of such allusions as *Loyalties,* Eugene Walter, and Mack Sennett?
3. The last sentence in paragraph 9 suddenly shifts the nature of what he is saying from seriousness to humor. What is the effect of this change upon the reader? Does he use the device elsewhere?

Suggestions for Writing

1. What Shakespearean play have you read most recently? Write an essay of 500 words in which you reconsider the play in the light of Benchley's essay. Consider the comic characters, the exit lines, and the Elizabethan stage conventions that applied to this kind of play. Are there awkwardnesses that would be hard to accept in a production of the play today?
2. Imitate Benchley's "attack" but call your essay "Looking Television Over." Try your hand at discussing some of the bad programs.
3. Write a 500-word essay entitled "On First Hearing Shakespeare." Use any stage or television performance you have witnessed. Discuss the great difference between reading and hearing drama.
4. Write a 400-word essay on "Theatricals in My Hometown" or "Our School's Dramatic Productions."

hyperbole: See Glossary.

PHYLLIS McGINLEY · *The Happy Exile*

After twenty-five years of writing poetry, much of which appeared in the New Yorker, *Phyllis McGinley published in 1959 a volume of short prose pieces which she called* The Province of the Heart. *"I have no excuse for this book," she says in her preface. She does not need one. Happily, but not surprisingly, her light prose is just as witty as her light verse.* Pocketful of Wry *she calls one volume of verse:* Stones from a Glass House *is another.* The Province of the Heart *continues in the same strain, a book in which, she says, she can "carry on a sort of running argument with those whose interpretation of life is different from [hers]."*

Miss McGinley is an opinionated woman, and she knows it. There is no shilly-shallying in these essays. If her version of the suburbs, for example, is "probably not the whole picture," it is at least the one she sees from her own window. "It is not an invention," she writes; "it is my seen facet of reality." But "The Happy Exile" is written to share a point of view, not force it. It investigates "the province of one mind and one heart." Her prose is too full of the grace of mind, the gentle wit, and the honest enthusiasm of her poetry to be called "argument." Let us call her essay, using another phrase in her own preface, a "personal reading of the truth."

[1] No one can describe quite accurately the province of the heart. Ask a man to tell you what his wife is like, and how can he say it? "She has pretty hands. Her hair is brown; one eyebrow grows higher than the other. She's never learned to read a road map, but she gets up twice at night to tuck the children in." He cannot re-create her

image for you because it is at once too familiar and too various.

² So how is one to define a region, an environment into which the spirit slips as easily and snugly as the foot into an old house slipper? The East is my home, although an adoptive one, and it is where I *feel* at home. It has made me welcome since our first encounter. I have known kinder climates, handsomer landscapes, skies more blue and exuberant. It has taken me years to grow used to a mountainless horizon and Aprils that are only intermittently spring. But it is the country of my choice; so I see it too affectionately, perhaps, for good reporting. I cannot even be sure exactly what portion of America the East comprises. When I was a child growing up in Colorado, Back East was Omaha. Now I go West to Cleveland. Taken as a coherent community, it includes, I should think, only the fairly narrow strip of the nation which lies along the Atlantic seaboard above Virginia. Perhaps only above Maryland. Below that is the South; beyond it is the Middle West, then the West, then the Coast—each with its own look and legend.

³ But if it is not a large area, it is a most diverse one. New York roars with a voice quite different from the prudent accents of Boston; Pennsylvania's lush farms are immoderately unlike the flinty pastures of New Hampshire. People speak with a broad A in Maine and a small one in New Jersey, nor does Rhode Island have much in common with Massachusetts. The East is a montage.° The pictures it calls to the mind are endless and bewildering—the stone fences of New England, New Haven's out-of-town openings, day lilies in June, cities taller and more fabulous than Troy. It is lakes and hills and whaling museums and subways and institutes of higher learning and nearly the world's best restaurants. It is Maine's wilderness and New York's Greenwich Vil-

montage: a composite picture made up of many smaller ones, each distinct yet blended into a whole, through techniques such as superimposition.

lage; prep schools and publishing houses and the Gloucester fishing fleet and factories and gentlemen's dairy farms and Walden Pond; clambakes and brownstones, dogwood and first nights and Ivy League football games; Amish cooking and the aromatic moors * of Nantucket. It is old and it is young, conservative and bursting with ardor, very green in summer, very white in winter, gregarious,° withdrawn, and at once both sophisticated and provincial. There is no one aspect to its face.

4   If Easterners have any traits in common, I can think of only two—a respect for tradition and a passion for privacy. Both influence our architecture, our social usages, our way of life. We put up fences; we let our hedges grow high; we cling to houses built in the colonial or the Georgian or the Federal manner. We are not quick to call acquaintances by their Christian names, nor are we happy about pulling down a tree or a building in the name of progress.

5   But a love of privacy (a commodity dear because it is difficult) does not imply unfriendliness. We value friendship too much to be spendthrift with it. We simply refuse to force camaraderie ° on our neighbors with the indiscriminate eagerness of a Newfoundland puppy. One has to get used to a more reticent * gesture than one encounters in the South or the West. You may find the Vermont farmer taciturn * to the point of silence if it's chat you're looking for. But get stuck in the snow some bitter night and he'll harness a team, pull you out of the drift, and make you a pot of hot coffee without asking to look at your wallet. The Bostonian may live next door to you for years without nodding good morning. But once you meet him properly, you'll know his is the most generous of friendships. Cape Codders are laconic ° only to tourists. The upstate Yankee is wide awake and comfortable as his opulent * valleys. Countrymen in Delaware

gregarious: sociable.   camaraderie: close friendship.
laconic: concise, expressing much in a few words.

have a touch of the South in their manner. Pennsylvanians resist change but are easy and hospitable on their native soil.

6   Environment has been shaping us here for a long time, and it is not a spectacular environment. Our mountains do not tower very high; our chasms do not cut deep. Everything comes on a less picturesque scale than it does beyond our borders. (New York City may make its claim for having the biggest of everything—buildings, prices, scandals, reputations—but New York is not, in itself, the East. It is unique, a New World monument rather than a local town.) We swim in a moderate ocean, drive small cars on less than endless roads. If we like hamburgers rare, we do not care for them raw. Our most persistent symbols are still our quiet elms, our lilac-shaded churchyards, and the fact that brisk marketing still goes on in a shabbily handsome building called Faneuil Hall.°

7   There is something very pleasant about accepting a natural background. I used to wonder why even the most faithful copy of an old house was so much less charming to look at than the original. My eye finally told me the reason. It is because the latter has warped a little with age. All its lines curve a bit to conform with the earth it stands on. Porches sag ever so slightly, foundations swing gently along the ground. Windows lean faintly toward the leaning landscape. The house has stopped doing battle with its surroundings and has become a part of them.

8   On the literal side, this grace of form explains why many an Easterner would rather spend his money on remodeling a dilapidated farmhouse into a residence than on building a new one at less expense. Figuratively, it accounts for what is most appealing in the East. This is a grown-up place. Here is the undemonstrative warmth of home.

9   The East is the hearthside of America. Like any home,

Faneuil Hall: the "Cradle of Liberty," in Boston, so called because this hall was used as a meeting place for American patriots during the Revolutionary period.

therefore, it has the defects of its virtues. Because it is a long-lived-in house, it bursts its seams, is inconvenient, needs constant refurbishing.* And some of the family resources have been spent. To attain the privacy that grown-up people find so desirable, Easterners live a harder life than people elsewhere. Today it is we and not the frontiersman who must be rugged to survive.

10   To live in a city we must pay much for little room and have not yet been able to wipe out our slums. To own a country background we must either commute ridiculous distances or make sacrifices of salary and advancement. We have our natural playgrounds, but they are not nearly spacious enough. Our climate is so inconsistent that we cannot even count on the clemency ° of the out-of-doors when we reach it. We have great universities and the finest of educational systems. But state-supported colleges are few and private secondary schools still outrank their public counterparts. We have population problems and tax problems, traffic jams and tent-caterpillars, high prices and too little sunlight.

11   What is there in the East, then, that holds us (even transplanted Westerners like me) so contentedly here?

12   I think the answer is the largeness of this little place. We own a freedom of mind and opportunity not available anywhere else in America. This is not a paradox. We are still rich in one great natural resource—human beings. So diverse is our population, so various its interests that, again like a family, we can have privacy without loneliness. Intellectual or extrovert, tycoon * or bohemian,* each can merge with his group. Among people of our own fortune and aspiration we can collect stamps, ride cross-country, compose for the oboe, preach on a soapbox, make a hundred million dollars, be an amateur painter or a professional one, play backgammon,* cultivate delphiniums, write poetry, or sell all we have and give to the poor. We will not be conspicuous against our skylines.

13   Moreover, we recognize more than one standard

clemency: mildness.

against which to measure success. Mature societies are usually tolerant societies; here there is more than one kind of competition, and a variety of rewards. Mink coats and air-conditioned automobiles and swimming pools and one's name in the paper are all good enough prizes, nor are we above appreciating family connections. But we have other values too. Our rules are flexible. Nowhere else in the country, I believe, is so much appreciation given to merit of mind and personality rather than to material prowess alone.

14 And for all our moderation, this is the most stimulating region on earth. It is old enough to be wise. It is not too old to have stopped experimenting.

15 Ungrudgingly, then, we admit to the Californian that he's a lucky fellow in the matter of weather. We tell the man from Alabama that we could certainly do with a few of those magnolias, and we agree with the Coloradan that he possesses some mighty elegant scenery. But we know that scenery is no substitute for conversation and art galleries and windows that open on the world. There are some of us who breathe more easily in a meadow full of daisies than on top of a mountain; and some of us who would rather explore the jungles of Madison Avenue than the Carlsbad Caverns.

16 A friend of mine who lives in Honolulu is spending a year in the East while her professor husband takes his sabbatical leave ° from his university. Her family is numerous and they have lived cramped in a city apartment during one of the foulest of our recent winters. I asked her the other day if she was not longing for the return to Hawaii and its spacious amenities.*

17 "Oh, no!" She sighed. "No, no, no. We're all so happy here. I suppose it's ungrateful of me not to miss Hawaii. But somehow I just don't want to go back to Paradise."

18 No, this is not Paradise or even close to it. But it is

sabbatical leave: a year, usually every seventh (thus the adjective), of freedom from teaching, granted to professors for study or travel.

home for a certain kind of moderate heart. And while I wouldn't visit here if you gave me the place, it's a wonderful region just to live in.

ANALYSIS

This essay might have been called "From Maine to Maryland" or "Where the Colonies Began." But Miss McGinley is not writing straight historical or geographical description. She says she sees it all "too affectionately, perhaps, for good reporting." The title she chooses is a paradox,° and she plays on this self-contradiction. This is a wholly personal essay—*her* exile, *her* new home, why *she* has come to love the East. Only by making her essay personal and meandering can she do justice to her feelings about this region of America and, in turn, tell us something about the East. Like the province of the heart, a whole section of a country is difficult to describe because it is "at once too familiar and too various." Yet she makes her feelings clear to us. How does she do it?

First, she limits the montage. In paragraph 3, she gives us the expected cross-section of the East, a series of flashing pictures, like a motion-picture sequence of scenes. But one paragraph is enough. She knows she cannot convey a sense of place by visual description alone.

Second, she settles on two aspects of the Easterner—a respect for tradition and a passion for privacy. Paragraphs 4–8 are occupied with elaborating this way of life. Some of the details are visual, of course (especially paragraph 7), but she also tries to define friendliness, to explain the *un*-spectacular, to defend old houses, and to suggest the "warmth of home." In this way we feel the aura, the distinctive character of a place, not simply its appearance.

Third, she recognizes the defects of the East and admits them bluntly. Paragraphs 9–10 are painfully true. The brevity of the charges does not lessen their seriousness.

Finally, she raises the question we have already anticipated: What holds her in this part of America? To answer she moves directly to the reason for her calling the East a mature society, the one great natural resource of

paradox: See Glossary.

this section of our country—the diversity of its people. And so once again she stresses feelings: privacy without loneliness, tolerance, flexibility, warmth of friendships. Even her final anecdote complements her whole point of view—"it's a wonderful region just to live in."

This is what we mean by a personal essay. Without apologies, it has Miss McGinley's stamp all over it. It begs for a rebuttal. Miss McGinley is prepared for that, too.

Questions on Content

1. What portion of the United States does Miss Mc-Ginley finally settle on as the boundaries of the East? Do you agree?
2. How does the Easterner show his passion for privacy?
3. Why does Miss McGinley find "even the most faithful copy of an old house much less charming to look at than the original"?
4. What stimulations does she find from the people of the East?
5. Where are Walden Pond, Gloucester, Nantucket, Carlsbad Caverns? Who are the Amish?

Add to your vocabulary: montage, moors, gregarious, reticent, taciturn, laconic, opulent, refurbishing, clemency, tycoon, bohemian, backgammon, amenities.

Questions on Technique

1. Miss McGinley might have described only her own home town, using it as a kind of focus for this large subject, the East Coast. What would she have lost in comparison with the organization she did choose?
2. She begins and ends this essay with brief "anecdotes." What do they contribute to the general pattern of the essay? What is the "twist" in the concluding anecdote? What effect does it have upon you?
3. What does she mean in paragraph 9 when she says "Like any home, therefore, [the East] has the defects of its virtues"?
4. What picture of Bostonians does the author suggest by the phrase "prudent accents"? What other adjective might she have chosen? What does she mean by "reticent gestures"?

Suggestions for Writing

1. Non-Easterners will want, very likely, to "answer" Miss McGinley. Write a 500-word essay called "I'm Happy Where I Live" in which you explore the character of your home town or the section of the United States in which you live. Do not feel you have to refute Miss McGinley's essay.

2. Reverse Miss McGinley's title. Write a 500-word essay on "The Unhappy Exile."

3. In paragraph 2, Miss McGinley talks of "an environment into which the spirit slips as easily and snugly as the foot into an old house slipper." Have you ever lived in such an environment, perhaps in a certain house your family occupied, at camp, at a relative's home? Describe it in 400 words.

4. Write a 400-word essay on "The Sense of Privacy" or "A Respect for Tradition" or "The Measure of Success."

5. You may want to talk, at random, about the people in your home town and the diversity of their interests. Call your essay, if you wish, "Some of My Best Friends."

6. Every community has its good and bad features. Write a 500-word essay on the good and/or bad features of your community. You may use satire ° and exaggeration, if you wish, to make your points.

E. B. WHITE · *Memorandum*

James Thurber once referred to E. B. White's work as "those silver and crystal sentences which have a ring like nobody else's sentences in the world." In a review of White's The Second Tree from the Corner *(1954), Irwin Edman, the late Columbia University philosopher, said "It is high time to declare roundly that E. B. White is the finest essayist in the United States." This kind of*

satire: See Glossary.

praise, from two highly qualified peers, White richly deserves.

After graduating from Cornell, E. B. White worked for the Seattle Times *and then took a job as a contributing editor of the* New Yorker. *In 1937 he and his family moved to Maine. For the five years following, he wrote a column for* Harper's *called "One Man's Meat." The essay we reprint here comes from the book of the same name, a collection of his* Harper's *pieces on Maine farms and farmers, on children, animals, war, and politics. More wise, political commentary appeared in White's* The Wild Flag *(1946). When, in 1960, he received the gold medal for essays and criticism from the American Academy of Arts and Letters, he said in reply: "A glance at the shelf of my published works leaves me wondering whether I am not simply a man of indecision. . . . My shelf begins with a thin volume of poems . . . and ends with a thin book of rules. In between are two works of fiction addressed to children who, as you know, will put up with almost anything. As for my essays, what is an essayist but a man who is too impatient to write a novel?"*

White is modest in the extreme. An essayist of his caliber is not a thwarted novelist. He is a master of exposition and of the art of brevity. White can make four pages more memorable than most men make forty. His admirers are not looking for a novel from his workshop, only more of the eloquent essays he has been writing for the last thirty years.

[1] Today I should carry the pumpkins and squash from the back porch to the attic. The nights are too frosty to leave them outdoors any longer. And as long as I am making some trips to the attic I should also take up the boat cushions and the charts and the stuff from the galley and also a fishing rod that belongs up in the attic. Today I should finish filling in the trench we dug for the water pipe and should haul two loads of beach gravel from the Naskeag ° bar to spread on top of the clay fill. And

Naskeag: Naskeag Point, near Brooklin, Maine.

I should stop in and pay the Reverend Mr. Smith for the gravel I got a month or two ago and ask him if he has seen a bear.

² I ought to finish husking the corn and wheel the old stalks out and dump them on the compost pile,° and while I am out there I should take a fork and pitch over the weeds that were thrown at the edge of the field last August and rake the little windfalls from under the apple tree and pitch them on to the heap too. I ought to go down to the shore at dead low water and hook on to the mooring with a chain and make the chain fast to the float, so that the tide will pick up the mooring rock and I can tow the whole thing ashore six hours later. I ought to knock the wedges out from the frames of the pier, put a line on the frames, and tow them in on the high water. First, though, I would have to find a line long enough to tie every frame. If I'm to do any work at the shore I ought first to put a cement patch on the leak in my right boot. After the frames are on the beach another fellow and myself ought to carry them up and stack them. And there is probably enough rockweed ° on the beach now, so that I ought to bring up a load or two for the sheep shed. I ought to find out who it is that is shooting coot ° down in the cove today, just to satisfy my own curiosity. He was out before daybreak with his decoys, but I do not think he has got any birds.

³ I ought to take up the wire fence round the chicken range today, roll it up in bundles, tie them with six-thread, and store them at the edge of the woods. Then I ought to move the range houses off the field and into the corner of the woods and set them up on blocks for the winter, but I ought to sweep them out first and clean the roosts with a wire brush. It would be a good idea to have a putty knife in my pocket, for scraping. I ought to add a bag of phosphate to the piles of hen dressing that

compost pile: a mixture of peat, manure, leaf mold, and lime, used for fertilizing or renovating land.
rockweed: any coarse seaweed.
coot: ducklike bird of the rail family. It is stupid and slow in flight.

have accumulated under the range houses and spread the mixture on the field, to get it ready for plowing. And I ought to decide whether to plow just the range itself or to turn over a little more on the eastern end. On my way in from the range I ought to stop at the henhouse long enough to climb up and saw off an overhanging branch from the apple tree—it might tear the paper roof in the first big wind storm. I shall have to get a ladder of course and a saw.

⁴ Today I certainly ought to go over to the mill and get four twelve-inch boards, twelve feet long and half an inch thick, to use in building three new hoppers for dry mash feeding to my pullets, which are now laying seventy-eight per cent and giving me about eighty dozen eggs a week. I should also need one board which would be an inch thick, for the end pieces and for making the ends of the reels. I shouldn't need anything for the stands because I have enough stuff round the place to build the stands—which I had better make twenty-three inches high from floor to perch. If I were to make them less than that, the birds on the floor would pick at the vents of the birds feeding.

⁵ I ought to get some shingle nails and some spikes while I am at it, as we are out of those things. And I ought to sharpen the blade of my plane if I am going to build some hoppers. I ought to take the cutting-off saw and have it filed, as long as I am going over to the mill anyway. On the way back I ought to stop in at Frank Hamilton's house and put in my application for government lime and super,° because I shall be passing his house and might just as well take advantage of it. Frank will ask me to sit down and talk a while, I imagine.

⁶ It is high time I raked up the bayberry brush which has been lying in the pasture since the August mowing. This would be a good chance to burn it today because we have had a rain and it is safe to burn. But before burning it I ought to find out whether it is really better

super: abbreviation of superphosphate, used to condition soil.

for the pasture to burn stuff like that or to let it rot for dressing. I suppose there is so much wood in it it wouldn't rot up quickly and should be burned. Besides, I was once told in high-school chemistry that no energy is ever lost to the world, and presumably the ashes from the fires will strengthen my pasture in their own way.

7 I ought to take the buck lamb out of the flock of lambs today, before he gets to work on the ewe lambs, because I don't want them to get bred. I don't know just where to put him, but I ought to decide that today, and put him there. I should send away today for some phenothiazine ° so that I can drench my sheep next week. It would probably be a good idea to try phenothiazine this time, instead of copper sulphate, which just gets the stomach worms and doesn't touch the nodular worms or the large-mouth bowel worms. And I ought to close the big doors on the north side of the barn cellar and board them up and bank them, so that the place won't be draughty down there at night when the sheep come in, as they are beginning to do. I have been thinking I ought to enlarge the south door so that I won't lose any lambs next spring from the ewes jamming through the narrow single opening, and this would be the time to do that.

8 Today I ought to start rebuilding the racks in the sheep shed, to fix them so the sheep can't pull hay out and waste it. There is a way to do this, and I know the way. So I am all set. Also I ought to fix up the pigpen down there in the barn cellar too and sweeten it up with a coat of whitening, so that I can get the pig indoors, because the nights are pretty cold now. The trough will probably not have to be rebuilt this year because last year I put a zinc binding all round the edges of it. (But if I *shouldn't* get round to fixing up the pen I should at least carry a forkful of straw down to the house where the pig now is—I should at least do that.)

9 This would be a good day to put in a new light in

phenothiazine: a yellowish crystalline compound formed by heat-
ing diphenylamine with sulphur.

the window in the woodshed, and also there is one broken in the shop and one in the henhouse, so the sensible thing would be to do them all at once, as long as I have the putty all worked up and the glass cutter out. I ought to hook up the stove in the shop today, and get it ready for winter use. And I ought to run up the road and see Bert and find out why he hasn't delivered the cord of slabwood he said he was going to bring me. At any rate, I ought to make a place in the cellar for it today, which will mean cleaning house down there a little and neating up, and finding a better place to keep my flats and fillers for my egg cases. Incidentally, I ought to collect eggs right now, so there won't be any breakage in the nests.

10 It just occurred to me that if I'm going to the mill today I ought to measure the truck and figure out what I shall need in the way of hardwood boards to build a set of sideboards and a headboard and a tailboard for my stakes. I ought to bring these boards back with me along with the pine for the hoppers. I shall need two bolts for the ends of each sideboard, and one bolt for the cleat in the middle, and two bolts for the ends of each of the head and tailboards, and there will be three of each of them, so that makes fifty-four bolts I shall need, and the stakes are about an inch and a half through and the boards will be three-quarters, so that makes two inches and a quarter, and allow another half inch for washer and nut. About a three-inch bolt would do it. I better get them today.

11 Another thing I ought to do is take that grass seed that the mice have been getting into in the barn and store it in a wash boiler or some pails or something. I ought to set some mousetraps tonight, I mustn't forget. I ought to set one upstairs, I guess, in the little northeast chamber where the pipe comes through from the set tubs in the back kitchen, because this is the Mouse Fifth Avenue, and it would be a good chance for a kill. I ought to gather together some old clothes and stuff for the rummage sale to raise money to buy books for the town library, and I ought to rake the barnyard and wheel the

dressing down into the barn cellar where it will be out of the weather, because there is a lot of good dressing there right now. I ought to note down on the calendar in my room that I saw the ewe named Galbreath go to buck day before yesterday, so I can have her lambing date. Hers will be the first lamb next spring, and it will be twins because she is a twinner. Which reminds me I ought to write Mike Galbreath a letter. I have been owing him one since before Roosevelt was elected for the third term. I certainly should do that, it has been such a long time. I should do it today while it is in my mind.

¹² One thing I ought to do today is to take a small Stillson wrench ° and go down cellar and tighten the packing nut on the water pump so it won't drip. I could do that when I am down there making a place for the slabwood—it would save steps to combine the two things. I also ought to stir the litter in the henpen in the barn where the Barred Rocks ° are, and in the henhouse where the crossbred birds are; and then fill some bushel baskets with shavings and add them to the litter in the places where it needs deepening. The dropping boards under the broody coops need cleaning and I should do that at the same time, since I should be out there anyway. As far as litter is concerned, a man could take and rake the lawn under the maples where there is such an accumulation of leaves and add these dry leaves to the litter in the houses for the birds to scratch around in. Anything to keep their minds occupied in healthy channels.

¹³ Today I intend to pull the young alders ° in the field on the north side, as they are beginning to get ahead

---

Stillson wrench: a monkey wrench with an adjustable jaw that grips pipes more tightly when pressure is exerted on the handle.

Barred Rocks: black and white chickens which lay brown eggs. They are bred chiefly in New England.

alders: shrubs or trees similar to the birch, of the family *Betulaceae*, genus *Alnus.*

of me. I must do that today, probably later on this afternoon. A bush hook would be a good tool for that. I
should also clean up the remaining garden trash and add
it to the compost, saving out whatever the sheep might
eat, and should remove the pipe from the well under the
apple tree and store it down below in the barn.

¹⁴ I also think I had better call up a buyer and get rid
of my ten old hens, since we have canned all we are going
to need. After the hens are gone I shall no longer need
the borrowed range house that they are living in and I
can get two long poles, lash them on behind the truck,
and load the house on and drag it up to Kenneth's house.
But it will be necessary to take an ax and flatten the
ends of the poles so they won't dig into the highway,
although the tar is so cold now they probably wouldn't
dig in much anyway. Still, the thing to do is do it right.

¹⁵ Another thing I should try to manage to do today
is to earmark the two pure-bred lambs. That will be
easy enough—it just means finding the ear tags that I put
away in a drawer or some place last spring and finding
the special pliers that you have to use in squeezing a tag
into a sheep's ear. I think I know where those pliers are,
I think they are right in my cabinet next to that jar of
rubber cement. I shall have to get the lambs up, but
they will come without much trouble now because they
are hungry. I *could* take the buck away at the same time
if I could think of a place to put him.

¹⁶ Today I want to get word to Walter about the plowing of the garden pieces, and I had also better arrange
down cellar about a bin for the roots, because on account
of the extra amount of potatoes we have it will mean a
little rearranging down there in order to get everything
in. But I can do that when I am down tightening the
nut on the pump. I ought to take the car into the village
today to get an inspection sticker put on it; however, on
second thought if I am going to the mill I guess it would
be better to go in the truck and have a sticker put on *that*
while I am seeing about the lumber, and then I can

bring the boards back with me. But I mustn't be away at low water otherwise I won't be able to hook on to the mooring.

17   Tomorrow is Tuesday and the egg truck will be coming through in the morning to pick up my cases, so I must finish grading and packing the eggs today—I have about fifty dozen packed and only ten to go to make up the two cases. Then I must nail up the cases and make out the tags and tack them on, and lug the cases over to the cellar door, ready to be taken out in the morning, as the expressman is apt to get here early. I've also got to write a letter today to a publisher who wrote me asking what happened to the book manuscript I was supposed to turn in a year ago last spring, and I also should take the green chair in the living room to Eliot Sweet so that he can put in some little buttons that keep coming out all the time. I can throw the chair into the truck and drop it by his shop on my way to town. If I am going to take the squashes and pumpkins up to the attic I had better take the old blankets which we have been covering them with nights, and hang them on the line to dry. I also ought to nail a pole up somewhere in the barn to hang grain sacks on so the rats won't be able to get at them and gnaw holes in them; empty sacks are worth ten cents for the heavy ones and five cents for the cotton ones, and they mount up quite fast and run into money. I mustn't forget to do that today—it won't take but a minute.

18   I've got to see about getting a birthday present for my wife today, but I can't think of anything. Her birthday is past anyway. There were things going on here at the time and I didn't get around to getting her a present but I haven't forgotten about it. Possibly when I am in the village I can find something.

19   If I'm going to rebuild the racks for the sheep it would be a good idea to have the mill rip out a lot of two-inch slats for me while I am there, as I shall need some stuff like that. I ought to make a list, I guess. And I mustn't forget shingle nails and the spikes. There is

a place on the bottom step of the stairs going down into the woodshed where the crocus sack which I nailed on to the step as a foot-wiper is torn off, and somebody might catch his foot in that and take a fall. I certainly should fix that today before someone has a nasty fall. The best thing would be to rip the old sack off and tack a new one on. A man should have some roofing nails if he is going to make a neat job of tacking a sack on to a step. I think I may have some but I'd better look. I can look when I go out to get the Stillson wrench that I shall need when I go down to tighten the packing nut on the pump, and if I haven't any I can get some when I go to town.

20　I've been spending a lot of time here typing, and I see it is four o'clock already and almost dark, so I had better get going. Specially since I ought to get a haircut while I am at it.

ANALYSIS

The French would call this essay a *tour de force*. The phrase means literally a feat of strength; but as we have extended its meaning, especially in critical writing, we use it to describe an adroit or ingenious accomplishment, a feat of skill. Applied to White's essay it would also suggest a highly individual performance. There is nothing like "Memorandum" anywhere in this book of models. In fact, it would be safe to say White never repeated the *form* of this essay in his own writing. The reasons are apparent. An author does not imitate himself if he can help it. The pattern of this essay is much too distinctive to be spoiled by repetition. Let us inspect it more closely.

The time is a Monday in autumn. The place is a farm in Maine. But all this could happen on any farm, anywhere. White needs no introduction to his memorandum. It is as though be began thinking after lunch about the chores to be done, now that the nights are frosty, or, put another way, as though he rolled a sheet into the typewriter and began typing. In paragraph 19, he says, shyly, "I ought to make a list, I guess." This whole essay is a list, mental or written, it does not matter. One task leads to another. One paragraph spills into the next, and by the time we are on the third page we sense the inevitable —it will be dark before he even gets started. There is enough work here for ten men.

White knows all this. It is his brand of humor. His style is perfectly adapted to casual understatement ° ("There is a way to do this, and I know the way. So I am all set.") He makes friendly asides to his audience ("Frank will ask me to sit down and talk awhile, I imagine."). He writes with "naive" earnestness ("But if I *shouldn't* get round to fixing up the pen I should at least carry a forkful of straw. . . ."). He mixes repairing his boat with writing Mike Galbreath a letter with earmarking two lambs with buying his wife's present with tightening the packing nut on the water pump with answering his publisher (the manuscript is eighteen months overdue!).

But do not be deceived. White has organized his recital beautifully. This is a casual essay carefully achieved. He mentions a neighbor from time to time (paragraphs 1, 5, 9, 11, 14, 16, 17). He becomes highly specific after talking in general details (four twelve-inch boards twelve feet long and a half inch thick, phenothiazine instead of copper sulphate for the sheep, pullets laying 78 percent, fifty-four bolts, a Stillson wrench, ear tags, special pliers, sixty dozen eggs to be packed). He interweaves his chores, moving from attic to cellar to barn to hen coop to pasture and back again. He works endless variations on I should, I ought, I intend, today I must, it is high time, this would be a good day to, it just occurred to me. And he saves the best understatement of all for his last sentence. *Tour de force* this essay certainly is, but do not underestimate its carefully balanced details. In what better way could White have shown us the variety of his day's work, the ease with which he can forget manuscripts and birthday presents, the joy of living close to the soil?

Questions on Content

This essay is so closely knit that it is difficult to question a reader on any one detail. Try making your own list of what constitutes this one farmer's chores.

understatement: See Glossary.

Questions on Technique

1. Let us suppose White had not adopted this "circular" technique, one chore leading to another, but had addressed a title such as "Farming Is Hard Work." How would *arguing* such a statement differ from *chatting* with his reader as he does in this memorandum?
2. Would you have organized the details of this essay beginning with the attic, then the cellar, then the farmyard and so on? Why? Do you think White gains or loses by his interweaving?
3. What particular details do you find add rural "color" to White's essay?

Suggestions for Writing

1. Have you ever lived or spent a vacation on a farm? Write an essay of 500 words called "On Doing Farm Chores."
2. The city dweller also has house problems. Saturday morning is a traditional time to tackle them. Write a 500-word essay called "Tomorrow We Clean Out the Attic [Basement, Garage]."
3. Imagine that White had reversed his seasons. It is early April. Spring is just breaking through. The ground is soft, the trees are pale gold, the air is balmy, and you thought you heard a nest of young birds. Write a 400-word essay in White's easy, colloquial ° language. Call it "Memorandum."
4. Write a 500-word essay on this altered maxim: Never do today what you can put off until tomorrow.
5. As a high school student you sometimes find yourself frantic because you have too many things to do: assignments due, work in school activities, sports, home chores, and so forth. Write an essay (400–500 words) in the White manner revealing your emotions as you face an overwhelming schedule.

colloquial: See Glossary.

SIR MAX BEERBOHM · *A Relic*

When Sir Max Beerbohm died in 1956, in Rapallo, Italy, where he had lived for many decades, England lost one of her finest essayists. "The Incomparable Max" he was called during the late 1890's and the Edwardian days. He had been one of the brilliant lights of the Yellow Book and had succeeded George Bernard Shaw as drama critic of the London Saturday Review. His satirical novel, Zuleika Dobson (1911), gained him more fame. It is likely, however, that his books of caricatures °—collections of witty drawings—and his eight volumes of essays will endure longer.

Beerbohm's books were always small books. He never believed in publishing much and certainly not before every line was polished with the greatest care. His education at Charterhouse and Oxford gave him a taste for tradition and urbanity. He liked his world well-ordered. His writing is a reflection of a strong distaste for commercialism, modernity, and speed. The titles of his essays suggest leisure and reflection—for example, "On Seeing People Off," "A Letter That Was Not Written," "Fashion and Her Bicycle," or "Going Back to School." But there is also a strain of the subtlest wit in everything Beerbohm writes, in a turn of phrase, a casual remark, a playful irony.° And he is not above making himself the butt of some of his keenest observations. "A Relic" demonstrates two sides of Beerbohm's talent; it is a simple reminiscence and an honest confession.

1 Yesterday I found in a cupboard an old, small, battered portmanteau ° which, by the initials on it, I recog-

caricatures: See Glossary.   irony: See Glossary.
portmanteau: a large suitcase.

"A Relic" from *And Even Now* by Max Beerbohm, E. P. Dutton and Co., Inc. Copyright 1921 by E. P. Dutton and Co., Inc. Reprinted by permission of the publisher.

nized as my own property. The lock appeared to have been forced. I dimly remembered having forced it myself, with a poker, in my hot youth, after some journey in which I had lost the key; and this act of violence was probably the reason why the trunk had so long ago ceased to travel. I unstrapped it, not without dust; it exhaled the faint scent of its long closure; it contained a tweed suit of Late Victorian pattern, some bills, some letters, a collar stud, and—something which, after I had wondered for a moment or two what on earth it was, caused me suddenly to murmur, "Down below, the sea rustled to and fro over the shingle." °

² Strange that these words had, year after long year, been existing in some obscure cell at the back of my brain!—forgotten but all the while existing, like the trunk in that cupboard. What released them, what threw open the cell door, was nothing but the fragment of a fan; just the butt-end of an inexpensive fan. The sticks are of white bone, clipped together with a semicircular ring that is not silver. They are neatly oval at the base, but variously jagged at the other end. The longest of them measures perhaps two inches. Ring and all, they have no market value; for a farthing ° is the least coin in our currency. And yet, though I had so long forgotten them, for me they are not worthless. They touch a chord . . . Lest this confession raise false hopes in the reader, I add that I did not know their owner.

³ I did once see her, and in Normandy, and by moonlight, and her name was Angélique. She was graceful, she was even beautiful. I was but nineteen years old. Yet even so I cannot say that she impressed me favorably. I was seated at a table of a café on the terrace of a casino. ° I sat facing the sea, with my back to the casino. I sat listening to the quiet sea, which I had crossed that morn-

shingle: a beach strewn with large stones.
farthing: a small British bronze coin, when still in existence worth one-fourth of a British penny.
casino: in Italy, a country house; more commonly, as Beerbohm uses it, a building used for dancing and gambling.

ing. The hour was late, there were few people about. I heard the swing-door behind me flap open, and was aware of a sharp snapping and crackling sound as a lady in white passed quickly by me. I stared at her erect thin back and her agitated elbows. A short fat man passed in pursuit of her—an elderly man in a black alpaca ° jacket that billowed. I saw that she had left a trail of little white things on the asphalt. I watched the efforts of the agonized short fat man to overtake her as she swept wraith-like * away to the distant end of the terrace. What was the matter? What had made her so spectacularly angry with him? The three or four waiters of the café were exchanging cynical smiles and shrugs, as waiters will. I tried to feel cynical, but was thrilled with excitement, with wonder and curiosity. The woman out yonder had doubled on her tracks. She had not slackened her furious speed, but the man waddlingly * contrived to keep pace with her now. With every moment they became more distinct, and the prospect that they would presently pass by me, back into the casino, gave me that physical tension which one feels on a wayside platform at the imminent passing of an express. In the rushingly enlarged vision I had of them, the wrath on the woman's face was even more saliently * the main thing than I had supposed it would be. That very hard Parisian face must have been as white as the powder that coated it. "Écoute, Angélique," gasped the perspiring bourgeois, "écoute, je te supplie—" ° The swing-door received them and was left swinging to and fro. I wanted to follow, but had not paid for my bock.° I beckoned my waiter. On his way to me he stooped down and picked up something which, with a smile and a shrug, he laid on my table: "Il semble que Mademoiselle ne s'en servira plus." ° This is the

alpaca: a thin kind of cloth made from the wool of a llama.
"Ecoute, Angélique . . . je te supplie": "Listen, Angélique, I beg of you."
bock: a kind of beer brewed usually in the spring. It tastes of an herb called wort.
"Il semble que Mademoiselle ne s'en servira plus." "It appears that Mademoiselle will not make use of this any more."

thing I now write of, and at sight of it I understood why there had been that snapping and crackling, and what the white fragments on the ground were.

⁴ I hurried through the rooms, hoping to see a continuation of that drama—a scene of appeasement,* perhaps, or of fury still implacable.* But the two oddly assorted players were not performing there. My waiter had told me he had not seen either of them before. I suppose they had arrived that day. But I was not destined to see either of them again. They went away, I suppose, next morning; jointly or singly; singly, I imagine.

⁵ They made, however, a prolonged stay in my young memory, and would have done so even had I not had that tangible * memento of them. Who were they, those two of whom that one strange glimpse had befallen me? What, I wondered, was the previous history of each? What, in particular, had all that tragic pother been about? Mlle. Angélique I guessed to be thirty years old, her friend perhaps fifty-five. Each of their faces was as clear to me as in the moment of actual vision—the man's fat shiny bewildered face; the taut white face of the woman, the hard red line of her mouth, the eyes that were not flashing, but positively dull, with rage. I presumed that the fan had been a present from him, and a recent present—bought perhaps that very day, after their arrival in the town. But what, *what* had he done that she should break it between her hands, scattering the splinters as who should sow dragon's teeth? ° I could not believe he had done anything much amiss. I imagined her grievance a trivial one. But this did not make the case less engrossing. Again and again I would take the fan-stump from my pocket, examining it on the palm of my hand, or between finger and thumb, hoping to read the mystery it had been mixed up in, so that I might reveal that mystery to the world. To the world, yes; nothing less than that. I was determined to make a story of what I had seen—a *conte* ° in the man-

sow dragon's teeth: stir up strife.
conte: a short story; at one time, a tale of adventure.

ner of the great Guy de Maupassant.° Now and again, in the course of the past year or so, it had occurred to me that I might be a writer. But I had not felt the impulse to sit down and write something. I did feel that impulse now. It would indeed have been an irresistible impulse if I had known just what to write.

6   I felt I might know at any moment, and had but to give my mind to it. Maupassant was an impeccable artist, but I think the secret of the hold he had on the young men of my day was not so much that we discerned * his cunning as that we delighted in the simplicity which his cunning achieved. I had read a great number of his short stories, but none that had made me feel as though I, if I were a writer, mightn't have written it myself. Maupassant had a European reputation. It was pleasing, it was soothing and gratifying, to feel that one could at any time win an equal fame if one chose to set pen to paper. And now, suddenly, the spring had been touched in me, the time was come. I was grateful for the fluke by which I had witnessed on the terrace that evocative * scene. I looked forward to reading the MS. of "The Fan"—tomorrow, at least. I was not wildly ambitious. I was not inordinately * vain. I knew I couldn't ever, with the best will in the world, write like Mr. George Meredith.° Those wondrous works of his, seething with wit, with poetry and philosophy and what not, never had beguiled * me with the sense that I might do something similar. I had full consciousness of not being a philosopher, of not being a poet, and of not being a wit. Well, Maupassant was none of these things. He was just an observer, like me. Of course he was a good deal older than I, and had observed a good deal more. But it seemed to me that he was not my superior in knowledge of life. I knew all about life through *him*.

Guy de Maupassant: French novelist and short story writer (1850–1893); "The Necklace" is one of his most famous stories.

George Meredith: British novelist and poet (1828–1909), author of *The Egoist*, *The Ordeal of Richard Feverel*, and other psychological studies.

7   Dimly, the initial paragraph of my tale floated in my mind. I—not exactly I myself, but rather that impersonal *je* ° familiar to me through Maupassant—was to be sitting at that table, with a bock before me, just as I *had* sat. Four or five short sentences would give the whole scene. One of these I had quite definitely composed. You have already heard it. "Down below, the sea rustled to and fro over the shingle."

8   These words, which pleased me much, were to do double duty. They were to recur. They were to be, by a fine stroke, the very last words of my tale, their tranquillity striking a sharp ironic contrast with the stress of what had just been narrated. I had, you see, advanced further in the form of my tale than in the substance. But even the form was as yet vague. What, exactly, was to happen after Mlle. Angélique and M. Joumand (as I provisionally called him) had rushed back past me into the casino? It was clear that I must hear the whole inner history from the lips of one or the other of them. Which? Should M. Joumand stagger out on to the terrace, sit down heavily at the table next to mine, bury his head in his hands, and presently, in broken words, blurt out to me all that might be of interest? . . .

9   " 'And I tell you I gave up everything for her—everything.' He stared at me with his old hopeless eyes. 'She is more than the fiend I have described to you. Yet I swear to you, monsieur, that if I had anything left to give, it should be hers.'

10   "Down below, the sea rustled to and fro over the shingle."

11   Or should the lady herself be my informant? For a while, I rather leaned to this alternative. It was more exciting, it seemed to make the writer more signally a man of the world. On the other hand, it was less simple to manage. Wronged persons might be ever so communicative, but I surmised that persons in the wrong were reticent. Mlle. Angélique, therefore, would have to be modified by me in appearance and behavior, toned down,

impersonal *je:* the impersonal "I," or first-person narrator.

touched up; and poor M. Joumand must look like a man
of whom one could believe anything. . . .

12   "She ceased speaking. She gazed down at the fragments of her fan, and then, as though finding in them an
image of her own life, whispered, 'To think what I once
was, monsieur!—what, but for him, I might be, even now!'
She buried her face in her hands, then stared out into the
night. Suddenly she uttered a short, harsh laugh.

13   "Down below, the sea rustled to and fro over the
shingle."

14   I decided that I must choose the first of these two
ways. It was the less chivalrous as well as the less lurid
way, but clearly it was the more artistic as well as the
easier. The "chose vue," ° the "tranche de la vie" °—this
was the thing to aim at. Honesty was the best policy. I
must be nothing if not merciless. Maupassant was nothing
if not merciless. He would not have spared Mlle. Angélique. Besides, why should I libel M. Joumand? Poor—no,
not *poor* M. Joumand! I warned myself against pitying
him. One touch of "sentimentality," and I should be lost.
M. Joumand was ridiculous. I must keep him so. But—
what was his position in life? Was he a lawyer perhaps?—
or the proprietor of a shop in the Rue de Rivoli? ° I
toyed with the possibility that he kept a fan shop—that
the business had once been a prosperous one, but had
gone down, down, because of his infatuation for this
woman to whom he was always giving fans—which she
always smashed. . . .

15   " 'Ah monsieur, cruel and ungrateful to me though
she is, I swear to you that if I had anything left to give, it
should be hers; but,' he stared at me with his old hopeless
eyes, 'the fan she broke tonight was the last—the last,
monsieur—of my stock.' Down below,"—but I pulled myself together, and asked pardon of my Muse.°

"chose vue": the thing seen or experienced.
"tranche de la vie": a slice of life.
Rue de Rivoli: a main street of Paris, noted for its shops.
Muse: one of the nine goddesses of song, poetry, arts, and sciences.
    Traditionally they are the source of inspiration.

[16] It may be that I had offended her ° by my fooling. Or it may be that she had a sisterly desire to shield Mlle. Angélique from my mordant ° art. Or it may be that she was bent on saving M. de Maupassant from a dangerous rivalry. Anyway, she withheld from me the inspiration I had so confidently solicited. I *could not* think what had led up to that scene on the terrace. I tried hard and soberly. I turned the "chose vue" over in my mind, day by day, and the fan-stump over and over in my hand. But the "chose à figurer" °—what, oh what, was that? Nightly I revisited the café, and sat there with an open mind—a mind wide-open to catch the idea that should drop into it like a ripe golden plum. The plum did not ripen. The mind remained wide-open for a week or more, but nothing except that phrase about the sea rustled to and fro in it.

[17] A full quarter of a century has gone by. M. Joumand's death, so far too fat was he all those years ago, may be presumed. A temper so violent as Mlle. Angélique's must surely have brought its owner to the grave, long since. But here, all unchanged, the stump of her fan is; and once more I turn it over and over in my hand, not learning its secret—no, nor even trying to, now. The chord this relic strikes in me is not one of curiosity as to that old quarrel, but (if you will forgive me) one of tenderness for my first effort to write, and for my first hopes of excellence.

ANALYSIS

To launch this reminiscence, Beerbohm uses one of the oldest devices known to the essayist: "Yesterday I found in a cupboard an old, small, battered portmanteau. . . ." How easy it is to think of similar openings for our own essays: "We were cleaning the attic last Saturday morning. . . ." or "The first day at the beach we wandered over to the deserted house. . . ." or "It was raining all afternoon, and rather than start the new novel I thought I would answer a few letters. At the bottom of the

offended her: that is, offended the muse that was inspiring him.
mordant: biting, sarcastic.   "chose à figurer": the thing imagined.

drawer. . . ." Beerbohm's first paragraph is an invitation
to listen while he unfolds his situation. But instead of
telling us what lies at the bottom of his dusty suitcase,
he murmurs a mysterious sentence: "Down below, the
sea rustled to and fro over the shingle." The word "shingle" attracts our attention. It is not an ordinary word.
But where is the relic his title announces? Surely a sentence is not lying in a portmanteau? In a certain sense
it is. The relic is a broken fan, all right, and he soon describes it. But Beerbohm is a subtle writer. This special
sentence is as much a relic as is "the butt-end of an inexpensive fan." Beerbohm would understand it if we
called his sentence "the butt-end of a youthful ambition."
Let us explain.

This is an open, simple essay. He finds a fan. It touches
a chord. He recalls Angélique and the nameless man.
Their brief encounter floods his memory. He recalls he
was going to write a story, a simple *conte* like one of
Maupassant's, not a philosophic novel like Meredith's.
He had the initial paragraph formed in his mind. He
debated the point of view he would adopt—who, that is,
would tell the story, whether Mlle. Angélique would
pour out her grief or M. Joumand (newly-named)
would "stagger out on to the terrace"—and then the
Muse left him. The plum did not ripen. The phrase
never flowered. Twenty-five years later, the stump of a
fan is all that remains.

We could call Beerbohm's essay a charming reminiscence of an old incident were it not for the twist *in the
last sentence*. Have you read the "Memorandum" by
E. B. White that precedes this essay? Recall his last paragraph: ". . . it is four o'clock already and almost dark,
so I had better get going. Specially since I ought to get
a haircut while I am at it." Do you remember how Miss
McGinley ends her essay: "And while I wouldn't visit
here if you gave me the place, it's a wonderful region
just to live in"? Or Robert Benchley: "I wouldn't be
surprised, if things keep on as they are, if Shakespeare
began to lose his hold on people. I give him ten centuries
more at the outside"? All three of these writers know
the virtues of a strong closing, an ironic ° turn of phrase

ironic: See Glossary.

or, as with White, a statement of fact so hopelessly honest that it reverses, turns over, undercuts in a playful way all that has gone before.

Beerbohm belongs in their company (or perhaps we should say *they* in *his* since he could have taught them the device). Beerbohm ends his reminiscence: "The chord this relic strikes in me is not one of curiosity as to that old quarrel, but (if you will forgive me) one of tenderness for my first effort to write, and for my first hopes of excellence." With *this* sentence in mind, reread his essay. Are, perhaps, some of Beerbohm's sentences double-edged; that is, do they tell us as much about Beerbohm as a young man as they do about his encounter in the casino? Keep this question in mind when you come to paragraphs 6–8, to such sentences as "Well, Maupassant was none of these things. He was just an observer, like me. Of course he was a good deal older than I. . . ." Or "I had, you see, advanced further in the form of my tale than in the substance. But even the form was as yet vague." Paragraph 14 is especially important, more as a reflection of Beerbohm than of his story. Beerbohm, we realize, had no story to write. He was not to be a Meredith, not even a Maupassant. He was scarcely aware, in his youth, of his condescension to Maupassant's skill. For this reason the stump of the fan was a cruel discovery at the bottom of that portmanteau.

He had no story, that is true. But he has a splendid essay to take its place, and its subject is "On Having No Story to Write."

Questions on Content

1. Where and how did Beerbohm find the fan?
2. What few details did he gather about the couple?
3. Why did he choose to imitate Maupassant rather than Meredith? What does the choice tell us about Beerbohm's concept of himself?
4. What difference would the choice of point of view (telling the story through Mlle. Angélique's or M. Joumand's eyes) have made to his tale?

Add to your vocabulary: wraith-like, waddlingly, saliently, appeasement, implacable, tangible, discerned, evocative, inordinately, beguiled, mordant.

Questions on Technique

1. Why do you think Beerbohm withheld the description of the fan until the second paragraph? Why did he not tell us about the fan first and the remembered sentence second?
2. Would you have had Beerbohm include more conversation than what we have been told in paragraph 3?
3. He gives us descriptive details of Mlle. Angélique and her friend in paragraph 5. Why not advance them to paragraph 3 when we *first* hear about the young lady?
4. What is wrong with the projected development of his story as he outlines it in paragraph 14?

Suggestions for Writing

1. Write an essay on Beerbohm's essay. Discuss in 500 words the effect this story has on you: you discover an essay about a man who discovers an old fan which reminds him. . . . What pictures do his words form for you; how curious are you about what happened on the terrace; how would you have written the story?
2. Imitate Beerbohm's form. Take an incident from your own life. Do *not* tell the story but write a 500-word essay on why the incident sticks in your memory.
3. Beerbohm plays with overheard conversations. Many of us have experienced something similar to what he describes. Write a 500-word essay on "The Pleasures (or Dangers) of Eavesdropping."
4. Write a 400-word essay on the subject "On Choosing a Subject to Write About."
5. You once had an idea for a play or a story which you thought would be a great success. Write about how you got this idea and what happened to it.
6. Although Beerbohm was unable to create a story about the mysterious man and woman who entered his life so briefly, many short story writers undoubtedly could have done so. Stories come to writers in many ways. One of the common ways is just such a chance meeting with interesting people who stir the author's imagination. You may have witnessed a scene between two persons or seen a mysterious character and wondered what his story was. Recall such an experience and write the story you created from it.

PART THREE

NARRATION

The urge to hear a story is strong within all of us. As children we sat enraptured while our parents, camp leaders, or friends our own age in the neighborhood told us tales of adventure or of fantasy or of ordinary happenings around us. As we grew older, we may have become more sceptical of what we heard, but our ears perked up at an anecdote just as quickly as our eyes were attracted to a picture. We wanted to know what happened to whom and when.

Narration is that kind of discourse which answers the question: "What happened?" It is concerned with action, with events in motion. Other kinds of writing—description and exposition, for example—may be employed in telling a story. As we said earlier in this book, *pure* description and *pure* exposition are rare. We will discover the same about pure narration. A writer inevitably will want to describe or explain in the course of his narrative. But a storyteller's main intention is to relate a connected series of events. Taken together they will make up a meaningful action. He may describe an island; he may explain why the army is invading it; he may fill in the background of the war. But *what* happened and *when*—that is, in what sequence—are his major concerns. They make the story.

Narration, then, is concerned with time. A series of events moves through time, and what connects these events is a plan or sequence: a beginning, a middle, and an end. A good narrative has unity. Without unity, it is a mere jumble of random happenings. With unity, it is complete in itself. A good narrative cannot tell us all of what happened—how many men took part in the attack, who commanded them, what part of the island was heavily defended—but it can select events and place them in order so that we have a feeling of progress toward a specific end.

Is *time* the narrator's only concern? Once his selected events are in motion does he face no more problems? Hardly. Let us look at the opening sentences of three well-known novels:

> I have just returned from a visit to my landlord—the solitary neighbor that I shall be troubled with. This is certainly a beautiful country! In all England, I do not believe that I could have fixed on a situation so completely removed from the stir of society.
> Emily Brontë, *Wuthering Heights*

> An unassuming young man was traveling, in midsummer, from his native city of Hamburg to Davos-Platz in the Canton of the Grisons, on a three weeks' visit.
> Thomas Mann, *The Magic Mountain*

> Strether's first question, when he reached the hotel, was about his friend; yet on learning that Waymarsh was apparently not to arrive till evening he was not wholly disconcerted. A telegram from him bespeaking a room "only if not noisy," with the answer paid, was produced for the inquirer at the office, so that the understanding that they should meet at Chester rather than Liverpool remained to that extent sound.
> Henry James, *The Ambassadors*

You will notice that all three excerpts place us at once in *time*. All three likewise tell us something about *setting*, that is, the physical background or atmosphere, and about *point of view*, that is, who is telling the story. Let us look briefly at these two additional problems of good narration.

Setting is handled in many different ways. In some stories it controls, almost dominates, the action. We feel sometimes that *place* is almost a character in the story, its influence is so strong. Such is the case with Emily Brontë's *Wuthering Heights*. The Yorkshire moors are very much removed from "the stir of society," as Mr. Lockwood, the narrator, will discover. Their isolation is overpowering. Wuthering Heights is the name of Heathcliff's dwelling. Why it is so called is part of the fascination of this first chapter. The title of Thomas Mann's novel also suggests immediately the importance of place. This story is set in Haus Berghof, a tuberculosis sanatarium in the Swiss Alps, near Davos-Platz. From the first sentence the hero is headed there. The "three weeks' visit" turns into a seven years' stay. Henry James is concerned with the influence of all of Europe on his character Strether, not just the influence of a house or a hospital. The novel opens in England (as "Chester rather than Liverpool" indicates) but moves eventually to Paris. James expends great effort in describing the atmosphere of that beguiling city. Not all stories weigh the setting so heavily in determining action, but setting is one way of bringing coherence to narration.

Point of view is equally vital in achieving coherence. When we use this term in discussing narrative technique, we mean "who is telling the story?" and "what is his relation to the action?" Emily Brontë narrates her novel in the first person. Mr. Lockwood is the new tenant at Thrushcross Grange and, as he tells us, he is curious about Heathcliff, the master of Wuthering Heights. His curiosity leads us directly into the story. But Heathcliff, not Lockwood, is the main character. We call Miss Brontë's method, therefore, first person point of view, the narrator's relation to the action being that of observer. If Heathcliff were to tell his own story—as do Huck Finn and Robinson Crusoe—we would call the technique first person point of view, the narrator's relation to the action being that of the main character or protagonist. And what a difference the shift would make.

James and Mann, on the other hand, tell their stories in the third person. Mann uses what is called the omniscient point of view. He roams wherever he wishes, into any character's mind, into any conversation, interpreting behavior if he so desires, commenting on action, telling us what his characters think and feel. He knows all. In *The Ambassadors*, James adopts what we call a limited omniscient point of view; that is, the author tells the story in the third person but he tells it from the viewpoint of *one* character in the story. James looks at all the events through Strether's eyes. He interprets Strether for us, but no other characters; he never leaves Strether's elbow. We see only what Strether and James see. We are given no knowledge of what other characters think and feel except as Strether knows these things. Quite obviously, these four different techniques—omniscient narrator, limited omniscient narrator, first person main character, first person observer—produce totally different kinds of stories. All four, however, are the author's way of establishing coherence in his narration.

Time, place, point of view are three important aspects of narration to watch for. One final aspect of narration, deserves mention. Let us call it *point of emphasis*. What is the author's motive in telling his story? All stories are made from characters in action (even when they are animals we call them characters). But some narratives stress character, some stress action (we call it "plot"), and some stress theme (the "point" or "meaning" of the story). In reading the five narratives that follow you will want to observe many things: who tells the story, what is happening, when, where—and after you have finished reading perhaps you will ask yourself "What was the author's major intention, his *point of emphasis?*" If you have already glanced at the chapter titles in this section, you will see that they offer abundant help in reaching a decision. One warning: types of exposition, as said much earlier, overlap each other: report into analysis, analysis into argument, and so on. Types of fiction merge just as easily. These narratives have been chosen for their high quality, not for easy pigeonholing. Enjoy the stories first. Analyze and classify them afterward.

CHAPTER 10

Simple narrative, first person

MARK TWAIN · *"I Sell a Dog"*

Ernest Hemingway believed modern American litera-
ture begins with Mark Twain, particularly one book,
Adventures of Huckleberry Finn. *Surely there is no doubt*
that Twain (or Samuel L. Clemens, as he was christened)
is one of our major nineteenth-century writers: humorist,
novelist, social critic, journalist, and short story writer. If
he had done no more than create Tom Sawyer and Huck
Finn he would have earned a permanent place in our
fiction.

In 1959, Charles Neider edited Twain's Autobiography.
It had appeared before, in 1924 and 1940, in piecemeal
fashion, but its confused publishing history need not con-
cern us. Neider's edition concentrates on "the more truly
autobiographical, the more purely literary and the more
characteristically humorous material" as Twain left
it. The last half of chapter 30, in his volume, is the
narrative that appears here. In November, 1867,
Twain had returned from a six-months tour of Europe.
A Hartford publisher had offered him a contract to
write a book on his adventures. He thought he could
write it in Washington, D. C. The story he tells here has

"I Sell a Dog" from *The Autobiography of Mark Twain,* edited by Charles
Neider. © 1959 by The Mark Twain Company. Reprinted by permission of
Harper & Brothers.

nothing to do with The Innocents Abroad, *as the book was called when it appeared in 1869, though you might feel, after you have read "I Sell a Dog," that Twain could also play the innocent at home. The title of the anecdote is ours; the humor of this story is all Twain's.*

1   I was out of money and I went down to Washington to see if I could earn enough there to keep me in bread and butter while I should write the book. I came across William Swinton, brother of the historian, and together we invented a scheme for our mutual sustenance; we became the fathers and originators of what is a common feature in the newspaper world now, the syndicate.° We became the old original first Newspaper Syndicate on the planet; it was on a small scale but that is usual with untried new enterprises. We had twelve journals on our list; they were all weeklies, all obscure and poor and all scattered far away among the back settlements. It was a proud thing for those little newspapers to have a Washington correspondent and a fortunate thing for us that they felt in that way about it. Each of the twelve took two letters a week from us, at a dollar per letter; each of us wrote one letter per week and sent off six duplicates of it to these benefactors, thus acquiring twenty-four dollars a week to live on, which was all we needed in our cheap and humble quarters.

2   Swinton was one of the dearest and loveliest human beings I have ever known, and we led a charmed existence together, in a contentment which knew no bounds. Swinton was refined by nature and breeding; he was a gentleman by nature and breeding; he was highly educated; he was of a beautiful spirit; he was pure in heart and speech. He was a Scotchman and a Presbyterian; a Presbyterian of the old and genuine school, being honest and sincere in his religion and loving it and finding serenity and peace in it. He hadn't a vice, unless a large and grateful

---

syndicate: a business concern which sells special articles, photographs, or comic strips to the press for simultaneous publication in a number of newspapers.

sympathy with Scotch whisky may be called by that name. I didn't regard it as a vice, because he was a Scotchman, and Scotch whiskey to a Scotchman is as innocent as milk is to the rest of the human race. In Swinton's case it was a virtue and not an economical one. Twenty-four dollars a week would really have been riches to us if we hadn't had to support that jug; because of the jug we were always sailing pretty close to the wind, and any tardiness in the arrival of any part of our income was sure to cause some inconvenience.

³ I remember a time when a shortage occurred; we had to have three dollars and we had to have it before the close of the day. I don't know now how we happened to want all that money at one time; I only know we had to have it. Swinton told me to go out and find it and he said he would also go out and see what he could do. He didn't seem to have any doubt that we would succeed but I knew that that was his religion working in him; I hadn't the same confidence; I hadn't any idea where to turn to raise all that bullion and I said so. I think he was ashamed of me, privately, because of my weak faith. He told me to give myself no uneasiness, no concern; and said in a simple, confident, and unquestioning way, "The Lord will provide." I saw that he fully believed the Lord would provide but it seemed to me that if he had had my experience —But never mind that; before he was done with me his strong faith had had its influence and I went forth from the place almost convinced that the Lord really would provide.

⁴ I wandered around the streets for an hour, trying to think up some way to get that money, but nothing suggested itself. At last I lounged into the big lobby of the Ebbitt House, which was then a new hotel, and sat down. Presently a dog came loafing along. He paused, glanced up at me and said with his eyes, "Are you friendly?" I answered with my eyes that I was. He gave his tail a grateful wag and came forward and rested his jaw on my knee and lifted his brown eyes to my face in a winningly affectionate way. He was a lovely creature, as beautiful as

a girl, and he was made all of silk and velvet. I stroked his smooth brown head and fondled his drooping ears and we were a pair of lovers right away. Pretty soon Brig.-Gen. Miles,° the hero of the land, came strolling by in his blue and gold splendors, with everybody's admiring gaze upon him. He saw the dog and stopped, and there was a light in his eye which showed that he had a warm place in his heart for dogs like this gracious creature; then he came forward and patted the dog and said.

⁵   "He is very fine—he is a wonder; would you sell him?"

⁶   I was greatly moved; it seemed a marvelous thing to me, the way Swinton's prediction had come true.

⁷   I said, "Yes."

⁸   The General said. "What do you ask for him?"

⁹   "Three dollars."

¹⁰   The General was manifestly surprised. He said, "Three dollars? Only three dollars? Why that dog is a most uncommon dog; he can't possibly be worth less than fifty. If he were mine, I wouldn't take a hundred for him. I'm afraid you are not aware of his value. Reconsider your price if you like, I don't wish to wrong you."

¹¹   But if he had known me he would have known that I was no more capable of wronging him than he was of wronging me. I responded with the same quiet decision as before.

¹²   "No, three dollars. That is his price."

¹³   "Very well, since you insist upon it," said the General, and he gave me three dollars and led the dog away and disappeared upstairs.

¹⁴   In about ten minutes a gentle-faced, middle-aged gentleman came along and began to look around here and there and under tables and everywhere, and I said to him, "Is it a dog you are looking for?"

¹⁵   His face had been sad before and troubled; but it lit up gladly now and he answered, "Yes—have you seen him?"

Brig.-Gen. Miles: Nelson Appleton Miles (1839–1925), American army commander in Indian wars, the War Between the States, and the Spanish-American War.

¹⁶ "Yes," I said, "he was here a minute ago and I saw him follow a gentleman away. I think I could find him for you if you would like me to try."

¹⁷ I have seldom seen a person look so grateful, and there was gratitude in his voice too when he conceded that he would like me to try. I said I would do it with great pleasure but that as it might take a little time I hoped he would not mind paying me something for my trouble. He said he would do it most gladly—repeating that phrase "most gladly"—and asked me how much.

¹⁸ I said, "Three dollars."

¹⁹ He looked surprised, and said, "Dear me, it is nothing! I will pay you ten, quite willingly."

²⁰ But I said, "No, three is the price," and I started for the stairs without waiting for any further argument, for Swinton had said that that was the amount that the Lord would provide and it seemed to me that it would be sacrilegious * to take a penny more than was promised.

²¹ I got the number of the General's room from the office clerk as I passed by his wicket,° and when I reached the room I found the General there caressing his dog and quite happy. I said, "I am sorry, but I have to take the dog again."

²² He seemed very much surprised and said, "Take him again? Why, he is my dog; you sold him to me and at your own price."

²³ "Yes," I said, "it is true—but I have to have him, because the man wants him again."

²⁴ "What man?"

²⁵ "The man that owns him; he wasn't my dog."

²⁶ The General looked even more surpised than before, and for a moment he couldn't seem to find his voice; then he said, "Do you mean to tell me that you were selling another man's dog—and knew it?"

²⁷ "Yes, I knew it wasn't my dog."

²⁸ "Then why did you sell him?"

²⁹ I said, "Well, that is a curious question to ask. I sold

wicket: a grilled or grated window.

him because you wanted him. You offered to buy the dog; you can't deny that. I was not anxious to sell him— I had not even thought of selling him—but it seemed to me that if it could be any accommodation to you—"

30 He broke me off in the middle, and said, *"Accommodation* to me? It is the most extraordinary spirit of accommodation I have ever heard of—the idea of your selling a dog that didn't belong to you—"

31 I broke him off there and said, "There is no relevance * about this kind of argument; you said yourself that the dog was probably worth a hundred dollars. I only asked you three; was there anything unfair about that? You offered to pay more, you know you did. I only asked you three; you can't deny it."

32 "Oh, what in the world has that to do with it! The crux of the matter is that you didn't own the dog—can't you see that? You seem to think that there is no impropriety ° in selling property that isn't yours provided you sell it cheap. Now then—"

33 I said, "Please don't argue about it any more. You can't get around the fact that the price was perfectly fair, perfectly reasonable—considering that I didn't own the dog—and so arguing about it is only a waste of words. I have to have him back again because the man wants him; don't you see that I haven't any choice in the matter? Put yourself in my place. Suppose you had sold a dog that didn't belong to you; suppose you—"

34 "Oh," he said, "don't muddle my brains any more with your idiotic reasoning! Take him along and give me a rest."

35 So I paid back the three dollars and led the dog downstairs and passed him over to his owner and collected three for my trouble.

36 I went away then with a good conscience, because I had acted honorably; I never could have used the three that I sold the dog for, because it was not rightly my own, but the three I got for restoring him to his rightful

---

impropriety: an improper act.

owner was righteously and properly mine, because I had earned it. That man might never have gotten that dog back at all, if it hadn't been for me. My principles have remained to this day what they were then. I was always honest; I know I can never be otherwise. It is as I said in the beginning—I was never able to persuade myself to use money which I had acquired in questionable ways.
³⁷ Now then, that is the tale. Some of it is true.

ANALYSIS

Twain is at home in the first-person narrative. It gives him leg-room, as it were. He was one of those writers who never seemed to know where fact left off and fiction began (nor did Tom and Huck), and so he liked to begin with the "story" as it happened and to make a few additions, or embellishments, as he went along. "Sort of shaping it a bit," he might have called it. Twain begins easily enough here. In two paragraphs he gives us a sufficient sense of place or situation. He tells us who Swinton is, what they live on, and why he enjoys his company. The action begins in paragraph 3, in a straight chronological progression.

Twain has a simple story to tell: he needs three dollars, he finds a dog, he sells him, he buys him back, he returns him to his owner, he reaps three dollars reward. A narrator with little talent would make a very dull story indeed of this experience. How does Twain turn it into pure delight? In paragraph 3, Twain writes that "[Swinton] told me to give myself no uneasiness, no concern; and said in a simple, confident, and unquestioning way, 'The Lord will provide.'" Twain adopts Swinton's manner throughout his narrative. Everything he writes is told "in a simple, confident, and unquestioning way." His story is as straightforward as he can make it. The style, that is, his choice of words and sentence structure, reflects the simple narrative method. The action is uncluttered, the reasoning logical. And the theme is apparent: honesty is a profitable policy.

If we look more closely we can see Twain's stylistic skill: "I hadn't any idea where to turn to raise all that bullion [three dollars!]"; "I lounged into the big lobby";

"I stroked his smooth brown head . . . and we were a pair of lovers right away"; "Brig.-Gen. Miles, the hero of the land, came strolling by in his blue and gold splendors." Twain can make a simple sentence light up by means of one well-chosen word.

Looking more closely at the action, we see it is a model of condensation and directness. Twain takes no time to analyze motives, to mull over alternatives. He finds a dog who likes him, a general who likes the dog, and a sale is made. When the real owner returns, Twain does *him* a favor and "finds" his dog. He returns the illegally-earned three dollars and keeps the three-dollar reward. The action of this narrative takes no more than twenty minutes.

But what of the "confident and unquestioning" reasoning and Twain's attendant theme? He zips through this story with such conviction that he does not allow us to analyze motives and logic. The humor of this piece lies in the last two paragraphs, of course, particularly in the sentence: "That man might never have gotten that dog back at all, if it hadn't been for me." What splendidly illogical logic! And Twain compounds it by finishing his story with a "straight face." He keeps his reward because he had "righteously and properly" earned it. But if it had not been for *him,* in the first place, the dog would have. . . . There is no need to finish it. *Some* of the story is true, he tells us. Which parts are true is your decision.

Questions on Content

1. What does Twain mean by "syndicate"?
2. Why is it important that Swinton be identified as a Scot?
3. Explain Twain's "logic" in paragraphs 29–35. What does he have to say about honesty in paragraph 36?

Add to your vocabulary: syndicate, sacrilegious, relevance, impropriety.

Questions on Technique

1. What does Twain accomplish in the first two paragraphs? Would the story have lost anything important if he had omitted them?

2. What part do "three dollars" play in the organization of this narrative? Why not make it "several dollars"?

3. How would you describe the dialogue? By specific references, show that the dialogue gives us an insight into the characters.

4. Would you have spent more time describing the characters, particularly the general and the dog's owner? Why?

Suggestions for Writing

1. Many of us have had pets. Narrate a story which involved your pet.

2. Write a short story called "I Buy a Dog [or other pet]."

3. Write a simple narrative in the first person, making yourself the main character. You might want to center the action around the first day at a new school, a rainy week at camp, a holiday at the seashore, a visit to an airfield. What happens should directly concern you, as narrator. All of it, as Twain would say, need not be true.

4. Retell Twain's story from paragraph 14 onward. Instead of writing "In about ten minutes a gentle-faced, middle-aged gentleman . . ," alter the plot.

5. Write a humorous account about a "deal" you once made: trading a bicycle or a boat, an agreement you made with a friend, and so forth.

CHAPTER II

Complex narrative,
third person

WILLIAM FAULKNER • *Barn Burning*

With this story we come to, in many ways, the most demanding selection in this book. We say "demanding" because William Faulkner makes few compromises with his reader. He is known as a master storyteller; but his method, as you will discover, makes Twain's narrative look like the ABC's. That is not a criticism disparaging Twain. One of the first aspects of narration you will want to observe is the way in which a good writer selects a vocabulary, a technique, a point of view° absolutely right for the story he has to tell. It would not be possible to tell Faulkner's story with Twain's method. Nor would Twain have been happy with Faulkner's vocabulary. Each writer seeks his own style and method.

"Barn Burning" first appeared in 1939 in Harper's Magazine. *Faulkner's reputation then was still maturing, even though he had published by that time what most critics think of as his major novels:* The Sound and the Fury, As I Lay Dying, Light in August, *and* Absalom, Absalom! *The story takes place in Yoknapatawpha County, a name Faulkner gives to a region created by his own fertile imagination. Since Faulkner was born in*

point of view: See Glossary.

*Oxford, Lafayette County, Mississippi, many readers see
a resemblance between Lafayette County and this im-
aginary world. On this subject Faulkner has little to say.
The wise novelist does not limit his fiction. He wants to
think he is writing about men and women, human
beings, anywhere, anytime. Man's nature does not change;
only the names, the dates, and the places he uses change
from one century to the next.*

*This story is about fear, hatred, stupidity, freedom,
justice, injustice, a kind of cowardice, and an indefinable
courage which leads to what you may feel is an overwhelming climax. It is a story about a ten-year old boy,
among other things. Faulkner calls him Colonel Sartoris
Snopes, an unlikely name. His mother calls him Sarty.
The story is told from the boy's point of view. He is not,
however, the only main character. You must meet Mr.
Abner Snopes, the boy's "pap," who is on trial as the
story opens. You will never forget him.*

¹ The store in which the Justice of the Peace's court
was sitting smelled of cheese. The boy, crouched on his
nail keg at the back of the crowded room, knew he
smelled cheese, and more: from where he sat he could
see the ranked shelves close-packed with the solid, squat,
dynamic shapes of tin cans whose labels his stomach read,
not from the lettering which meant nothing to his mind
but from the scarlet devils and the silver curve of fish—
this, the cheese which he knew he smelled and the hermetic ° meat which his intestines believed he smelled
coming in intermittent gusts momentary and brief between the other constant one, the smell and sense just a
little of fear because mostly of despair and grief, the old
fierce pull of blood. He could not see the table where the
Justice sat and before which his father and his father's
enemy (*our enemy* he thought in that despair; *ourn!
mine and hisn both! He's my father!*) stood, but he could
hear them, the two of them that is, because his father had
said no word yet:

hermetic: airtight, as in a sealed can.

2 "But what proof have you, Mr. Harris?"

3 "I told you. The hog got into my corn. I caught it up and sent it back to him. He had no fence that would hold it. I told him so, warned him. The next time I put the hog in my pen. When he came to get it I gave him enough wire to patch up his pen. The next time I put the hog up and kept it. I rode down to his house and saw the wire I gave him still rolled on to the spool in his yard. I told him he could have the hog when he paid me a dollar pound fee.° That evening a Negro came with the dollar and got the hog. He was a strange Negro. He said, 'He say to tell you wood and hay kin burn.' I said, 'What?' 'That whut he say to tell you,' the Negro said. 'Wood and hay kin burn.' That night my barn burned. I got the stock out but I lost the barn."

4 "Where is the Negro? Have you got him?"

5 "He was a strange Negro, I tell you. I don't know what became of him."

6 "But that's not proof. Don't you see that's not proof?"

7 "Get that boy up here. He knows." For a moment the boy thought too that the man meant his older brother until Harris said, "Not him. The little one. The boy," and, crouching, small for his age, small and wiry like his father, in patched and faded jeans even too small for him, with straight, uncombed, brown hair and eyes gray and wild as storm scud,° he saw the men between himself and the table part and become a lane of grim faces, at the end of which he saw the Justice, a shabby, collarless, graying man in spectacles, beckoning him. He felt no floor under his bare feet; he seemed to walk beneath the palpable weight of the grim turning faces. His father, stiff in his black Sunday coat donned not for the trial but for the moving, did not even look at him. *He aims for me to lie,* he thought, again with that frantic grief and despair. *And I will have to do hit.*

8 "What's your name, boy?" the Justice said.

pound fee: money for keeping an animal in an enclosure, usually
   when the animal is caught trespassing.
storm scud: vapory clouds driven swiftly by the wind.

⁹ "Colonel Sartoris Snopes," the boy whispered.

¹⁰ "Hey?" the Justice said. "Talk louder. Colonel Sartoris? I reckon anybody named for Colonel Sartoris in this country can't help but tell the truth, can they?" The boy said nothing. *Enemy—Enemy!* he thought; for a moment he could not even see, could not see that the Justice's face was kindly nor discern that his voice was troubled when he spoke to the man named Harris: "Do you want me to question this boy?" But he could hear, and during those subsequent long seconds while there was absolutely no sound in the crowded little room save that of quiet and intent breathing it was as if he had swung outward at the end of a grape vine, over a ravine, and at the top of the swing had been caught in a prolonged instant of mesmerized ° gravity, weightless in time.

¹¹ "No!" Harris said violently, explosively. "Damnation! Send him out of here!" Now time, the fluid world, rushed beneath him again, the voices coming to him again through the smell of cheese and sealed meat, the fear and despair and the old grief of blood:

¹² "This case is closed. I can't find against you, Snopes, but I can give you advice. Leave this country and don't come back to it."

¹³ His father spoke for the first time, his voice cold and harsh, level, without emphasis: "I aim to. I don't figure to stay in a country among people who . . ." he said something unprintable and vile, addressed to no one.

¹⁴ "That'll do," the Justice said. "Take your wagon and get out of this country before dark. Case dismissed."

¹⁵ His father turned, and he followed the stiff black coat, the wiry figure walking a little stiffly from where a Confederate provost's ° man's musket ball had taken him in the heel on a stolen horse thirty years ago, followed the two backs now, since his older brother had appeared from somewhere in the crowd, no taller than the father but thicker, chewing tobacco steadily between the

mesmerized: hypnotized.
provost: an officer of the military police.

two lines of grim-faced men and out of the store and across the worn gallery and down the sagging steps and among the dogs and half-grown boys in the mild May dust, where as he passed a voice hissed:

16 "Barn burner!"

17 Again he could not see, whirling; there was a face in a red haze, moonlike, bigger than the full moon, the owner of it half again his size, he leaping in the red haze toward the face, feeling no blow, feeling no shock when his head struck the earth, scrabbling up and leaping again, feeling no blow this time either and tasting no blood, scrabbling up to see the other boy in full flight and himself already leaping into pursuit as his father's hand jerked him back, the harsh, cold voice speaking above him: "Go get in the wagon."

18 It stood in a grove of locusts and mulberries across the road. His two hulking sisters in their Sunday dresses and his mother and her sister in calico and sunbonnets were already in it, sitting on and among the sorry residue of the dozen and more movings which even the boy could remember—the battered stove, the broken beds and chairs, the clock inlaid with mother-of-pearl, which would not run, stopped at some fourteen minutes past two o'clock of a dead and forgotten day and time, which had been his mother's dowry. She was crying, though when she saw him she drew her sleeve across her face and began to descend from the wagon. "Get back," the father said.

19 "He's hurt. I got to get some water and wash his . . ."

20 "Get back in the wagon," his father said. He got in too, over the tail-gate. His father mounted to the seat where the older brother already sat and struck the gaunt mules two savage blows with the peeled willow, but without heat. It was not even sadistic; ° it was exactly that same quality which in later years would cause his descendants to overrun the engine before putting a motor car into motion, striking and reining back in the same

sadistic: enjoying being cruel.

movement. The wagon went on, the store with its quiet crowd of grimly watching men dropped behind; a curve in the road hid it. *Forever* he thought. *Maybe he's done satisfied now, now that he has . . .* stopping himself. His mother's hand touched his shoulder.

21 "Does hit hurt?" she said.

22 "Naw," he said. "Hit don't hurt. Lemme be."

23 "Can't you wipe some of the blood off before hit dries?"

24 "I'll wash tonight," he said. "Lemme be, I tell you."

25 The wagon went on. He did not know where they were going. None of them ever did or ever asked, because it was always somewhere, always a house of sorts waiting for them a day or two days or even three days away. Likely his father had already arranged to make a crop on another farm before he . . . Again he had to stop himself. He (the father) always did. There was something about his wolflike independence and even courage when the advantage was at least neutral which impressed strangers, as if they got from his latent * ravening ° ferocity not so much a sense of dependability as a feeling that his ferocious conviction in the rightness of his own actions would be of advantage to all whose interest lay with his.

26 That night they camped, in a grove of oaks and beeches where a spring ran. The nights were still cool and they had a fire against it, of a rail lifted from a near-by fence and cut into lengths—a small fire, neat, niggard * almost, a shrewd fire; such fires were his father's habit and custom always, even in freezing weather. Older, the boy might have remarked this and wondered why not a big one; why should not a man who had not only seen the waste and extravagance of war, but who had in his blood an inherent voracious * prodigality ° with material not his own, have burned everything in sight? Then he might have gone a step farther and thought that that was the reason: that niggard blaze was the living fruit of nights passed during those four years in the woods hiding

ravening: devouring, rapacious.   prodigality: extravagance, waste.

from all men, blue or gray, with his strings of horses (captured horses, he called them). And older still, he might have divined the true reason: that the element of fire spoke to some deep mainspring of his father's being, as the element of steel or of powder spoke to other men, as the one weapon for the preservation of integrity, else breath were not worth the breathing, and hence to be regarded with respect and used with discretion.

²⁷ But he did not think this now and he had seen those same niggard blazes all his life. He merely ate his supper beside it and was already half asleep over his iron plate when his father called him, and once more he followed the stiff back, the stiff and ruthless limp, up the slope and on to the starlit road where, turning, he could see his father against the stars but without face or depth—a shape black, flat, and bloodless as though cut from tin in the iron folds of the frockcoat which had not been made for him, the voice harsh like tin and without heat like tin:

²⁸ "You were fixing to tell them. You would have told him." He didn't answer. His father struck him with the flat of his hand on the side of the head, hard but without heat, exactly as he had struck the two mules at the store, exactly as he would strike either of them with any stick in order to kill a horse fly, his voice still without fear or anger: "You're getting to be a man. You got to learn. You got to learn to stick to your own blood or you ain't going to have any blood to stick to you. Do you think either of them, any man there this morning, would? Don't you know all they wanted was a chance to get at me because they knew I had them beat? Eh?" Later, twenty years later, he was to tell himself, "If I had said they wanted only truth, justice, he would have hit me again." But now he said nothing. He was not crying. He just stood there. "Answer me," his father said.

²⁹ "Yes," he whispered. His father turned.

³⁰ "Get on to bed. We'll be there tomorrow."

³¹ Tomorrow they were there. In the early afternoon the wagon stopped before a paintless two-room house

identical almost with the dozen others it had stopped before even in the boy's ten years, and again, as on the other dozen occasions, his mother and aunt got down and began to unload the wagon, although his two sisters and his father and brother had not moved.

32   "Likely hit ain't fitten for hawgs," one of the sisters said.

33   "Nevertheless, fit it will and you'll hog it and like it," his father said. "Get out of them chairs and help your Ma unload."

34   The two sisters got down, big, bovine,° in a flutter of cheap ribbons; one of them drew from the jumbled wagon bed a battered lantern, the other a worn broom. His father handed the reins to the older son and began to climb stiffly over the wheel. "When they get unloaded, take the team to the barn and feed them." Then he said, and at first the boy thought he was still speaking to his brother: "Come with me."

35   "Me?" he said.

36   "Yes," his father said. "You."

37   "Abner," his mother said. His father paused and looked back—the harsh level stare beneath the shaggy, graying, irascible ° brows.

38   "I reckon I'll have a word with the man that aims to begin tomorrow owning me body and soul for the next eight months."

39   They went back up the road. A week ago—or before last night, that is—he would have asked where they were going, but not now. His father had struck him before last night but never before had he paused afterward to explain why; it was as if the blow and the following calm, outrageous voice still rang, repercussed, divulging nothing to him save the terrible handicap of being young, the light weight of his few years, just heavy enough to prevent his soaring free of the world as it seemed to be ordered but not heavy enough to keep him footed solid in it, to resist it and try to change the course of its events.

bovine: cowlike, sluggish.   irascible: prone to anger.

[40] Presently he could see the grove of oaks and cedars and the other flowering trees and shrubs where the house would be, though not the house yet. They walked beside a fence massed with honeysuckle and Cherokee roses ° and came to a gate swinging open between two brick pillars, and now, beyond a sweep of drive, he saw the house for the first time and at that instant he forgot his father and the terror and despair both, and even when he remembered his father again (who had not stopped) the terror and despair did not return. Because, for all the twelve movings, they had sojourned until now in a poor country, a land of small farms and fields and houses, and he had never seen a house like this before. *Hit's big as a courthouse* he thought quietly, with a surge of peace and joy whose reason he could not have thought into words, being too young for that: *They are safe from him. People whose lives are a part of this peace and dignity are beyond his touch, he no more to them than a buzzing wasp: capable of stinging for a little moment but that's all; the spell of this peace and dignity rendering even the barns and stable and cribs which belong to it impervious ° to the puny flames he might contrive . . .* this, the peace and joy, ebbing for an instant as he looked again at the stiff black back, the stiff and implacable limp of the figure which was not dwarfed by the house, for the reason that it had never looked big anywhere and which now, against the serene columned backdrop, had more than ever that impervious quality of something cut ruthlessly from tin, depthless, as though, sidewise to the sun, it would cast no shadow. Watching him, the boy remarked the absolutely undeviating course which his father held and saw the stiff foot come squarely down in a pile of fresh droppings where a horse had stood in the drive and which his father could have avoided by a simple change of stride. But it ebbed only for a moment, though he could not have thought this into words either,

Cherokee roses: a Chinese climbing rose. It is the state flower of Georgia.
impervious: impenetrable.

walking on in the spell of the house, which he could even want but without envy, without sorrow, certainly never with that ravening and jealous rage which unknown to him walked in the ironlike black coat before him: *Maybe he will feel it too. Maybe it will even change him now from what maybe he couldn't help but be.*

⁴¹ They crossed the portico. Now he could hear his father's stiff foot as it came down on the boards with clocklike finality, a sound out of all proportion to the displacement of the body it bore and which was not dwarfed either by the white door before it, as though it had attained to a sort of vicious and ravening minimum not to be dwarfed by anything—the flat, wide, black hat, the formal coat of broadcloth which had once been black but which had now that friction-glazed greenish cast of the bodies of old house flies, the lifted sleeve which was too large, the lifted hand like a curled claw. The door opened so promptly that the boy knew the Negro must have been watching them all the time, an old man with neat grizzled hair, in a linen jacket, who stood barring the door with his body, saying, "Wipe yo foots, white man, fo you come in here. Major ain't home nohow."

⁴² "Get out of my way," his father said, without heat too, flinging the door back and the Negro also and entering, his hat still on his head. And now the boy saw the prints of the stiff foot on the doorjamb and saw them appear on the pale rug behind the machinelike deliberation of the foot which seemed to bear (or transmit) twice the weight which the body compassed. The Negro was shouting "Miss Lula! Miss Lula!" somewhere behind them, then the boy, deluged as though by a warm wave by a suave * turn of carpeted stair and a pendant ° glitter of chandeliers and a mute gleam of gold frames, heard the swift feet and saw her too, a lady—perhaps he had never seen her like before either—in a gray, smooth gown with lace at the throat and an apron tied at the waist and the sleeves turned back, wiping cake or biscuit dough

pendant: suspended, also spelled "pendent."

from her hands with a towel as she came up the hall, looking not at his father at all but at the tracks on the blond rug with an expression of incredulous amazement.

⁴³ "I tried," the Negro cried. "I tole him to . . ."

⁴⁴ "Will you please go away?" she said in a shaking voice. "Major de Spain is not at home. Will you please go away?"

⁴⁵ His father had not spoken again. He did not speak again. He did not even look at her. He just stood stiff in the center of the rug, in his hat, the shaggy iron-gray brows twitching slightly above the pebble-colored eyes as he appeared to examine the house with brief deliberation. Then with the same deliberation he turned; the boy watched him pivot on the good leg and saw the stiff foot drag round the arc of the turning, leaving a final long and fading smear. His father never looked at it, he never once looked down at the rug. The Negro held the door. It closed behind them, upon the hysteric and indistinguishable woman-wail. His father stopped at the top of the steps and scraped his boot clean on the edge of it. At the gate he stopped again. He stood for a moment, planted stiffly on the stiff foot, looking back at the house. "Pretty and white, ain't it?" he said. "That's sweat. Negro sweat. Maybe it ain't white enough yet to suit him. Maybe he wants to mix some white sweat with it."

⁴⁶ Two hours later the boy was chopping wood behind the house within which his mother and aunt and the two sisters (the mother and aunt, not the two girls, he knew that; even at this distance and muffled by walls the flat loud voices of the two girls emanated ° an incorrigible ° idle inertia) were setting up the stove to prepare a meal, when he heard the hooves and saw the linen-clad man on a fine sorrel ° mare, whom he recognized even before he saw the rolled rug in front of the Negro youth following on a fat bay ° carriage horse—a suffused, angry face

emanated: issued forth.   incorrigible: uncorrectable.
sorrel: a brown color, red-yellow in hue, sometimes (of horses) called bright chestnut.
bay: reddish brown.

vanishing, still at full gallop, beyond the corner of the house where his father and brother were sitting in the two tilted chairs; and a moment later, almost before he could have put the ax down, he heard the hooves again and watched the sorrel mare go back out of the yard, already galloping again. Then his father began to shout one of the sisters' names, who presently emerged backward from the kitchen door dragging the rolled rug along the ground by one end while the other sister walked behind it.

⁴⁷ "If you ain't going to tote,° go on and set up the wash pot," the first said.

⁴⁸ "You, Sarty!" the second shouted. "Set up the wash pot!" His father appeared at the door, framed against that shabbiness, as he had been against that other bland perfection, impervious to either, the mother's anxious face at his shoulder.

⁴⁹ "Go on," the father said. "Pick it up." The two sisters stooped, broad, lethargic; stooping, they presented an incredible expanse of pale cloth and a flutter of tawdry ribbons.

⁵⁰ "If I thought enough of a rug to have to git hit all the way from France I wouldn't keep hit where folks coming in would have to tromp on hit," the first said. They raised the rug.

⁵¹ "Abner," the mother said. "Let me do it."

⁵² "You go back and git dinner," his father said. "I'll tend to this."

⁵³ From the woodpile through the rest of the afternoon the boy watched them, the rug spread flat in the dust beside the bubbling wash pot, the two sisters stooping over it with that profound and lethargic reluctance, while the father stood over them in turn, implacable and grim, driving them though never raising his voice again. He could smell the harsh homemade lye they were using; he saw his mother come to the door once and look toward them with an expression not anxious now but very like

tote: carry.

despair; he saw his father turn, and he fell to with the ax and saw from the corner of his eye his father raise from the ground a flattish fragment of field stone and examine it and return to the pot, and this time his mother actually spoke: "Abner. Abner. Please don't. Please, Abner."

⁵⁴ Then he was done too. It was dusk; the whippoorwills had already begun. He could smell coffee from the room where they would presently eat the cold food remaining from the mid-afternoon meal, though when he entered the house he realized they were having coffee again probably because there was a fire on the hearth, before which the rug now lay spread over the backs of the two chairs. The tracks of his father's foot were gone. Where they had been were now long, water-cloudy scoriations ° resembling the sporadic ° course of a Lilliputian ° mowing machine.

⁵⁵ It still hung there while they ate the cold food and then went to bed, scattered without order or claim up and down the two rooms, his mother in one bed, where his father would later lie, the older brother in the other, himself, the aunt, and the two sisters on pallets on the floor. But his father was not in bed yet. The last thing the boy remembered was the depthless, harsh silhouette of the hat and coat bending over the rug and it seemed to him that he had not even closed his eyes when the silhouette was standing over him, the fire almost dead behind it, the stiff foot prodding him awake. "Catch up the mule," his father said.

⁵⁶ When he returned with the mule his father was standing in the black door, the rolled rug over his shoulder. "Ain't you going to ride?" he said.

⁵⁷ "No. Give me your foot."

scoriations: a manufactured word, from *scoria,* the refuse left after smelting metals.
sporadic: occurring occasionally or in scattered instances.
Lilliputian: dwarfed, diminutive, from the island Lilliput, in Swift's *Gulliver's Travels,* where the inhabitants are six inches tall.

⁵⁸ He bent his knee into his father's hand, the wiry, surprising power flowed smoothly, rising, he rising with it, on to the mule's bare back (they had owned a saddle once; the boy could remember it though not when or where) and with the same effortlessness his father swung the rug up in front of him. Now in the starlight they retraced the afternoon's path, up the dusty road rife * with honeysuckle, through the gate and up the black tunnel of the drive to the lightless house, where he sat on the mule and felt the rough warp of the rug drag across his thighs and vanish.

⁵⁹ "Don't you want me to help?" he whispered. His father did not answer and now he heard again that stiff foot striking the hollow portico with that wooden and clocklike deliberation, that outrageous overstatement of the weight it carried. The rug, hunched, not flung (the boy could tell that even in the darkness) from his father's shoulder struck the angle of wall and floor with a sound unbelievably loud, thunderous, then the foot again, unhurried and enormous; a light came on in the house and the boy sat, tense, breathing steadily and quietly and just a little fast, though the foot itself did not increase its beat at all, descending the steps now; now the boy could see him.

⁶⁰ "Don't you want to ride now?" he whispered. "We kin both ride now," the light within the house altering now, flaring up and sinking. *He's coming down the stairs now,* he thought. He had already ridden the mule up beside the horse block; presently his father was up behind him and he doubled the reins over and slashed the mule across the neck, but before the animal could begin to trot the hard, thin arm came round him, the hard, knotted hand jerking the mule back to a walk.

⁶¹ In the first red rays of the sun they were in the lot, putting plow gear on the mules. This time the sorrel mare was in the lot before he heard it at all, the rider collarless and even bareheaded, trembling, speaking in a shaking voice as the woman in the house had done, his father merely looking up once before stooping again

to the hame ° he was buckling, so that the man on the mare spoke to his stooping back:

62 "You must realize you have ruined that rug. Wasn't there anybody here, any of your women . . ." he ceased, shaking, the boy watching him, the older brother leaning now in the stable door, chewing, blinking slowly and steadily at nothing apparently. "It cost a hundred dollars. But you never had a hundred dollars. You never will. So I'm going to charge you twenty bushels of corn against your crop. I'll add it in your contract and when you come to the commissary ° you can sign it. That won't keep Mrs. de Spain quiet but maybe it will teach you to wipe your feet off before you enter her house again."

63 Then he was gone. The boy looked at his father, who still had not spoken or even looked up again, who was now adjusting the loggerhead in the hame.

64 "Pap," he said. His father looked at him—the inscrutable * face, the shaggy brows beneath which the gray eyes glinted coldly. Suddenly the boy went toward him, fast, stopping as suddenly. "You done the best you could!" he cried. "If he wanted hit done different why didn't he wait and tell you how? He won't git no twenty bushels! He won't git none! We'll gether hit and hide hit! I kin watch . . ."

65 "Did you put the cutter back in that straight stock like I told you?"

66 "No, sir," he said.

67 "Then go do it."

68 That was Wednesday. During the rest of that week he worked steadily, at what was within his scope and some which was beyond it, with an industry that did not need to be driven nor even commanded twice; he had this from his mother, with the difference that some at least of what he did he liked to do, such as splitting wood with the half-size ax which his mother and aunt had earned, or saved money somehow, to present him with at Christmas. In company with the two older women (and

hame: one of the two curved pieces in a harness.

commissary: a store supplying equipment and provisions.

on one afternoon, even one of the sisters), he built pens for the shoat ° and the cow which were a part of his father's contract with the landlord, and one afternoon, his father being absent, gone somewhere on one of the mules, he went to the field.

⁶⁹ They were running a middle buster now, his brother holding the plow straight while he handled the reins, and walking beside the straining mule, the rich black soil shearing cool and damp against his bare ankles, he thought *Maybe this is the end of it. Maybe even that twenty bushels that seems hard to have to pay for just a rug will be a cheap price for him to stop forever and always from being what he used to be;* thinking, dreaming now, so that his brother had to speak sharply to him to mind the mule: *Maybe he even won't collect the twenty bushels. Maybe it will all add up and balance and vanish—corn, rug, fire; the terror and grief, the being pulled two ways like between two teams of horses—gone, done with for ever and ever.*

⁷⁰ Then it was Saturday; he looked up from beneath the mule he was harnessing and saw his father in the black coat and hat. "Not that," his father said. "The wagon gear." And then, two hours later, sitting in the wagon bed behind his father and brother on the seat, the wagon accomplished a final curve, and he saw the weathered paintless store with its tattered tobacco and patent-medicine posters and the tethered * wagons and saddle animals below the gallery. He mounted the gnawed steps behind his father and brother, and there again was the lane of quiet, watching faces for the three of them to walk through. He saw the man in spectacles sitting at the plank table and he did not need to be told this was a Justice of the Peace; he sent one glare of fierce, exultant, partisan ° defiance at the man in collar and cravat now, whom he had seen but twice before in his life, and that on a galloping horse, who now wore on his face an expression not of rage but of amazed unbe-

shoat: a young hog.   partisan: devoted to one party or faction.

lief which the boy could not have known was at the incredible circumstance of being sued by one of his own tenants, and came and stood against his father and cried at the Justice: "He ain't done it! He ain't burnt . . ."

71 "Go back to the wagon," his father said.

72 "Burnt?" the Justice said. "Do I understand this rug was burned too?"

73 "Does anybody here claim it was?" his father said. "Go back to the wagon." But he did not, he merely retreated to the rear of the room, crowded as that other had been, but not to sit down this time, instead, to stand pressing among the motionless bodies, listening to the voices:

74 "And you claim twenty bushels of corn is too high for the damage you did to the rug?"

75 "He brought the rug to me and said he wanted the tracks washed out of it. I washed the tracks out and took the rug back to him."

76 "But you didn't carry the rug back to him in the same condition it was in before you made the tracks on it."

77 His father did not answer, and now for perhaps half a minute there was no sound at all save that of breathing, the faint, steady suspiration ° of complete and intent listening.

78 "You decline to answer that, Mr. Snopes?" Again his father did not answer. "I'm going to find against you, Mr. Snopes. I'm going to find that you were responsible for the injury to Major de Spain's rug and hold you liable for it. But twenty bushels of corn seems a little high for a man in your circumstances to have to pay. Major de Spain claims it cost a hundred dollars. October corn will be worth about fifty cents. I figure that if Major de Spain can stand a ninety-five dollar loss on something he paid cash for, you can stand a five-dollar loss you haven't earned yet. I hold you in damages to Major de Spain to the amount of ten bushels of corn over and above your contract with him, to be paid to him out of your crop at gathering time. Court adjourned."

suspiration: breathing.

⁷⁹ It had taken no time hardly, the morning was but half begun. He thought they would return home and perhaps back to the field, since they were late, far behind all other farmers. But instead his father passed on behind the wagon, merely indicating with his hand for the older brother to follow with it, and crossed the road toward the blacksmith shop opposite, pressing on after his father, overtaking him, speaking, whispering up at the harsh, calm face beneath the weathered hat: "He won't git no ten bushels neither. He won't git one. We'll . . ." until his father glanced for an instant down at him, the face absolutely calm, the grizzled ° eyebrows tangled above the cold eyes, the voice almost pleasant, almost gentle:

⁸⁰ "You think so? Well, we'll wait till October anyway."

⁸¹ The matter of the wagon—the setting of a spoke or two and the tightening of the tires—did not take long either, the business of the tires accomplished by driving the wagon into the spring branch ° behind the shop and letting it stand there, the mules nuzzling into the water from time to time, and the boy on the seat with the idle reins, looking up the slope and through the sooty tunnel of the shed where the slow hammer rang and where his father sat on an upended cypress bolt, easily, either talking or listening, still sitting there when the boy brought the dripping wagon up out of the branch and halted it before the door.

⁸² "Take them on to the shade and hitch," his father said. He did so and returned. His father and the smith and a third man squatting on his heels inside the door were talking, about crops and animals; the bay, squatting too in the ammoniac dust and hoof-parings and scales of rust, heard his father tell a long and unhurried story out of the time before the birth of the older brother even when he had been a professional horsetrader. And then his father came up beside him where he stood before a tattered last year's circus poster on the other side of

grizzled: streaked with gray.   branch: stream.

the store, gazing rapt and quiet at the scarlet horses, the incredible poisings and convolutions of tulle ° and tights and the painted leers of comedians, and said, "It's time to eat."

83   But not at home. Squatting beside his brother against the front wall, he watched his father emerge from the store and produce from a paper sack a segment of cheese and divide it carefully and deliberately into three with his pocket knife and produce crackers from the same sack. They all three squatted on the gallery and ate, slowly, without talking; then in the store again, they drank from a tin dipper tepid * water smelling of the cedar bucket and of living beech trees. And still they did not go home. It was a horse lot this time, a tall rail fence upon and along which men stood and sat and out of which one by one horses were led, to be walked and trotted and then cantered back and forth along the road while the slow swapping and buying went on and the sun began to slant westward, they—the three of them—watching and listening, the older brother with his muddy eyes and his steady, inevitable tobacco, the father commenting now and then on certain of the animals, to no one in particular.

84   It was after sundown when they reached home. They ate supper by lamplight, then, sitting on the doorstep, the boy watched the night fully accomplish, listening to the whippoorwills and the frogs, when he heard his mother's voice: "Abner! No! No! Oh, God. Oh, God. Abner!" and he rose, whirled, and saw the altered light through the door where a candle stub now burned in a bottle neck on the table and his father, still in the hat and coat, at once formal and burlesque as though dressed carefully for some shabby and ceremonial violence, emptying the reservoir of the lamp back into the five-gallon kerosene can from which it had been filled, while the mother tugged at his arm until he shifted the lamp to the other hand and flung her back, not savagely or

tulle: a thin net.

viciously, just hard, into the wall, her hands flung out against the wall for balance, her mouth open and in her face the same quality of hopeless despair as had been in her voice. Then his father saw him standing in the door.

⁸⁵ "Go to the barn and get that can of oil we were oiling the wagon with," he said. The boy did not move. Then he could speak.

⁸⁶ "What . . ." he cried. "What are you . . ."

⁸⁷ "Go get that oil," his father said. "Go."

⁸⁸ Then he was moving, running, outside the house, toward the stable: this the old habit, the old blood which he had not been permitted to choose for himself, which had been bequeathed him willy nilly and which had run for so long (and who knew where, battening ° on what of outrage and savagery and lust) before it came to him. *I could keep on, he thought. I could run on and on and never look back, never need to see his face again. Only I can't. I can't,* the rusted can in his hand now, the liquid sploshing in it as he ran back to the house and into it, into the sound of his mother's weeping in the next room, and handed the can to his father.

⁸⁹ "Ain't you going to even send a Negro?" he cried. "At least you sent a Negro before!"

⁹⁰ This time his father didn't strike him. The hand came even faster than the blow had, the same hand which had set the can on the table with almost excruciating * care flashing from the can toward him too quick for him to follow it, gripping him by the back of his shirt and on to tiptoe before he had seen it quit the can, the face stooping at him in breathless and frozen ferocity, the cold, dead voice speaking over him to the older brother who leaned against the table, chewing with that steady, curious, sidewise motion of cows:

⁹¹ "Empty the can into the big one and go on. I'll catch up with you."

⁹² "Better tie him up to the bedpost," the brother said.

⁹³ "Do like I told you," the father said. Then the boy

battening: thriving, growing.

was moving, his bunched shirt and the hard, bony hand between his shoulder-blades, his toes just touching the floor, across the room and into the other one, past the sisters sitting in the two chairs over the cold hearth, and to where his mother and aunt sat side by side on the bed, the aunt's arms about his mother's shoulders.

94 "Hold him," the father said. The aunt made a startled movement. "Not you," the father said. "Lennie. Take hold of him. I want to see you do it." His mother took him by the wrist. "You'll hold him better than that. If he gets loose don't you know what he is going to do? He will go up yonder." He jerked his head toward the road. "Maybe I'd better tie him."

95 "I'll hold him," his mother whispered.

96 "See you do then." Then his father was gone, the stiff foot heavy and measured up the boards, ceasing at last.

97 Then he begun to struggle. His mother caught him in both arms, he jerking and wrenching at them. He would be stronger in the end, he knew that. But he had no time to wait for it. "Lemme go!" he cried. "I don't want to have to hit you!"

98 "Let him go!" the aunt said. "If he don't go, before God, I am going up there myself!"

99 "Don't you see I can't?" his mother cried. "Sarty! Sarty! No! No! Help me, Lizzie!"

100 Then he was free. His aunt grasped at him but it was too late. He whirled, running, his mother stumbled forward on to her knees behind him, crying to the nearer sister: "Catch him, Net! Catch him!" But that was too late too, the sister (the sisters were twins, born at the same time, yet either of them now gave the impression of being, encompassing as much living meat and volume and weight as any other two of the family) not yet having begun to rise from the chair, her head, face, alone merely turned, presenting to him in the flying instant an astonishing expanse of young female features untroubled by any surprise even, wearing only an expression of bovine interest. Then he was out of the room, out

of the house, in the mild dust of the starlit road and
the heavy rifeness of honeysuckle, the pale ribbon un-
spooling with terrific slowness under his running feet,
reaching the gate at last and turning in, running, his
heart and lungs drumming, on up the drive toward the
lighted house, the lighted door. He did not knock, he
burst in, sobbing for breath, incapable for the moment
of speech; he saw the astonished face of the Negro in
the linen jacket without knowing when the Negro had
appeared.

101   "De Spain!" he cried, panted. "Where's . . ." then
he saw the white man too emerging from a white door
down the hall. "Barn!" he cried. "Barn!"

102   "What?" the white man said. "Barn?"

103   "Yes!" the boy cried. "Barn!"

104   "Catch him!" the white man shouted.

105   But it was too late this time too. The Negro grasped
his shirt, but the entire sleeve, rotten with washing,
carried away, and he was out that door too and in the
drive again, and had actually never ceased to run even
while he was screaming into the white man's face.

106   Behind him the white man was shouting, "My
horse! Fetch my horse!" and he thought for an instant of
cutting across the park and climbing the fence into the
road, but he did not know the park nor how high the
vine-massed fence might be and he dared not risk it. So
he ran on down the drive, blood and breath roaring;
presently he was in the road again though he could not
see it. He could not hear either: the galloping mare was
almost upon him before he heard her, and even then he
held his course, as if the very urgency of his wild grief
and need must in a moment more find him wings, waiting until the ultimate instant to hurl himself aside and
into the weed-choked roadside ditch as the horse thun-
dered past and on, for an instant in furious silhouette
against the stars, the tranquil early summer night sky
which, even before the shape of the horse and rider
vanished, stained abruptly and violently upward: a long,
swirling roar incredible and soundless, blotting the stars,

and he springing up and into the road again, running
again, knowing it was too late yet still running even after
he heard the shot and, an instant later, two shots, pausing now without knowing he had ceased to run, crying
"Pap! Pap!", running again before he knew he had begun to run, stumbling, tripping over something and
scrabbling up again without ceasing to run, looking
backward over his shoulder at the glare as he got up,
running on among the invisible trees, panting, sobbing,
"Father! Father!"

[107]   At midnight he was sitting on the crest of a hill. He
did not know it was midnight and he did not know how
far he had come. But there was no glare behind him
now and he sat now, his back toward what he had called
home for four days anyhow, his face toward the dark
woods which he would enter when breath was strong
again, small, shaking steadily in the chill darkness, hugging himself into the remainder of his thin, rotten shirt,
the grief and despair now no longer terror and fear but
just grief and despair. *Father. My father,* he thought.
"He was brave!" he cried suddenly, aloud but not loud,
no more than a whisper: "He was! He was in the war!
He was in Colonel Sartoris' cav'ry!" not knowing that
his father had gone to that war a private in the fine old
European sense, wearing no uniform, admitting the
authority of and giving fidelity to no man or army or
flag, going to war as Malbrouck ° himself did: for booty
—it meant nothing and less than nothing to him if it
were enemy booty or his own.

[108]   The slow constellations wheeled on. It would be
dawn and then sunup after a while and he would be
hungry. But that would be tomorrow and now he was
only cold, and walking would cure that. His breathing was easier now and he decided to get up and go on,

Malbrouck: Faulkner probably has in mind the eighteenth-century
French nursery ditty, sung to the tune of "For He's a Jolly Good
Fellow." It begins: "Malbrouck s'en va-t-en guerre" (Malbrouck
is off to war). Malbrouck is the French version of the English
name Marlborough.

and then he found that he had been asleep because he knew it was almost dawn, the night almost over. He could tell that from the whippoorwills. They were everywhere now among the dark trees below him, constant and inflectioned and ceaseless, so that, as the instant for giving over to the day birds drew nearer and nearer, there was no interval at all between them. He got up. He was a little stiff, but walking would cure that too as it would the cold, and soon there would be the sun. He went on down the hill, toward the dark woods within which the liquid silver voices of the birds called unceasing—the rapid and urgent beating of the urgent and choiring heart of the late spring night. He did not look back.

ANALYSIS

This story is so rich in detail one could analyze its local color at length. Rather than concentrate on any one aspect, however, let us outline the story briefly in terms of the *four* approaches to narrative analysis we discussed a few pages back.

Time: The story begins in time present. Faulkner makes it no more specific than that, though we know from paragraph 15 ("a Confederate . . . musket ball had taken him in the heel . . . thirty years ago") that it must be the 1890's. The narrative covers less than a week and moves in straight chronological progression. Faulkner notes times changes carefully:

Paragraph 26: "That night they camped. . . ."
Paragraph 31: "Tomorrow they were there. In the early afternoon the wagon stopped. . . ."
Paragraph 46: "Two hours later the boy was chopping wood behind the house. . . ."
Paragraph 53: "From the woodpile through the rest of the afternoon the boy watched them. . . . ."
Paragraph 54: "Then he was done too. It was dusk. . . ."
Paragraph 55: "It still hung there while they ate the cold food and then went to bed . . . the silhouette

was standing over him . . . the stiff foot prodding him awake."

Paragraph 61: "In the first red rays of the sun they were in the lot. . . ."

Paragraph 68: "That was Wednesday. During the rest of that week he worked steadily. . . ."

Paragraph 70: "Then it was Saturday. . . ."

Paragraph 79: "It had taken no time hardly, the morning was but half begun. . . ."

Paragraph 107: "At midnight he was sitting on the crest of a hill. . . ."

Paragraph 108 (the last): "The slow constellations wheeled on. It would be dawn and then sunup after a while and he would be hungry. But that would be tomorrow and now he was only cold. . . ."

The boy's liberation comes on a Sunday. He moves out and away from this desperate clan to which he is kin. In this week he has matured. When he hears Major de Spain's shots he cries "Pap! Pap!" but before the paragraph ends he is "panting, sobbing, 'Father! Father!'" Is it an accident that this story ends on Sunday? Is Sarty perhaps unconsciously asking God for help? We said earlier that Faulkner is writing about mankind, not just one boy. Does Sarty, at this moment, stand for all men who follow their own beliefs and fight injustice?

Place: We can only guess where the story occurs; Faulkner never tells us. The dialogue suggests the South, certainly. Abner Snopes fought for the Confederacy. When we read Faulkner's novels, some of which concern the characters in this story, we learn that Major de Spain's home is in Jefferson, Mississippi, but specific place is unimportant in this story.

Point of view: Faulkner makes an especially wise choice in his point-of-view character. Since his climax is centered on the liberation of young Sarty, it is right that we should see the action through his eyes. Sarty is only ten years old. To tell his story in the first person would have meant making him a fairly wise young boy (like Huck Finn) or reducing all the action to the child's level. Faulkner chose limited omniscient narration, giving himself a wider range of vocabulary, a larger scale of emotions (the whole family is involved in barn burning, like it or not), and an opportunity to comment on Sarty's reactions to the trial, the spotted rug, the defiance of de Spain, and the final outrage.

Point of emphasis: This story is not about a stray hog or a soiled rug. It is concerned, as its title suggests, with a mad kind of revenge. But it is *most* concerned with a young boy. Sentence two says: "The boy, crouched on his nail keg at the back of the crowded room, knew he smelled cheese, and more. . . ." What more he smells, whether he knows it or not at this juncture, is deceit and treachery and blind defiance and a wickedness that will drive him into the "dark woods within which the liquid silver voices of the birds called unceasing. . . ." This story ends with one of Faulkner's simplest sentences: "He did not look back." If we feel Faulkner needs to tell us more explicitly than that what this story is about, where its main emphasis lies, then we had better reread it. He gives us guideposts on every page.

Questions on Content

1. The story opens in the court of a Justice of the Peace. Who is on trial and what is the Justice's decision? Why?
2. How many members are there in the Snopes family? What are Sarty's brother and sisters like? What is his mother's role in the story?
3. Why does the judge consider Major de Spain's penalty of twenty bushels of corn exorbitant?
4. Reread paragraph 106. Do we know *exactly* what happened?

Add to your vocabulary: mesmerized, sadistic, latent, niggard, voracious, bovine, irascible, impervious, suave, pendant, emanated, incorrigible, sporadic, rife, inscrutable, tethered, tepid, battening, excruciating.

Questions on Technique

1. Faulkner is noted for his long and intricate sentences. Paragraph 1 contains a fine example. Find four others. What does this ornate style contribute to the telling of the story?

2. The father-son relationship in this story is vital. Faulkner begins describing it in paragraph 7. Where does he continue it and how?

3. In paragraph 1, Faulkner uses, for the first time, italicized phrases. By paragraph 7 they are whole sentences. They occur throughout the story. How would you describe this device? In what way is it effective writing?

4. We seldom hear Abner Snopes speak, but when he does he makes his family jump. How would you describe his manner of speaking?

5. Paragraphs 107–108 are quiet and almost solemn compared with what goes immediately before. Why is this a memorable way to end this story?

Suggestions for Writing

1. Narrate in 600 words a memorable incident from your childhood, writing from a limited omniscient point of view. Make yourself the main character but write in the third person. Remember, we see all of what happens through this child's eyes, but you are free to comment on what happens.

2. Write a story in which the main action covers several days, paying particular attention to the passage of time. Your subject might be a vacation trip, a visit to friends, the first week of school, the first days on a summer job. Build your action chronologically, developing a climax from what happens over a series of days. You will have to select very carefully the incidents you tell in detail, for you obviously cannot tell everything.

3. Describe in 400 words a single incident in your life with particular concern for vocabulary. Pay attention here to choosing the exact word with the greatest impact on your reader. Rewrite the story several times, if possible. You will discover that one word can often make or ruin a sentence.

4. Write a single incident which will reveal the central character as a recognizable type: a bully, a sissy, a flirt, a bookworm, a big athlete, a musician, a joiner, or any other familiar type. Let the action and dialogue reveal the character's personality.

CHAPTER 12

Narrative and characterization

KATHERINE MANSFIELD · *Miss Brill*

Katherine Mansfield Beauchamp was born in New Zealand but went to Queen's College, London, for her education. With John Middleton Murry, whom she married in 1913, and the novelist D. H. Lawence, she founded a literary review. Success with her own writing came slowly. Not until 1920, three years before her death, did a volume called Bliss and Other Stories *bring her the acclaim that was her due.* The Garden Party *(1922) and* The Doves' Nest *(1923) established her reputation as one of the most important short-story writers of the twentieth century.*

In discussing types of fiction, we frequently speak of a "New Yorker story," meaning a brief sketch with ordinary but sensitive characters, perceptive dialogue, and understated theme,° and without strong plot ° or climax. Three authors might be said to be the models for this kind of fiction: Anton Chekhov, the nineteenth-century Russian doctor who wrote of frustrated middle-class lives in the Russian provinces; James Joyce, the Irish exile

theme: See Glossary.   plot: See Glossary.

*who wrote all his life about middle-class Dubliners; and
Katherine Mansfield. Irony and pathos are terms that recur in criticism of their work. By "irony" we mean the
contradiction between the literal and the intended meaning, since one thing is said and another is implied. By
"pathos" we mean simply the sense of pity. You will want
to consider whether either applies to "Miss Brill."*

¹ Although it was so brilliantly fine—the blue sky
powdered with gold and great spots of light like white
wine splashed over the Jardins Publiques °—Miss Brill
was glad that she had decided on her fur. The air was
motionless, but when you opened your mouth there was
just a faint chill, like a chill from a glass of iced water
before you sip, and now and again a leaf came drifting—
from nowhere, from the sky. Miss Brill put up her hand
and touched her fur. Dear little thing! It was nice to
feel it again. She had taken it out of its box that afternoon, shaken out the moth powder, given it a good
brush, and rubbed the life back into the dim little eyes.
"What has been happening to me?" said the sad little
eyes. Oh, how sweet it was to see them snap at her again
from the red eiderdown! ° . . . But the nose, which was
of some black composition, wasn't at all firm. It must
have had a knock, somehow. Never mind—a little dab
of black sealing wax when the time came—when it was
absolutely necessary. . . . Little rogue! Yes, she really
felt like that about it. Little rogue biting its tail just by
her left ear. She could have taken if off and laid it on
her lap and stroked it. She felt a tingling in her hands
and arms, but that came from walking, she supposed.
And when she breathed, something light and sad—no,
not sad, exactly—something gentle seemed to move in
her bosom.

² There were a number of people out this afternoon,
far more than last Sunday. And the band sounded louder
and gayer. That was because the Season had begun. For

Jardins Publiques: public gardens.
eiderdown: a quilt filled with duck feathers.

although the band played all the year round on Sundays, out of season it was never the same. It was like some one playing with only the family to listen; it didn't care how it played if there weren't any strangers present. Wasn't the conductor wearing a new coat, too? She was sure it was new. He scraped with his foot and flapped his arms like a rooster about to crow, and the bandsmen sitting in the green rotunda blew out their cheeks and glared at the music. Now there came a little "flutey" bit—very pretty!—a little chain of bright drops. She was sure it would be repeated. It was; she lifted her head and smiled.

3   Only two people shared her "special" seat: a fine old man in a velvet coat, his hands clasped over a huge carved walking-stick, and a big old woman, sitting upright, with a roll of knitting on her embroidered apron. They did not speak. This was disappointing, for Miss Brill always looked forward to the conversation. She had become really quite expert, she thought, at listening as though she didn't listen, at sitting in other people's lives just for a minute while they talked round her.

4   She glanced, sideways, at the old couple. Perhaps they would go soon. Last Sunday, too, hadn't been as interesting as usual. An Englishman and his wife, he wearing a dreadful Panama hat and she button boots. And she'd gone on the whole time about how she ought to wear spectacles; she knew she needed them; but that it was no good getting any; they'd be sure to break and they'd never keep on. And he'd been so patient. He'd suggested everything—gold rims, the kind that curved round your ears, little pads inside the bridge. No, nothing would please her. "They'll always be sliding down my nose!" Miss Brill had wanted to shake her.

5   The old people sat on the bench, still as statues. Never mind, there was always the crowd to watch. To and fro, in front of the flowerbeds and the band rotunda, the couples and groups paraded, stopped to talk, to greet, to buy a handful of flowers from the old beggar who had his tray fixed to the railings. Little children ran among

them, swooping and laughing; little boys with big white
silk bows under their chins, little girls, little French
dolls, dressed up in velvet and lace. And sometimes a
tiny staggerer came suddenly rocking into the open from
under the trees, stopped, stared, as suddenly sat down
"flop," until its small high-stepping mother, like a young
hen, rushed scolding to its rescue. Other people sat on
the benches and green chairs, but they were nearly
always the same, Sunday after Sunday, and—Miss Brill
had often noticed—there was something funny about
nearly all of them. They were odd, silent, nearly all old,
and from the way they stared they looked as though
they'd just come from dark little rooms or even—even
cupboards!

⁶ Behind the rotunda the slender trees with yellow
leaves down drooping, and through them just a line of
sea, and beyond the blue sky with gold-veined clouds.

⁷ Tum-tum-tum tiddle-um! tiddle-um! tum tiddley-um
tum ta! blew the band.

⁸ Two young girls in red came by and two young soldiers in blue met them, and they laughed and paired and
went off arm-in-arm. Two peasant women with funny
straw hats passed, gravely, leading beautiful smoke-
colored donkeys. A cold, pale nun hurried by. A beautiful woman came along and dropped her bunch of violets,
and a little boy ran after to hand them to her, and she
took them and threw them away as if they'd been poisoned. Dear me! Miss Brill didn't know whether to admire that or not! And now an ermine toque ° and a
gentleman in grey met just in front of her. He was tall,
stiff, dignified, and she was wearing the ermine toque
she'd bought when her hair was yellow. Now everything,
her hair, her face, even her eyes, was the same color as
the shabby ermine, and her hand, in its cleaned glove,
lifted to dab her lips, was a tiny yellowish paw. Oh, she
was so pleased to see him—delighted! She rather thought

toque: a hat with little or no brim and a full crown.

they were going to meet that afternoon. She described where she'd been—everywhere, here, there, along by the sea. The day was so charming—didn't he agree? And wouldn't he, perhaps? . . . But he shook his head, lighted a cigarette, slowly breathed a great deep puff into her face, and, even while she was still talking and laughing, flicked the match away and walked on. The ermine toque was alone; she smiled more brightly than ever. But even the band seemed to know what she was feeling and played more softly, played tenderly, and the drum beat, "The Brute! The Brute!" over and over. What would she do? What was going to happen now? But as Miss Brill wondered, the ermine toque turned, raised her hand as though she'd seen some one else, much nicer, just over there, and pattered away. And the band changed again and played more quickly, more gaily than ever, and the old couple on Miss Brill's seat got up and marched away, and such a funny old man with long whiskers hobbled along in time to the music and was nearly knocked over by four girls walking abreast.

⁹ Oh, how fascinating it was! How she enjoyed it! How she loved sitting here, watching it all! It was like a play. It was exactly like a play. Who could believe the sky at the back wasn't painted? But it wasn't till a little brown dog trotted on solemn and then slowly trotted off, like a little "theater" dog, a little dog that had been drugged, that Miss Brill discovered what it was that made it so exciting. They were all on the stage. They weren't only the audience, not only looking on; they were acting. Even she had a part and came every Sunday. No doubt somebody would have noticed if she hadn't been there; she was part of the performance after all. How strange she'd never thought of it like that before! And yet it explained why she made such a point of starting from home at just the same time each week—so as not to be late for the performance—and it also explained why she had quite a queer, shy feeling at telling her English pupils how she spent her Sunday afternoons. No wonder!

Miss Brill nearly laughed out loud. She was on the stage. She thought of the old invalid gentleman to whom she read the newspaper four afternoons a week while he slept in the garden. She had got quite used to the frail head on the cotton pillow, the hollowed eyes, the open mouth and the high pinched nose. If he'd been dead she mightn't have noticed for weeks; she wouldn't have minded. But suddenly he knew he was having the paper read to him by an actress! "An actress!" The old head lifted; two points of light quivered in the old eyes. "An actress—are ye?" And Miss Brill smoothed the newspaper as though it were the manuscript of her part and said gently: "Yes, I have been an actress for a long time."

10   The band had been having a rest. Now they started again. And what they played was warm, sunny, yet there was just a faint chill—a something, what was it?—not sadness—no, not sadness—a something that made you want to sing. The tune lifted, lifted, the light shone; and it seemed to Miss Brill that in another moment all of them, all the whole company, would begin singing. The young ones, the laughing ones who were moving together, they would begin, and the men's voices, very resolute and brave, would join them. And then she too, she too, and the others on the benches—they would come in with a kind of accompaniment—something low, that scarcely rose or fell, something so beautiful—moving. . . . And Miss Brill's eyes filled with tears and she looked smiling at all the other members of the company. Yes, we understand, we understand, she thought—though what they understood she didn't know.

11   Just at that moment a boy and a girl came and sat down where the old couple had been. They were beautifully dressed; they were in love. The hero and heroine, of course, just arrived from his father's yacht. And still soundlessly singing, still with that trembling smile, Miss Brill prepared to listen.

12   "No, not now," said the girl. "Not here, I can't."

13   "But why? Because of that stupid old thing at the end there?" asked the boy. "Why does she come here at

all—who wants her? Why doesn't she keep her silly old mug at home?"

14   "It's her fu-fur which is so funny," giggled the girl. "It's exactly like a fried whiting." °

15   "Ah, be off with you!" said the boy in an angry whisper. Then: "Tell me, ma petite chère——" °

16   "No, not here," said the girl. "Not *yet*."

.   .   .   .

17   On her way home she usually bought a slice of honey cake at the baker's. It was her Sunday treat. Sometimes there was an almond in her slice, sometimes not. It made a great difference. If there was an almond it was like carrying home a tiny present—a surprise—something that might very well not have been there. She hurried on the almond Sundays and struck the match for the kettle in quite a dashing way.

18   But today she passed the baker's by, climbed the stairs, went into the little dark room—her room like a cupboard—and sat down on the red eiderdown. She sat there for a long time. The box that the fur came out of was on the bed. She unclasped the necklet quickly; quickly, without looking, laid it inside. But when she put the lid on she thought she heard something crying.

ANALYSIS

In comparison with "Barn Burning," Miss Mansfield's story is easy reading. She uses many sensitive strokes in this portrait, and the play of light on them illuminates every detail. The climax, if we can call it that, is so openly and deftly arrived at that it wants nothing more than careful reading. Let us look chiefly at her diction, that is, her choice of words. In this way we can watch an artist at work.

Rather than tell us *about* Miss Brill, she puts her into action. She *shows* us this spinster on a Sunday afternoon in the park. "Jardins Publiques" at once suggests France; Miss Brill is a stranger here. There is a "faint chill" in

whiting: a European fish of the cod family.
ma petite chère——: my little dear. . . .

the air and (we are still in paragraph 1) "something light and sad—no, not sad, exactly—something gentle" moves her. Keep these words "chill" and "sad" in mind. By the end of the story we might want to say that something cold and ungentle and decidedly sad happens to this lady. But we anticipate. We read, in paragraph 1, a description of the fur, the "dear little thing," with its "dim little eyes" and a nose that "must have had a knock, somehow." Will the fur have something to do with the action, we might ask.

Paragraph 2 tells us the "Season" has begun. This is a kind of "first Sunday" in her weekly ritual, not "opening night" but "opening matinee." Everything is gay and bright. The flute notes are "a little chain of bright drops." The band seems to be playing for her. Paragraphs 3 and 4 plant the idea that Miss Brill is accustomed to hearing all the conversations around her, "listening as though she didn't listen." Eavesdropping is her vicarious pleasure, her substitute for the real thing. Paragraph 5 suggests that she also judges her park companions. The young mother is "like a young hen." The "other people" are "odd, silent, nearly all old." They look "as though they'd just come from dark little rooms or even—even cupboards!" "Cupboards" is another planted word. Miss Mansfield will use it again.

Paragraph 8 introduces what, with hindsight, we could call a "parallel" character. She has no name. Miss Mansfield calls her "the ermine toque" and notes that it was bought "when her hair was yellow." She and her hat are old. Her hand is a "paw" dabbing her lips. Her friend is rude to her. He breathes slowly (the adverb makes it ruder) "a great deep puff [of smoke] into her face." The "ermine toque" smiles at the offense. But does "smiled more brightly than ever" suggest the alternative to crying? What would Miss Brill have done? We will have a chance to hear when a "parallel" action happens to her. The overheard conversation (paragraphs 12–16) will come like a "puff of smoke" in her face.

Paragraph 9 uses a natural simile: ° sitting in the park is like playing a role on stage. "Yes," Miss Brill hears herself saying to her invalid friend, "I have been

simile: See Glossary

an actress for a long time." Paragraph 10 extends the simile. It seems as though they would all sing together, they would all understand. But a "something, what [is] it?" creeps in. Again the "faint chill" appears. And later she has more doubts: "Yes, we understand, we understand, she thought—though what they understood she didn't know."

With paragraph 11 the "hero and heroine" come on stage. They are no hero and heroine, of course. Calling them that is part of Miss Brill's make-believe world. Reality, when it appears, comes crashing in: "her silly old mug," "fu-fur which is so funny," "like a fried whiting." Miss Mansfield has chosen the words carefully. They are cruel but apt. They are words that come naturally to a young boy and girl. And Miss Brill, who (as paragraph 3 told us) "had become really quite expert at listening," hears every one.

What next? Taking these cues, reread paragraphs 17 and 18; then finish the analysis. Is Miss Brill on stage now? Can she accept her role or is life *not* a play? What has honey cake to do with sorrow? You will want to raise and answer several other questions.

Questions on Content

1. Why does Miss Mansfield not tell us exactly in what city or country this story occurs? Does it matter that Miss Brill is a stranger here?
2. What makes where Miss Brill sits in the park her "special" seat?
3. What details (and how far along in the story) do we hear about Miss Brill's occupation?

Questions on Technique

1. Miss Mansfield has Miss Brill talk *about* conversation she hears, but she does not record any before paragraph 12. Why do you suppose she waits so long?
2. How does Miss Mansfield employ the band and its music throughout the story?
3. In how much detail are the other visitors to the park described? What details do you find especially effective?
4. Between paragraphs 16 and 17, Miss Mansfield makes

a decided break in the narrative. Why is it necessary to get Miss Brill back to her room?

Suggestions for Writing

1. Rewrite this story making it an American park and making the main character a young girl or boy who is lonely or unhappy or worried with indecision.
2. Narrate an incident involving an overheard telephone conversation. You can hear, however, only one half of the conversation. As author, you will have to have your main character imagining the rest.
3. From your own experience, narrate an incident that involved one or more of the following: mistaken identity, eavesdropping, sudden change of mood, a meeting in a park or on the boardwalk, a quarrel between two people observed at a distance. Keep the story in the third person.
4. Write a short story emphasizing one emotion—fear, happiness, hate, pleasure.

JOSEPHINE JOHNSON · *Alexander to the Park*

The Middle West is home country to Josephine Winslow Johnson. She is a native of Missouri, was educated in St. Louis, taught at the People's Art Center in that city, worked as a reporter, and has lived for years on a farm in Ohio. Her Pulitzer prize novel, Now in November *(1934), is, not surprisingly, about farm life in the Middle West.*

"Alexander to the Park" has no particular locale. It contains one main character, three minor ones, and assorted animals and birds. The temptation to contrast it with Katherine Mansfield's "Miss Brill" ought to be strong. Yield to it. Not only contrast the two stories but

"Alexander to the Park" by Josephine Johnson, from *Harper's Bazaar*, September 1941. Copyright 1941 by Hearst Magazines, Inc. Reprinted by permission of the author.

*note how they complement each other. The last para-
graphs of Miss Mansfield's story are pure pathos.° Miss
Johnson begins with defeatism, irritability, and what
Mark Twain would call "cussedness"—not pathos, surely,
since we do not know Ivan well enough to feel pity for
him. But whereas Miss Brill's spirits fall in her story,
Ivan's, we feel, can do nothing but rise. How this comes
about is the action of the narrative.*

1   "Would you mind very much," his sister said, "would
you mind taking Alexander to the park?"

2   The park in autumn, Ivan thought. A sad place full
of mangy coyotes. But he smiled and took Alexander by
the hand.

3   Alexander was a year and a half and looked older. He
was a nice child but not brilliant. His hair was straight
and a coffee color, and he had big pink cheeks.

4   It was a Saturday in October, and a yellow sun, but
Ivan felt old and papery. Autumn in the park . . . autumn in the park . . . it was where he ought to go all
right. A place full of caged beasts and molting birds and
quince-faced nurses.

5   He held Alexander with one hand and adjusted his
spotted tie from the marked-down counter. He was
twenty and thin and dark and worked as a clerk in a
department store . . . I ought to be able to say Alexander is a fine sweet child, a good boy, a nephew to be proud
of. But I am sorry. I have a date. This is Saturday, Anne,
this is Saturday, and I have a date . . . But not being
able to say this, having no basis in truth for saying this,
Alexander and I are on our way to the park to see the
soiled pigeons and the nurses like pale lemons in a cape.

6   Alexander trudged along in happy silence, his eyes
entranced by every creeping bug and autumn butterfly
in bronze and blue.

7   "Bugs will devour the world someday, Alexander,"
Ivan said with gloomy relish. "Floods and floods of fluttering bugs will gnaw the world to dust. The pillars of

pathos: See Glossary.

the elephant house will lie like mounds of powder in the streets."

⁸ "Boogs?" said Alexander joyfully. "Boogs?"

⁹ "Yes, bugs," Ivan said. "Not fire, not flood, but bugs."

¹⁰ They turned into the park path and ahead of them loomed the Doric columns ° of the great elephant house and the great arch of the aviary.° Ivan was convinced he could smell coyotes on the air. "Well, Alexander," he said dourly, "here we are. Here is the park."

¹¹ Alexander said nothing.

¹² Ivan sighed. Other children talk, he thought, but not Alexander.

¹³ The paths were deep with fallen leaves, and the little boy plowed through them, shouting. Ivan sighed and thought of winter coming and of all things huddled up in dark and hidden holes. Badgers and woodchucks coiled in sleep.

¹⁴ They stopped first at the owl cage and watched the frowzy birds open and shut their yellow eyes. Wisdom, thought Ivan scornfully, is an attitude. A pontifical ° position of the feathers. Nothing more.

¹⁵ Alexander seized the bars and tried to push his large pink face inside. The owl stared at him coldly, a glassy fierceness in his eyes. He thinks Alexander is an enormous mouse, Ivan reflected. Fat and rosy and full of delicious juices. Come away. Come away, little boy. Before the bird makes up his mind to devour!

¹⁶ Suddenly the owl was gone, drifting upward like a great soft feather.

¹⁷ "Let's go see the parrots," Ivan said. "The talking birds in the house."

¹⁸ "Boids," Alexander murmured softly. "Boids."

¹⁹ They stepped inside the warm white building with its slightly fetid smell of birds and wild shrieking sound of cockatoos.° Birds too much like people. People like

Doric columns: the simplest of the Greek orders of column design.
aviary: a house or enclosure in which birds are kept.
pontifical: having the dignity of a bishop or pontiff.
cockatoos: brilliant-colored parrots.

birds. Sharp and feathery, with bright peering eyes. Cockatoos with white scalloped wings and pink naked eyes peered at him coldly.

20   He stopped in front of a cage of cockatoos and observed them sadly. They were the color of old blue-black umbrellas or elbows of worn suits. They looked like schoolteachers who had reached their prime in 1880— pupil-pouncing teachers in dresses of dead silk. It was not, he explained to no one, that he disliked women. He held no brief for men; but out of the vast and cynical storehouse of his sex he felt the findings justified the placing of women under the head of Predatory Fowl. Snatching, scratching, hatching, beak and claw forever active in the gravelly affairs of life. Man the scurrying valiant beetle; man the gold corn disappearing down the craw.

21   The coarse nasal voices of parrots broke the air like the crashing of enormous pans, and Alexander shouted at the wild confusion of blue and orange and scarlet feathers beating on the bars. Then he seized a bit of mashed banana fallen from the cage and crammed it down his mouth. Ivan thought vaguely of various tropical diseases Alexander might develop: tularemia ° and tarantulas ° and trachoma.° All, he thought with a sense of life's confused and furious intent, all because of a bit of mashed banana!

22   They went outside and, passing the animal cages, Ivan averted his eyes from the rachitic ° hyenas and the sinister floating shapes of the wild dogs, bored, lonely beasts that prowled and lay and prowled again.

23   The sea lions sneezed and coughed in the cold pool waters and he shivered as they plunged and snarled, the water flashing from their whiskers in the autumn air. He

---

tularemia: a disease transmitted by horse flies and producing a
   fever.
tarantulas: large venomous spiders.
trachoma: contagious form of conjunctivitis (inflammation of the
   mucous membrane lining the inner surface of the eyelid).
rachitic: having rickets, a disease of the bones.

hauled Alexander up the long stone steps of the elephant house and they stared at the rhinoceros, who lifted his back legs like a goose, his hide covered with rusty patches like the joints of ancient armor. For a brief minute Ivan lived through the thunder of the mammoth hoofs, the dry hot grasses parting, the wild black native cries, and himself—Ivan—with the great tusk boring in his groin. He wiped the damp beads from his forehead with a shuddering hand. It was like that precisely to look up and see the doors opening and a Man of Importance standing there—a Head of the Department, enormous, lowering,* a gray suit partially hiding the rhinocerian hide. Books in order? Books in order? . . . and the small and bloodshot eyes.

24   He shuddered and looked thankfully at the enormous wet obscenity of a hippopotamus, a great gray blubber sighing like a steamboat in the lukewarm waters, behind which a painted jungle scene fooled no one, not even Alexander. "Pickshure!" he said, pointing with a fat, soiled finger. "Pickshure." The concept of a hippopotamus he could not grasp; the vast areas of bobbing flesh were but gray blobs of space. And then suddenly one rose with the bellow of a foghorn and opened its vast liver-and-pink-mottled mouth, and Alexander, backing away in terror, fell and sobbed with pain of concrete on his knees.

25   Ivan picked him up and hugged him sadly. It was all one with autumn and the glowering porcine beasts—all this, and Alexander sobbing with wet pants in front of the bronze placard of a pygmy hippopotamus, captured 1925, and presented to Calvin Coolidge; an inhabitant of South African jungles.

26   "Don't cry, Alexander," he said. "Don't cry. You'll be all right." He rocked him back and forth in his arms and felt the dampness coming through his shirt. "Let's go out in the sun." he said. "Let's go out in the nice bright sun." And get us an autumn sunstroke, he thought savagely. An autumn sunstroke in the fall.

27   Gloomily they descended the shining steps, Alexander murmuring "Awwet" and Ivan adjusting his twisted tie.
28   At the path they paused and looked about. People went by and did not notice the damp spot spreading on Alexander's bottom. People walked leisurely, cheerfully. To Ivan they all appeared slightly bored but pleasant; as though they forever expected life to be other than it had always been. They are living in a dream, Ivan pondered. They expect a beautiful girl or a handsome man or a check in the mail or a headline in the paper. If not today, why, then tomorrow, and if not tomorrow, why, then sometime soon. "They don't know," he said aloud. "They don't know it never happens here."
29   Alexander had found a sewer grating and was very happy dropping bits of gravel down between the bars. It interested him a great deal more than the animals, but Ivan took him firmly by the hand. "We came to the park to see the animals, Alexander," he explained. "Nobody pays taxes to drop gravel down the sewer. Not as a regular thing." He stepped out briskly toward the monkey house, and Alexander plodded patiently at his side, his mind a mystery without end.
30   The monkeys were all being very active, very entertaining. But Ivan felt depressed. "This is the way we probably look to God," he reflected. "Jumping around with silly grins." The orangutan regarded him with grave and speculative eyes. Her baby clambered in and out the bars like a red hairy spider, a pot-bellied autumn spider. He was an ugly little mug!
31   "Pretty?" said Alexander doubtfully. "Pretty?"
32   Watching the wild grinning and grimacing caricatures ° of himself, Ivan's feeling of depression and loneliness rose to that heated simmering rumble which precedes the volcanic roar. "We swing, we bow, we crouch, we swing," he muttered. "We say, Yes, madam, No, madam, Yes, miss, No, miss. Yes, sir, No, sir—we show our

caricatures: See Glossary.

teeth in smiles more meaningless than any apes. We scrunch our toast and gulp our coffee, and some of us have stomach trouble and others have relatives, and some of us go into the Army and others of us sell blue-striped ties, and some of us have girls and others have wives, and one out of a hundred has a Cause, and the other ninety-nine have bunions and bills and go to the movies and take their nephews to the park . . . To what purpose and what end?" he murmured. "Spring and fall and winter?—and the dour ° leaves falling in the park . . ."

33 He was about to remove Alexander from the railing and start the long trek homeward when he felt a harsh tug at his trousers. Looking down, he saw a child, a wide, aggressive little girl of Alexander's size, who wanted to get "up" she shouted hopefully. She had firm yellow hair and a firm cleft in her shining chin. Startled, Ivan looked behind him to determine her source and saw a girl. She must have just come, he thought confusedly. First we were alone. And now—this.

34 The girl was round and small, with sleek, pale, shining hair parted in the middle with a bun behind, and dark blue eyes. He did not think that she was real. How like a pretty bird! he thought vaguely. How like a yellow dove!

35 She tugged at the child with some embarrassment. "Let go of the gentleman, Jacqueline!" she kept saying. But Jacqueline clung like an infuriated barnacle * and roared. "Would you mind to put her up?" the girl asked timidly. "Otherwise she will go on roaring."

36 She had such a nice voice!

37 "Oh, not at all, not at all," Ivan said. "There's room—there's room," he stuttered, and waved his arms. "I venture to say there's room for *all* of the roaring children in the world!" Then he blushed and lifted Jacqueline—not so lightly—to the rail. Alexander gave her a laconic glance and went on staring at the monkeys. Jacqueline was subdued with pleasure.

dour: sour or sullen in appearance.

³⁸ "She's a cute c-h-i-l-d," Ivan said politely. "I mean, a c-u-t-e child!" He blushed again with fever.

³⁹ The girl smiled with sweet kindness. "She wouldn't understand anyway," she said. "Jacqueline's too young. They look cute together, don't they?" she added. "They're just the same size. Like a pair of shoes. Maybe you would sell him to match Jacqueline."

⁴⁰ Suns danced before Ivan's eyes. "I couldn't sell Alexander!" he blurted. "He isn't mine! I mean, not that I would if he were, if I could—no!"

⁴¹ She laughed again, and his frenzy uncoiled and sank away. She had—thank God—not a laugh like a chill silver tinkle or a breeze battling the blossoms or such tripe, but a warm motherly sound, like the smell of a bakery on a winter night.

⁴² "Jacqueline isn't mine, either," she said, "but sometimes I could sell her when she beats her heels! But mostly she is good."

⁴³ "It is only evil spirits in them." Ivan said. "Devils to be exorcised." °

⁴⁴ She looked a little puzzled. It was evident that she thought he meant exercised but was too kind to correct him. She is no pedant,° Ivan thought gratefully. His heart rose and flooded like gold, like molten sun—like torrents of burning butter. He looked up and noticed the October sun glittering and flashing between the golden leaves. He looked around and the waters of the seal pool shone with amethystine ° lights.

⁴⁵ "My name is Ivan," he said. "We have just been visiting the elephant house. And then," he added with simple dignity, "we came up here."

⁴⁶ She nodded gently, "My name is Mary. We came the other way around. By the pink rocks and the kangaroos."

⁴⁷ There was a long pause, and Mary pushed a pin into the bun at her neck and straightened the cuffs of her pink sweater. They both stared at the cage.

exorcised: driven off by solemn oaths.
pedant: one who displays learning.
amethystine: bluish-purple.

⁴⁸ "Oh, look!" Mary cried. "Look at the gibbons! °
Look how beautifully they swing!"

⁴⁹ Ivan watched them intently. They swung back and
forth on long hairy arms and twisted and swung with
such artless and consummate * skill they took his breath
away. They were like long furry ropes blown back and
forth in wind. He had never noticed how beautiful they
were before. "Amazing!" he murmured. "Simply amazing!" He wanted to stand there watching them forever.

⁵⁰ Alexander did not want to stay forever. Nor did
Jacqueline. They whimpered to get down—get on—find
something new. A monkey's power to please is a transitory * thing.

⁵¹ Now, thought Ivan in despair, she will go the one
way and I will go the other, and this is the end.

⁵² They both stood there uncertainly, and Ivan, looking wildly about, saw a Chinese pagoda on the hill and
in the pagoda a man with popcorn and ice cream.

⁵³ "I was just going to buy a cone for Alexander," he
said fiercely. "Could I induce you to share a cone with
me? I mean—ha-ha!—I mean, could I buy us *all* a cone?"

⁵⁴ "I should love one," she said. Her sweet face turned
up at him like a rosy mallow ° flower. He could see
himself reflected standing there, chattering, chattering,
drowning in her dark blue eyes.

⁵⁵ "Ise!" Jacqueline shouted. "Ise!"

⁵⁶ Alexander stared at her uncomprehendingly. He
pointed up at the sky: "Boid?" He pointed at his foot:
"Shu?"

⁵⁷ "Ice-cre-eam-co-one." Ivan said. He separated the
syllables carefully, the way he understood that children
should be taught. "Ice-cre-eam-co-one." Dear God, make
Alexander smarter!

⁵⁸ Alexander pointed at some bright gold quinces on a
bush. "Kow?" he said distinctly. "Kow!" He opened his
mouth to an enormous size.

gibbons: smallest of the anthropoid apes.
mallow: a family of herbs and shrubs including the okra, holly-
    hock, althea, hibiscus, etc.

⁵⁹ Ivan heard her laugh again, a kind and pleasant sound. Ah God, the patience of women! the sweetness, the—"Shall we go?" he suggested gaily. "Shall we go and get the ice-cream cones?"

⁶⁰ They walked up the path, Jacqueline ahead, marching determinedly, her white chin set, her eyes fixed with ferocious delight on the ice-cream man. Alexander trailed dreamily behind her. "Awwet, awwet," he muttered from time to time and shook his head.

⁶¹ "Isn't it a lovely autumn day?" Mary said.

⁶² He looked up at the fluttering golden leaves, the sycamore leaves like small gold frog paws in the wind. The sky was a blazing blue. The birds in the pool were shouting, the sea lions braying and moving in the green sapphire waters; the pillars of the elephant house glittered like sun on snow.

⁶³ "Don't you love the park?" she said. "Don't you love it, Ivan?"

⁶⁴ "Oh, I do!—I do indeed!" Ivan almost shouted. He threw up his arms, and hundreds of white pigeons flew upward in the golden air. Slightly soiled park pigeons, but Ivan watched their fanning flight with dazzled eyes. "Aren't they beautiful?" he said. Like doves, like cockatoos, like flying flowers! O Mary, Mary, Mary!

ANALYSIS

There are several ways of approaching any work of art, and all readers will not agree on which is the right one. We looked at "Miss Brill" with our attention on stylistic virtues. Each word seemed to be carefully laid into place, all aimed at creating a character toward whom we have real feeling by the time the story concludes. We could do the same here; Miss Johnson uses words with care. But it may be more rewarding to inspect "Alexander to the Park" for its point of view. In fact, Ivan, the point-of-view ° character, *is* the story.

Miss Johnson chooses limited omniscient narration. We see this park as Ivan sees it, alas! Ingeniously she

point of view: See Glossary.

makes Alexander too young to speak much, so we hear only Ivan's embittered comments on the state of the world as he wanders through a zoo. The park is a "sad place full of mangy coyotes" (paragraph 2), a "place full of caged beasts and molting birds and quince-faced nurses" (paragraph 4), full of "rachitic hyenas and the sinister floating shapes of the wild dogs, bored, lonely beasts that prowled and lay and prowled again" (paragraph 22). The cockatoos remind him of "pupil-pouncing teachers in dresses of dead silk" (paragraph 20), the hippopotamus of a "steam-boat in lukewarm waters" (paragraph 24). His coming to the monkey house is inevitable. "This is the way we probabably look to God," he reflects. "Jumping around with silly grins." (paragraph 30)

It is here in paragraph 30 that we are given the first real explanation—if we can call it that—of Ivan's misanthropy. We learned in paragraph 5 that he was "twenty and thin and dark and worked as a clerk in a department store," wearing a "spotted tie from the marked-down counter." Now we hear Ivan explode with anger at his own "feeling of depression and loneliness." He sees no purpose and no end in life, only "dour leaves falling in the park." Ivan does not know it, but what his life lacks is love, someone with whom to share the world. Paragraph 33 alters the course of the action, and not a moment too soon.

Perhaps the turning point is too pat, too inevitable. Miss Johnson, nevertheless, makes it come off. Ivan's similes ° alter as his spirits rise: Mary looks "like a yellow dove," she has "a laugh . . . like the smell of a bakery on a winter night," his heart floods with "torrents of burning butter," her sweet face turns up at him like "a rosy mallow flower." The Ivan who, in paragraph 4, had felt "old and papery" now sees the sycamore leaves looking "like small gold frog paws in the wind." Is all this really happening? Can he really watch the "slightly soiled park pigeons" with "*dazzled* eyes"? Mary has shown him how. The point-of-view character shifts his point of view. He now sees the world through her eyes. Ivan's transformation does not get him a new job or dry Alex-

similes: See Glossary.

ander's pants, but somehow that matters less as he shouts inside himself "O Mary, Mary, Mary!"

Questions on Content

1. Why did Ivan not refuse his sister when she asked him to take Alexander to the park?
2. What animals and birds other than those we just mentioned above serve as good "springboards" for describing Ivan's resentment?
3. What causes Ivan to blush and stammer when Jacqueline tugs at his trousers and asks to be lifted up?
4. What part does an ice-cream cone play in this story?

Add to your vocabulary: pontifical, lowering, dour, barnacle, pedant, consummate, transitory.

Questions on Technique

1. Alexander could be an eight-year old boy with whom Ivan could have conversation as they wander through the zoo. Why do you suppose Miss Johnson makes him so young?
2. Analyze paragraph 20. Ivan puts women "under the head of Predatory Fowl." Do we know the cause of Ivan's harsh judgment of women?
3. How does Miss Johnson create an effective image of the "Man of Importance . . . —a Head of the Department" in paragraph 23?
4. Reread Ivan's impression of Mary (paragraphs 34–59). Could exaggeration play a part in it? Why is exaggeration acceptable here, or do you not agree?
5. Miss Johnson apparently enjoys creating striking images ° and similes. Some of them delighted you; others may have seemed strained or forced. Find five similes or images and evaluate each explaining your reaction to it.

Suggestions for Writing

1. Take Miss Johnson's form and adapt it to an experience you have had with a small child. Tell your story in the third person. Set the story at a circus, at a fire, in an amusement park, at the county fair, during a blizzard, after midnight, or some other occasion that

images: See Glossary.

will produce reactions. Another adult need not enter
your story.

2. Rewrite Miss Johnson's story, in about 500 words,
   from paragraph 33 onward. Have someone other than
   Jacqueline tug at Ivan's trousers.

3. Write a simplified version of this story in the first
   person. Make Mary the narrator.

CHAPTER 13

Narrative and theme

WALTER VAN TILBURG CLARK · *The Portable Phonograph*

This Part closes with one of the most disturbing short stories of the last few decades. In 1941, Walter Van Tilburg Clark was so moved by newspaper headlines full of war and destruction that, in order to dispel his emotions, he began writing this story. It was published that fall. In 1945, the world witnessed the first military use of an atomic bomb, over Hiroshima and Nagasaki. The destruction was so enormous that man faced for the first time, in what is now called the Atomic Age, the possibility of wiping himself off the face of the earth. The apprehension that Clark says he had felt in 1941 had multiplied tenfold.

Clark is a novelist. He published The Ox-Bow Incident *in 1940 and two other novels since then. He knew that if he wanted to capture a universality of apprehension for other generations to ponder over he would have to project it through human beings in action, through a meaningful incident. It would not suffice to talk about the end of the world. "One cannot afford," he wrote later, "to speak seriously of the end of the world." One could suggest it, however, pictorially, in a fiction that would lie close to truth. "I just began to write," he says.*

"I can't remember exactly what set me off. . . . In this case it was the prairie, the vast, desolated backdrop of the dugout, which first appeared, accompanied by a feeling that such a scene implied in itself all that one could afford to say directly about a final war." His theme ° is man's fight for survival. His method is narration. Watch how he slowly develops one through the other.

¹ The red sunset, with narrow, black cloud strips like threats across it, lay on the curved horizon of the prairie. The air was still and cold, and in it settled the mute darkness and greater cold of night. High in the air there was wind, for through the veil of the dusk the clouds could be seen gliding rapidly south and changing shapes. A queer sensation of torment, of two-sided, unpredictable nature, arose from the stillness of the earth air beneath the violence of the upper air. Out of the sunset, through the dead, matted grass and isolated weed stalks of the prairie, crept the narrow and deeply rutted remains of a road. In the road, in places, there were crusts of shallow, brittle ice. There were little islands of an old oiled pavement in the road too, but most of it was mud, now frozen rigid. The frozen mud still bore the toothed impress of great tanks, and a wanderer on the neighboring undulations ° might have stumbled, in this light, into large, partially filled-in and weed-grown cavities, their banks channelled and beginning to spread into badlands. These pits were such as might have been made by falling meteors, but they were not. They were the scars of gigantic bombs, their rawness already made a little natural by rain, seed, and time. Along the road, there were rakish * remnants of fence. There was also, just visible, one portion of tangled and multiple barbed wire still erect, behind which was a shelving ditch with small caves, now very quiet and empty, at intervals in its back wall. Otherwise there was no structure or remnant of a structure visible over the dome of the darkling earth, but only, in

theme: See Glossary.   undulations: wavelike curves or elevations.

sheltered hollows, the darker shadows of young trees trying again.

2   Under the wuthering ° arch of the high wind a V of wild geese fled south. The rush of their pinions ° sounded briefly, and the faint, plaintive notes of their expeditionary talk. Then they left a still greater vacancy. There was the smell and expectation of snow, as there is likely to be when the wild geese fly south. From the remote distance, toward the red sky, came faintly the protracted howl and quick yap-yap of a prairie wolf.

3   North of the road, perhaps a hundred yards, lay the parallel and deeply intrenched course of a small creek, lined with leafless alders ° and willows. The creek was already silent under ice. Into the bank above it was dug a sort of cell, with a single opening, like the mouth of a mine tunnel. Within the cell there was a little red of fire, which showed dully through the opening, like a reflection or a deception of the imagination. The light came from the chary burning of four blocks of poorly aged peat,° which gave off a petty warmth and much acrid ° smoke. But the precious remnants of wood, old fence posts and timbers from the long-deserted dugouts, had to be saved for the real cold, for the time when a man's breath blew white, the moisture in his nostrils stiffened at once when he stepped out, and the expansive blizzards paraded for days over the vast open, swirling and settling and thickening, till the dawn of the cleared day when the sky was thin blue-green and the terrible cold, in which a man could not live for three hours unwarmed, lay over the uniformly drifted swell of the plain.

4   Around the smoldering peat, four men were seated cross-legged. Behind them, traversed by their shadows,

wuthering: a provincial adjective from Yorkshire, England, meaning hostile, fierce, tumultuous.

pinions: terminal sections of a bird's wings.

alders: shrubs or trees similar to the birch, of the family *Betulaceae*, genus *Alnus*.

peat: a soil of partially decomposed vegetable matter which is drained, cultivated, cut, and then dried for fuel.

acrid: stinging, irritating.

was the earth bench, with two old and dirty army blankets, where the owner of the cell slept. In a niche in the opposite wall were a few tin utensils which caught the glint of the coals. The host was rewrapping in a piece of daubed ° burlap four fine, leather-bound books. He worked slowly and very carefully, and at last tied the bundle securely with a piece of grass-woven cord. The other three looked intently upon the process, as if a great significance lay in it. As the host tied the cord, he spoke. He was an old man, his long, matted beard and hair gray to nearly white. The shadows made his brows and cheekbones appear gnarled, his eyes and cheeks deeply sunken. His big hands, rough with frost and swollen by rheumatism, were awkward but gentle at their task. He was like a prehistoric priest performing a fateful ceremonial rite. Also his voice had in it a suitable quality of deep, reverent despair, yet perhaps at the moment, a sharpness of selfish satisfaction.

⁵ "When I perceived what was happening," he said, "I told myself, 'It is the end. I cannot take much; I will take these.'

⁶ "Perhaps I was impractical," he continued. "But for myself, I do not regret, and what do we know of those who will come after us? We are the doddering remnant of a race of mechanical fools. I have saved what I love; the soul of what was good in us is here; perhaps the new ones will make a strong enough beginning not to fall behind when they become clever."

⁷ He rose with slow pain and placed the wrapped volumes in the niche with his utensils. The others watched him with the same ritualistic gaze.

⁸ "Shakespeare, the Bible, *Moby-Dick,*° the *Divine Comedy,*" ° one of them said softly. "You might have done worse, much worse."

daubed: covered over with mud or paste.

Moby-Dick: an American novel (1851) written by Herman Melville. Moby Dick is an elusive white whale.

Divine Comedy: an epic poem by Dante Alighieri, divided into three parts: *Inferno* (1300), *Purgatory* (1308), and *Paradise* (1311).

9 "You will have a little soul left until you die," said another harshly. "That is more than is true of us. My brain becomes thick, like my hands." He held the big, battered hands, with their black nails, in the glow to be seen.

10 "I want paper to write on," he said. "And there is none."

11 The fourth man said nothing. He sat in the shadow farthest from the fire, and sometimes his body jerked in its rags from the cold. Although he was still young, he was sick and coughed often. Writing implied a greater future than he now felt able to consider.

12 The old man seated himself laboriously, and reached out, groaning at the movement, to put another block of peat on the fire. With bowed heads and averted eyes, his three guests acknowledged his magnanimity.

13 "We thank you, Doctor Jenkins, for the reading," said the man who had named the books.

14 They seemed then to be waiting for something. Doctor Jenkins understood, but was loath to comply. In an ordinary moment he would have said nothing. But the words of *The Tempest*,° which he had been reading, and the religious attention of the three made this an unusual occasion.

15 "You wish to hear the phonograph," he said grudgingly.

16 The two middle-aged men stared into the fire, unable to formulate and expose the enormity of their desire.

17 The young man, however, said anxiously, between suppressed coughs, "Oh, please," like an excited child.

18 The old man rose again in his difficult way, and went to the back of the cell. He returned and placed tenderly upon the packed floor, where the firelight might fall upon it, an old portable phonograph in a black case. He smoothed the top with his hand, and then opened it. The lovely green-felt-covered disk became visible.

19 "I have been using thorns as needles," he said. "But

The Tempest: Shakespeare's last comedy (1611). It takes place on an island.

tonight, because we have a musician among us"—he bent
his head to the young man, almost invisible in the
shadow—"I will use a steel needle. There are only three
left."

20   The two middle-aged men stared at him in speechless
adoration. The one with the big hands, who wanted to
write, moved his lips, but the whisper was not audible.

21   "Oh, don't!" cried the young man, as if he were hurt.
"The thorns will do beautifully."

22   "No," the old man said. "I have become accustomed
to the thorns, but they are not really good. For you, my
young friend, we will have good music tonight."

23   "After all," he added generously, and beginning to
wind the phonograph, which creaked, "they can't last
forever."

24   "No, nor we," the man who needed to write said
harshly. "The needle, by all means."

25   "Oh, thanks," said the young man. "Thanks," he said
again in a low, excited voice, and then stifled his coughing with a bowed head.

26   "The records, though," said the old man when he
had finished winding, "are a different matter. Already
they are very worn. I do not play them more than once
a week. One, once a week, that is what I allow myself.

27   "More than a week I cannot stand it; not to hear
them," he apologized.

28   "No, how could you?" cried the young man. "And
with them here like this."

29   "A man can stand anything," said the man who
wanted to write, in his harsh, antagonistic voice.

30   "Please, the music," said the young man.

31   "Only the one," said the old man. "In the long run,
we will remember more that way."

32   He had a dozen records with luxuriant gold and red
seals. Even in that light the others could see that the
threads of the records were becoming worn. Slowly he
read out the titles and the tremendous, dead names of
the composers and the artists and the orchestras. The
three worked upon the names in their minds, carefully.

It was difficult to select from such a wealth what they would at once most like to remember. Finally, the man who wanted to write named Gershwin's "New York." °

33 "Oh, no," cried the sick young man, and then could say nothing more because he had to cough. The others understood him, and the harsh man withdrew his selection and waited for the musician to choose.

34 The musician begged Doctor Jenkins to read the titles again, very slowly, so that he could remember the sounds. While they were read, he lay back against the wall, his eyes closed, his thin, horny hand pulling at his light beard, and listened to the voices and the orchestras and the single instruments in his mind.

35 When the reading was done he spoke despairingly. "I have forgotten," he complained; "I cannot hear them clearly.

36 "There are things missing," he explained.

37 "I know," said Doctor Jenkins. "I thought that I knew all of Shelley ° by heart. I should have brought Shelley."

38 "That's more soul than we can use," said the harsh man. *"Moby-Dick* is better.

39 "We can understand that," he emphasized.

40 The Doctor nodded.

41 "Still," said the man who had admired the books, "we need the absolute if we are to keep a grasp on anything.

42 "Anything but these sticks and peat clods and rabbit snares," he said bitterly.

43 "Shelley desired an ultimate absolute," said the harsh man. "It's too much," he said. "It's no good; no earthly good."

Gershwin's "New York": George Gershwin (1898–1937), American composer, played his "Second Rhapsody for Orchestra with Piano" for the first time in 1932, with the Boston Symphony Orchestra. While being composed it was often referred to as the "New York Rhapsody" or the "Manhattan Rhapsody."

Shelley: Percy Bysshe Shelley (1792–1822), English poet of the Romantic period.

⁴⁴ The musician selected a Debussy ° nocturne. The others considered and approved. They rose to their knees to watch the Doctor prepare for the playing, so that they appeared to be actually in an attitude of worship. The peat glow showed the thinness of their bearded faces, and the deep lines in them, and revealed the condition of their garments. The other two continued to kneel as the old man carefully lowered the needle onto the spinning disk, but the musician suddenly drew back against the wall again, with his knees up, and buried his face in his hands.

⁴⁵ At the first notes of the piano the listeners were startled. They stared at each other. Even the musician lifted his head in amazement, but then quickly bowed it again, strainingly, as if he were suffering from a pain he might not be able to endure. They were all listening deeply, without movement. The wet, blue-green notes tinkled forth from the old machine, and were individual, delectable * presences in the cell. The individual, delectable presences swept into a sudden tide of unbearably beautiful dissonance,* and then continued fully the swelling and ebbing of that tide, the dissonant inpourings, and the resolutions, and the diminishments, and the little, quiet wavelets of interlude lapping between. Every sound was piercing and singularly sweet. In all the men except the musician, there occurred rapid sequences of tragically heightened recollection. He heard nothing but what was there. At the final, whispering disappearance, but moving quietly so that the others would not hear him and look at him, he let his head fall back in agony, as if it were drawn there by the hair, and clenched the fingers of one hand over his teeth. He sat that way while the others were silent, and until they began to breathe again normally. His drawn-up legs were trembling violently.

⁴⁶ Quickly Doctor Jenkins lifted the needle off, to save it and not to spoil the recollection with scraping. When he had stopped the whirling of the sacred disc, he

Debussy: Claude Debussy (1862–1918), French impressionist composer.

courteously left the phonograph open and by the fire, in sight.

47 The others, however, understood. The musician rose last, but then abruptly, and went quickly out at the door without saying anything. The others stopped at the door and gave their thanks in low voices. The Doctor nodded magnificently.

48 "Come again," he invited, "in a week. We will have the 'New York.' "

49 When the two had gone together, out toward the rimed ° road, he stood in the entrance, peering and listening. At first, there was only the resonant * boom of the wind overhead, and then far over the dome of the dead, dark plain, the wolf cry lamenting. In the rifts of clouds the Doctor saw four stars flying. It impressed the Doctor that one of them had just been obscured by the beginning of a flying cloud at the very moment he heard what he had been listening for, a sound of suppressed coughing. It was not near-by, however. He believed that down against the pale alders he could see the moving shadow.

50 With nervous hands he lowered the piece of canvas which served as his door, and pegged it at the bottom. Then quickly and quietly, looking at the piece of canvas frequently, he slipped the records into the case, snapped the lid shut, and carried the phonograph to his couch. There, pausing often to stare at the canvas and listen, he dug earth from the wall and disclosed a piece of board. Behind this there was a deep hole in the wall, into which he put the phonograph. After a moment's consideration, he went over and reached down his bundle of books and inserted it also. Then, guardedly, he once more sealed up the hole with the board and the earth. He also changed his blankets, and the grass-stuffed sack which served as a pillow, so that he could lie facing the entrance. After carefully placing two more blocks of peat upon the fire, he stood for a long time watching the

rimed: covered with a rough, white ice, formed not by frost but by fog.

stretched canvas, but it seemed to billow naturally with the first gusts of a lowering wind. At last he prayed, and got in under his blankets, and closed his smoke-smarting eyes. On the inside of the bed, next the wall, he could feel with his hand the comfortable piece of lead pipe.

ANALYSIS

Not every storyteller will want to begin with so over-powering a sense of *place,* particularly when it is to be nameless. But the method Clark uses works beautifully for the theme he wants to expound. In a long, full opening paragraph we learn that "there was no structure or remnant of a structure visible over the dome of the darkling earth." The time is sunset, in autumn, and the cold night and a colder winter are approaching. How right that end of day and end of growing season should be the *time* of the story. The only sound is the rush of geese overhead and the howl of a prairie wolf. The only color is "a little red of fire" in "a sort of cell." The air smells of "poorly aged peat" making "acrid smoke." It is paragraph 4 before we meet living human beings.

Clark has set his stage meticulously. In fact, the story begins as though a curtain were rising slowly on a mammoth, desolate stage and the audience were invited to contemplate empty shadows before hearing a man's voice. When the voice finally comes, it too is anonymous. We know him as "the host" at first. Later he is called Doctor Jenkins, the professor. He has been reading Shakespeare to "the other three." And who are they? In time we meet them as the writer, and the musician, and the man with the unknown past. That is all we need to know. Clearly the story is about survival, not about these four men. The *point of emphasis* ° is the theme or underlying meaning.

Clark works his theme into the action; he does not superimpose it on an incredible series of events. How believable it is that the professor should save the great works of man's imagination (Dante, Shakespeare, Melville), that the phonograph should be portable (this

point of emphasis: See Glossary.

idea was a happy invention on Clark's part), that the records should be played only once a week, that already Jenkins has learned how to substitute thorns for needles, that the musician should select Debussy, not Gershwin. These are homely but important details, and through them Clark is able to make powerful implications about man's spirit. But does he also suggest that man's body will, in time, make its demands? And will these demands overpower the longings of the spirit?

Reread his solemn, frightening, last paragraph. We see Jenkins lower "the piece of canvas which served as his door and [peg] it at the bottom." But man can endure cold. What are his greater fears? Jenkins works with "nervous" hands. He "quickly and quietly" slips the records into the case. He pauses to stare and listen. He "guardedly" seals up the hole. He changes his blankets to "lie facing the entrance." For a long time he stands "watching the stretched canvas." Then comes the final sentence, even more effective than Faulkner's "He did not look back" or Miss Johnson's "O Mary, Mary, Mary!" or Miss Mansfield's "She thought she heard something crying."

Clark recalls (see his essay in the *Pacific Spectator,* Summer, 1949) that "that sentence plucked the proper closing note, one that might linger for a time with a tenuous but moving reminder of the whole intention. If so, it was so, happily, by means of the very least phrase, and particularly by means of the one word 'comfortable.' Nothing in the phrase was considered, not 'comfortable' any more than the rest, but even as it came, that 'comfortable' tickled me, not so much because of its immediate implication, in which the paradox ° was clear enough, as for some remote, redoubling connotation.°"

Here we have it all said, and in the author's own words. The last sentence is a "moving reminder of the whole intention"; the theme of the story, *survival,* is summed up in five words. The adjective is a paradox; Jenkins is anything but comfortable, having just closed "his smoke-smarting eyes." But Clark and the careful reader sense "some more remote, redoubling connotation." Clark tells us he borrowed the word, uncon-

paradox: See Glossary.   connotation: See Glossary.

sciously, from *Romeo and Juliet:* "Remember how Juliet, waking in the tomb, and not yet aware that Romeo is dead, murmurs drowsily to the gentle Friar Lawrence, 'Oh, comfortable Friar—'?" Most of us will not remember. But our imaginations *will* go to work on why Jenkins finds his lead pipe "comfortable," what connotations surround the word. Survival implies self-preservation. Does self-preservation imply fighting for protection? Against wild animals? Against one's neighbors? But fighting one's neighbors is war, and war has just brought Jenkins to this low state. Will man never learn? Is his fate on earth not struggle for food or warmth but struggle to master his own base passions?

Questions on Content

1. What specific indications of war (now past) does Clark give us in paragraph 1?
2. What book has Jenkins been reading from? Does the choice of specific play tell us anything about the situation?
3. Does the musician listen to Debussy in the same way as all the other men? What makes him different?
4. Why does Jenkins use a real needle instead of a thorn for the playing of Debussy?

Add to your vocabulary: rakish, delectable, dissonance, resonant.

Questions on Technique

1. Clark could have begun his story with Doctor Jenkins' taking out his books in anticipation of the arrival of guests? Why do you think he sets the stage first?
2. In paragraph 4, what effect does Clark wish to achieve with adjectives like "smoldering" peat, "dirty" army blankets, "tin" utensils, "daubed" burlap, "grass-woven" cord, and the like?
3. In paragraph 10, we learn that there is no paper to write on. How do you react to this simple fact? Does this sentence, like "comfortable lead pipe," also have connotations? Is it connected with using thorns for needles?
4. What irony lies behind the sentence (paragraph 32),

"It was difficult to select from such a wealth. . . ."?
Are twelve records "wealth"?
5. In paragraph 49, what use does Clark make of "a sound of suppressed coughing" and a "moving shadow"?

Suggestions for Writing

1. Rewrite this story for experience in creating dialogue. Open it with Jenkins talking to the other men. Cut description to a minimum. Try to convey the feeling of desolation through the conversation.
2. From your own experience, build a narrative, in 600 words, around a special place: a cabin in the woods, a camp site, a beach house, a hotel room, your family's new home. Make the description of *place* the major aspect of the story.
3. Stretch your imagination. *You* have just landed on the moon, the first human being (earthman, at least) to have done so. Describe, in the first person, all you see.
4. Write your own short story of survival after a nuclear war. Perhaps your ideas of what life would be like are different from Clark's. How would the experience of the four survivors have been different if they had been in the ruins of a large city?

PART FOUR

MODELS
WITHOUT
ANALYSIS

If you have studied the first three Parts of this book, you have looked closely at three kinds of writing: description, exposition, and narration. Now it is time to examine four models without analysis, without editorial comment on who is writing, what is the main subject, and what techniques are demonstrated. You will have a chance to discover for yourself how the writer organizes his material and what he emphasizes. You will want to evaluate these pieces critically.

The selections, all by established American writers, differ vastly from each other. James Agee's memories of a childhood in Tennessee may recall Thomas Sancton's essay in the first chapter of this book. Loren Eiseley's essay begs for contrast with E. G. F. Sauer's; S. I. Hayakawa will compare easily with the six models of definition. The Stephen Crane story, published more than sixty years ago and now a classic, will probably stand by itself, unlike any of the five narratives in Part Three. But discount these suggestions, if you wish, or disprove them by bringing other essays and narratives you have studied in this volume into comparison or contrast with the models that follow. Better still, ask yourself these questions: James Agee describes his hometown with affection; does he also write expository prose, a kind of reporting? The Eiseley and the Hayakawa essays demonstrate two kinds of analytical prose; but does Loren Eiseley also depend heavily on narrative? And what is Stephen Crane's prose, ultimately: a simple narrative, an elaborate description? Or both?

CHAPTER 14

Description

JAMES AGEE · *Knoxville: Summer, 1915*

1 We are talking now of summer evenings in Knoxville,
Tennessee in the time that I lived there so successfully
disguised to myself as a child. It was a little bit mixed
sort of block, fairly solidly lower middle class, with one
or two juts apiece on either side of that. The houses corresponded: middle-sized gracefully fretted wood houses
built in the late nineties and early nineteen hundreds,
with small front and side and more spacious back yards,
and trees in the yards, and porches. These were soft-
wooded trees, poplars, tulip trees, cottonwoods. There
were fences around one or two of the houses, but mainly
the yards ran into each other with only now and then a
low hedge that wasn't doing very well. There were few
good friends among the grown people, and they were
not poor enough for the other sort of intimate acquaintance, but everyone nodded and spoke, and even might
talk short times, trivially, and at the two extremes of the
general or the particular, and ordinarily next door neighbors talked quite a bit when they happened to run into
each other, and never paid calls. The men were mostly
small businessmen, one or two very modestly executives,
one or two worked with their hands, most of them
clerical, and most of them between thirty and forty-five.

² But it is of these evenings, I speak.

³ Supper was at six and was over by half past. There was still daylight, shining softly and with a tarnish, like the lining of a shell; and the carbon lamps lifted at the corners were on in the light, and the locusts were started, and the fireflies were out, and a few frogs were flopping in the dewy grass, by the time the fathers and the children came out. The children ran out first hell bent and yelling those names by which they were known; then the fathers sank out leisurely in crossed suspenders, their collars removed and their necks looking tall and shy. The mothers stayed back in the kitchen washing and drying, putting things away, recrossing their traceless footsteps like the lifetime journeys of bees, measuring out the dry cocoa for breakfast. When they came out they had taken off their aprons and their skirts were dampened and they sat in rockers on their porches quietly.

⁴ It is not of the games children play in the evening that I want to speak now, it is of a contemporaneous atmosphere that has little to do with them: that of the fathers of families, each in his space of lawn, his shirt fishlike pale in the unnatural light and his face nearly anonymous, hosing their lawns. The hoses were attached at spiggots that stood out of the brick foundations of the houses. The nozzles were variously set but usually so there was a long sweet stream of spray, the nozzle wet in the hand, the water trickling the right forearm and the peeled-back cuff, and the water whishing out a long loose and low-curved cone, and so gentle a sound. First an insane noise of violence in the nozzle, and then the still irregular sound of adjustment, then the smoothing into steadiness and a pitch as accurately tuned to the size and style of stream as any violin. So many qualities of sound out of one hose: so many choral differences out of those several hoses that were in earshot. Out of any one hose, the almost dead silence of the release, and the short still arch of the separate big drops, silent as a held breath, and the only noise the flattering noise on leaves and the slapped grass at the fall of each big drop. That, and the

intense hiss with the intense stream; that, and that same intensity not growing less but growing more quiet and delicate with the turn of the nozzle, up to that extreme tender whisper when the water was just a wide bell of film. Chiefly, though, the hoses were set much alike, in a compromise between distance and tenderness of spray, (and quite surely a sense of art behind this compromise, and a quiet deep joy, too real to recognize itself), and the sounds therefore were pitched much alike; pointed by the snorting start of a new hose; decorated by some man playful with the nozzle; left empty, like God by the sparrow's fall, when any single one of them desists: and all, though near alike, of various pitch; and in this unison. These sweet pale streamings in the light lift out their pallors and their voices all together, mothers hushing their children, the hushing unnaturally prolonged, the men gentle and silent and each snail-like withdrawn into the quietude of what he singly is doing, tasting the mean goodness of their living like the last of their suppers in their mouths; while the locusts carry on this noise of hoses on their much higher and sharper key. The noise of the locust is dry, and it seems not to be rasped or vibrated but urged from him as if through a small orifice by a breath that can never give out. Also there is never one locust but an illusion of at least a thousand. The noise of each locust is pitched in some classic locust range out of which none of them varies more than two full tones: and yet you seem to hear each locust discrete from all the rest, and there is a long, slow, pulse in their noise, like the scarcely defined arch of a long and high set bridge. They are all around in every tree, so that the noise seems to come from nowhere and everywhere at once, from the whole shell heaven, shivering in your flesh and teasing your eardrums, the boldest of all the sounds of night. And yet it is habitual to summer nights, and is of the great order of noises, like the noises of the sea and of the blood her precocious grandchild, which you realize you are hearing only when you catch yourself listening. Meantime from low in the dark, just outside the swaying horizons of the hoses, conveying always grass in the damp of dew and its strong green-black smear of smell, the regular yet spaced noises of the crickets, each a sweet cold silver noise three-noted, like the slipping each time of three matched links of a small chain.

⁵ But the men by now, one by one, have silenced their hoses and drained and coiled them. Now only two, and now only one, is left, and you see only ghostlike shirt with the sleeve garters, and sober mystery of his mild face like the lifted face of large cattle enquiring of your presence in a pitch-dark pool of meadow; and now he too is gone; and it has become that time of evening when people sit on their porches, rocking gently and talking gently and watching the street and the standing up into their sphere of possession of the trees, of birds' hung havens, hangars. People go by; things go by. A horse, drawing a buggy, breaking his hollow iron music on the asphalt; a loud auto; a quiet auto; people in pairs, not in a hurry, scuffling, switching their weight of aestival ° body, talking casually, the taste hovering over them of vanilla, strawberry, pasteboard and starched milk, the image upon them of lovers and horsemen, squared with clowns in hueless amber. A street car raising its iron moan; stopping, belling and starting; stertorous; ° rousing and raising again its iron increasing moan and swimming its gold windows and straw seats on past and past and past, the bleak spark crackling and cursing above it like a small malignant spirit set to dog its tracks; the iron whine rises on rising speed; still risen, faints; halts; the faint stinging bell; rises again, still fainter; fainting, lifting, lifts, faints forgone: forgotten. Now is the night one blue dew.

Now is the night one blue dew, my father has drained, he has coiled the hose.

aestival: of summer.   stertorous: characterized by heavy snoring.

Low on the length of lawns, a frailing of fire who
    breathes.
Content, silver, like peeps of light, each cricket makes his
    comment over and over in the drowned grass.
A cold toad thumpily flounders.
Within the edges of damp shadows of side yards are hov-
    ering children nearly sick with joy of fear, who watch
    the unguarding of a telephone pole.
Around white carbon corner lamps bugs of all sizes are
    lifted elliptic, solar systems. Big hardshells bruise
    themselves, assailant: he is fallen on his back, legs
    squiggling.
Parents on porches: rock and rock: From damp strings
    morning glories: hang their ancient faces.
The dry and exalted noise of the locusts from all the air
    at once enchants my eardrums.

6   On the rough wet grass of the back yard my father and
mother have spread quilts. We all lie there, my mother,
my father, my uncle, my aunt, and I too am lying there.
First we were sitting up, then one of us lay down, and
then we all lay down, on our stomachs, or on our sides,
or on our backs, and they have kept on talking. They are
not talking much, and the talk is quiet, of nothing in particular, of nothing at all in particular, of nothing at all.
The stars are wide and alive, they seem each like a smile
of great sweetness, and they seem very near. All my people are larger bodies than mine, quiet, with voices gentle
and meaningless like the voices of sleeping birds. One is
an artist, he is living at home. One is a musician, she is
living at home. One is my mother who is good to me. One
is my father who is good to me. By some chance, here they
are, all on this earth; and who shall ever tell the sorrow
of being on this earth, lying, on quilts, on the grass, in a
summer evening, among the sounds of the night. May
God bless my people, my uncle, my aunt, my mother, my
good father, oh, remember them kindly in their time of
trouble; and in the hour of their taking away.

[7] After a little I am taken in and put to bed. Sleep, soft smiling, draws me unto her: and those receive me, who quietly treat me, as one familiar and well-beloved in that home: but will not, oh, will not, not now, not ever; but will not ever tell me who I am.

CHAPTER 15

Exposition

LOREN C. EISELEY · *The Bird and the Machine*

¹ I suppose their little bones have years ago been lost among the stones and winds of those high glacial pastures. I suppose their feathers blew eventually into the piles of tumbleweed beneath the straggling cattle fences and rotted there in the mountain snows, along with dead steers and all the other things that drift to an end in the corners of the wire. I do not quite know why I should be thinking of birds over the New York *Times* at breakfast, particularly of the birds of my youth half a continent away. It is a funny thing what the brain will do with memories and how it will treasure them and finally bring them into odd juxtapositions with other things, as though it wanted to make a design, or get some meaning out of them, whether you want it or not, or even see it.

² It used to seem marvelous to me, but I read now that there are machines that can do these things in a small way, machines that can crawl about like animals, and that it may not be long now until they do more things—maybe even make themselves—I saw that piece in the *Times* just now and then they will, maybe—well, who knows—but you read about it more and more with no one making any protest, and already they can add better than we and

reach up and hear things through the dark and finger the guns over the night sky.

³ This is the new world that I read about at breakfast. This is the world that confronts me in my biological books and journals, until there are times when I sit quietly in my chair and try to hear the little purr of the cogs in my head and the tubes flaring and dying as the messages go through them and the circuits snap shut or open. This is the great age, make no mistake about it; the robot has been born somewhat appropriately along with the atom bomb, and the brain they say now is just another type of more complicated feedback system. The engineers have its basic principles worked out; it's mechanical, you know; nothing to get superstitious about; and man can always improve on nature once he gets the idea. Well, he's got it all right and that's why, I guess, that I sit here in my chair, with the article crunched in my hand, remembering those two birds and that blue mountain sunlight. There is another magazine article on my desk that reads "Machines Are Getting Smarter Every Day." I don't deny it, but I'll still stick with the birds. It's life I believe in, not machines.

⁴ Maybe you don't believe there is any difference. A skeleton is all joints and pulleys, I'll admit. And when man was in his simpler stages of machine building in the eighteenth century, he quickly saw the resemblances. "What," wrote Hobbes,° "is the heart but a spring, and the nerves so many strings, and the joints but so many wheels, giving motion to the whole body?" Tinkering about in their shops it was inevitable in the end that men would see the world as a huge machine "subdivided into an infinite number of lesser machines."

⁵ The idea took on with a vengeance. Little automatons toured the country—dolls controlled by clockwork. Clocks described as little worlds were taken on tours by their designers. They were made up of moving figures, shifting scenes, and other remarkable devices. The life of the cell was unknown. Man, whether he was conceived as posses-

Hobbes: Thomas Hobbes (1588–1679), British philosopher.

sing a soul or not, moved and jerked about like these tiny puppets. A human being thought of himself in terms of his own tools and implements. He had been fashioned like the puppets he produced and was only a more clever model made by a greater designer.

6 Then in the nineteenth century, the cell was discovered, and the single machine in its turn was found to be the product of millions of infinitesimal machines—the cells. Now, finally, the cell itself dissolves away into an abstract chemical machine—and that into some intangible, inexpressible flow of energy. The secret seems to lurk all about, the wheels get smaller and smaller, and they turn more rapidly, but when you try to seize it the life is gone —and so, by popular definition, some would say that life was never there in the first place. The wheels and the cogs are the secret and we can make them better in time—machines that will run faster and more accurately than real mice to real cheese.

7 I have no doubt it can be done, though a mouse harvesting seeds on an autumn thistle is to me a fine sight and more complicated, I think, in his multiform activity, than a machine "mouse" running a maze. Also, I like to think of the possible shape of the future brooding in mice, just as it brooded once in a rather ordinary mousy insectivore ° who became a man. It leaves a nice fine indeterminate sense of wonder that even an electronic brain hasn't got, because you know perfectly well that if the electronic brain changes it will be because of something man has done to it. But what man will do to himself he doesn't really know. A certain scale of time and a ghostly intangible thing called change are ticking in him. Powers and potentialities like the oak in the seed, or a red and awful ruin. Either way, it's impressive; and the mouse has it, too. Or those birds, I'll never forget those birds—yet before I measured their significance, I learned the lesson of time first of all. I was young then and left alone in a great desert—part of an expedition that had scattered its men over several hundred miles in order to carry on research

insectivore: any animal or plant that feeds on insects.

more effectively. I learned there that time is a series of planes existing superficially in the same universe. The tempo is a human illusion, a subjective clock ticking in our kind of protoplasm.

8   As the long months passed, I began to live on the slower planes and to observe more readily what passed for life there. I sauntered, I passed more and more slowly up and down the canyons in the dry baking heat of midsummer. I slumbered for long hours in the shade of huge brown boulders that had gathered in tilted companies out on the flats. I had forgotten the world of men and the world had forgotten me. Now and then I found a skull in the canyons, and these justified my remaining there. I took a serene cold interest in these discoveries. I had come, like many a naturalist before me, to view life with a wary and subdued attention. I had grown to take pleasure in the divested bone.

9   I sat once on a high ridge that fell away before me into a waste of sand dunes. I sat through hours of a long afternoon. Finally, as I glanced beside my boot an indistinct configuration caught my eye. It was a coiled rattlesnake, a big one. How long he had sat with me I do not know. I had not frightened him. We were both locked in the sleep-walking tempo of the earlier world, baking in the same high air and sunshine. Perhaps he had been there when I came. He slept on as I left, his coils, so ill discerned by me, dissolving once more among the stones and gravel from which I had barely made him out.

10   Another time I got on a higher ridge, among some tough little wind-warped pines half covered over with sand in a basin-like depression that caught everything carried by the air up to those heights. There were a few thin bones of birds, some cracked shells of indeterminable age, and the knotty fingers of pine roots bulged out of shape from their long and agonizing grasp upon the crevices of the rock. I lay under the pines in the sparse shade and went to sleep once more.

11   It grew cold finally, for autumn was in the air by then, and the few things that lived thereabouts were sinking

down into an even chillier scale of time. In the moments between sleeping and waking I saw the roots about me and slowly, slowly, a foot in what seemed many centuries, I moved by sleep-stiffened hands over the scaling bark and lifted my numbed face after the vanishing sun. I was a great awkward thing of knots and aching limbs, trapped up there in some long, patient endurance that involved the necessity of putting living fingers into rock and by slow, aching expansion bursting those rocks asunder. I suppose, so thin and slow was the time of my pulse by then, that I might have stayed on to drift still deeper into the lower cadences of the frost, or the crystalline life that glisters in pebbles or shines in a snow flake, or dreams in the meteoric iron between the worlds.

[12]   It was a dim descent, but time was present in it. Somewhere far down in that scale the notion struck me that one might come the other way. Not many months thereafter I joined some colleagues heading higher into a remote windy tableland where huge bones were reputed to protrude like boulders from the turf. I had drowsed with reptiles and moved with the century-long pulse of trees; now, lethargically, I was climbing back up some invisible ladder of quickening hours. There had been talk of birds in connection with my duties. Birds are intense, fast-living creatures—reptiles, I suppose one might say, that have escaped out of the heavy sleep of time, transformed fairy creatures dancing over sunlit meadows. It is a youthful fancy, no doubt, but because of something that happened up there among the escarpments of that range, it remains with me a life-long impression. I can never bear to see a bird imprisoned.

[13]   We came into that valley through the trailing mists of a spring night. It was a place that looked as though it might never have known the foot of man, but our scouts had been ahead of us and we knew all about the abandoned cabin of stone that lay far up on one hillside. It had been built in the land rush of the last century and then lost to the cattlemen again as the marginal soils failed to take to the plow.

14 There were spots like this all over that country. Lost graves marked by unlettered stones and old corroding rim-fire cartridge cases lying where somebody had made a stand among the boulders that rimmed the valley. They are all that remain of the range wars; the men are under the stones now. I could see our cavalcade winding in and out through the mist below us: torches, the reflection of the truck lights on our collecting tins, and the far-off bumping of a loose dinosaur thigh bone in the bottom of a trailer. I stood on a rock a moment looking down and thinking what it cost in money and equipment to capture the past.

15 We had, in addition, instructions to lay hands on the present. The word had come through to get them alive— birds, reptiles, anything. A zoo somewhere abroad needed restocking. It was one of those reciprocal matters in which science involves itself. Maybe our museum needed a stray ostrich egg and this was the payoff. Anyhow, my job was to help capture some birds and that was why I was there before the trucks.

16 The cabin had not been occupied for years. We intended to clean it out and live in it, but there were holes in the roof and the birds had come in and were roosting in the rafters. You could depend on it in a place like this where everything blew away and even a bird needed some place out of the weather and away from coyotes. A cabin going back to nature in a wild place draws them till they come in, listening at the eaves, I imagine, pecking softly among the shingles till they find a hole and then suddenly the place is theirs and man is forgotten.

17 Sometimes of late years I find myself thinking the most beautiful sight in the world might be the birds taking over New York after the last man has run away to the hills. I will never live to see it, of course, but I know just how it will sound because I've lived up high and I know the sort of watch birds keep on us. I've listened to sparrows tapping tentatively on the outside of air conditioners when they thought no one was listening, and I

know how other birds test the vibrations that come up to them through the television aerials.

18 "Is he gone?" they ask, and the vibrations come up from below, "Not yet, not yet."

19 Well, to come back, I got the door open softly and I had the spotlight all ready to turn on and blind whatever birds there were so they couldn't see to get out through the roof. I had a short piece of ladder to put against the far wall where there was a shelf on which I expected to make the biggest haul. I had all the information I needed just like any skilled assassin. I pushed the door open, the hinges squeaking only a little. A bird or two stirred—I could hear them—but nothing flew and there was a faint starlight through the hole in the roof.

20 I padded across the floor, got the ladder up, and the light ready, and slithered up the ladder till my head and arms were over the shelf. Everything was dark as pitch except for the starlight at a little place back of the shelf near the eaves. With the light to blind them, they'd never make it. I had them. I reached my arm carefully over in order to be ready to seize whatever was there and I put the flash on the edge of the shelf where it would stand by itself when I turned it on. That way I'd be able to use both hands.

21 Everything worked perfectly except for one detail—I didn't know what kind of birds were there. I never thought about it at all and it wouldn't have mattered if I had. My orders were to get something interesting. I snapped on the flash and sure enough there was a great beating and feathers flying, but instead of my having them, they, or rather he, had me. He had my hand, that is, and for a small hawk not much bigger than my fist he was doing all right. I heard him give one short metallic cry when the light went on and my hand descended on the bird beside him; after that he was busy with his claws and his beak was sunk in my thumb. In the struggle I knocked the lamp over on the shelf and his mate got her sight back and whisked neatly through the hole in the roof and off among the stars outside. It all happened in

fifteen seconds and you might think I would have fallen down the ladder, but no, I had a professional assassin's reputation to keep up, and the bird, of course, made the mistake of thinking the hand was the enemy and not the eyes behind it. He chewed my thumb up pretty effectively and lacerated my hand with his claws, but in the end I got him, having two hands to work with.

22 He was a sparrow hawk and a fine young male in the prime of life. I was sorry not to catch the pair of them, but as I dripped blood and folded his wings carefully, holding him by the back so that he couldn't strike again, I had to admit the two of them might have been more than I could have handled under the circumstances. The little fellow had saved his mate by diverting me, and that was that. He was born to it, and made no outcry now, resting in my hand hopelessly, but peering toward me in the shadows behind the lamp with a fierce, almost indifferent glance. He neither gave nor expected mercy and something out of the high air passed from him to me, stirring a faint embarrassment.

23 I quit looking into that eye and managed to get my huge carcass with its fist full of prey back down the ladder. I put the bird in a box too small to allow him to injure himself by struggle and walked out to welcome the arriving trucks. It had been a long day, and camp was still to make in the darkness. In the morning that bird would be just another episode. He would go back with the bones in the truck to a small cage in a city where he would spend the rest of his life. And a good thing, too. I sucked my aching thumb and spat out some blood. An assassin has to get used to these things. I had a professional reputation to keep up.

24 In the morning, with the change that comes on suddenly in that high country, the mist that had hovered below us in the valley was gone. The sky was a deep blue, and one could see for miles over the high outcroppings of stone. I was up early and brought the box in which the little hawk was imprisoned out onto the grass where I was building a cage. A wind as cool as a mountain spring ran

over the grass and stirred my hair. It was a fine day to be alive. I looked up and all around and at the hole in the cabin roof out of which the other little hawk had fled. There was no sign of her anywhere that I could see.

25 "Probably in the next county by now," I thought cynically, but before beginning work I decided I'd have a look at my last night's capture.

26 Secretively, I looked again all around the camp and up and down and opened the box. I got him right out in my hand with his wings folded properly and I was careful not to startle him. He lay limp in my grasp and I could feel his heart pound under the feathers but he only looked beyond me and up.

27 I saw him look that last look away beyond me into a sky so full of light that I could not follow his gaze. The little breeze flowed over me again, and nearby a mountain aspen shook all its tiny leaves. I suppose I must have had an idea then of what I was going to do, but I never let it come up into consciousness. I just reached over and laid the hawk on the grass.

28 He lay there a long minute without hope, unmoving, his eyes still fixed on that blue vault above him. It must have been that he was already so far away in heart that he never felt the release from my hand. He never even stood. He just lay with his breast against the grass.

29 In the next second after that long minute he was gone. Like a flicker of light, he had vanished with my eyes full on him, but without actually seeing even a premonitory ° wing beat. He was gone straight into that towering emptiness of light and crystal that my eyes could scarcely bear to penetrate. For another long moment there was silence. I could not see him. The light was too intense. Then from far up somewhere a cry came ringing down.

30 I was young then and had seen little of the world, but when I heard that cry my heart turned over. It was not the cry of the hawk I had captured; for, by shifting my position against the sun, I was now seeing further up. Straight out of the sun's eye, where she must have been

premonitory: giving warning in advance.

soaring restlessly above us for untold hours, hurtled his mate. And from far up, ringing from peak to peak of the summits over us, came a cry of such unutterable and ecstatic joy that it sounds down across the years and tingles among the cups on my quiet breakfast table.

31 I saw them both now. He was rising fast to meet her. They met in a great soaring gyre ° that turned to a whirling circle and a dance of wings. Once more, just once, their two voices, joined in a harsh wild medley of question and response, struck and echoed against the pinnacles of the valley. Then they were gone forever somewhere into those upper regions beyond the eyes of men.

32 I am older now, and sleep less, and have seen most of what there is to see and am not very much impressed any more, I suppose, by anything. "What Next in the Attributes of Machines?" my morning headline runs. "It Might Be the Power to Reproduce Themselves."

33 I lay the paper down and across my mind a phrase floats insinuatingly: "It does not seem that there is anything in the construction, constituents, or behavior of the human being which it is essentially impossible for science to duplicate and synthesize. On the other hand . . ."

34 All over the city the cogs in the hard, bright mechanisms have begun to turn. Figures move through computers, names are spelled out, a thoughtful machine selects the fingerprints of a wanted criminal from an array of thousands. In the laboratory an electronic mouse runs swiftly through a maze toward the cheese it can neither taste nor enjoy. On the second run it does better than a living mouse.

35 "On the other hand . . ." Ah, my mind takes up, on the other hand the machine does not bleed, ache, hang for hours in the empty sky in a torment of hope to learn the fate of another machine, nor does it cry out with joy nor dance in the air with the fierce passion of a bird. Far off, over a distance greater than space, that remote cry from the heart of heaven makes a faint buzzing among my breakfast dishes and passes on and away.

gyre: a circular or spiral motion.

S. I. HAYAKAWA · *Words, Meanings, and Contexts*

(On being asked to define New Orleans jazz): "Man, when you got to ask what it is, you'll never get to know."

LOUIS ARMSTRONG

Dictionary definitions frequently offer verbal substitutes for an unknown term which only conceal a lack of real understanding. Thus a person might look up a foreign word and be quite satisfied with the meaning "bullfinch" without the slightest ability to identify or describe this bird. Understanding does not come through dealings with words alone, but rather with the things for which they stand. Dictionary definitions permit us to hide from ourselves and others the extent of our ignorance.

H. R. HUSE,
The Illiteracy of the Literate °

[1] It is an almost universal belief that every word has a correct meaning, that we learn these meanings principally from teachers and grammarians (except that most of the time we don't bother to, so that we ordinarily speak "sloppy English"), and that dictionaries and grammars are the supreme authority in matters of meaning and usage. Few people ask by what authority the writers of dictionaries and grammars say what they say. The docility with which most people bow down to the dictionary is amazing, and the person who says, "Well, the dictionary is wrong!" is looked upon as out of his mind.

[2] Let us see how dictionaries are made and how the

° From the *Illiteracy of the Literate* by H. R. Huse, copyright, 1933, by D. Appleton-Century Company, Inc. Reprinted by permission of Appleton-Century-Crofts, Inc.

"Words, Meanings, and Contexts" by S. I. Hayakawa from *Language in Thought and Action.* Copyright, 1939, 1940, by S. I. Hayakawa, copyright, 1941, 1949, by Harcourt, Brace & World, Inc.

editors arrive at definitions. What follows applies, incidentally, only to those dictionary offices where first-
hand, original research goes on—not those in which
editors simply copy existing dictionaries. The task of
writing a dictionary begins with the reading of vast
amounts of the literature of the period or subject that it
is intended to cover. As the editors read, they copy on
cards every interesting or rare word, every unusual or
peculiar occurence of a common word, a large number
of common words in their ordinary uses, and also the
sentences in which each of these words appears, thus:

> pail
>
> The dairy *pails* bring home increase of milk
>> Keats, *Endymion*
>> I, 44–45

[3] That is to say, the context of each word is collected,
along with the word itself. For a really big job of dictionary writing, such as the *Oxford English Dictionary* (usually bound in about twenty-five volumes), millions of
such cards are collected, and the task of editing occupies
decades. As the cards are collected, they are alphabetized
and sorted. When the sorting is completed, there will be
for each word anywhere from two to three to several
hundred illustrative quotations, each on its card.
[4] To define a word, then, the dictionary editor places
before him the stack of cards illustrating that word; each
of the cards represents an actual use of the word by a
writer of some literary or historical importance. He reads
the cards carefully, discards some, rereads the rest, and
divides up the stack according to what he thinks are the
several senses of the word. Finally, he writes his definitions, following the hard-and-fast rule that each definition
must be based on what the quotations in front of him reveal about the meaning of the word. The editor cannot

be influenced by what *he* thinks a given word *ought* to mean. He must work according to the cards, or not at all.

⁵ The writing of a dictionary, therefore, is not a task of setting up authoritative statements about the "true meanings" of words, but a task of *recording,* to the best of one's ability, what various words *have meant* to authors in the distant or immediate past. *The writer of a dictionary is a historian, not a lawgiver.* If, for example, we had been writing a dictionary in 1890, or even as late as 1919, we could have said that the word "broadcast" means "to scatter" (seed and so on) but we could not have decreed that from 1921 on, the commonest meaning of the word should become "to disseminate audible messages, etc., by wireless telephony." To regard the dictionary as an "authority," therefore, is to credit the dictionary writer with gifts of prophecy which neither he nor anyone else possesses. In choosing our words when we speak or write, we can be *guided* by the historical record afforded us by the dictionary, but we cannot be *bound* by it, because new situations, new experiences, new inventions, new feelings, are always compelling us to give new uses to old words. Looking under a "hood," we should ordinarily have found, five hundred years ago, a monk; today, we find a motorcar engine.

⁶ The way in which the dictionary writer arrives at his definitions is merely the systematization of the way in which we all learn the meanings of words, beginning at infancy, and continuing for the rest of our lives. Let us say that we have never heard the word "oboe" before, and we overhear a conversation in which the following sentences occur:

⁷ He used to be the best *oboe* player in town. . . . Whenever they came to that *oboe* part in the third movement, he used to get very excited. . . . I saw him one day at the music shop, buying a new reed for his *oboe.* . . . He never liked to play the clarinet after he started playing the *oboe.* . . . He said it wasn't much fun, because it was too easy.

⁸ Although the word may be unfamiliar, its meaning

becomes clear to us as we listen. After hearing the first sentence, we know that an "oboe" is "played," so that it must be either a game or a musical instrument. With the second sentence the possibility of its being a game is eliminated. With each succeeding sentence the possibilities as to what an "oboe" may be are narrowed down until we get a fairly clear idea of what is meant. This is how we learn by *verbal context*.

⁹ But even independently of this, we learn by physical and social context. Let us say that we are playing golf and that we have hit the ball in a certain way with certain unfortunate results, so that our companion says to us, "That's a bad *slice*." He repeats this remark every time our ball fails to go straight. If we are reasonably bright, we learn in a very short time to say, when it happens again, "That's a bad slice." On one occasion, however, our friend says to us, "That's not a *slice* this time; that's a *hook*." In this case we consider what has happened, and we wonder what is different about the last stroke from those previous. As soon as we make the distinction, we have added still another word to our vocabulary. The result is that after nine holes of golf, we can use both these words accurately—and perhaps several others as well, such as "divot," "number-five iron," "approach shot," *without ever having been told what they mean*. Indeed, we may play golf for years without ever being able to give a dictionary definition of "to slice": "To strike (the ball) so that the face of the club draws inward across the face of the ball, causing it to curve toward the right in flight (with a right-handed player)" (*Webster's New International Dictionary*). But even without being able to give such a definition, we should still be able to use the word accurately whenever the occasion demanded.

¹⁰ We learn the meanings of practically all our words, not from dictionaries, not from definitions, but from hearing these noises as they accompany actual situations in life and learning to associate certain noises with certain

situations. Even as dogs learn to recognize "words," as for example by hearing "biscuit" at the same time as an actual biscuit is held before their noses, so do we all learn to interpret language by being aware of the happenings that accompany the noises people make at us--by being aware, in short, of contexts.

11 The definitions given by little children in school show clearly how they associate words with situations; they almost always define in terms of physical and social contexts: "Punishment is when you have been bad and they put you in a closet and don't let you have any supper." "Newspapers are what the paper boy brings and you wrap up the garbage with it." These are good definitions. The main reason that they cannot be used in dictionaries is that they are too specific; it would be impossible to list the myriads of situations in which every word has been used. For this reason, dictionaries give definitions on a high level of abstraction; that is, with particular references left out for the sake of conciseness. This is another reason why it is a great mistake to regard a dictionary definition as telling us all about a word.

12 From this point on, it will be necessary to employ some special terms in talking about meaning: *extensional meaning,* which will also be referred to as *denotation,* and *intensional meaning*—note the *s*—which will also be referred to as connotation. Briefly explained, the extensional meaning of an utterance is that which it *points to* or denotes in the extensional world. That is to say, the extensional meaning is something that *cannot be expressed in words,* because it is that which words stand for. An easy way to remember this is to put your hand over your mouth and point whenever you are asked to give an extensional meaning.

13 The *intensional meaning* of a word or expression, on the other hand, is that which is *suggested* (connoted) inside one's head. Roughly speaking, whenever we express the meaning of words by uttering more words, we are giving intensional meaning, or connotations. To remem-

ber this, put your hand over your eyes and let the words spin around in your head.

¹⁴ Utterances may have, of course, both extensional and intensional meaning. If they have no intensional meaning at all—that is, if they start no notions whatever spinning about in our heads—they are meaningless noises, like foreign languages that we do not understand. On the other hand, it is possible for utterances to have no extensional meaning at all, in spite of the fact that they may start many notions spinning about in our heads. The statement, "Angels watch over my bed at night," is one that has intensional but no extensional meaning. This does not mean that there are no angels watching over my bed at night. When we say that the statement has no extensional meaning, we are merely saying that we cannot see, touch, photograph, or in any scientific manner detect the presence of angels. The result is that, if an argument begins on the subject whether or not angels watch over my bed, *there is no way of ending the argument to the satisfaction of all disputants,* the Christians and the non-Christians, the pious and the agnostic, the mystical and the scientific. Therefore, whether we believe in angels or not, knowing in advance that any argument on the subject will be both endless and futile, we can avoid getting into fights about it.

¹⁵ When, on the other hand, statements have extensional content, as when we say, "This room is fifteen feet long," arguments can come to a close. No matter how many guesses there are about the length of the room, all discussion ceases when someone produces a tape measure. This, then, is the important difference between extensional and intensional meanings: namely, when utterances have extensional meanings, discussion can be ended and agreement reached; when utterances have intensional meanings only and no extensional meanings, arguments may, and often do, go on indefinitely. Such arguments can result only in irreconcilable conflict. Among individuals, they may result in the breaking up of friendships; in society, they often split organizations into bit-

terly opposed groups; among nations, they may aggravate existing tensions so seriously as to become real obstacles to the peaceful settling of disputes.

16 Arguments of this kind may be termed "non-sense arguments," because they are based on utterances about which no sense data can be collected. Needless to say, there are occasions when the hyphen may be omitted— that depends on one's feelings toward the particular argument under consideration. The reader is requested to provide his own examples of "non-sense arguments." Even the foregoing examples of the angels may give offense to some people, in spite of the fact that no attempt is made to deny or affirm the existence of angels. He can imagine, therefore, the uproar that might result from giving a number of examples from theology, politics, law, economics, literary criticism, and other fields in which it is not customary to distinguish clearly sense from non-sense.

17 Everyone, of course, who has ever given any thought to the meanings of words has noticed that they are always shifting and changing in meaning. Usually, people regard this as a misfortune, because it "leads to sloppy thinking" and "mental confusion." To remedy this condition, they are likely to suggest that we should all agree on "one meaning" for each word and use it only with that meaning. Thereupon it will occur to them that we simply cannot make people agree in this way, even if we could set up an ironclad dictatorship under a committee of lexicographers who would place censors in every newspaper office and microphones in every home. The situation, therefore, appears hopeless.

18 Such an impasse is avoided when we start with a new premise altogether—one of the premises upon which modern linguistic thought is based: namely, that *no word ever has exactly the same meaning twice*. The extent to which this premise fits the facts can be demonstrated in a number of ways. First, if we accept the proposition that the contexts of an utterance determine its meaning, it becomes apparent that since no two contexts are ever *ex-*

actly the same, no two meanings can ever be exactly the same. How can we "fix the meaning" even for so common an expression as "to believe in" when it can be used in such sentences as the following:

I believe in you (I have confidence in you) .
I believe in democracy (I accept the principles implied by the term democracy) .
I believe in Santa Claus (It is my opinion that Santa Claus exists) .

[19] Secondly, we can take, for example, a word of "simple" meaning like "kettle." But when John says "kettle," its intensional meanings to him are the common characteristics of all the kettles John remembers. When Peter says "kettle," however, its intensional meaning to him are the common characteristics of all the kettles he remembers. *No matter how small or how negligible the differences may be between John's "kettle" and Peter's "kettle," there is some difference.*

[20] Finally, let us examine utterances in terms of extensional meanings. If John, Peter, Harold, and George each say "my typewriter," we would have to point to four different typewriters to get the extensional meaning in each case: John's new Underwood, Peter's old Corona, Harold's L. C. Smith, and the undenotable intended "typewriter" that George plans some day to buy: "My typewriter, when I buy one, will be a noiseless." Also, if John says "my typewriter" today, and again "my typewriter" tomorrow, the extensional meaning is different in the two cases, because the typewriter is not exactly the same from one day to the next (nor from one minute to the next) : slow processes of wear, change, and decay are going on constantly. Although we can say, then, that the differences in the meanings of a word on one occasion, on another occasion a minute later, and on still another occasion another minute later, are negligible, we cannot say that the meanings are *exactly* the same.

[21] To say dogmatically that we know what a word means

in advance of its utterance is nonsense. All we can know in advance is *approximately* what it will mean. After the utterance, we interpret what has been said in the light of both verbal and physical contexts and act according to our interpretation. An examination of the verbal context of an utterance, as well as the examination of the utterance itself, directs us to the intensional meanings; an examination of the physical context directs us to the extensional meanings. When John says to James, "Bring me that book, will you?" James looks in the direction of John's pointed finger (physical context) and sees a desk with several books on it (physical context); he thinks back over their previous conversation (verbal context) and knows which of those books is being referred to.

²² Interpretation *must* be based, therefore, on the totality of contexts. If it were otherwise, we should not be able to account for the fact that even if we fail to use the right (customary) words in some situations, people can very frequently understand us. For example:

A: Gosh, look at the second baseman go!
B (looking): You mean the shortstop?
A: Yes, that's what I mean.

A: There must be something wrong with the oil line; the engine has started to balk.
B: Don't you mean "gas line"?
A: Yes—didn't I say gas line?

Contexts sometimes indicate so clearly what we mean that often we do not even have to say what we mean in order to be understood.

²³ It is clear, then, that the ignoring of contexts in any act of interpretation is at best a stupid practice. At its worst, it can be a vicious practice. A common example is the sensational newspaper story in which a few words by a public personage are torn out of their context and made the basis of a completely misleading account. There is the incident of an Armistice Day speaker, a university teacher, who declared before a high-school assembly that

the Gettysburg Address was "a powerful piece of propaganda." The context clearly revealed that "propaganda" was being used according to its dictionary meanings rather than according to its popular meanings; it also revealed that the speaker was a very great admirer of Lincoln's. However, the local newspaper, completely ignoring the context, presented the account in such a way as to convey the impression that the speaker had called Lincoln a liar. On this basis, the newspaper began a campaign against the instructor. The speaker remonstrated with the editor of the newspaper, who replied, in effect, "I don't care what else you said. You said the Gettysburg Address was propaganda, didn't you?" This appeared to the editor complete proof that Lincoln had been maligned and that the speaker deserved to be discharged from his position at the university. Similar practices may be found in advertisements. A reviewer may be quoted on the jacket of a book as having said, "A brilliant work," while reading of the context may reveal that what he really said was, "It just falls short of being a brilliant work." There are some people who will always be able to find a defense for such a practice in saying, "But he did use the words, 'a brilliant work,' didn't he?"

24   People in the course of argument very frequently complain about words meaning different things to different people. Instead of complaining, they should accept it as a matter of course. It would be startling indeed if the word "justice," for example, were to have the same meaning to the nine justices of the United States Supreme Court; we should get nothing but unanimous decisions. It would be even more startling if "justice" meant the same to President Truman as to Joseph Stalin.° If we can get deeply into our consciousness the principle that no word ever has the same meaning twice, we will develop the habit of automatically examining contexts, and this enables us to understand better what others are saying. As it is, however, we are all too likely, when a word

Stalin: President Truman and Joseph Stalin were leaders of the United States and Russia respectively when this piece was written.

sounds familiar, to assume that we understand it even when we don't. In this way we read into people's remarks meanings that were never intended. Then we waste energy in angrily accusing people of "intellectual dishonesty" or "abuse of words," when their only sin is that they use words in ways unlike our own, as they can hardly help doing, especially if their background has been widely different from ours. There are cases of intellectual dishonesty and the abuse of words, of course, but they do not always occur in the places where people think they do.

25 In the study of history or of cultures other than our own, contexts take on special importance. To say, "There was no running water or electricity in the house," does not condemn an English house in 1570, but says a great deal against a house in Chicago in 1949. Again, if we wish to understand the Constitution of the United States, it is not enough, as our historians now tell us, merely to look up all the words in the dictionary and to read the interpretations written by Supreme Court justices. We must see the Constitution in its historical context: the conditions of life, the current ideas, the fashionable prejudices, and the probable interests of the people who drafted the Constitution. After all, the words "The United States of America" stood for quite a different-sized nation and a different culture in 1790 from what they stand for today. When it comes to very big subjects, the range of contexts to be examined, verbal, social, and historical, may become very large indeed.

26 All this is not to say, however, that the reader might just as well throw away his dictionary, since contexts are so important. Any word in a sentence—any sentence in a paragraph, any paragraph in a larger unit—whose meaning is revealed by its context, is itself part of the context of the rest of the text. To look up a word in a dictionary, therefore, frequently explains not only the word itself, but the rest of the sentence, paragraph, conversation, or essay in which it is found. All words within a given context interact upon one another.

[27] Realizing, then, that a dictionary is a historical work, we should understand the dictionary thus: "The word *mother* has most frequently been used in the past among English-speaking people to indicate a female parent." From this we can safely infer, "If that is how it has been used, that is what it *probably* means in the sentence I am trying to understand." This is what we normally do, of course; after we look up a word in the dictionary, we re-examine the context to see if the definition fits. If the context reads, "Mother began to form in the bottle," one may have to look at the dictionary more carefully.

[28] A dictionary definition, therefore, is an invaluable guide to interpretation. Words do not have a single "correct meaning"; they apply to *groups* of similar situations, which might be called *areas of meaning*. It is for definition in terms of areas of meaning that a dictionary is useful. In each use of any word, we examine the particular context and the extensional events denoted (if possible) to discover the *point* intended within the area of meaning.

CHAPTER 16

Narration

STEPHEN CRANE · *The Open Boat*

A Tale Intended to be after the Fact:
Being the Experience of Four Men
from the Sunk Steamer Commodore

I

1   None of them knew the color of the sky. Their eyes glanced level, and were fastened upon the waves that swept toward them. These waves were of the hue of slate, save for the tops, which were of foaming white, and all of the men knew the colors of the sea. The horizon narrowed and widened, and dipped and rose, and at all times its edge was jagged with waves that seemed thrust up in points like rocks.

2   Many a man ought to have a bathtub larger than the boat which here rode upon the sea. These waves were most wrongfully and barbarously abrupt and tall, and each froth-top was a problem in small boat navigation.

3   The cook squatted in the bottom and looked with both eyes at the six inches of gunwale which separated him from the ocean. His sleeves were rolled over his fat forearms, and the two flaps of his unbuttoned vest dangled as he bent to bail out the boat. Often he said: "Gawd! That was a narrow clip." As he remarked it he invariably gazed eastward over the broken sea.

4   The oiler, steering with one of the two oars in the boat,

sometimes raised himself suddenly to keep clear of water that swirled in over the stern. It was a thin little oar and it seemed often ready to snap.

5   The correspondent, pulling at the other oar, watched the waves and wondered why he was there.

6   The injured captain, lying in the bow, was at this time buried in that profound dejection and indifference which comes, temporarily at least, to even the bravest and most enduring when, willy nilly, the firm fails, the army loses, the ship goes down. The mind of the master of a vessel is rooted deep in the timbers of her, though he command for a day or a decade, and this captain had on him the stern impression of a scene in the greys of dawn of seven turned faces, and later a stump of a topmast with a white ball on it that slashed to and fro at the waves, went lower and lower, and down. Thereafter there was something strange in his voice. Although steady, it was deep with mourning, and of a quality beyond oration or tears.

7   "Keep 'er a little more south, Billie," said he.

8   "A little more south, sir," said the oiler in the stern.

9   A seat in this boat was not unlike a seat upon a bucking broncho, and, by the same token, a broncho is not much smaller. The craft pranced and reared, and plunged like an animal. As each wave came, and she rose for it, she seemed like a horse making at a fence outrageously high. The manner of her scramble over these walls of water is a mystic thing, and, moreover, at the top of them were ordinarily these problems in white water, the foam racing down from the summit of each wave, requiring a new leap, and a leap from the air. Then, after scornfully bumping a crest, she would slide, and race, and splash down a long incline, and arrive bobbing and nodding in front of the next menace.

10   A singular disadvantage of the sea lies in the fact that after successfully surmounting one wave you discover that there is another behind it just as important and just as nervously anxious to do something effective in the way of swamping boats. In a ten-foot dingey ° one can get an

dingey: a small boat, also spelled "dinghy."

idea of the resources of the sea in the line of waves that is not probable to the average experience which is never at sea in a dingey. As each slatey wall of water approached, it shut all else from the view of the men in the boat, and it was not difficult to imagine that this particular wave was the final outburst of the ocean, the last effort of the grim water. There was a terrible grace in the move of the waves, and they came in silence, save for the snarling of the crests.

11   In the wan light, the faces of the men must have been gray. Their eyes must have glinted in strange ways as they gazed steadily astern. Viewed from a balcony, the whole thing would doubtless have been weirdly picturesque. But the men in the boat had no time to see it, and if they had had leisure there were other things to occupy their minds. The sun swung steadily up the sky, and they knew it was broad day because the color of the sea changed from slate to emerald-green, streaked with amber lights, and the foam was like tumbling snow. The process of the breaking day was unknown to them. They were aware only of this effect upon the color of the waves that rolled toward them.

12   In disjointed sentences the cook and the correspondent argued as to the difference between a lifesaving station and a house of refuge. The cook had said: "There's a house of refuge just north of the Mosquito Inlet Light, and as soon as they see us, they'll come off in their boat and pick us up."

13   "As soon as who see us?" said the correspondent.

14   "The crew," said the cook.

15   "Houses of refuge don't have crews," said the correspondent. "As I understand them, they are only places where clothes and grub are stored for the benefit of shipwrecked people. They don't carry crews."

16   "Oh, yes, they do," said the cook.

17   "No, they don't," said the correspondent.

18   "Well, we're not there yet, anyhow," said the oiler, in the stern.

19   "Well," said the cook, "perhaps it's not a house of ref-

uge that I'm thinking of as being near Mosquito Inlet Light. Perhaps it's a lifesaving station."

²⁰ "We're not there yet," said the oiler, in the stern.

II

²¹ As the boat bounced from the top of each wave, the wind tore through the hair of the hatless men, and as the craft plopped her stern down again the spray splashed past them. The crest of each of these waves was a hill, from the top of which the men surveyed, for a moment, a broad tumultuous expanse, shining and wind-driven. It was probably splendid. It was probably glorious this play of the free sea, wild with lights of emerald and white and amber.

²² "Bully good thing it's an on-shore wind," said the cook, "If not, where would we be? Wouldn't have a show."

²³ "That's right," said the correspondent.

²⁴ The busy oiler nodded his assent.

²⁵ Then the captain, in the bow, chuckled in a way that expressed humor, contempt, tragedy, all in one. "Do you think we've got much of a show now, boys?" said he.

²⁶ Whereupon the three were silent, save for a trifle of hemming and hawing. To express any particular optimism at this time they felt to be childish and stupid, but they all doubtless possessed this sense of the situation in their mind. A young man thinks doggedly at such times. On the other hand, the ethics of their condition was decidedly against any open suggestion of hopelessness. So they were silent.

²⁷ "Oh, well," said the captain, soothing his children, "we'll get ashore all right."

²⁸ But there was that in his tone which made them think, so the oiler quoth: "Yes! If this wind holds!"

²⁹ The cook was bailing: "Yes! If we don't catch hell in the surf."

³⁰ Canton flannel gulls flew near and far. Sometimes they sat down on the sea, near patches of brown seaweed that rolled over the waves with a movement like carpets

on a line in a gale. The birds sat comfortably in groups, and they were envied by some in the dingey, for the wrath of the sea was no more to them than it was to a covey of prairie chickens a thousand miles inland. Often they came very close and stared at the men with black bead-like eyes. At these times they were uncanny and sinister in their unblinking scrutiny, and the men hooted angrily at them, telling them to be gone. One came, and evidently decided to alight on the top of the captain's head. The bird flew parallel to the boat and did not circle, but made short sidelong jumps in the air in chicken-fashion. His black eyes were wistfully fixed upon the captain's head. "Ugly brute," said the oiler to the bird. "You look as if you were made with a jackknife." The cook and the correspondent swore darkly at the creature. The captain naturally wished to knock it away with the end of the heavy painter; ° but he did not dare do it, because anything resembling an emphatic gesture would have capsized this freighted boat, and so with his open hand, the captain gently and carefully waved the gull away. After it had been discouraged from the pursuit the captain breathed easier on account of his hair, and others breathed easier because the bird struck their minds at this time as being somehow gruesome and ominous.

31 In the meantime the oiler and the correspondent rowed. And also they rowed.

32 They sat together in the same seat, and each rowed an oar. Then the oiler took both oars; then the correspondent took both oars; then the oiler; then the correspondent. They rowed and they rowed. The very ticklish part of the business was when the time came for the reclining one in the stern to take his turn at the oars. By the very last star of truth, it is easier to steal eggs from under a hen than it was to change seats in the dingey. First the man in the stern slid his hand along the thwart ° and moved with care, as if he were of Sèvres.° Then the man

painter: the rope used to make a boat fast.
thwart: a rower's seat reaching athwart a boat.
Sèvres: a costly French porcelain.

in the rowing seat slid his hand along the other thwart. It was all done with the most extraordinary care. As the two sidled past each other, the whole party kept watchful eyes on the coming wave, and the captain cried: "Look out now! Steady there!"

33 The brown mats of seaweed that appeared from time to time were like islands, bits of earth. They were traveling, apparently, neither one way nor the other. They were, to all intents, stationary. They informed the men in the boat that it was making progress slowly toward the land.

34 The captain, rearing cautiously in the bow, after the dingey soared on a great swell, said that he had seen the lighthouse at Mosquito Inlet. Presently the cook remarked that he had seen it. The correspondent was at the oars then, and for some reason he too wished to look at the lighthouse, but his back was toward the far shore and the waves were important, and for some time he could not seize an opportunity to turn his head. But at last there came a wave more gentle than the others, and when at the crest of it he swiftly scoured the western horizon.

35 "See it?" said the captain.

36 "No," said the correspondent slowly, "I didn't see anything."

37 "Look again," said the captain. He pointed. "It's exactly in that direction."

38 At the top of another wave, the correspondent did as he was bid, and this time his eyes chanced on a small still thing on the edge of the swaying horizon. It was precisely like the point of a pin. It took an anxious eye to find a lighthouse so tiny.

39 "Think we'll make it, captain?"

40 "If this wind holds and the boat don't swamp, we can't do much else," said the captain.

41 The little boat, lifted by each towering sea, and splashed viciously by the crests, made progress that in the absence of seaweed was not apparent to those in her. She seemed just a wee thing wallowing, miraculously top up,

at the mercy of five oceans. Occasionally, a great spread of water, like white flames, swarmed into her.

⁴² "Bail her, cook," said the captain serenely.

⁴³ "All right, captain," said the cheerful cook.

III

⁴⁴ It would be difficult to describe the subtle brotherhood of men that was here established on the seas. No one said that it was so. No one mentioned it. But it dwelt in the boat, and each man felt it warm him. They were a captain, an oiler, a cook, and a correspondent, and they were friends, friends in a more curiously iron-bound degree than may be common. The hurt captain, lying against the water-jar in the bow, spoke always in a low voice and calmly, but he could never command a more ready and swiftly obedient crew than the motley three of the dingey. It was more than a mere recognition of what was best for the common safety. There was surely in it a quality that was personal and heartfelt. And after this devotion to the commander of the boat there was this comradeship that the correspondent, for instance, who had been taught to be cynical of men, knew even at the time was the best experience of his life. But no one said that it was so. No one mentioned it.

⁴⁵ "I wish we had a sail," remarked the captain. "We might try my overcoat on the end of an oar and give you two boys a chance to rest." So the cook and the correspondent held the mast and spread wide the overcoat. The oiler steered, and the little boat made good way with her new rig. Sometimes the oiler had to scull° sharply to keep a sea from breaking into the boat, but otherwise sailing was a success.

⁴⁶ Meanwhile the lighthouse had been growing slowly larger. It had now almost assumed color, and appeared like a little gray shadow on the sky. The man at the oars could not be prevented from turning his head rather often to try for a glimpse of this little gray shadow.

scull: to propel a boat by means of oars.

⁴⁷ At last, from the top of each wave the men in the tossing boat could see land. Even as the lighthouse was an upright shadow on the sky, this land seemed but a long black shadow on the sea. It certainly was thinner than paper. "We must be about opposite New Smyrna," said the cook, who had coasted this shore often in schooners. "Captain, by the way, I believe they abandoned that lifesaving station there about a year ago."

⁴⁸ "Did they?" said the captain.

⁴⁹ The wind slowly died away. The cook and the correspondent were not now obliged to slave in order to hold high the oar. But the waves continued their old impetuous swooping at the dingey, and the little craft, no longer under way, struggled woundily over them. The oiler or the correspondent took the oars again.

⁵⁰ Shipwrecks are apropos of nothing. If men could only train for them and have them occur when the men had reached pink condition, there would be less drowning at sea. Of the four in the dingey none had slept any time worth mentioning for two days and two nights previous to embarking in the dingey, and in the excitement of clambering about the deck of a foundering ship they had also forgotten to eat heartily.

⁵¹ For these reasons, and for others, neither the oiler nor the correspondent was fond of rowing at this time. The correspondent wondered ingenuously how in the name of all that was sane could there be people who thought it amusing to row a boat. It was not an amusement; it was a diabolical punishment, and even a genius of mental aberrations could never conclude that it was anything but a horror to the muscles and a crime against the back. He mentioned to the boat in general how the amusement of rowing struck him, and the weary-faced oiler smiled in full sympathy. Previously to the foundering, by the way, the oiler had worked double-watch in the engine-room of the ship.

⁵² "Take her easy, now, boys," said the captain. "Don't spend yourselves. If we have to run a surf you'll need

all your strength, because we'll sure have to swim for it. Take your time."

⁵³ Slowly the land arose from the sea. From a black line it became a line of black and a line of white, trees and sand. Finally, the captain said that he could make out a house on the shore. "That's the house of refuge, sure," said the cook. "They'll see us before long, and come out after us."

⁵⁴ The distant lighthouse reared high. "The keeper ought to be able to make us out now, if he's looking through a glass," said the captain. "He'll notify the life-saving people."

⁵⁵ "None of those other boats could have got ashore to give word of the wreck," said the oiler, in a low voice. "Else the lifeboat would be out hunting us."

⁵⁶ Slowly and beautifully the land loomed out of the sea. The wind came again. It had veered from the north-east to the southeast. Finally, a new sound struck the ears of the men in the boat. It was the low thunder of the surf on the shore. "We'll never be able to make the light-house now," said the captain. "Swing her head a little more north, Billie."

⁵⁷ "A little more north, sir," said the oiler.

⁵⁸ Whereupon the little boat turned her nose once more down the wind, and all but the oarsman watched the shore grow. Under the influence of this expansion doubt and direful apprehension was leaving the minds of the men. The management of the boat was still most absorb-ing, but it could not prevent a quiet cheerfulness. In an hour, perhaps, they would be ashore.

⁵⁹ Their backbones had become thoroughly used to balancing in the boat, and they now rode this wild colt of a dingey like circus men. The correspondent thought that he had been drenched to the skin, but happening to feel in the top pocket of his coat, he found therein eight cigars. Four of them were soaked with sea-water; four were perfectly scatheless. After a search, somebody produced three dry matches, and thereupon the four waifs rode impudently in their little boat, and with an

assurance of an impending rescue shining in their eyes, puffed at the big cigars and judged well and ill of all men. Everybody took a drink of water.

IV

⁶⁰ "Cook," remarked the captain, "there don't seem to be any signs of life about your house of refuge."

⁶¹ "No," replied the cook. "Funny they don't see us!"

⁶² A broad stretch of lowly coast lay before the eyes of the men. It was of low dunes topped with dark vegetation. The roar of the surf was plain, and sometimes they could see the white lip of a wave as it spun up the beach. A tiny house was blocked out black upon the sky. Southward, the slim lighthouse lifted its little gray length.

⁶³ Tide, wind, and waves were swinging the dingey northward. "Funny they don't see us," said the men.

⁶⁴ The surf's roar was here dulled, but its tone was, nevertheless, thunderous and mighty. As the boat swam over the great rollers, the men sat listening to this roar. "We'll swamp sure," said everybody.

⁶⁵ It is fair to say here that there was not a lifesaving station within twenty miles in either direction, but the men did not know this fact, and in consequence they made dark and opprobrious remarks concerning the eyesight of the nation's lifesavers. Four scowling men sat in the dingey and surpassed records in the invention of epithets.

⁶⁶ "Funny they don't see us."

⁶⁷ The light-heartedness of a former time had completely faded. To their sharpened minds it was easy to conjure pictures of all kinds of incompetency and blindness and, indeed, cowardice. There was the shore of the populous land, and it was bitter and bitter to them that from it came no sign.

⁶⁸ "Well," said the captain, ultimately, "I suppose we'll have to make a try for ourselves. If we stay out here too long, we'll none of us have strength left to swim after the boat swamps."

⁶⁹ And so the oiler, who was at the oars, turned the boat

straight for the shore. There was a sudden tightening of muscles. There was some thinking.

70 "If we don't all get ashore—" said the captain. "If we don't all get ashore, I suppose you fellows know where to send news of my finish?"

71 They then briefly exchanged some addresses and admonitions. As for the reflections of the men, there was a great deal of rage in them. Perchance they might be formulated thus: "If I am going to be drowned—if I am going to be drowned—if I am going to be drowned, why, in the name of the seven mad gods who rule the sea, was I allowed to come thus far and contemplate sand and trees? Was I brought here merely to have my nose dragged away as I was about to nibble the sacred cheese of life? It is preposterous. If this old ninny-woman, Fate, cannot do better than this, she should be deprived of the management of men's fortunes. She is an old hen who knows not her intention. If she has decided to drown me, why did she not do it in the beginning and save me all this trouble? The whole affair is absurd. . . . But no, she cannot mean to drown me. She dare not drown me. She cannot drown me. Not after all this work." Afterward the man might have had an impulse to shake his fist at the clouds: "Just you drown me, now, and then hear what I call you!"

72 The billows that came at this time were more formidable. They seemed always just about to break and roll over the little boat in a turmoil of foam. There was a preparatory and long growl in the speech of them. No mind unused to the sea would have concluded that the dingey could ascend these sheer heights in time. The shore was still afar. The oiler was a wily surfman. "Boys," he said swiftly, "she won't live three minutes more, and we're too far out to swim. Shall I take her to sea again, captain?"

73 "Yes! Go ahead!" said the captain.

74 This oiler, by a series of quick miracles, and fast and steady oarsmanship, turned the boat in the middle of the surf and took her safely to sea again.

⁷⁵   There was a considerable silence as the boat bumped over the furrowed sea to deeper water. Then somebody in gloom spoke. "Well, anyhow, they must have seen us from the shore by now."

⁷⁶   The gulls went in slanting flight up the wind toward the gray desolate east. A squall, marked by dingy clouds, and clouds brick-red, like smoke from a burning building, appeared from the southeast.

⁷⁷   "What do you think of those lifesaving people? Ain't they peaches?"

⁷⁸   "Funny they haven't seen us."

⁷⁹   "Maybe they think we're out here for sport! Maybe they think we're fishin'. Maybe they think we're fools."

⁸⁰   It was a long afternoon. A changed tide tried to force them southward, but wind and wave said northward. Far ahead, where coastline, sea, and sky formed their mighty angle, there were little dots which seemed to indicate a city on the shore.

⁸¹   "St. Augustine?"

⁸²   The captain shook his head. "Too near Mosquito Inlet."

⁸³   And the oiler rowed, and then the correspondent rowed. Then the oiler rowed. It was a weary business. The human back can become the seat of more aches and pains than are registered in books for the composite anatomy of a regiment. It is a limited area, but it can become the theater of innumerable muscular conflicts, tangles, wrenches, knots, and other comforts.

⁸⁴   "Did you ever like to row, Billie?" asked the correspondent.

⁸⁵   "No," said the oiler. "Hang it."

⁸⁶   When one exchanged the rowing-seat for a place in the bottom of the boat, he suffered a bodily depression that caused him to be careless of everything save an obligation to wiggle one finger. There was cold sea-water swashing to and fro in the boat, and he lay in it. His head, pillowed on a thwart, was within an inch of the swirl of a wave crest, and sometimes a particularly ob-

streperous sea came in-board and drenched him once more. But these matters did not annoy him. It is almost certain that if the boat had capsized he would have tumbled comfortably out upon the ocean as if he felt sure that it was a great soft mattress.

87 "Look! There's a man on the shore!"

88 "Where?"

89 "There! See 'im? See 'im?"

90 "Yes, sure! He's walking along."

91 "Now he's stopped. Look! He's facing us!"

92 "He's waving at us!"

93 "So he is! By thunder!"

94 "Ah, now we're all right! Now we're all right! There'll be a boat out here for us in half an hour."

95 "He's going on. He's running. He's going up to that house there."

96 The remote beach seemed lower than the sea, and it required a searching glance to discern the little black figure. The captain saw a floating stick and they rowed to it. A bathtowel was by some weird chance in the boat, and, trying this on the stick, the captain waved it. The oarsman did not dare turn his head, so he was obliged to ask questions.

97 "What's he doing now?"

98 "He's standing still again. He's looking, I think. . . . There he goes again. Toward the house. . . . Now he stopped again."

99 "Is he waving at us?"

100 "No, not now! he was, though."

101 "Look! There comes another man!"

102 "He's running."

103 "Look at him go, would you."

104 "Why, he's on a bicycle. Now he's met the other man. They're both waving at us. Look!"

105 "There comes something up the beach."

106 "What the devil is that thing?"

107 "Why, it looks like a boat."

108 "Why, certainly it's a boat."

109 "No, it's on wheels."

¹¹⁰ "Yes, so it is. Well, that must be the lifeboat. They drag them along shore on a wagon.

¹¹¹ "That's the lifeboat, sure."

¹¹² "No, it's—it's an omnibus."

¹¹³ "I tell you it's a lifeboat."

¹¹⁴ "It is not! It's an omnibus. I can see it plain. See? One of these big hotel omnibuses."

¹¹⁵ "By thunder, you're right. It's an omnibus, sure as fate. What do you suppose they are doing with an omnibus? Maybe they are going around collecting the lifecrew, hey?"

¹¹⁶ "That's it, likely. Look! There's a fellow waving a little black flag. He's standing on the steps of the omnibus. There come those other two fellows. Now they're all talking together. Look at the fellow with the flag. Maybe he ain't waving it."

¹¹⁷ "That ain't a flag, is it? That's his coat. Why, certainly, that's his coat."

¹¹⁸ "So it is. It's his coat. He's taken it off and is waving it around his head. But would you look at him swing it."

¹¹⁹ "Oh, say, there isn't any lifesaving station there. That's just a winter resort hotel omnibus that has brought over some of the boarders to see us drown."

¹²⁰ "What's that idiot with the coat mean? What's he signaling, anyhow?"

¹²¹ "It looks as if he were trying to tell us to go north. There must be a lifesaving station up there."

¹²² "No! He thinks we're fishing. Just giving us a merry hand. See? Ah, there, Willie."

¹²³ "Well, I wish I could make something out of those signals. What do you suppose he means?"

¹²⁴ "He don't mean anything. He's just playing."

¹²⁵ "Well, if he'd just signal us to try the surf again, or to go to sea and wait, or go north, or go south, or go to Hell—there would be some reason in it. But look at him. He just stands there and keeps his coat revolving like a wheel. The ass!"

¹²⁶ "There come more people."

[127] "Now there's quite a mob. Look! Isn't that a boat?"

[128] "Where? Oh, I see where you mean. No, that's no boat."

[129] "That fellow is still waving his coat."

[130] "He must think we like to see him do that. Why don't he quit it? It don't mean anything."

[131] "I don't know. I think he is trying to make us go north. It must be that there's a lifesaving station there somewhere."

[132] "Say, he ain't tired yet. Look at 'im wave."

[133] "Wonder how long he can keep that up. He's been revolving his coat ever since he caught sight of us. He's an idiot. Why aren't they getting men to bring a boat out? A fishing boat—one of those big yawls—could come out here all right. Why don't he do something?"

[134] "Oh, it's all right, now."

[135] "They'll have a boat out here for us in less than no time, now that they've seen us."

[136] A faint yellow tone came into the sky over the low land. The shadows on the sea slowly deepened. The wind bore coldness with it, and the men began to shiver.

[137] "Holy smoke!" said one, allowing his voice to express his impious mood, "if we keep on monkeying out here! If we've got to flounder out here all night!"

[138] "Oh, we'll never have to stay here all night! Don't you worry. They've seen us now, and it won't be long before they'll come chasing out after us."

[139] The shore grew dusky. The man waving a coat blended gradually into this gloom, and it swallowed in the same manner the omnibus and the group of people. The spray, when it dashed uproariously over the side, made the voyagers shrink and swear like men who were being branded.

[140] "I'd like to catch the chump who waved that coat. I feel like soaking him one, just for luck."

[141] "Why? What did he do?"

[142] "Oh, nothing, but then he seemed so cheerful."

[143] In the meantime the oiler rowed, and then the correspondent rowed, and then the oiler rowed. Gray-faced

and bowed forward, they mechanically, turn by turn, plied the leaden oars. The form of the lighthouse had vanished from the southern horizon, but finally a pale star appeared, just lifting from the sea. The streaked saffron in the west passed before the all-merging darkness, and the sea to the east was black. The land had vanished, and was expressed only by the low and drear thunder of the surf.

144 "If I am going to be drowned—if I am going to be drowned—if I am going to be drowned, why, in the name of the seven mad gods who rule the sea, was I allowed to come thus far and contemplate sand and trees? Was I brought here merely to have my nose dragged away as I was about to nibble the sacred cheese of life?"

145 The patient captain, drooped over the water-jar, was sometimes obliged to speak to the oarsman.

146 "Keep her head up! Keep her head up!"

147 " 'Keep her head up,' sir." The voices were weary and low.

148 This was surely a quiet evening. All save the oarsman lay heavily and listlessly in the boat's bottom. As for him, his eyes were just capable of noting the tall black waves that swept forward in a most sinister silence, save for an occasional subdued growl of a crest.

149 The cook's head was on a thwart, and he looked without interest at the water under his nose. He was deep in other scenes. Finally he spoke. "Billie," he murmured, dreamfully, "what kind of pie do you like best?"

v

150 "Pie," said the oiler and the correspondent, agitatedly. "Don't talk about those things, blast you!"

151 "Well," said the cook, "I was just thinking about ham sandwiches, and—"

152 A night on the sea in an open boat is a long night. As darkness settled finally, the shine of the light, lifting from the sea in the south, changed to full gold. On the northern horizon a new light appeared, a small bluish gleam on the edge of the waters. These two lights were the fur-

niture of the world. Otherwise there was nothing but waves.

153   Two men huddled in the stern, and distances were so magnificent in the dingey that the rower was enabled to keep his feet partly warmed by thrusting them under his companions. Their legs indeed extended far under the rowing-seat until they touched the feet of the captain forward. Sometimes, despite the efforts of the tired oarsman, a wave came piling into the boat, an icy wave of the night, and the chilling water soaked them anew. They would twist their bodies for a moment and groan, and sleep the dead sleep once more, while the water in the boat gurgled about them as the craft rocked.

154   The plan of the oiler and the correspondent was for one to row until he lost the ability, and then arouse the other from his sea-water couch in the bottom of the boat.

155   The oiler plied the oars until his head drooped forward, and the overpowering sleep blinded him. And he rowed yet afterward. Then he touched a man in the bottom of the boat, and called his name. "Will you spell me for a little while?" he said meekly.

156   "Sure, Billie," said the correspondent, awakening and dragging himself to a sitting position. They exchanged places carefully, and the oiler, cuddling down in the sea-water at the cook's side, seemed to go to sleep instantly.

157   The particular violence of the sea had ceased. The waves came without snarling. The obligation of the man at the oars was to keep the boat headed so that the tilt of the rollers would not capsize her, and to preserve her from filling when the crests rushed past. The black waves were silent and hard to be seen in the darkness. Often one was almost upon the boat before the oarsman was aware.

158   In a low voice the correspondent addressed the captain. He was not sure that the captain was awake, although this iron man seemed to be always awake. "Captain, shall I keep her making for that light north, sir?"

159   The same steady voice answered him. "Yes. Keep it about two points off the port bow."

[160] The cook had tied a lifebelt around himself in order to get even the warmth which this clumsy cork contrivance could donate, and he seemed almost stovelike when a rower, whose teeth invariably chattered wildly as soon as he ceased his labor, dropped down to sleep.

[161] The correspondent, as he rowed, looked down at the two men sleeping underfoot. The cook's arm was around the oiler's shoulders, and, with their fragmentary clothing and haggard faces, they were the babes of the sea, a grotesque rendering of the old babes in the wood.

[162] Later he must have grown stupid at his work, for suddenly there was a growling of water, and a crest came with a roar and a swash into the boat, and it was a wonder that it did not set the cook afloat in his lifebelt. The cook continued to sleep, but the oiler sat up, blinking his eyes and shaking with the new cold.

[163] "Oh, I'm awful sorry, Billie," said the correspondent, contritely.

[164] "That's all right, old boy," said the oiler, and lay down again and was asleep.

[165] Presently it seemed that even the captain dozed, and the correspondent thought that he was the one man afloat on all the oceans. The wind had a voice as it came over the waves, and it was sadder than the end.

[166] There was a long, loud swishing astern of the boat, and a gleaming trail of phosphorescence, like blue flame, was furrowed on the black waters. It might have been made by a monstrous knife.

[167] Then there came a stillness, while the correspondent breathed with the open mouth and looked at the sea.

[168] Suddenly there was another swish and another long flash of bluish light, and this time it was alongside the boat, and might almost have been reached with an oar. The correspondent saw an enormous fin speed like a shadow through the water, hurling the crystalline spray and leaving the long glowing trail.

[169] The correspondent looked over his shoulder at the captain. His face was hidden, and he seemed to be asleep. He looked at the babes of the sea. They certainly were

asleep. So, being bereft of sympathy, he leaned a little way to one side and swore softly into the sea.

170   But the thing did not then leave the vicinity of the boat. Ahead or astern, on one side or the other, at intervals long or short, fled the long sparkling streak, and there was to be heard the whiroo of the dark fin. The speed and power of the thing was greatly to be admired. It cut the water like a gigantic and keen projectile.

171   The presence of this biding thing did not affect the man with the same horror that it would if he had been a picnicker. He simply looked at the sea dully and swore in an undertone.

172   Nevertheless, it is true that he did not wish to be alone with the thing. He wished one of his companions to awaken by chance and keep him company with it. But the captain hung motionless over the water-jar, and the oiler and the cook in the bottom of the boat were plunged in slumber.

VI

173   "If I am going to be drowned—if I am going to be drowned—if I am going to be drowned, why, in the name of the seven mad gods who rule the sea, was I allowed to come thus far and contemplate sand and trees?"

174   During this dismal night, it may be remarked that a man would conclude that it was really the intention of the seven mad gods to drown him, despite the abominable injustice of it. For it was certainly an abominable injustice to drown a man who had worked so hard, so hard. The man felt it would be a crime most unnatural. Other people had drowned at sea since galleys swarmed with painted sails, but still--

175   When it occurs to a man that nature does not regard him as important, and that she feels she would not maim the universe by disposing of him, he at first wishes to throw bricks at the temple, and he hates deeply the fact that there are no bricks and no temples. Any visible expression of nature would surely be pelleted with his jeers.

176   Then, if there be no tangible thing to hoot he feels,

perhaps, the desire to confront a personification and indulge in pleas, bowed to one knee, and with hands supplicant, saying: "Yes, but I love myself."

177   A high cold star on a winter's night is the word he
feels that she says to him. Thereafter he knows the pathos
of his situation.

178   The men in the dingey had not discussed these matters, but each had, no doubt, reflected upon them in silence and according to his mind. There was seldom any
expression upon their faces save the general one of complete weariness. Speech was devoted to the business of the
boat.

179   To chime the notes of his emotion, a verse mysteriously entered the correspondent's head. He had even forgotten that he had forgotten this verse, but it suddenly
was in his mind.

A soldier of the Legion lay dying in Algiers,
There was lack of woman's nursing, there was dearth of
*   woman's tears;*
But a comrade stood beside him, and he took that com
*   rade's hand,*
And he said: "I never more shall see my own, my native
*   land."*

180   In his childhood, the correspondent had been made
acquainted with the fact that a soldier of the Legion lay
dying in Algiers, but he had never regarded the fact as
important. Myriads of his school-fellows had informed
him of the soldier's plight, but the dinning had naturally
ended by making him perfectly indifferent. He had never
considered it his affair that a soldier of the Legion lay
dying in Algiers, nor had it appeared to him as a matter
for sorrow. It was less to him than the breaking of a pencil's point.

181   Now, however, it quaintly came to him as a human,
living thing. It was no longer merely a picture of a few
throes in the breast of a poet, meanwhile drinking tea
and warming his feet at the grate; it was an actuality—
stern, mournful, and fine.

¹⁸² The correspondent plainly saw the soldier. He lay on the sand with his feet out straight and still. While his pale left hand was upon his chest in an attempt to thwart the going of his life, the blood came between his fingers. In the far Algerian distance, a city of low square forms was set against a sky that was faint with the last sunset hues. The correspondent, plying the oars and dreaming of the slow and slower movements of the lips of the soldier, was moved by a profound and perfectly impersonal comprehension. He was sorry for the soldier of the Legion who lay dying in Algiers.

¹⁸³ The thing which had followed the boat and waited had evidently grown bored at the delay. There was no longer to be heard the slash of the cutwater, and there was no longer the flame of the long trail. The light in the north still glimmered, but it was apparently no nearer to the boat. Sometimes the boom of the surf rang in the correspondent's ears, and he turned the craft seaward then and rowed harder. Southward, someone had evidently built a watch-fire on the beach. It was too low and too far to be seen, but it made a shimmering, roseate reflection upon the bluff back of it, and this could be discerned from the boat. The wind came stronger, and sometimes a wave suddenly raged out like a mountain-cat, and there was to be seen the sheen and sparkle of a broken crest.

¹⁸⁴ The captain, in the bow, moved on his water-jar and sat erect. "Pretty long night," he observed to the correspondent. He looked at the shore. "Those lifesaving people take their time."

¹⁸⁵ "Did you see that shark playing around?"

¹⁸⁶ "Yes, I saw him. He was a big fellow, all right."

¹⁸⁷ "Wish I had known you were awake."

¹⁸⁸ Later the correspondent spoke into the bottom of the boat.

¹⁸⁹ "Billie!" There was a slow and gradual disentanglement. "Billie, will you spell me?"

¹⁹⁰ "Sure," said the oiler.

¹⁹¹ As soon as the correspondent touched the cold com-

fortable sea-water in the bottom of the boat, and had huddled close to the cook's lifebelt he was deep in sleep, despite the fact that his teeth played all the popular airs. This sleep was so good to him that it was but a moment before he heard a voice call his name in a tone that demonstrated the last stages of exhaustion. "Will you spell me?"

192 "Sure, Billie."

193 The light in the north had mysteriously vanished, but the correspondent took his course from the wide-awake captain.

194 Later in the night they took the boat farther out to sea, and the captain directed the cook to take one oar at the stern and keep the boat facing the seas. He was to call out if he should hear the thunder of the surf. This plan enabled the oiler and the correspondent to get respite together. "We'll give those boys a chance to get into shape again," said the captain. They curled down and, after a few preliminary chatterings and trembles, slept once more the dead sleep. Neither knew they had bequeathed to the cook the company of another shark, or perhaps the same shark.

195 As the boat caroused on the waves, spray occasionally bumped over the side and gave them a fresh soaking, but this had no power to break their repose. The ominous slash of the wind and the water affected them as it would have affected mummies.

196 "Boys," said the cook, with the notes of every reluctance in his voice, "she's drifted in pretty close. I guess one of you had better take her to sea again." The correspondent, aroused, heard the crash of the toppled crests.

197 As he was rowing, the captain gave him some whisky-and-water, and this steadied the chills out of him. "If I ever get ashore and anybody shows me even a photograph of an oar—"

198 At last there was a short conversation.

199 "Billie . . . Billie, will you spell me?"

200 "Sure," said the oiler.

VII

201 When the correspondent again opened his eyes, the sea and the sky were each of the gray hue of the dawning. Later, carmine and gold was painted upon the waters. The morning appeared finally, in its splendor, with a sky of pure blue, and the sunlight flamed on the tips of the waves.

202 On the distant dunes were set many little black cottages, and a tall white windmill reared above them. No man, nor dog, nor bicycle appeared on the beach. The cottages might have formed a deserted village.

203 The voyagers scanned the shore. A conference was held in the boat. "Well," said the captain, "if no help is coming, we might better try a run through the surf right away. If we stay out here much longer we will be too weak to do anything for ourselves at all." The others silently acquiesced in this reasoning. The boat was headed for the beach. The correspondent wondered if none ever ascended the tall wind-tower, and if then they never looked seaward. This tower was a giant, standing with its back to the plight of the ants. It represented in a degree, to the correspondent, the serenity of nature amid the struggles of the individual—nature in the wind, and nature in the vision of men. She did not seem cruel to him then, nor beneficent, nor treacherous, nor wise. But she was indifferent, flatly indifferent. It is, perhaps, plausible that a man in this situation, impressed with the unconcern of the universe, should see the innumerable flaws of his life, and have them taste wickedly in his mind and wish for another chance. A distinction between right and wrong seems absurdly clear to him, then, in this new ignorance of the grave-edge, and he understands that if he were given another opportunity he would mend his conduct and his words, and be better and brighter during an introduction or at a tea.

204 "Now, boys," said the captain, "she is going to swamp sure. All we can do is to work her in as far as possible, and then when she swamps, pile out and scramble for the beach. Keep cool now, and don't jump until she swamps sure."

205 The oiler took the oars. Over his shoulders he scanned the surf. "Captain," he said, "I think I'd better bring her about, and keep her head-on to the seas and back her in."

206 "All right, Billie," said the captain. "Back her in." The oiler swung the boat then and, seated in the stern, the cook and the correspondent were obliged to look over their shoulders to contemplate the lonely and indifferent shore.

207 The monstrous in-shore rollers heaved the boat high until the men were again enabled to see the white sheets of water scudding up the slanted beach. "We won't get in very close," said the captain. Each time a man could wrest his attention from the rollers, he turned his glance toward the shore, and in the expression of the eyes during this contemplation there was a singular quality. The correspondent, observing the others, knew that they were not afraid, but the full meaning of their glances was shrouded.

208 As for himself, he was too tired to grapple fundamentally with the fact. He tried to coerce his mind into thinking of it, but the mind was dominated at this time by the muscles, and the muscles said they did not care. It merely occurred to him that if he should drown it would be a shame.

209 There were no hurried words, no pallor, no plain agitation. The men simply looked at the shore. "Now, remember to get well clear of the boat when you jump," said the captain.

210 Seaward the crest of a roller suddenly fell with a thunderous crash, and the long white comber ° came roaring down upon the boat.

211 "Steady now," said the captain. The men were silent. They turned their eyes from the shore to the comber and

comber: a long curling **wave**.

waited. The boat slid up the incline, leaped at the furious top, bounced over it, and swung down the long back of the waves. Some water had been shipped and the cook bailed it out.

212   But the next crest crashed also. The tumbling boiling flood of white water caught the boat and whirled it almost perpendicular. Water swarmed in from all sides. The correspondent had his hands on the gunwale ° at this time, and when the water entered at that place he swiftly withdrew his fingers, as if he objected to wetting them.

213   The little boat, drunken with this weight of water, reeled and snuggled deeper into the sea.

214   "Bail her out, cook! Bail her out," said the captain.

215   "All right, captain," said the cook.

216   "Now, boys, the next one will do for us, sure," said the oiler. "Mind to jump clear of the boat."

217   The third wave moved forward, huge, furious, implacable. It fairly swallowed the dingey, and almost simultaneously the men tumbled into the sea. A piece of lifebelt had lain in the bottom of the boat, and as the correspondent went overboard he held this to his chest with his left hand.

218   The January water was icy, and he reflected immediately that it was colder than he had expected to find it off the coast of Florida. This appeared to his dazed mind as a fact important enough to be noted at the time. The coldness of the water was sad; it was tragic. This fact was somehow so mixed and confused with his opinion of his own situation that it seemed almost a proper reason for tears. The water was cold.

219   When he came to the surface he was conscious of little but the noisy water. Afterward he saw his companions in the sea. The oiler was ahead in the race. He was swimming strongly and rapidly. Off to the correspondent's left, the cook's great white and corked back bulged out of the water, and in the rear the captain was hanging with his one good hand to the keel of the overturned dingey.

220   There is a certain immovable quality to a shore, and

gunwale: the upper edge of a boat's side.

the correspondent **wondered** at it amid the confusion of the sea.

221 It seemed also very attractive, but the correspondent knew that it was a long journey, and he paddled leisurely. The piece of life preserver lay under him, and sometimes he whirled down the incline of a wave as if he were on a hand-sled.

222 But finally he arrived at a place in the sea where travel was beset with difficulty. He did not pause swimming to inquire what manner of current had caught him, but there his progress ceased. The shore was set before him like a bit of scenery on a stage, and he looked at it and understood with his eyes each detail of it.

223 As the cook passed, much farther to the left, the captain was calling to him, "Turn over on your back, cook! Turn over on your back and use the oar."

224 "All right, sir." The cook turned on his back, and, paddling with an oar, went ahead as if he were a canoe.

225 Presently the boat also passed to the left of the correspondent with the captain clinging with one hand to the keel.° He would have appeared like a man raising himself to look over a board fence, if it were not for the extraordinary gymnastics of the boat. The correspondent marvelled that the captain could still hold to it.

226 They passed on, nearer to shore—the oiler, the cook, the captain—and following them went the water-jar, bouncing gaily over the seas.

227 The correspondent remained in the grip of this strange new enemy—a current. The shore, with its white slope of sand and its green bluff, topped with little silent cottages, was spread like a picture before him. It was very near to him then, but he was impressed as one who in a gallery looks at a scene from Brittany or Algiers.

228 He thought: "I am going to drown? Can it be possible? Can it be possible? Can it be possible?" Perhaps an individual must consider his own death to be the final phenomenon of nature.

keel: the longitudinal timber extending along the center of the bottom of a boat.

329   But later a wave perhaps whirled him out of this small deadly current, for he found suddenly that he could again make progress toward the shore. Later still, he was aware that the captain, clinging with one hand to the keel of the dingey, had his face turned away from the shore and toward him, and was calling his name, "Come to the boat! Come to the boat!!"

330   In his struggle to reach the captain and the boat, he reflected that when one gets properly wearied, drowning must really be a comfortable arrangement, a cessation of hostilities accompanied by a large degree of relief, and he was glad of it, for the main thing in his mind for some moments had been horror of the temporary agony. He did not wish to be hurt.

331   Presently he saw a man running along the shore. He was undressing with most remarkable speed. Coat, trousers, shirt, everything flew magically off him.

332   "Come to the boat," called the captain.

333   "All right, captain." As the correspondent paddled, he saw the captain let himself down to bottom and leave the boat. Then the correspondent performed his one little marvel of the voyage. A large wave caught him and flung him with ease and supreme speed completely over the boat and far beyond it. It struck him even then as an event in gymnastics, and a true miracle of the sea. An overturned boat in the surf is not a plaything to a swimming man.

334   The correspondent arrived in water that reached only to his waist, but his condition did not enable him to stand for more than a moment. Each wave knocked him into a heap, and the undertow pulled at him.

335   Then he saw the man who had been running and undressing, and undressing and running, come bounding into the water. He dragged ashore the cook, and then waded toward the captain, but the captain waved him away, and sent him to the correspondent. He was naked, naked as a tree in winter, but a halo was about his head, and he shone like a saint. He gave a strong pull, and a long drag, and a bully heave at the correspondent's hand.

The correspondent, schooled in the minor formulæ, said: "Thanks, old man." But suddenly the man cried: "What's that?" He pointed a swift finger. The correspondent said: "Go."

[236] In the shallows, face downward, lay the oiler. His forehead touched sand that was periodically, between each wave, clear of the sea.

[237] The correspondent did not know all that transpired afterward. When he achieved safe ground he fell, striking the sand with each particular part of his body. It was as if he had dropped from a roof, but the thud was grateful to him.

[238] It seems that instantly the beach was populated with men, with blankets, clothes, and flasks, and women with coffeepots and all the remedies sacred to their minds. The welcome of the land to the men from the sea was warm and generous, but a still and dripping shape was carried slowly up the beach, and the land's welcome for it could only be the different and sinister hospitality of the grave.

[239] When it came night, the white waves paced to and fro in the moonlight, and the wind brought the sound of the great sea's voice to the men on shore, and they felt that they could then be interpreters.

GLOSSARY

Analogy. An agreement or likeness between two things (because of some point or points held in common); sometimes called extended comparison. For example, the analogy between sleep and death lies in passivity and serenity. Analogies can be made between the heart and a pump, between the eyes of a man and the windows of a house, and so forth.

Caricature. A picture or description characterized by gross exaggeration or distortion.

Cliché. A stale, worn-out phrase or idea; for example, "accidents will happen" or "easy come, easy go" or "last but not least."

Climax. The highest point or culmination of an argument or an action. We use the term *anticlimax* to describe those arguments or actions which are markedly of less importance than the climax which preceded.

Coherence. The continuity or logical flow from one point to another in a composition; the interrelation of the various parts of a composition and of the ideas within those parts.

Colloquialism. An expression acceptable in ordinary conversation, friendly letters, or informal writing but unsuited to formal speech or writing; for example, "He's done a *bang-up* job" or "Early that morning we *hit the road*."

Connotation. The suggestions or associations, often emotional, aroused by a word, beyond its dictionary definition. "Home" connotes family, tradition, continuity. "Red" connotes anger, passion, danger, and Communist Russia.

Deduction. Reasoning from the general to the particular or from a given premise to a logical conclusion.

Denotation. The primary or dictionary definition of a word, as opposed to its connotations or associated meanings.

Diction. Choice of words or mode of expression.

Emphasis. The arrangement of the various elements of a composition in an order best calculated to make the reader aware of, and sympathetic to, the writer's purpose.

Hyperbole. A figure of speech based on exaggeration: "mountainous waves" or "millions of friends."

Hypothesis. A tentative theory or proposition offered as the explanation of certain phenomena.

Idiom. The form of expression or construction peculiar to a language, approved by usage, and sometimes having a meaning other than its grammatical or logical one; for example, "He *carried out* his assignment" or "When you come to town, please *drop in*."

Imagery. The representation of any sense experience; not merely word pictures but also sounds, smells, and tastes put into words.

Induction. Reasoning from the particular to the general or from a series of established facts numerous and convincing enough to lead to a general conclusion.

Irony. A mode of expression which involves a contrast between what is said or stated and what is suggested or understood. Ironic statements say one thing and imply the opposite. An example is Antony's repeated statement, "Brutus is an honorable man," in his famous oration in *Julius Caesar*. They sometimes employ *un-*

derstatement (saying less than the situation warrants, such as describing a hurricane as a small shower) or *paradox* (making statements seemingly contradictory or opposed to common sense but which, on examination, prove to be true).

Linguistics. The study of human speech including the origin, structure, and modification of language.

Metaphor. An implied comparison between essentially unlike things; for example, "His mind is an unweeded garden" or "Jealousy is a green-eyed monster."

Objective. An *objective* treatment implies a certain detachment on the author's part toward the material of the essay or story. He is not likely to involve himself or his personal feelings in the matter discussed. A *subjective* treatment is often highly colored by the author's own feelings, impressions, or memory. *Purely* objective or subjective writing is, of course, rare.

Paradox. See *irony*.

Pathos. The sense of pity or sympathetic sorrow. When a writer tries to elicit pathos from a situation or character that does not legitimately induce this reaction, we call the effect *bathos*.

Personification. The attributing of human characteristics to inanimate objects or abstract ideas; for example, "The land shows its ravaged face" or "The streets wander aimlessly about."

Plot. The sequence, plan, or structure which the author chooses in arranging the events of his narrative so as to make the meaning clear and the incidents exciting.

Point of emphasis. The author's primary motive for writing his narrative; for example, to relate a chain of events, to describe a character or place, to stress a theme, or to propound a moral.

Point of view. The relationship of the narrator to the story being told. The simplest method is *first person main character:* the narrator tells his own story. Three other methods are *first person observer:* the narrator tells a story he has observed; *limited omniscient narrator:* the author tells the story but from the viewpoint of only one character in the story; and *omniscient narrator:* the author tells the story, recording the thoughts of all characters, commenting on any part of the action, describing anything he wishes.

Sarcasm. Harsh or taunting remarks, expressing contempt, usually ironical.

Satire. A method of writing in which vices and abuses are held up for ridicule. The satirist generally wishes to correct that which he scorns. In the course of writing his satire, he may employ *irony* and/or *sarcasm.*

Semantics. The study of the meanings of words, changes of meanings, and human responses to meanings.

Sensory impressions. Strong effects produced in the intellect or feelings by way of the five senses.

Setting. The physical place or locale of a story.

Simile. An explicit comparison between two essentially unlike things, introduced by *like* or *as;* for example, "Her skin was as soft as a cloud" or "She had a voice like the north wind in January."

Style. A comprehensive term, indicating the author's distinctive mode of expression, that which marks his work with individual characteristics. An author might be known for his terse style (exceedingly clear and concise) or his ornate style (excessively embellished with figures of speech) .

Subjective. See *objective.*

Syllogism. In logic, deductive reasoning is framed in a syllogism, that is, in the form of two statements or premises that are so connected that the third statement or conclusion necessarily follows. For example, "All men are mortal; John is a man; therefore, John is mortal." The formula can be written: $A = B$, $C = A$, therefore, $C = B$.

Symbol. An object or character which *stands for* something else; a material object representing something immaterial; an emblem, token, or sign. In chemistry, Cl stands for chlorine; in mathematics ∞ stands for infinity. In art and literature, white is usually a symbol of purity or innocence; the serpent is a symbol of evil or Satan or temptation; the lion is a symbol of strength, St. Mark, and Great Britain, among other things.

Theme. The main or central point of a composition. The theme unites a composition as the topic sentence unites a paragraph.

Tone. A term most frequently used when speaking of music and acoustics or of color. But it is also used in writing to mean the manner of expression the author uses, his attitude toward his subject. His tone may be flippant or formal or insulting, for example.

Topic sentence. The sentence in the paragraph, usually the first, which announces the subject of the paragraph.

Understatement. See *irony*.

Unity. The consistent relationship of all the elements of a composition to the central theme. The root principles of unity are (1) a clearly defined purpose, and (2) an orderly means of achieving that purpose.

Whimsy. A capricious kind of wit, the product of an odd and playful fancy.

INDEX

M   7
N   8
O   9
P   0
    1

CAPITALIZATION STYLE SHEET

Mexico City — a city in Mexico
Ocala National Forest — our national forests
Twenty-ninth Street — across the street
the South — a mile south
North America — northern Wisconsin
the Explorers' Club — a club for explorers
Ford Motor Company — an automobile company
Central High School — a new high school
Pomona College — four years in college
the American Revolution — a successful revolution
the Wrigley Building — a Chicago building
the Fourth of July — the fifth of July
the Freshman Class — freshman classes
English, French, Latin — social studies, physics, art
History II — a course in world history
Winter's frosty breath — spring, summer, winter, fall
Principal Langley — Mr. Langley, the principal
the President (U.S.) — the president of our club
God made His will known — tribal gods of the Indians
Don't tell Mother (or mother) — Don't tell my mother
Ivory soap
the Democratic party
a Negro, a Presbyterian, a Swede
The Last of the Mohicans, the Reader's Digest

PUNCTUATION STYLE SHEET
Comma

Fred, Harry, and Joe or Fred, Harry and Joe
Fred and Harry and Joe
A tall, thin, emaciated man
A tall, thin young man
My brother George, a freshman at Cornell, went ...
I knew, therefore, that he was right.
I therefore knew that he was right.
Address me at 222 Twin Oaks Road, Akron 3, Ohio, after March 10.
A student who is late must stay after school.
John, who was late, must stay after school.
When the weather is bad, we practice indoors.
We practice indoors when the weather is bad.
Sensing the danger, the dog barked.
Helen offered to help, but she did not show up.
Helen offered to help but did not show up.
The football team won all but two games, and one of these was a tie.

Semicolon

The football team won all but two games; one of these was a tie.
Each student takes several standardized tests; for example, the D
STEP, SAT, and ACE.
The delegates were Carol Woodson, High School of Commerce; Rand
Howe, Technical Trade School; and Ellery Glaeser, Classical Sen
High School.

Colon

They asked me to bring the following items: flashlight, raincoat, blank
and matches.

Apostrophe

It's late.
I like its lines.
Let's go!
a man's hat
men's clothing
a girl's coat
two girls' coats
Ulysses' pen

Hyphen

dem-on-strate (not demonstr-ate)
com-mand, hap-py
will-ing, at-ten-tion
thirty-three students
a two-thirds majority
two thirds of the students
a second-story room
a room in the second story

Italics and Quotation Marks

A Tale of Two Cities
the Saturday Evening Post
the New York Times, or New York Times
"Casey at the Bat" (poem)
"The Devil and Daniel Webster" (story)
Mother said, "You may drive."
Mother said I might drive.
"Drive carefully," he warned. "Speed causes accidents."
"Drive carefully," he warned, "because speed causes accidents."
"We won!" Jack shouted. "Did you hear Bill say, 'We won!'?"

CORRECTION SYMBOLS

ms	error in manuscript form or neatness	**nc**	not clear
cap	error in use of capital letters	**‖**	run-on sentence or begin sentence here
	error in punctuation	**gr**	error in grammar
sp	error in spelling	**w**	error in word choice
frag	sentence fragment	**¶**	Begin a new paragraph here.
ss	error in sentence structure	**t**	error in tense
ref	unclear or incorrect reference of pronoun	**∧**	You have omitted something.
	awkward sentence		

The errors ms, sp, ss, k, nc should be rewritten on a separate correction sheet attached to the composition, or, if there is space, on the final page of the composition. Each error requiring rewriting should be numbered in the margin of the composition and marked with the same number on the correction sheet. As indicated in the "Passage Corrected by the Student" on the opposite page, errors which do not require writing a whole sentence are to be corrected on the composition at the place where the error occurs.

Example of Symbols in Margin of a Composition

∧ sp   Our games are lessons noble liveing. The

frag   playing field is in truth a school. Which

teaches the laws of honor. They ring through

‖   every game, they are blazoned above every

playing field. They are among the oldest and

p gr   the most enduring things in the World. Underlaying

p   every sport however often men may forget

it is the maxim "a fair field and no

ss   favor." Learned on the field, a player can

apply the lessons in honorable behavior during

ref   the rest of their life.

YMBOLS

ript form	**nc**	not clear
	‖	run-on sentence or begin sentence here
apital letters	**gr**	error in grammar
tion	**w**	error in word choice
	¶	Begin a new paragraph here.
ent		
e structure	**t**	error in tense
rect reference of	**∧**	You have omitted something.
ce		

, **k, nc** should be rewritten on a separate correc-
the composition, or, if there is space, on the final
tion. Each error requiring rewriting should be
n of the composition and marked with the same
on sheet. As indicated in the "Passage Corrected
he opposite page, errors which do not require
ence are to be corrected on the composition at
ror occurs.

in Margin of a Composition

ames are lessons noble liveing.   The

eld is in truth a school.   Which

he laws of honor.   They ring through

e, they are blazoned above every

ield.   They are among the oldest and

enduring things in the World. Underlaying

t however often men may forget

maxim "a fair field and no

Learned on the field, a player can

lessons in honorable behavior during

of their life.

Passage Corrected by the Student

∧ sp   Our games are lessons ∧_in noble *living* ~~liveing~~.   The

frag   playing field is in truth a school, ^w Which

teaches the laws of honor.   They ring throug**h**

‖   every game; ᴊ ~~t~~hey are blazoned above every

playing field.   They are among the oldest and

Cap gr   the most enduring things in the ^w World. ~~Underlay~~ *Underlyin*

⊙ p   every sport, however often men may forget

it, is the maxim "a fair field and no

⊙ SS   favor."   Learned on the field, a player can

apply the lessons in honorable behavior durin**g**

ref   the rest of *his* ~~their~~ life.

Correction Sheet

living, living, living, living, living

⊙ *A player can apply during the rest*
of his life the lessons in honorable
behavior learned on the field.

Passage Corrected by the Student

∧ sp   Our games are lessons ∧*in* noble *living* ~~liveing~~. **The**

frag   playing field is in truth a school, *w* ~~W~~hich

        teaches the laws of honor. They ring through

|| every game; ~~t~~hey are blazoned above every

        playing field. They are among the oldest and

Cap gr   the most enduring things in the *w* ~~W~~orld. ~~Underlay~~ *Underlying*

-p   every sport, however often men may forget

        it, is the maxim "a fair field and no

① SS   favor." Learned on the field, a player can

        apply the lessons in honorable behavior during

ref   the rest of ~~their~~ *his* life.

Correction Sheet

living, living, living, living, living

①   *A player can apply during the rest of his life the lessons in honorable behavior learned on the field.*

CORRECTION SYMBOLS

ms	error in manuscript form or neatness	**nc**	not clear
cap	error in use of capital letters	**‖**	run-on sentence or begin sentence here
p	error in punctuation	**gr**	error in grammar
sp	error in spelling	**w**	error in word choice
frag	sentence fragment	**¶**	Begin a new paragraph here.
ss	error in sentence structure		
ref	unclear or incorrect reference of pronoun	**t**	error in tense
k	awkward sentence	**∧**	You have omitted something.

The errors **ms, sp, ss, k, nc** should be rewritten on a separate correction sheet attached to the composition, or, if there is space, on the final page of the composition. Each error requiring rewriting should be numbered in the margin of the composition and marked with the same number on the correction sheet. As indicated in the "Passage Corrected by the Student" on the opposite page, errors which do not require rewriting a whole sentence are to be corrected on the composition at the place where the error occurs.

Example of Symbols in Margin of a Composition

∧ sp	Our games are lessons noble liveing. The
frag	playing field is in truth a school. Which
	teaches the laws of honor. They ring through
‖	every game, they are blazoned above every
	playing field. They are among the oldest and
ap gr	the most enduring things in the World. Underlaying
p	every sport however often men may forget
	it is the maxim "a fair field and no
ss	favor." Learned on the field, a player can
	apply the lessons in honorable behavior during
ref	the rest of their life.

FREE TEXTBOOK RECORD

This Textbook is the property of the State of Georgia for use in the Cobb County System. Students and their parents are responsible for loss or all damage to this book by careless use.

Name of School _____ Book # 16690

Name of Student

Faye Crowder

JAMES S. PETERS
CHAIRMAN,
STATE BOARD OF EDUCATION

CLAUDE PURCELL
STATE SUPERINTENDENT
OF SCHOOLS